INFINITUM

An Afrofuturist Tale

TIM FIELDER

AMISTAD

An Imprint of HarperCollins*Publishers*

INFINITUM. Copyright © 2021 by Dieselfunk Studios.

For information, address
HarperCollins Publishers
195 Broadway, New York, NY 10007.

HarperCollins books may be purchased for educational, business, or sales promotional use. For information, please email the Special Markets Department at SPsales@harpercollins.com.

Design: Boston for URB ALT Media

FIRST EDITION

Library of Congress Cataloging-in-Publication Data

Names: Fielder, Tim, author, artist.
Title: Infinitum : an Afrofuturist tale / Tim Fielder.
Description: First edition. | New York : Amistad, 2021.
Identifiers: LCCN 2019060233 | ISBN 9780062964083 (hardcover) | ISBN 9780062964090 (trade paperback) | ISBN 9780062964113 (ebook)
Subjects: LCSH: Graphic novels.
Classification: LCC PN6727.F477 I54 2020 | DDC 741.5/973—dc23
LC record available at https://lccn.loc.gov/2019060233

21 22 23 24 25 IMAGO 10 9 8 7 6 5 4 3 2 1

other graphic novels by
Tim Fielder

Matty's Rocket
Black Metropolis

For my Boys, now Men,
Jacob Fielder and Maximilius Fielder:

You Saved Me.

introduction ■ *on birth of an OG*

Illustration: Stacey Robinson

Greetings, Dieselfunkateers! I was with my brother a few years back setting up my career retrospective exhibition, "Black Metropolis: 30 Years of Afrofuturism, Comics, Music, Animation, Decapitated Chickens, Heroes, Villains, and Negroes."

One of the young curators was excitedly sorting the stacks of work to be mounted on the wall. As she got deeper into the pile she suddenly blurted out, "Oh my God, you're like some kind of OG Afrofuturist!"

Bro and I stopped to look at the curator's realization. Sensing the unintended levity in the situation, I replied, "Hey, man, did she just call me old?" The curator was horrified at the notion of an unintentional slight. But before she could apologize I chuckled and stopped her mid-sentence. "Yes, yes, I am an OG Afrofuturist."

One of my good friends visited my studio as I was deep into production on this book. He questioned my direction of producing a fully rendered story when simpler drawings would do. "Smells like ego to me," he said. I pondered the notion and replied, "Yes, yes, it is ego."

Black people deserve to see themselves in fully rendered visual narratives with big themes. Why only one black guy in the universe? Why does the black guy have to always die? Even more extreme, do black women exist at all in science fiction? I draw Negroes in Spaceships.

With that, I present to you my labor of long-sought and passionate love. INFINITUM.

Tim Fielder, 2020

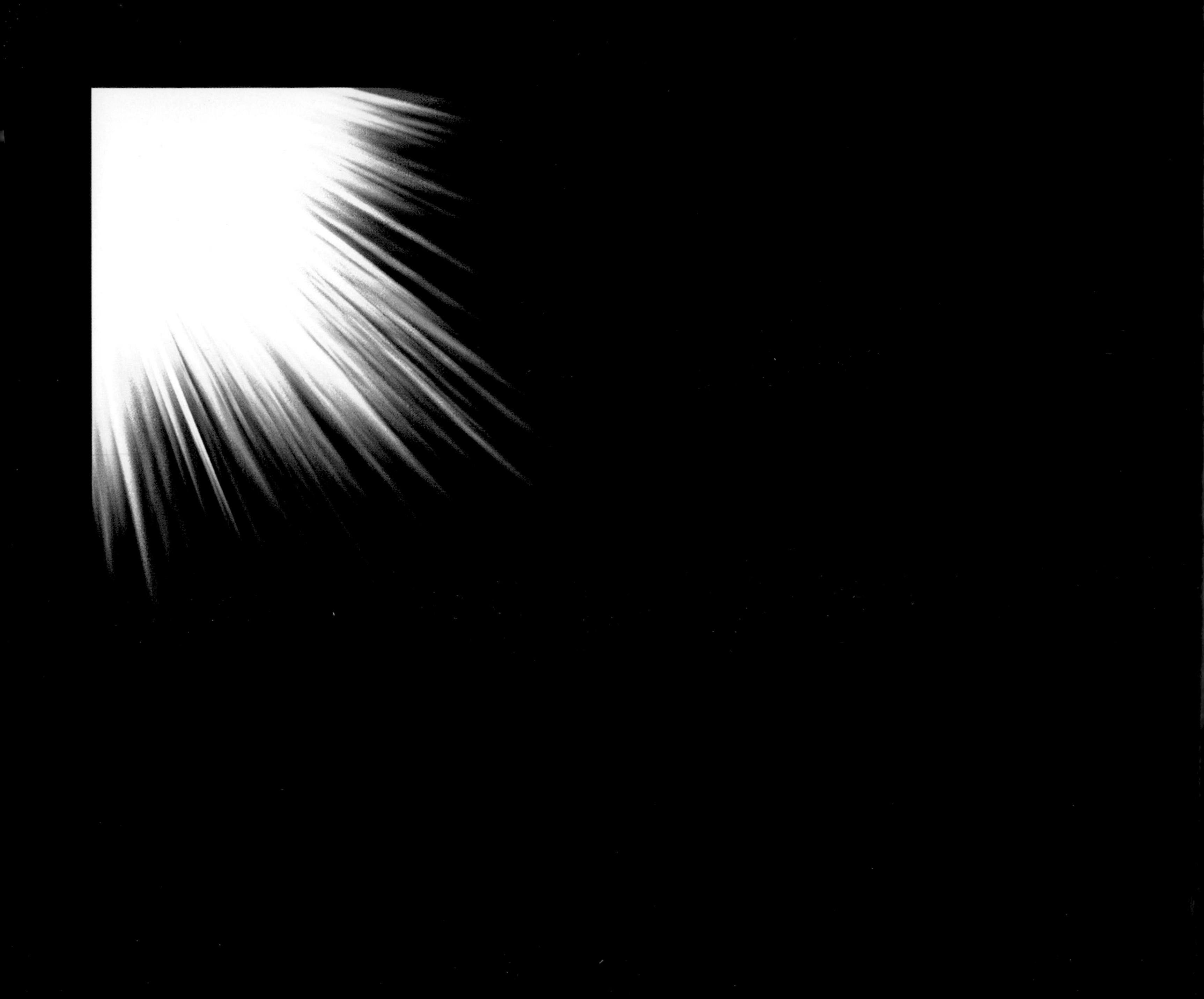

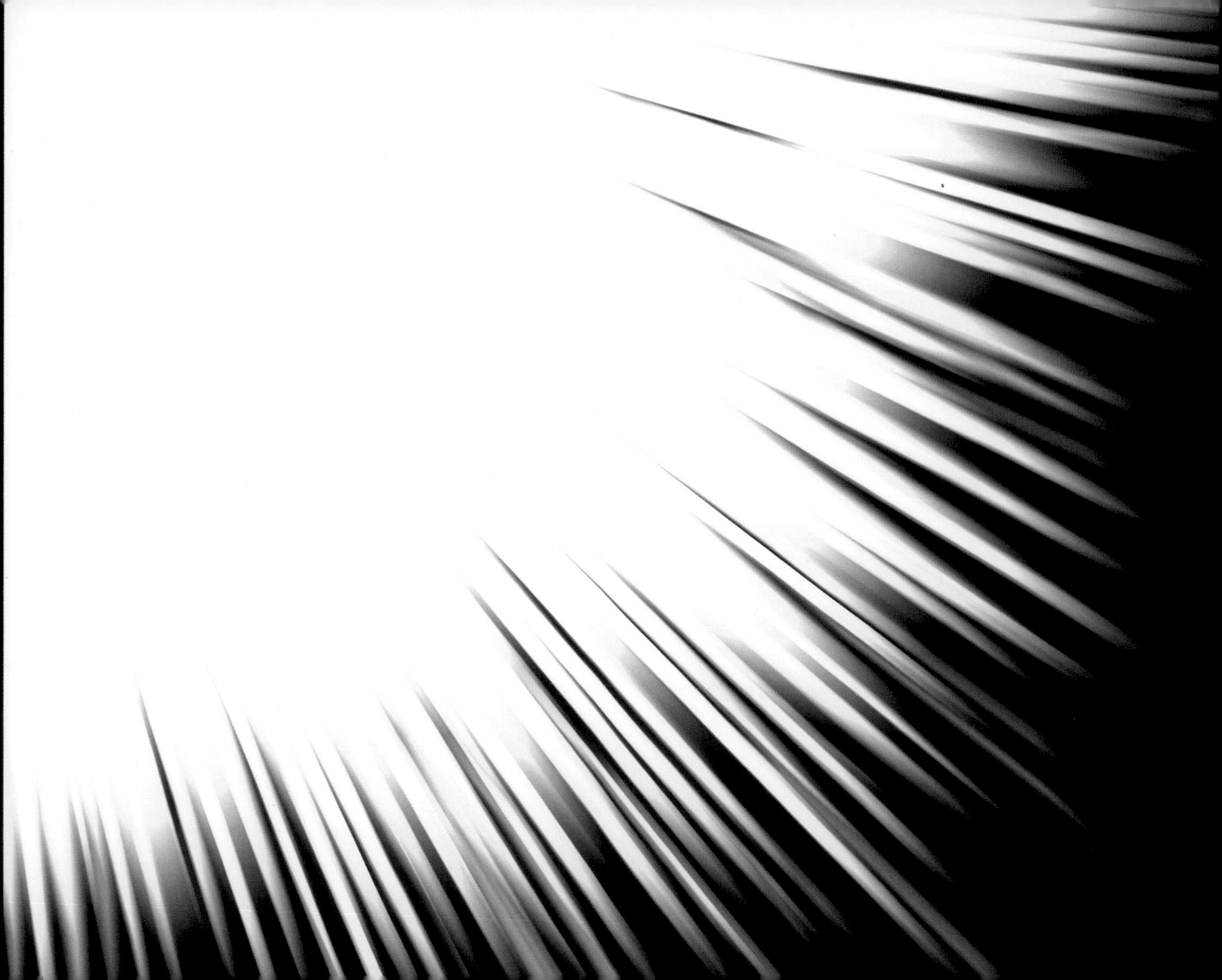

The Birth of The Universe...

Came and Went.

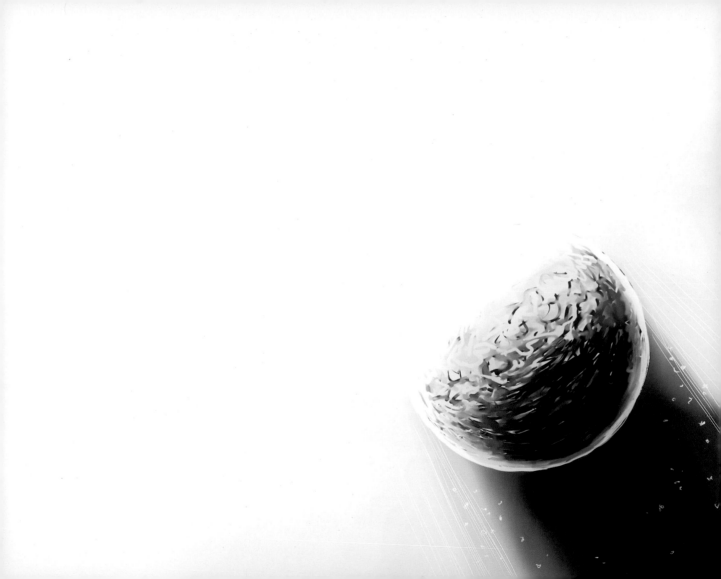

All the young Earth could do was try — **try to sustain life** — as was its imperative. First to appear were microbic creatures swimming in fluid — the foundation and blood of life. Eventually primitive land and air creatures flourished in the hotbed of biomass — sometimes benevolent, sometimes malevolent...most always carnivorous.

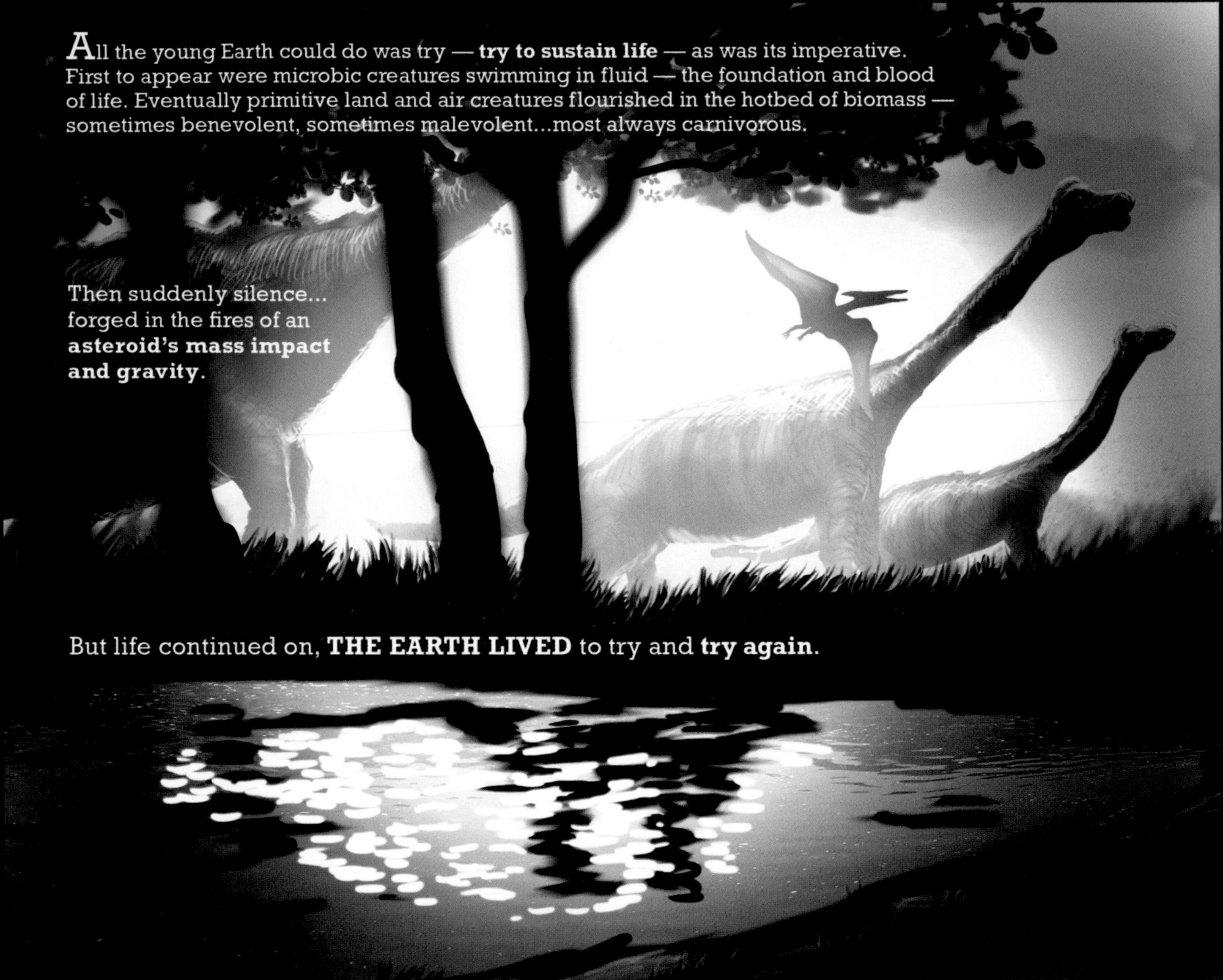

Then suddenly silence... forged in the fires of an **asteroid's mass impact and gravity**.

But life continued on, **THE EARTH LIVED** to try and **try again**.

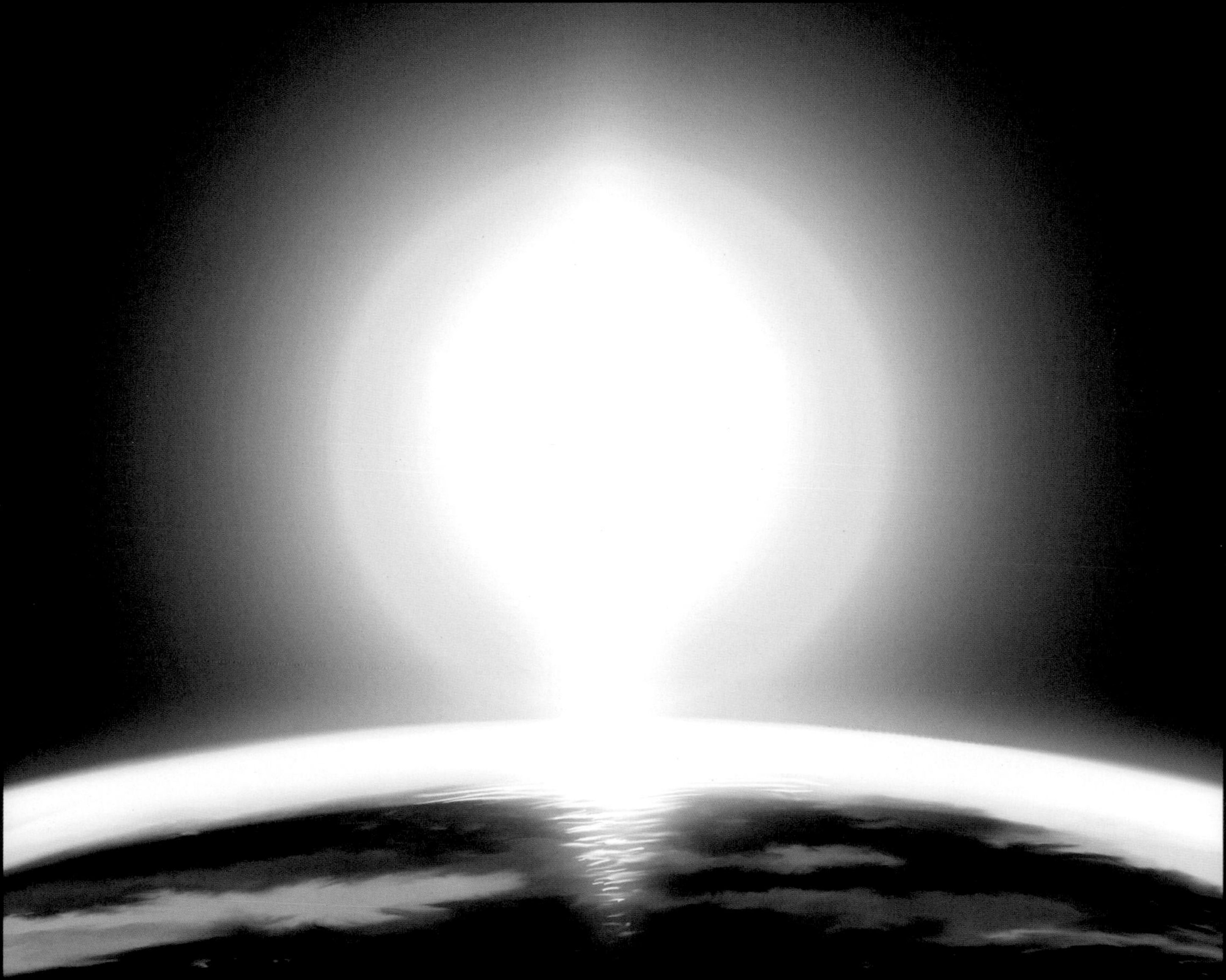

INFINITUM

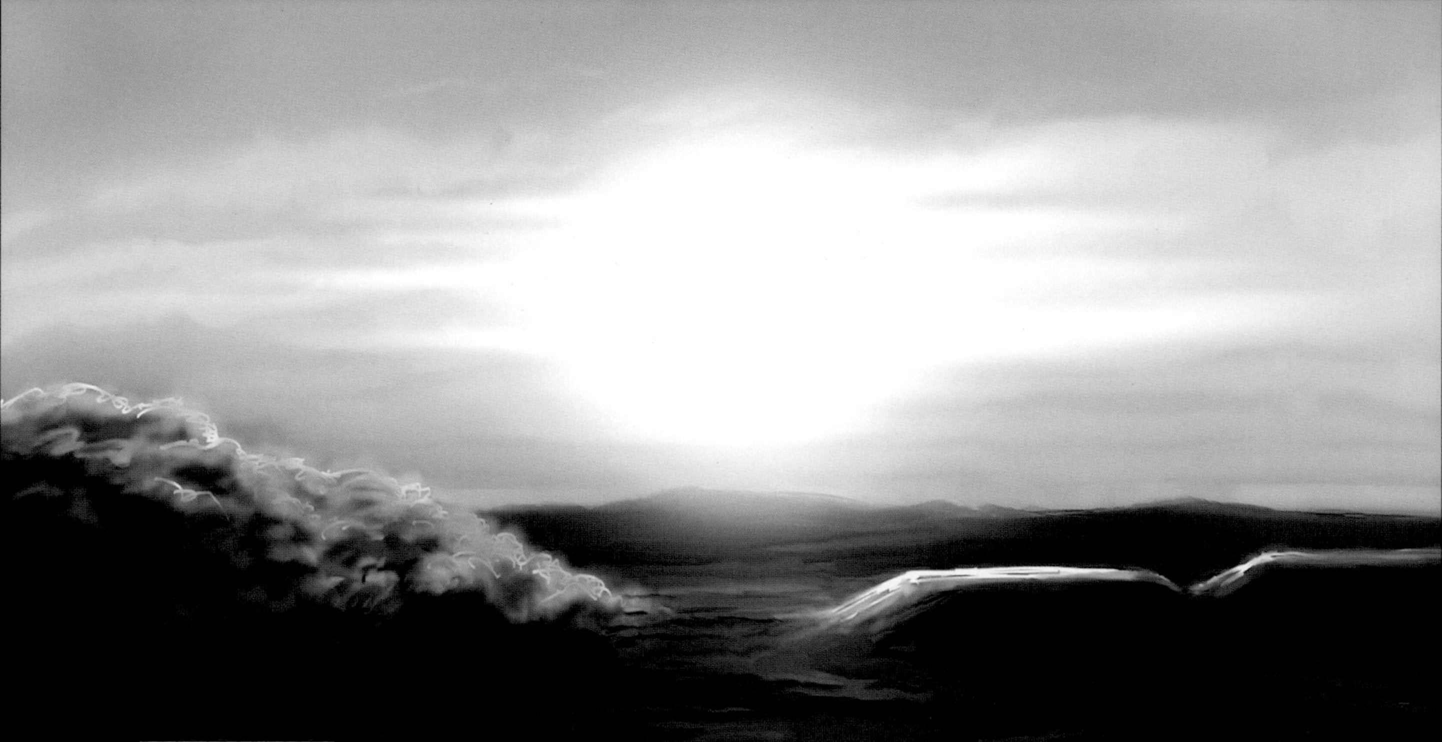

In the time of the Great African Kingdoms
there lived a very Powerful King...

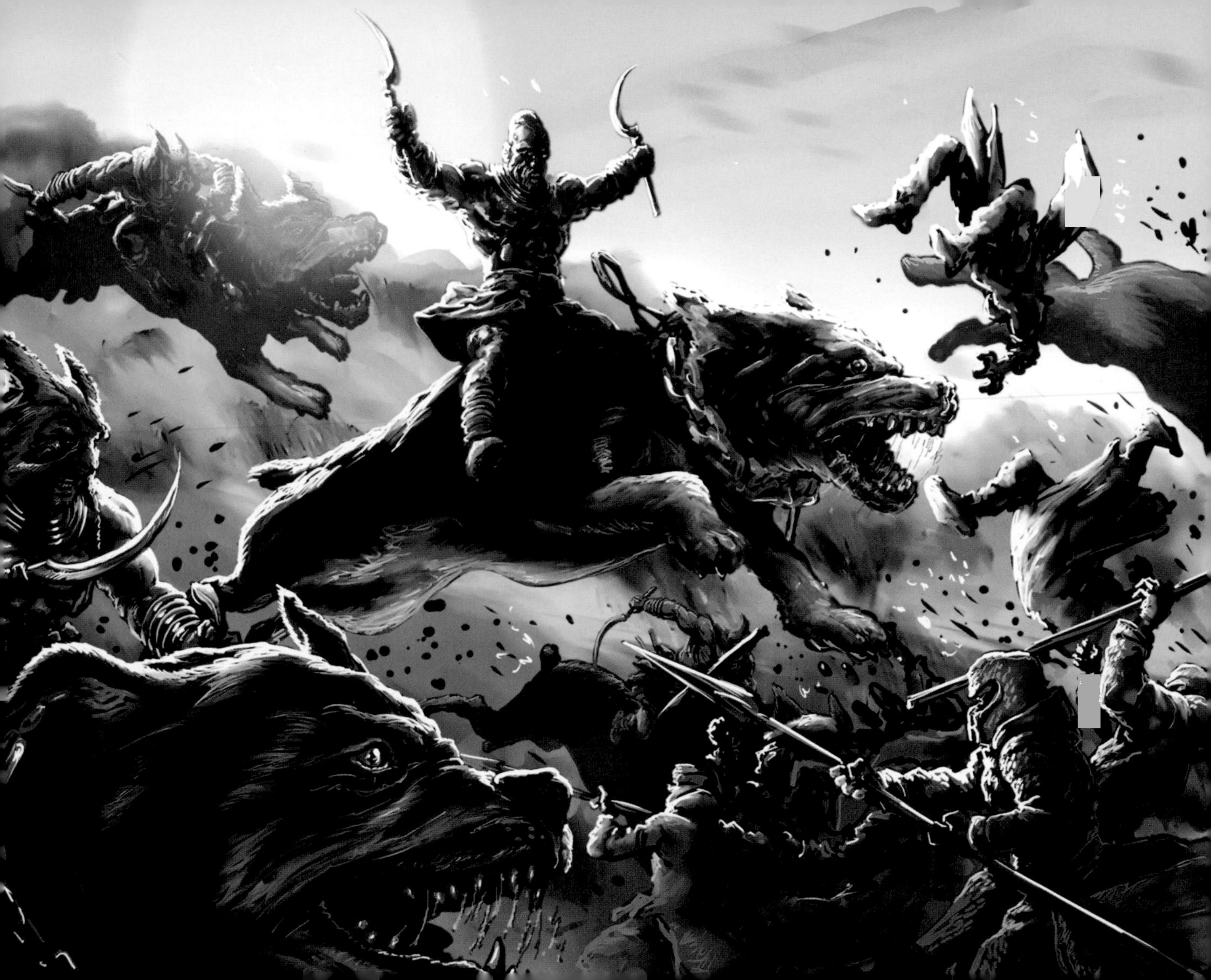

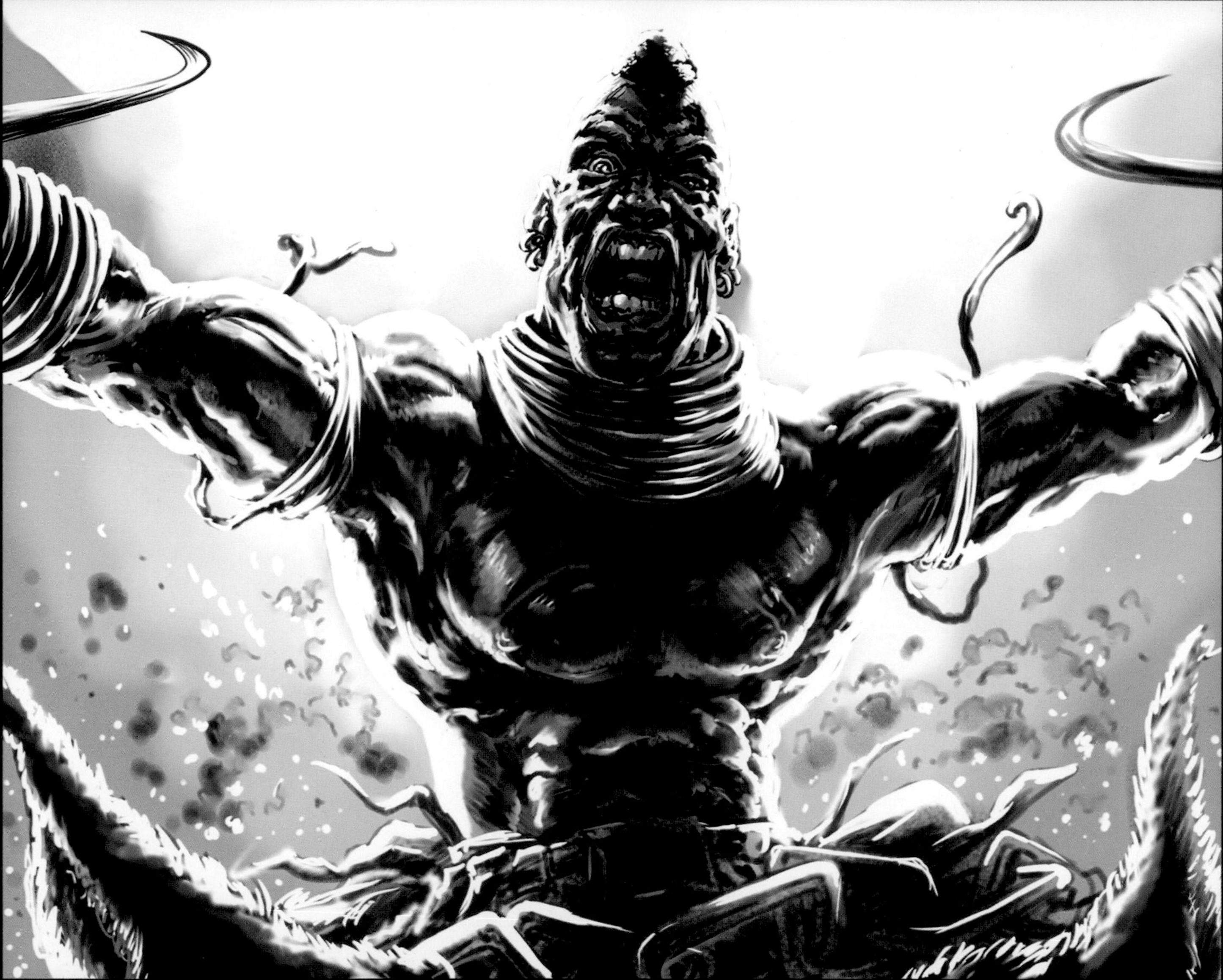

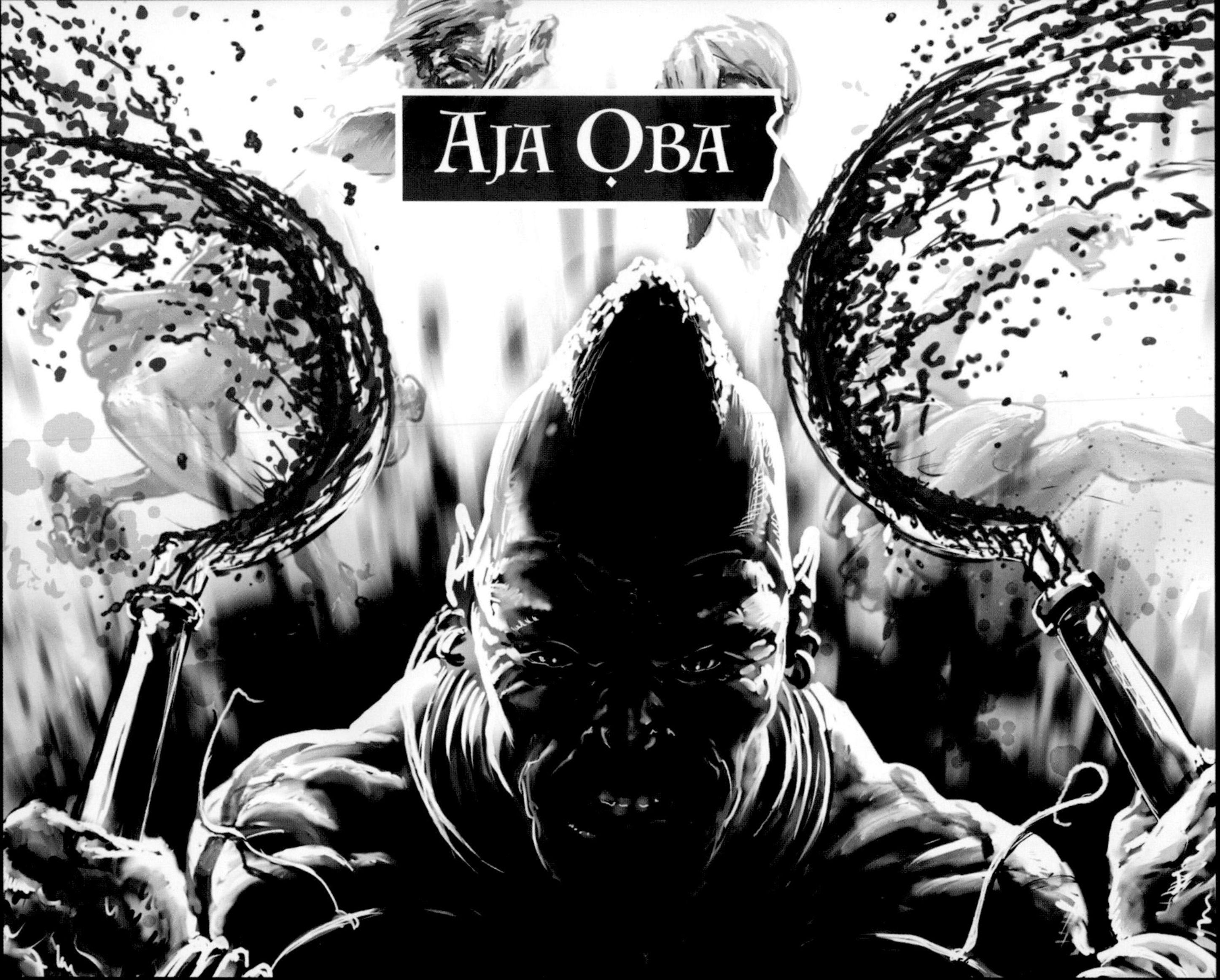
AJA ỌBA

Aja **Ọ**ba was a **WARLORD**. He ruled his kingdom with an iron fist. His **Dog Troops**, known for their capacity to wage war by **land or sea**, held the unique characteristic of riding abnormally **large canines** in battle.

The Troops' ruthlessness across the **African Continent** made them feared by all: Kush, Persia, Axum, Songhai, Mesopotamia, Babylonia, Mutapa, Zimbabwe, and so on.

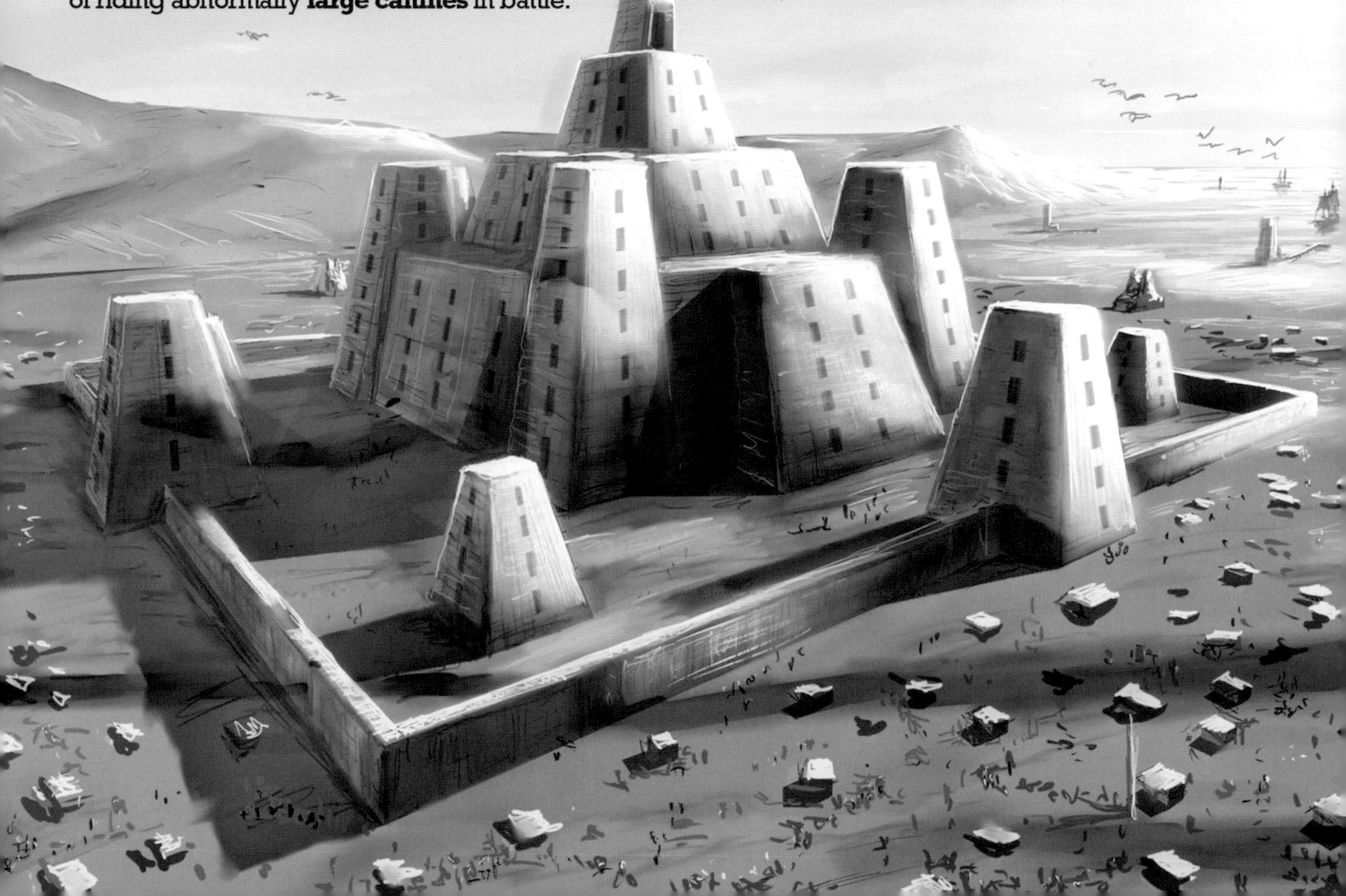

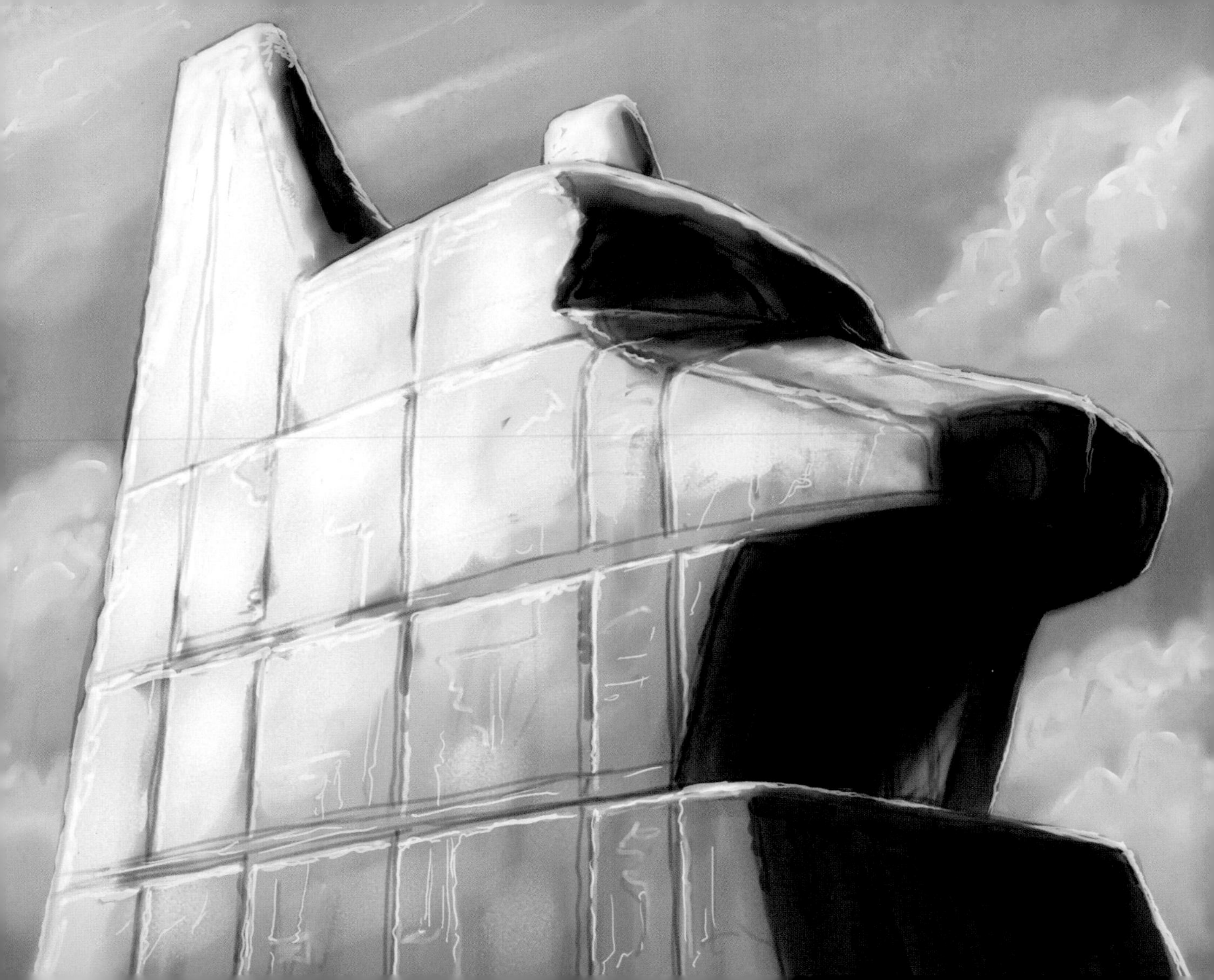

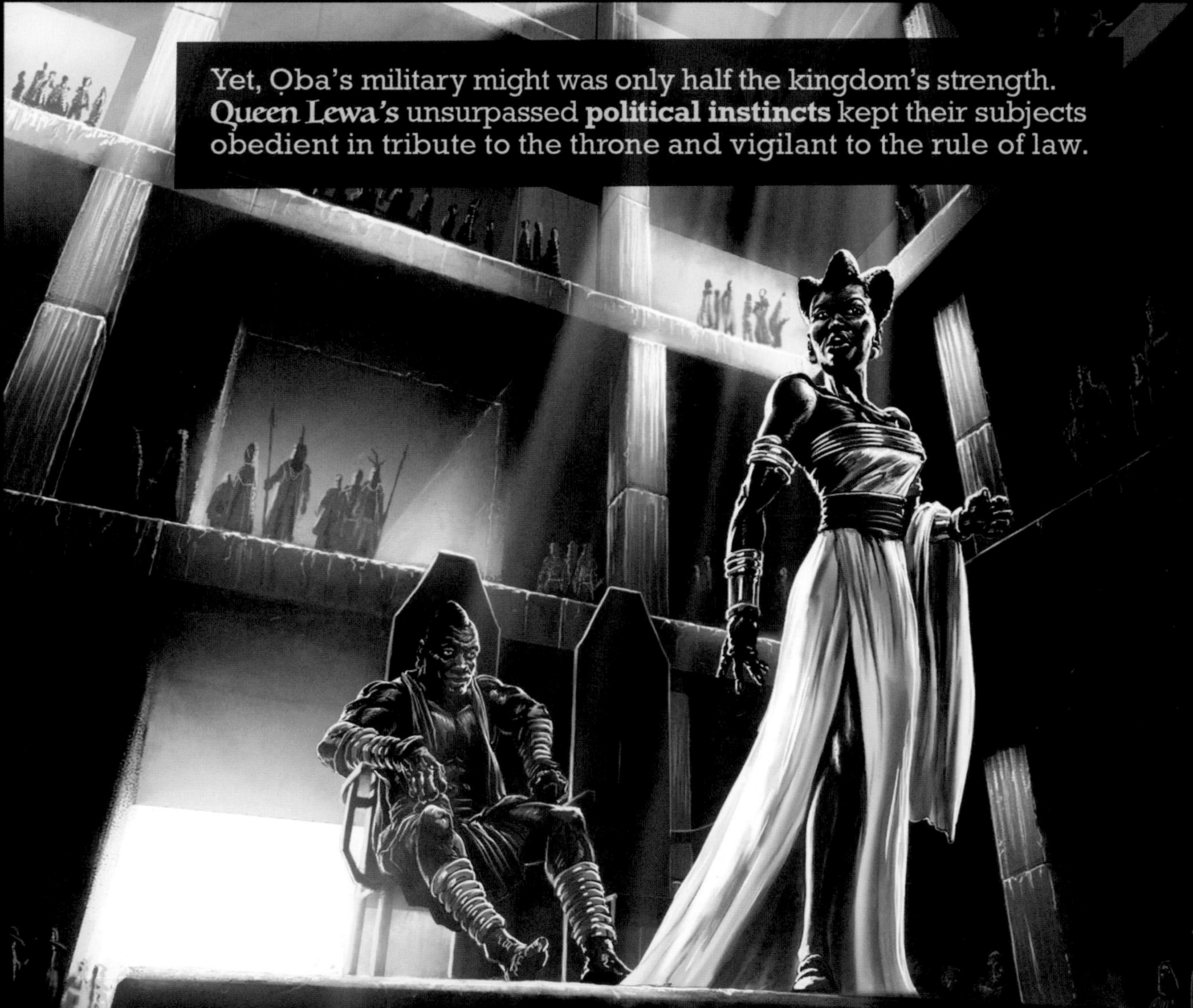
Yet, Ọba's military might was only half the kingdom's strength. **Queen Lewa's** unsurpassed **political instincts** kept their subjects obedient in tribute to the throne and vigilant to the rule of law.

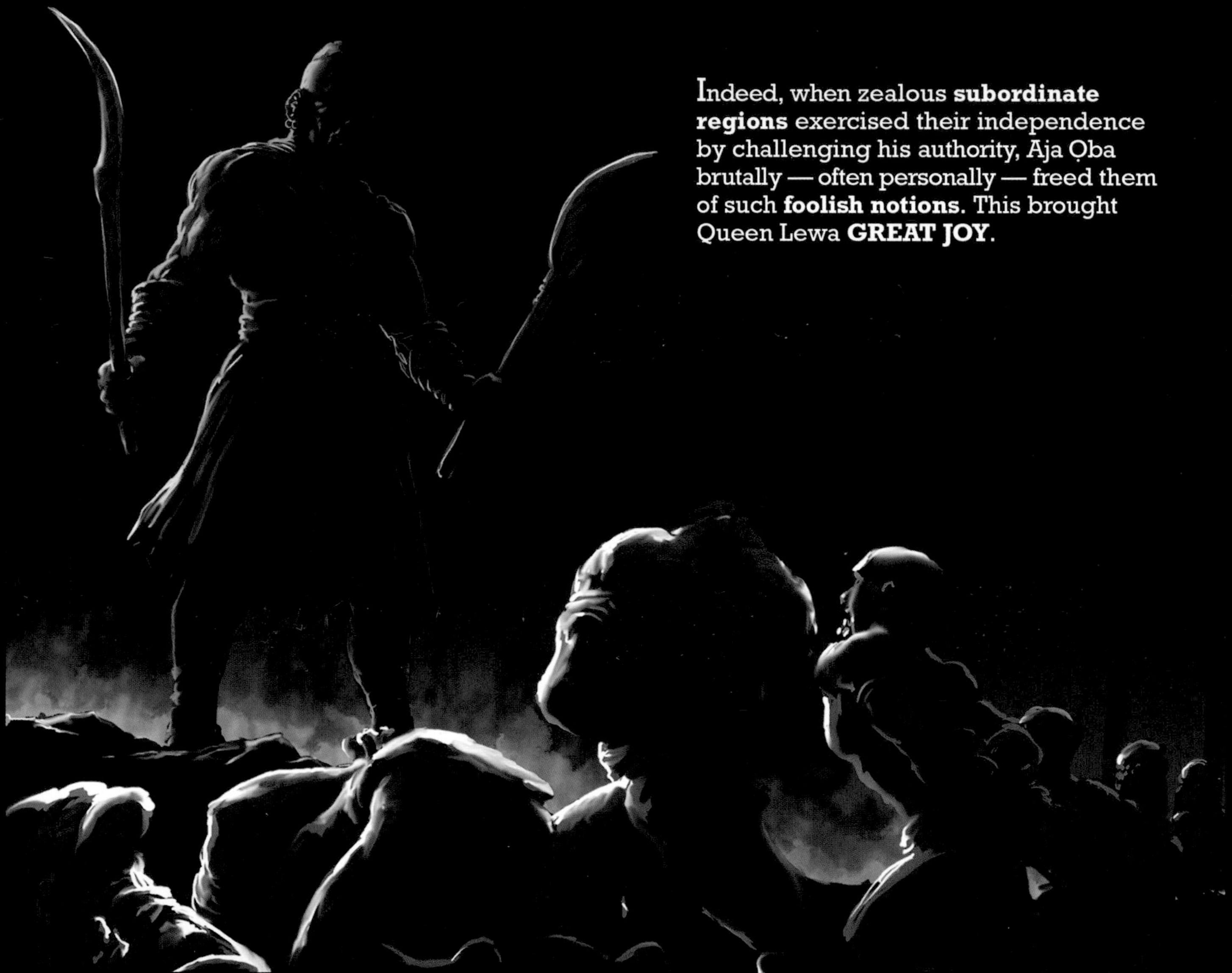

Indeed, when zealous **subordinate regions** exercised their independence by challenging his authority, Aja Ọba brutally — often personally — freed them of such **foolish notions**. This brought Queen Lewa **GREAT JOY**.

They owned a vast global network of fertile **Gold Mines**. This beget commercial alliances as far away as Peru, Kaminaljuyu, Knossos, Hatti, Teotihuacan, and Olmec.

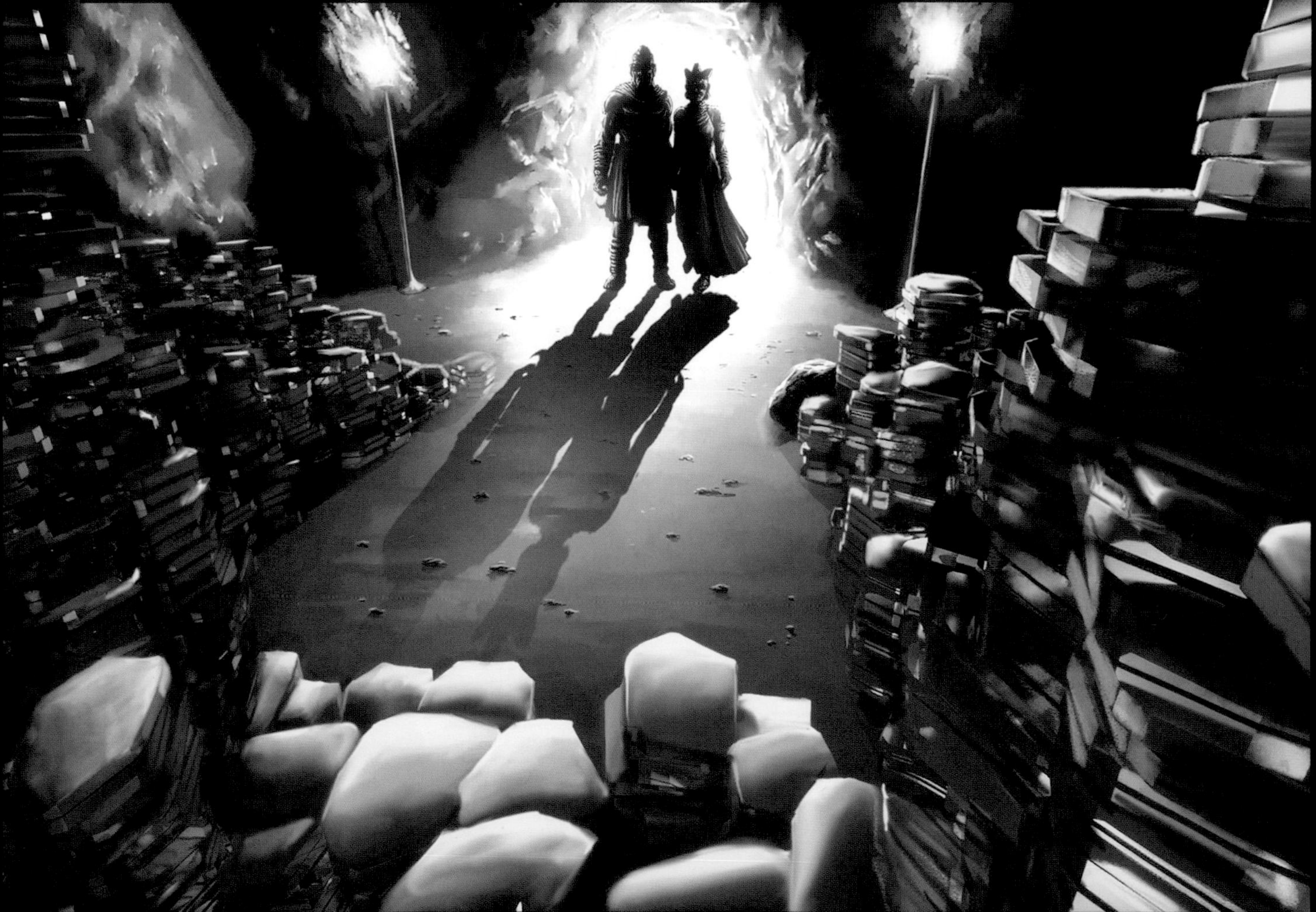

It would be an insincere claim to suggest **Lewa** was my first love. I was not hers, either. But it was **Queen Lewa** who made me a **Great King**, just as I made her **Ruler Over All Lands** upon which her eyes fell.

Initially ours was a cold marriage of sovereign convenience between **warring monarchies**. Every public proclamation as royal couple was strategized to embrace pliable enemies or to militarily suffocate factions who continued to wage war against us. **I killed men in Lewa's name.**

Our desire for **Absolute Reign** was mutual, so with patience and the treasure of time, **Queen Lewa** and I ultimately grew to love one another.

Ours was The Kingdom of Aja Ọba.

Queen Lewa

Puzzles fascinate me. Remove one piece from the equation and the story is incomplete.

I was raised to rule. My progenitors amassed power across Africa over hundreds of years. I was four years a Queen when I first met Ọba at an assembly of state heads with his beloved father and mother, Aja Jacub and Queen Riwena. Five times my loyal soldiers had pushed Ọba's troops out of our seaports during sieges. Our defiance earned his grudging respect. His parents were feeble but still radiated the brutal intelligence of career warriors. It was clear that Ọba's obsession with combat was inherited as was his spiritual link to them. After several tense conferences, we proposed merging our monarchies through marriage to avoid sustained conflict. So, with the blessings of forebears and the public, we wed. Rival nations were rightly intimidated by our combined might.

I've learned to truly appreciate Aja Ọba's physical beauty. His exquisite onyx skin and muscular form are well-suited for offspring — future rulers. As a lover, he is equally fierce, frightening, and exposed. Ọba and I are intent on conceiving a child. We consume arcane potions and meals provided daily by our doctors and the high priestesses of Aje Juress. My womb is consecrated by prayers of protection.

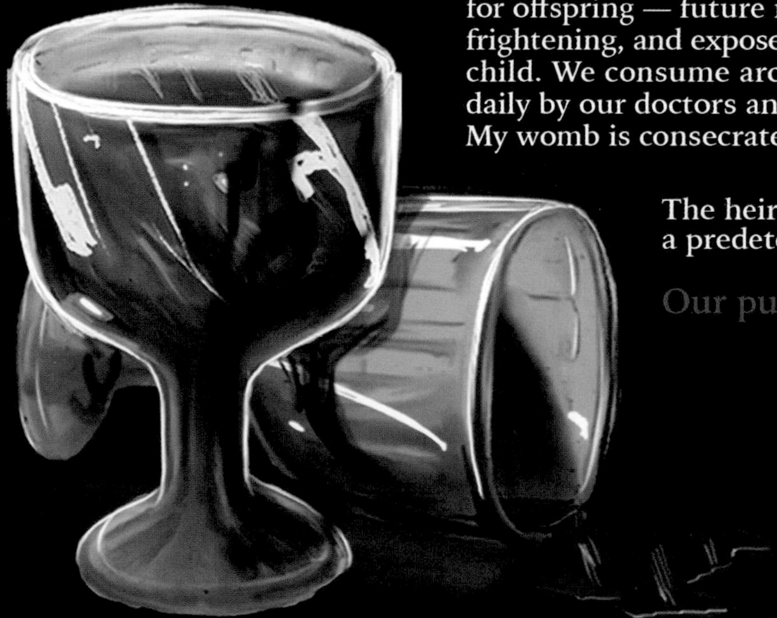

The heir of our dreams is as real as the sky is a predetermined blue. He will come.

Our puzzle will be COMPLETE.

But, Aja Ọba and Queen Lewa's dream was **broken**....

They could **not** have Children.

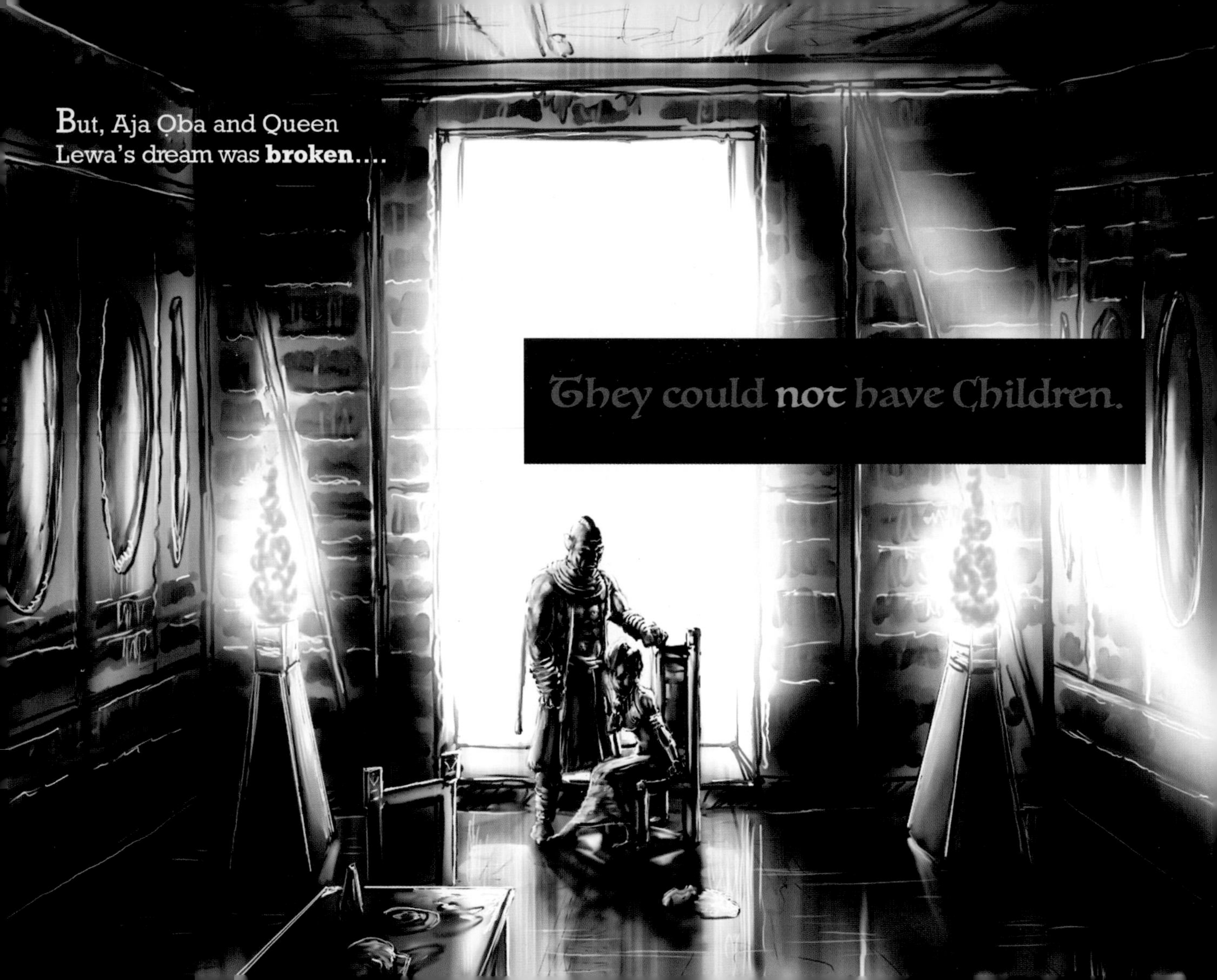

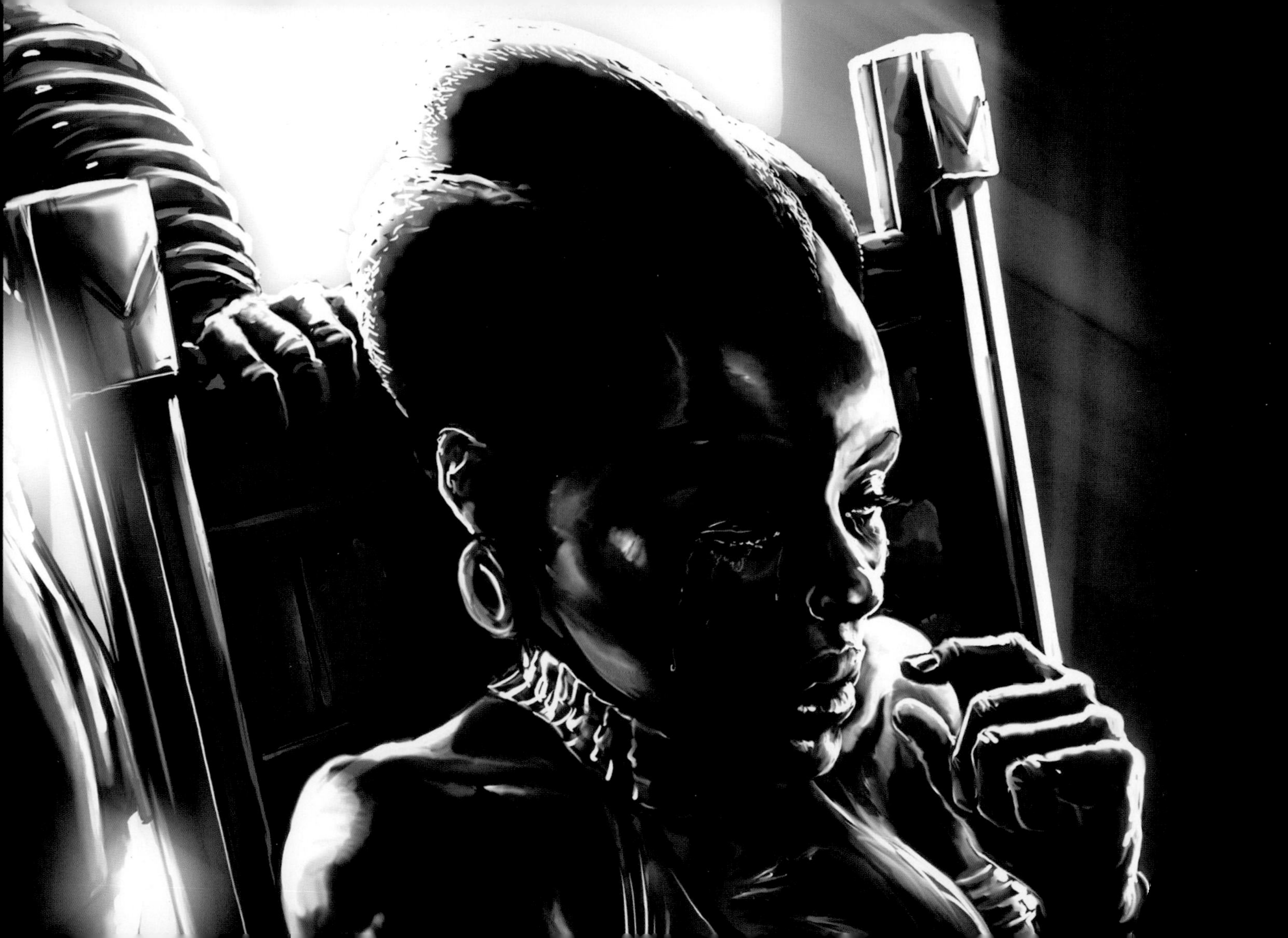

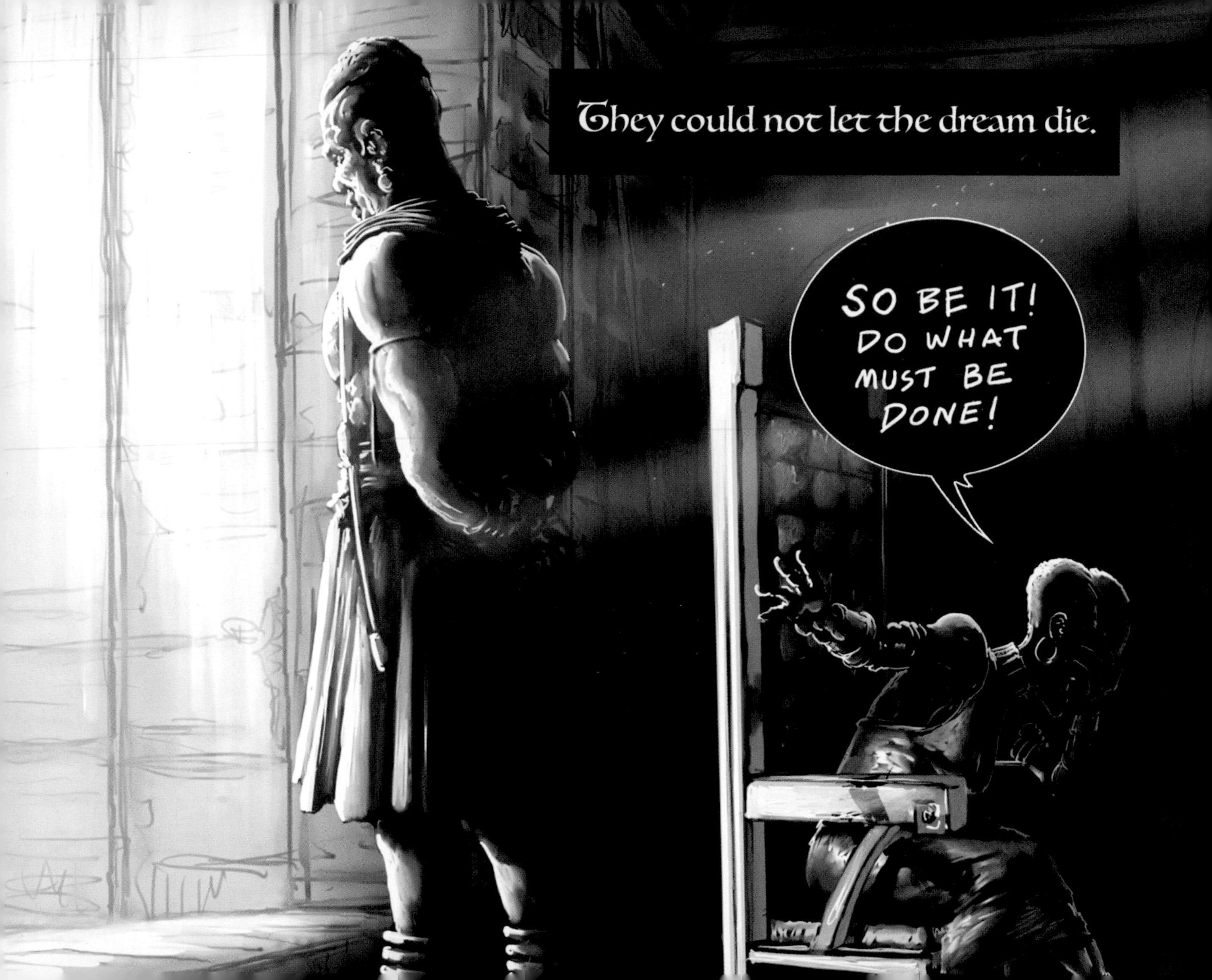
They could not let the dream die.
SO BE IT! DO WHAT MUST BE DONE!

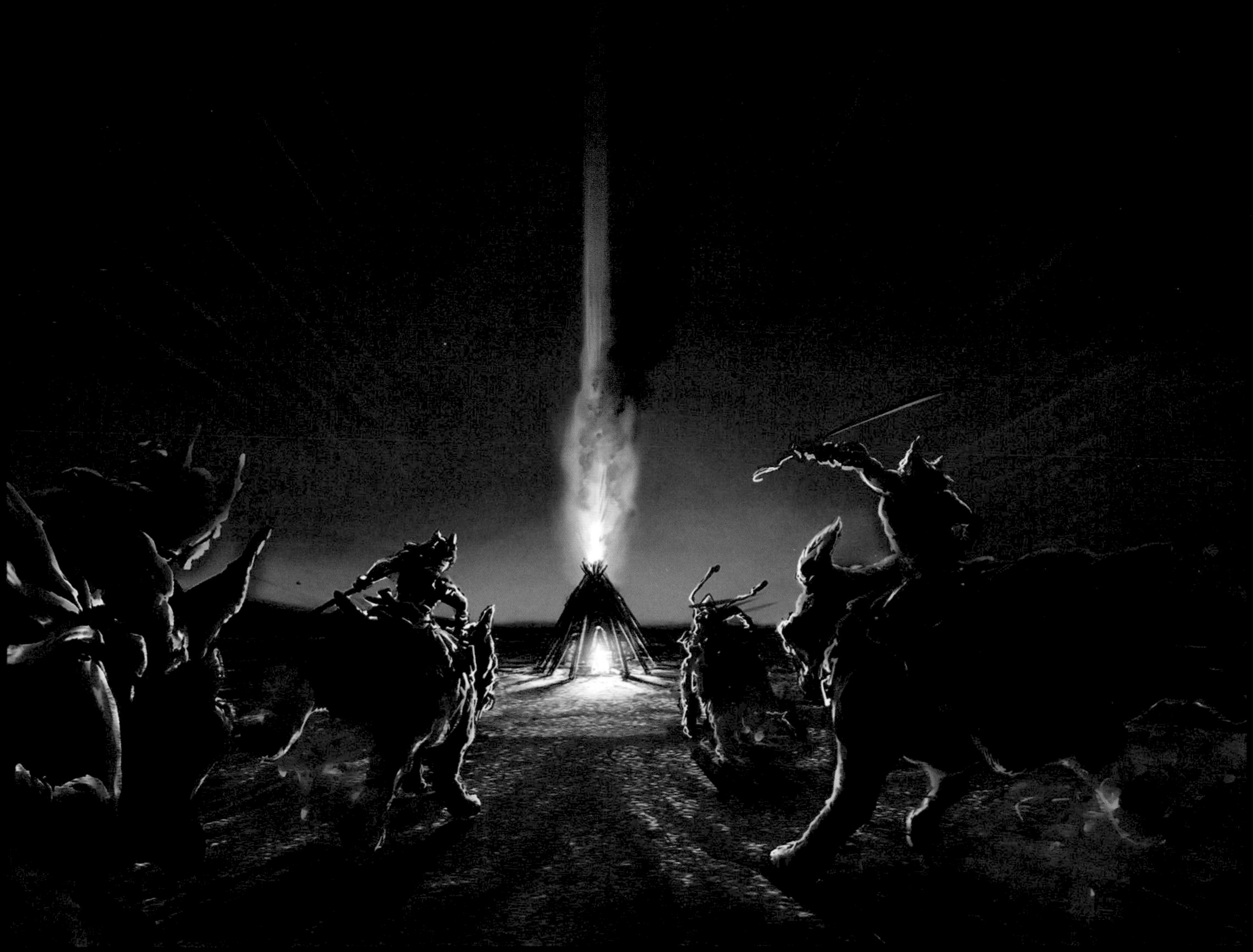

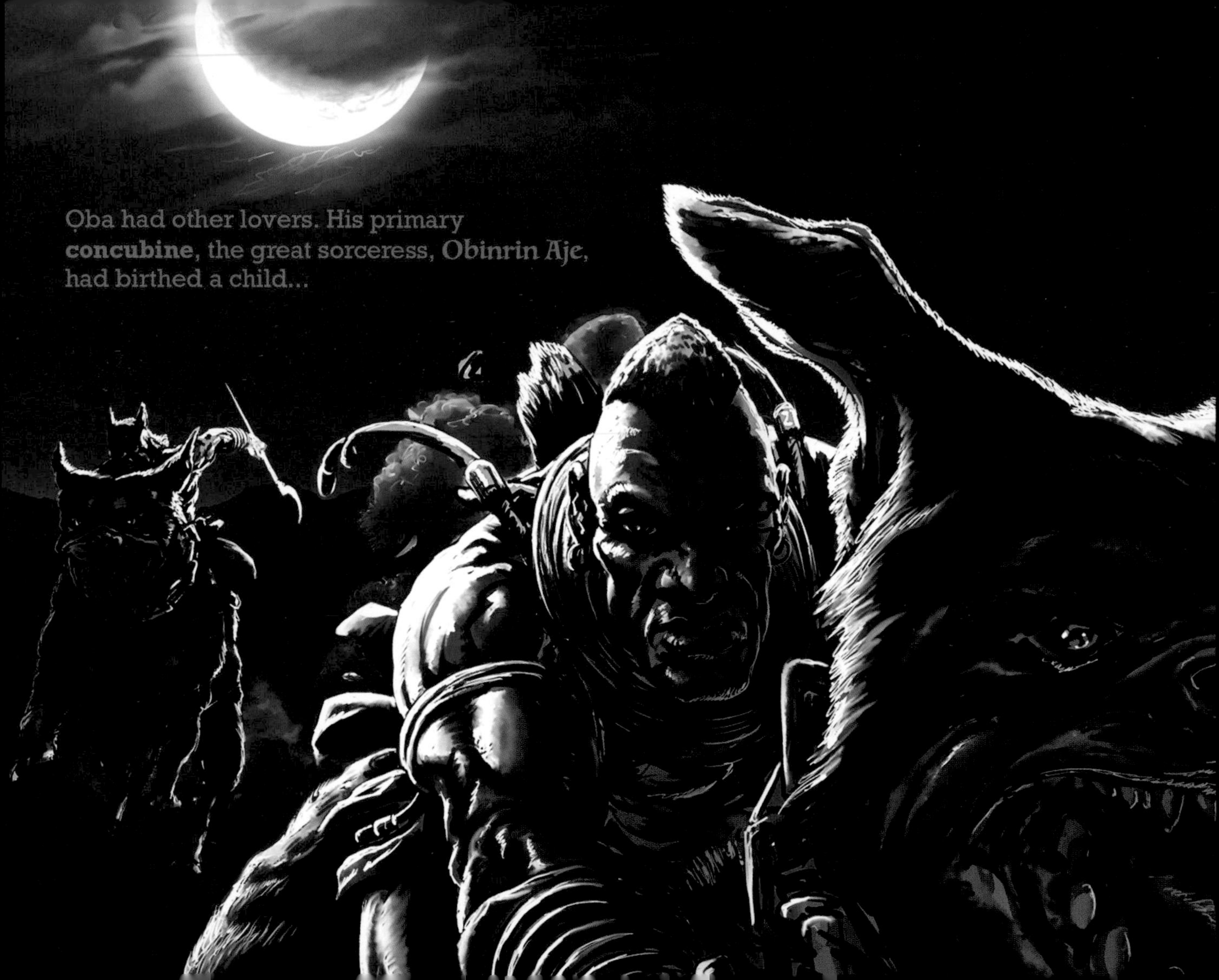
Ọba had other lovers. His primary **concubine**, the great sorceress, Obinrin Aje, had birthed a child…

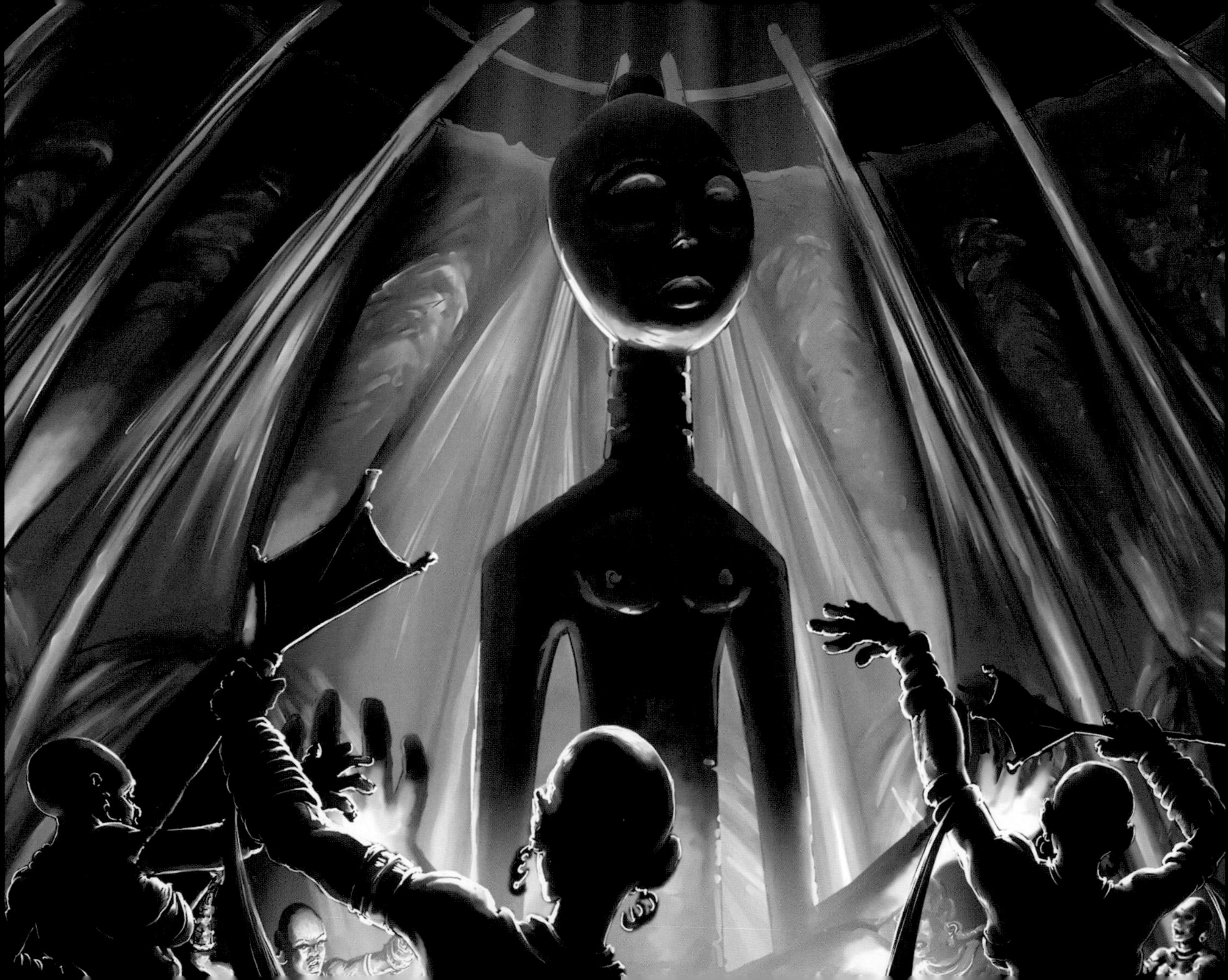

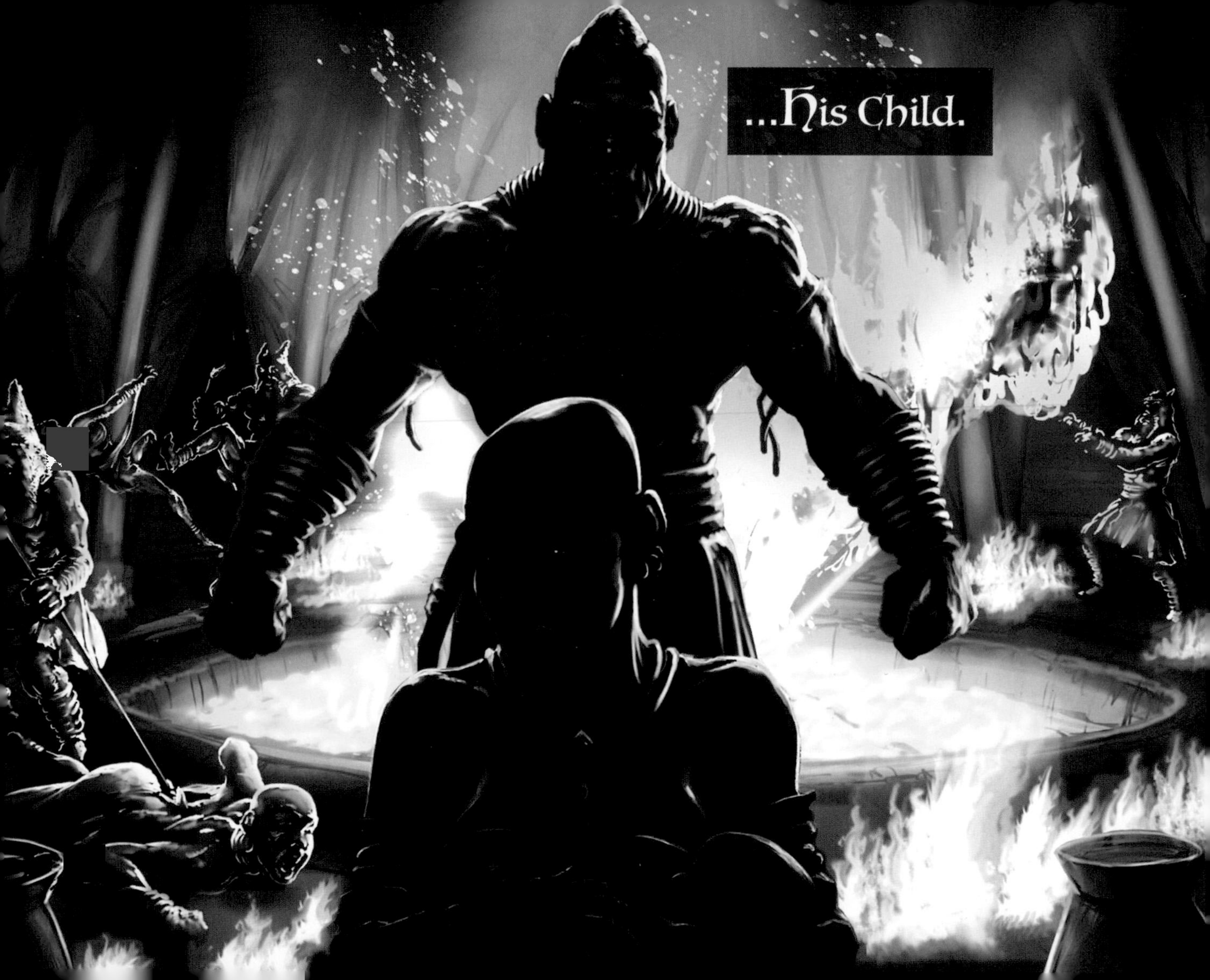
...His Child.

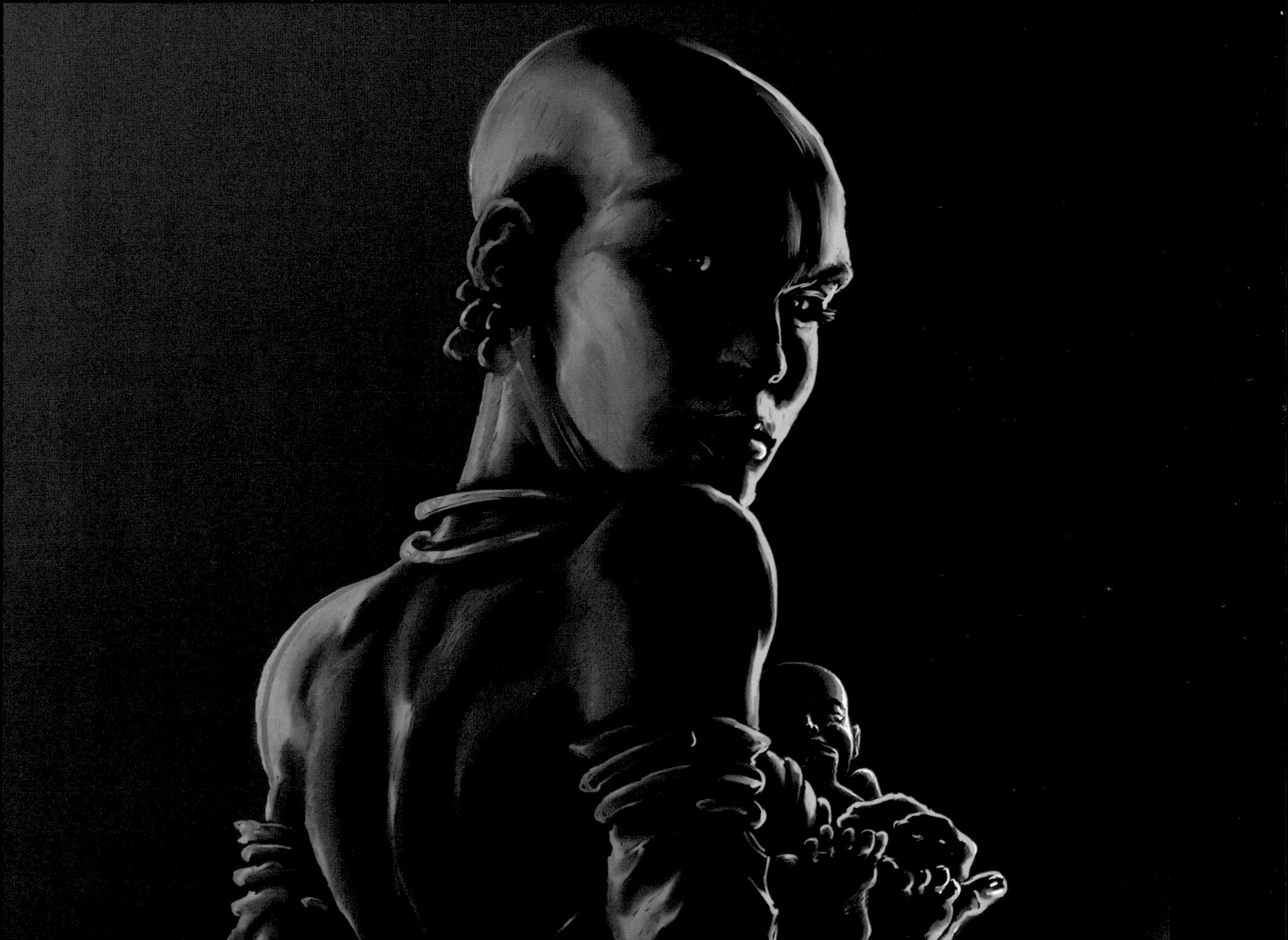

Obinrin Aje was the leader of a long line of conjure women called **Aje Juress**. These mighty shamans were the spiritual trustees between life and death for **The Kingdom of Aja Ọba**. **Obinrin** was a master alchemist whose Myths and Magic made our borders impenetrable and **The Throne** transcendent.

Obinrin and I had found ourselves passionate lovers since childhood who fate would **separate yet bind forever**. The Queen and I heard rumblings of an **Aje Juress** plot to **sterilize the throne**. Imagine my fury and relief to unearth that my troublesome affair with **the witch** bore salvation for my lineage.

I knew what I must do.

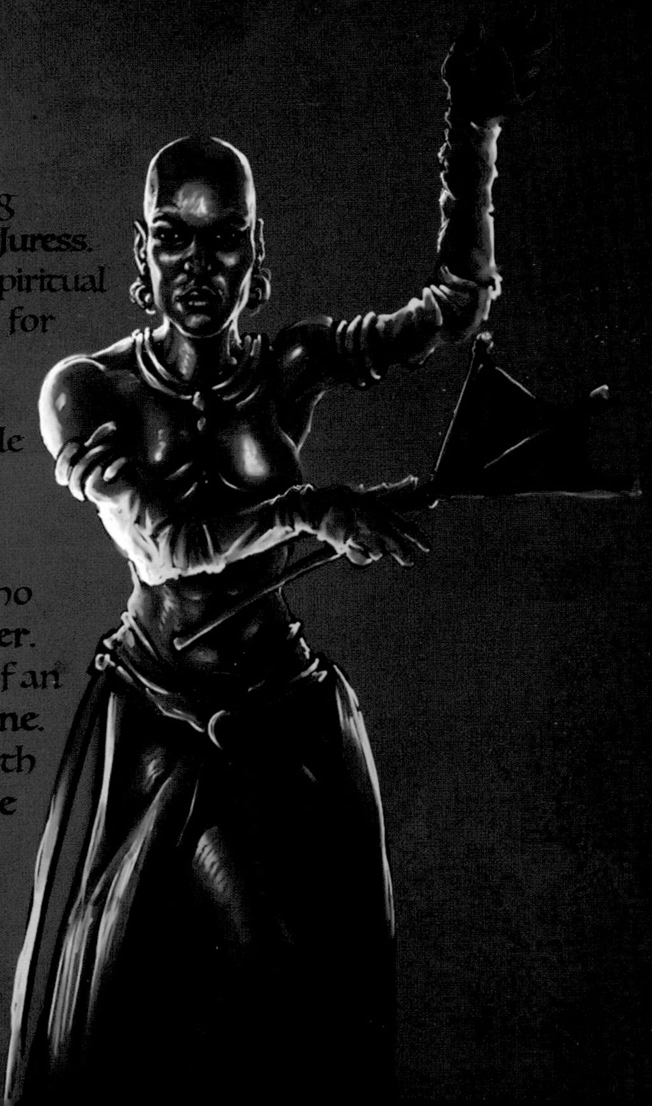

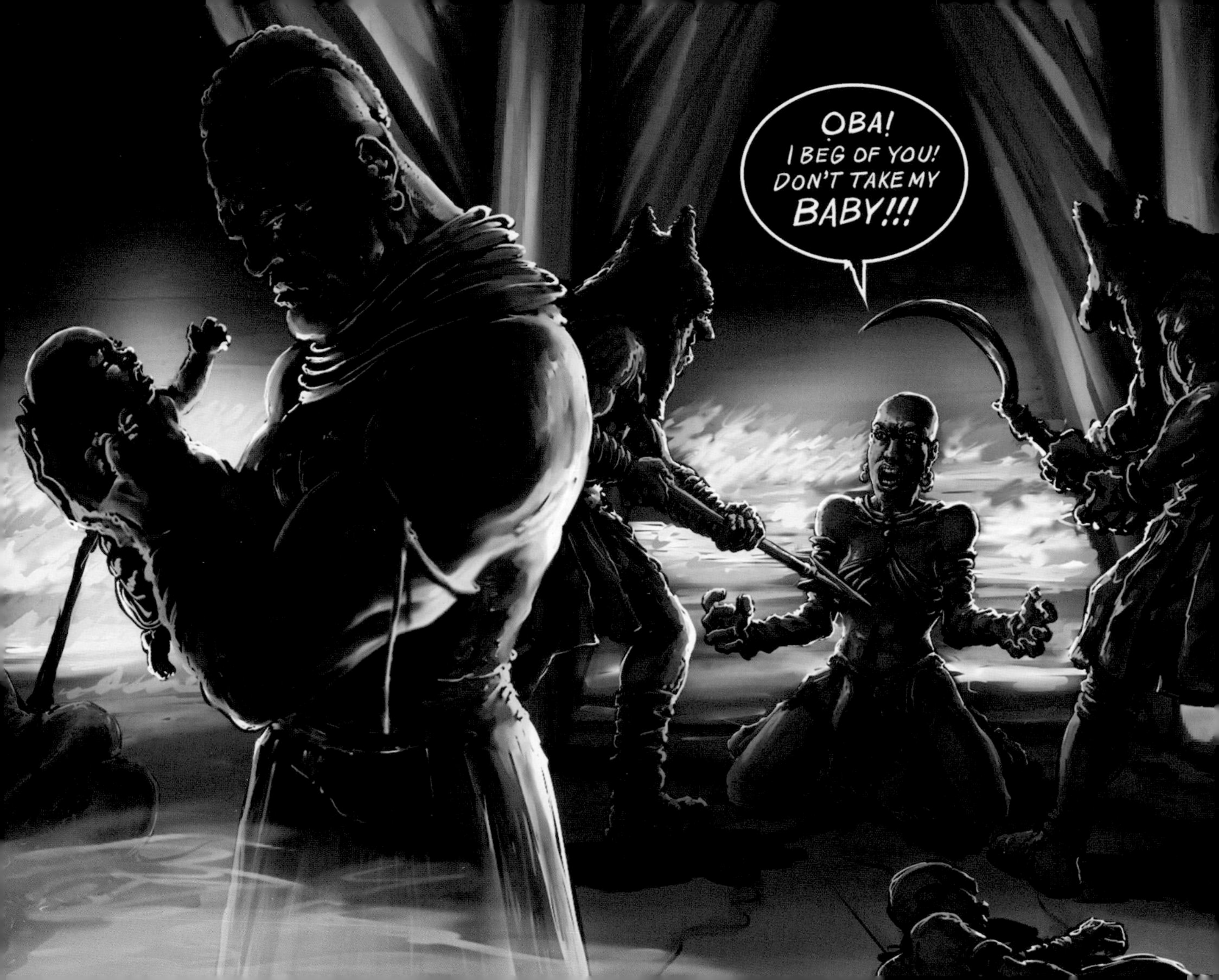
ỌBA! I BEG OF YOU! DON'T TAKE MY BABY!!!

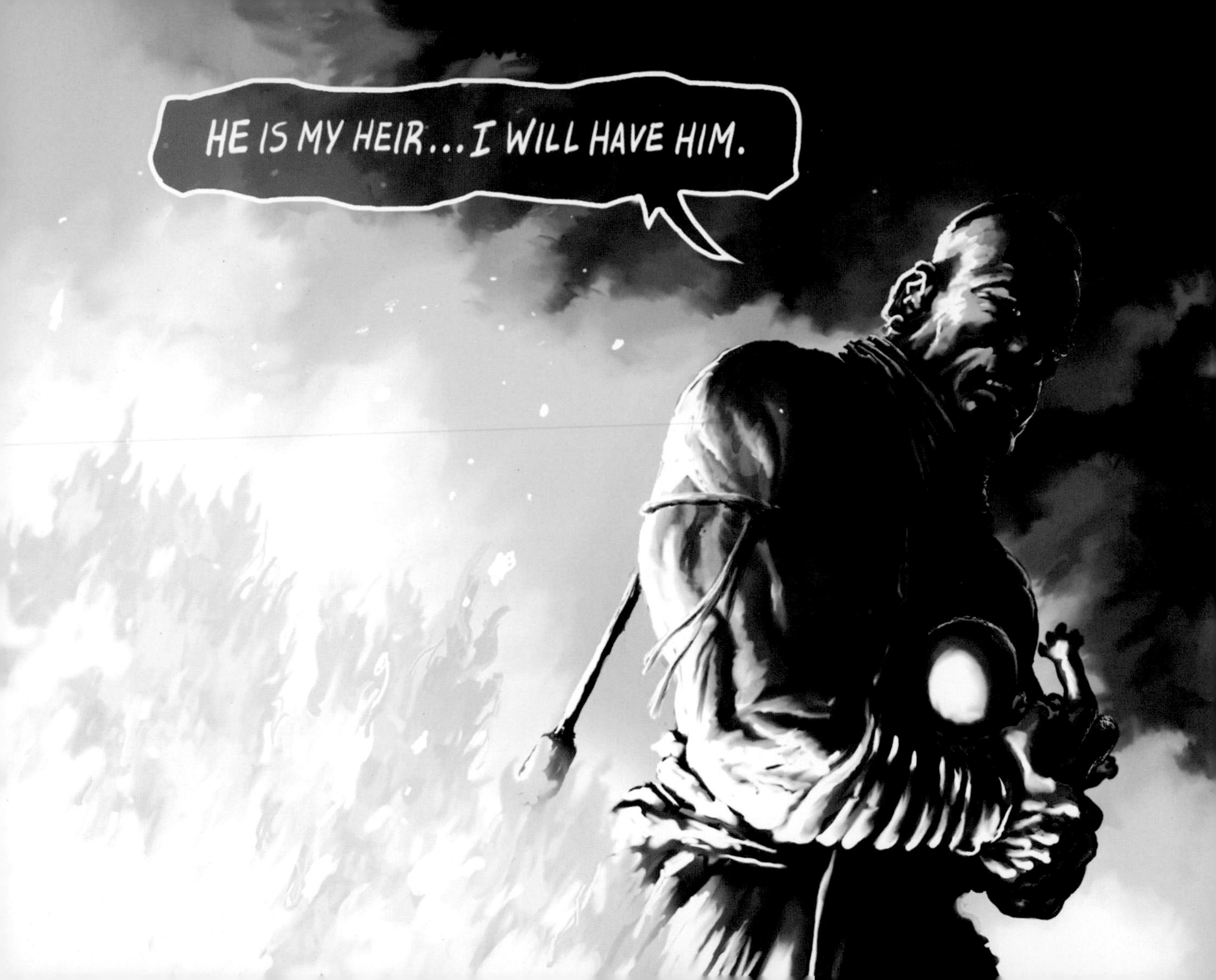
HE IS MY HEIR...I WILL HAVE HIM.

Women of the Aje Juress bridge the isolation of divination study with the invitation to community. Our alchemy and oral traditions direct the populace toward the Gods. Yet, we're also focused on wielding secular influence in The Kingdom of Aja Ọba. Some Aje Juress train to be captains of industry while others serve in the military. Even more carry cryptic societal titles such as Judge of Culture or Shepherd of Mercy.

My yearnings were unique in that I, a master soothsayer, was secretly ordained by the Monarchy and Aje Juress to be the future bride of Prince Ọba. To perpetuate this union, he and I were raised in close proximity, sharing the playful bonding experiences of young children. This led to familiar physical attractions and, finally, to sexual exploration. I knew the history of every scar on Ọba's body. His battles were my wars. What was marked upon him was surely marked upon me. We are twin fires in every way.

Ah, but life is heartless. As we neared the age of matrimony, fate intervened. Ọba's clashes with a nation to the South saw waters ripple red with the blood of soldiers from both sides. The Kingdom of Ọba's war council was strangely seduced by the sturdy resistance. Thus, without consulting the Aje Juress, Ọba was promised to the young Queen of the defiant land. This was a fracturing of centuries-old covenants between Shrine and State.

More deeply for me, it was a damn personal betrayal.

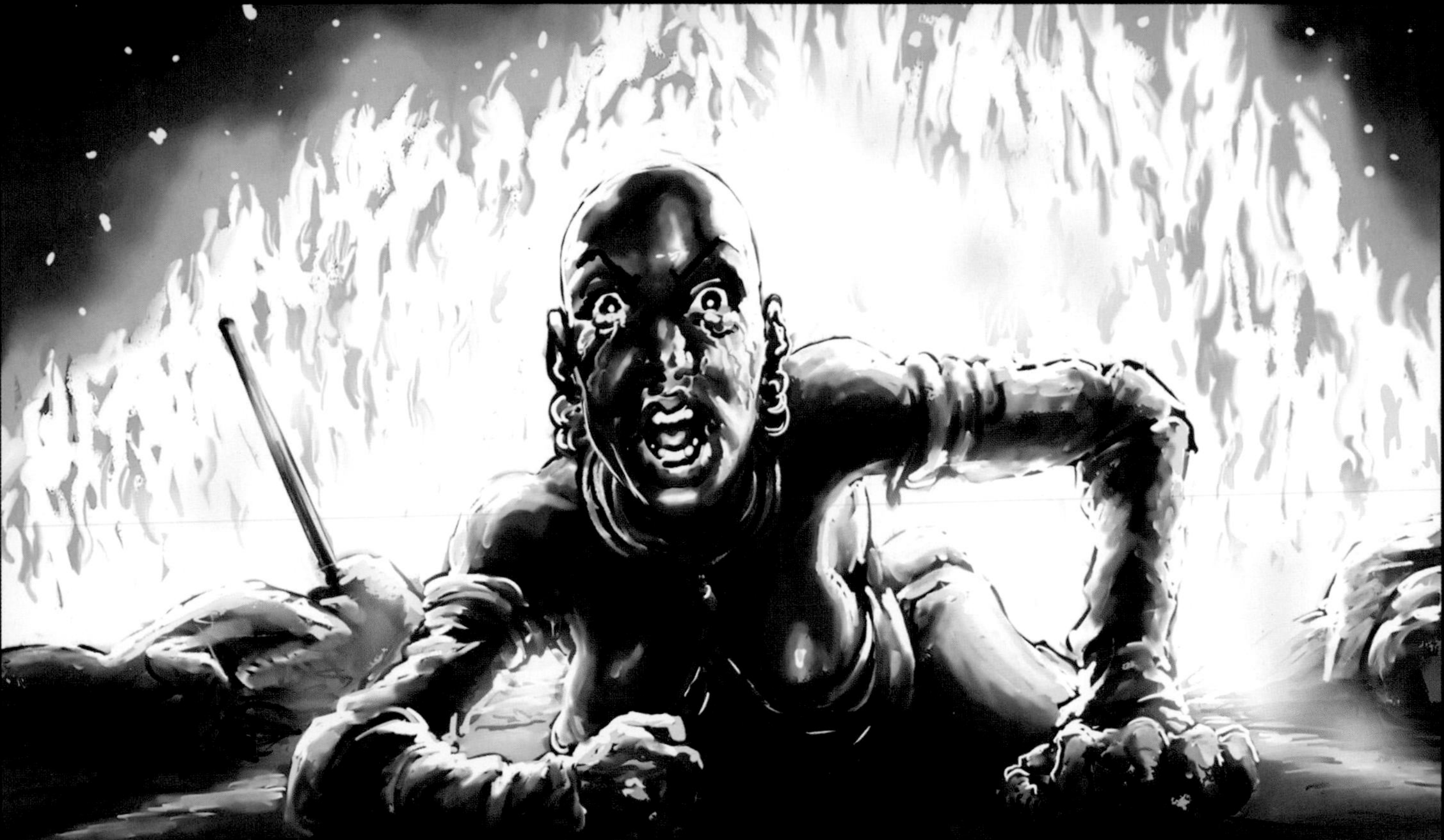

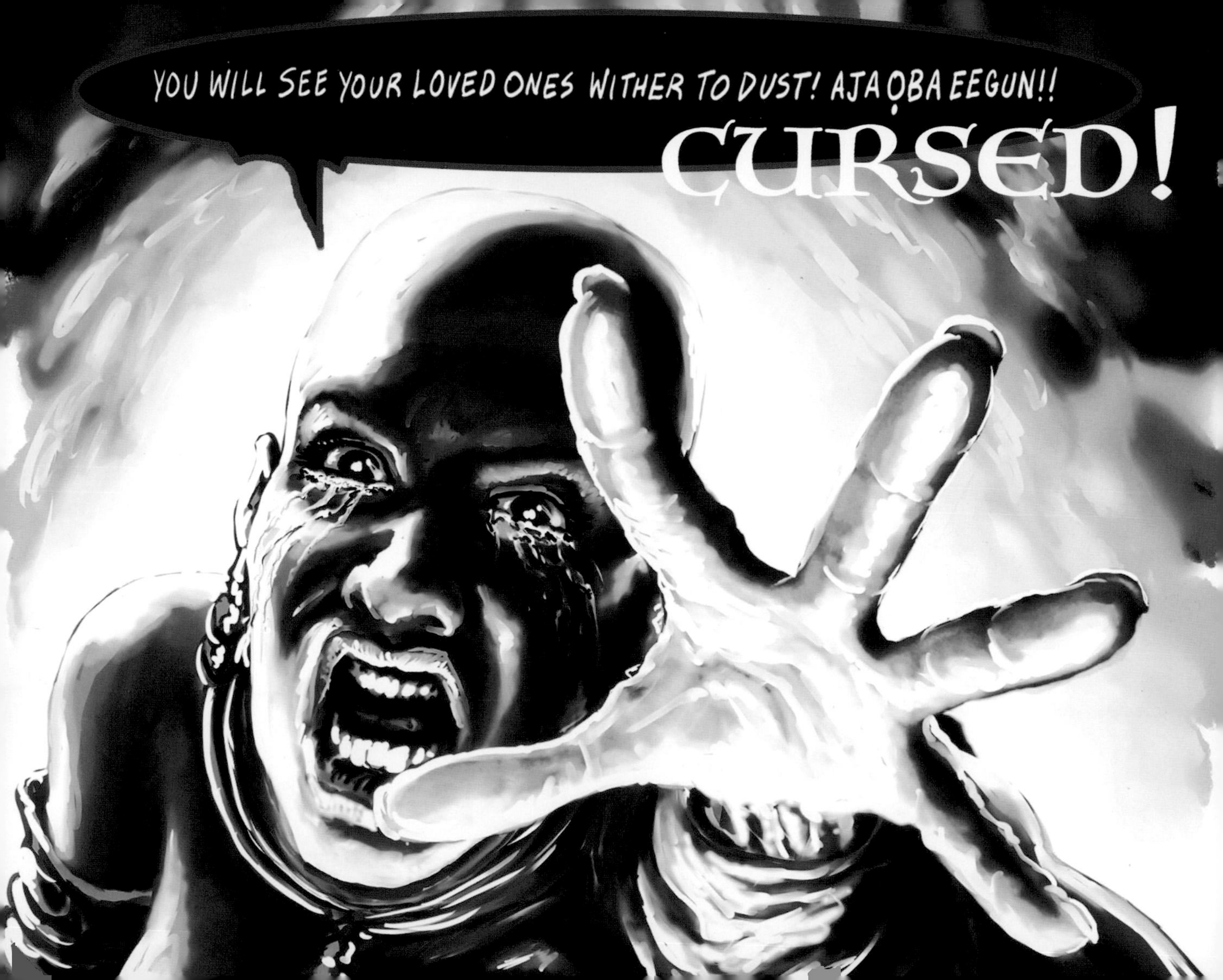
YOU WILL SEE YOUR LOVED ONES WITHER TO DUST! AJA ỌBA EEGUN!!
CURSED!

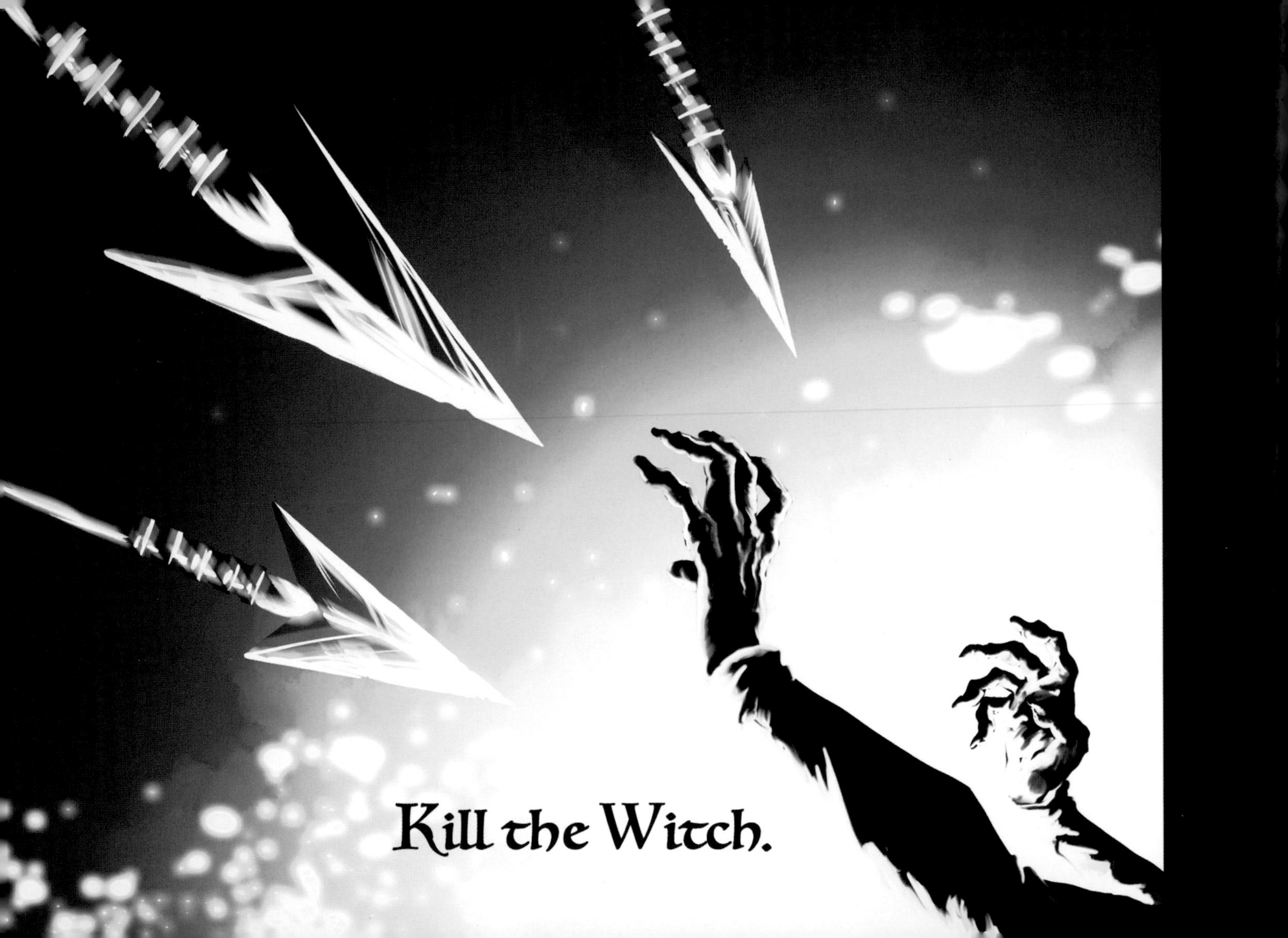
Kill the Witch.

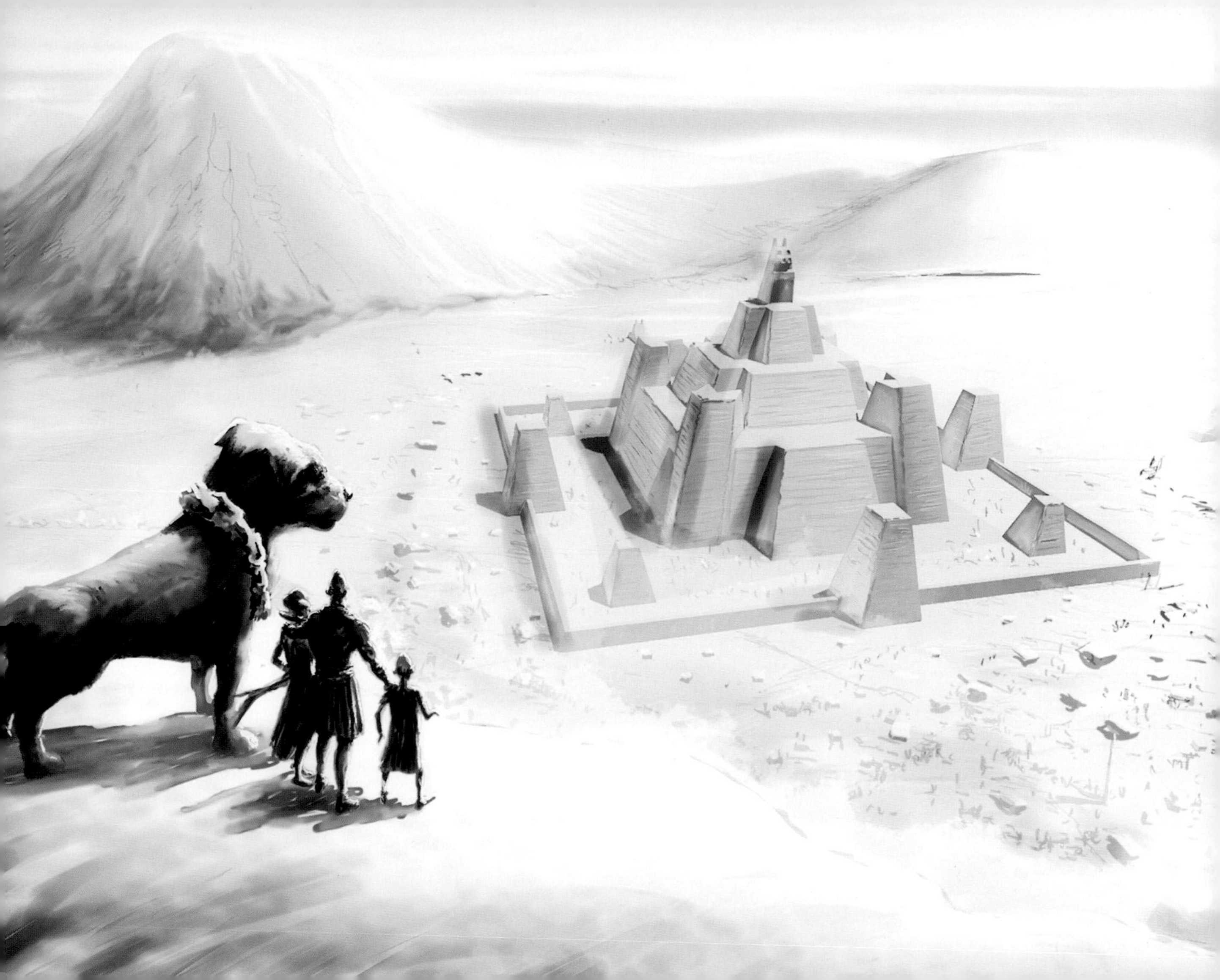

Ignoring the final outrage of his **concubine**, the King **did indeed** take the Child Heir to raise with his beloved Queen. They were a blessed **FAMILY**.

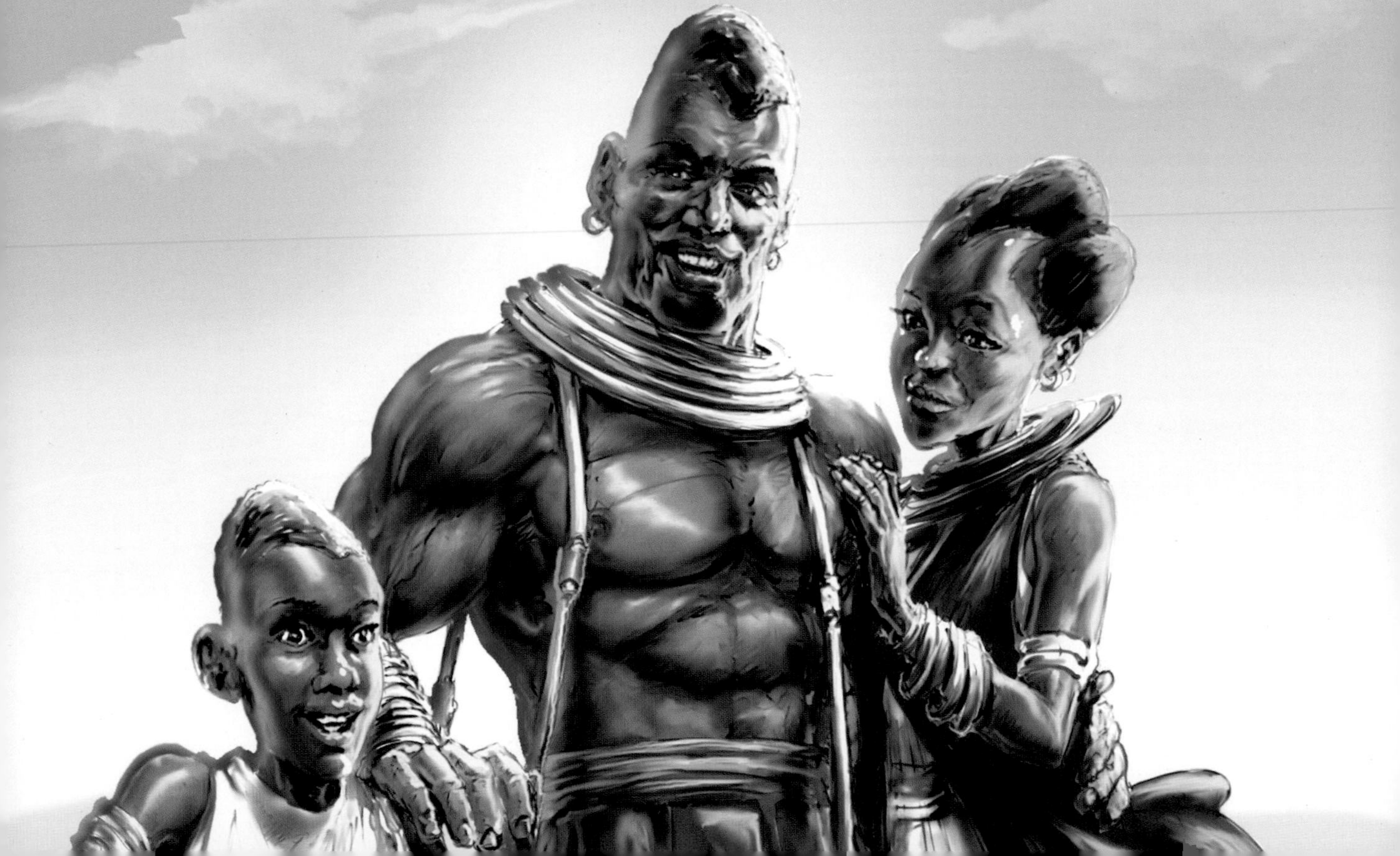

Thus, **The Royal House** grew in power, stature, and riches. This brought Ọba great pride. Yet, over the years **the Queen and Heir clearly aged**.

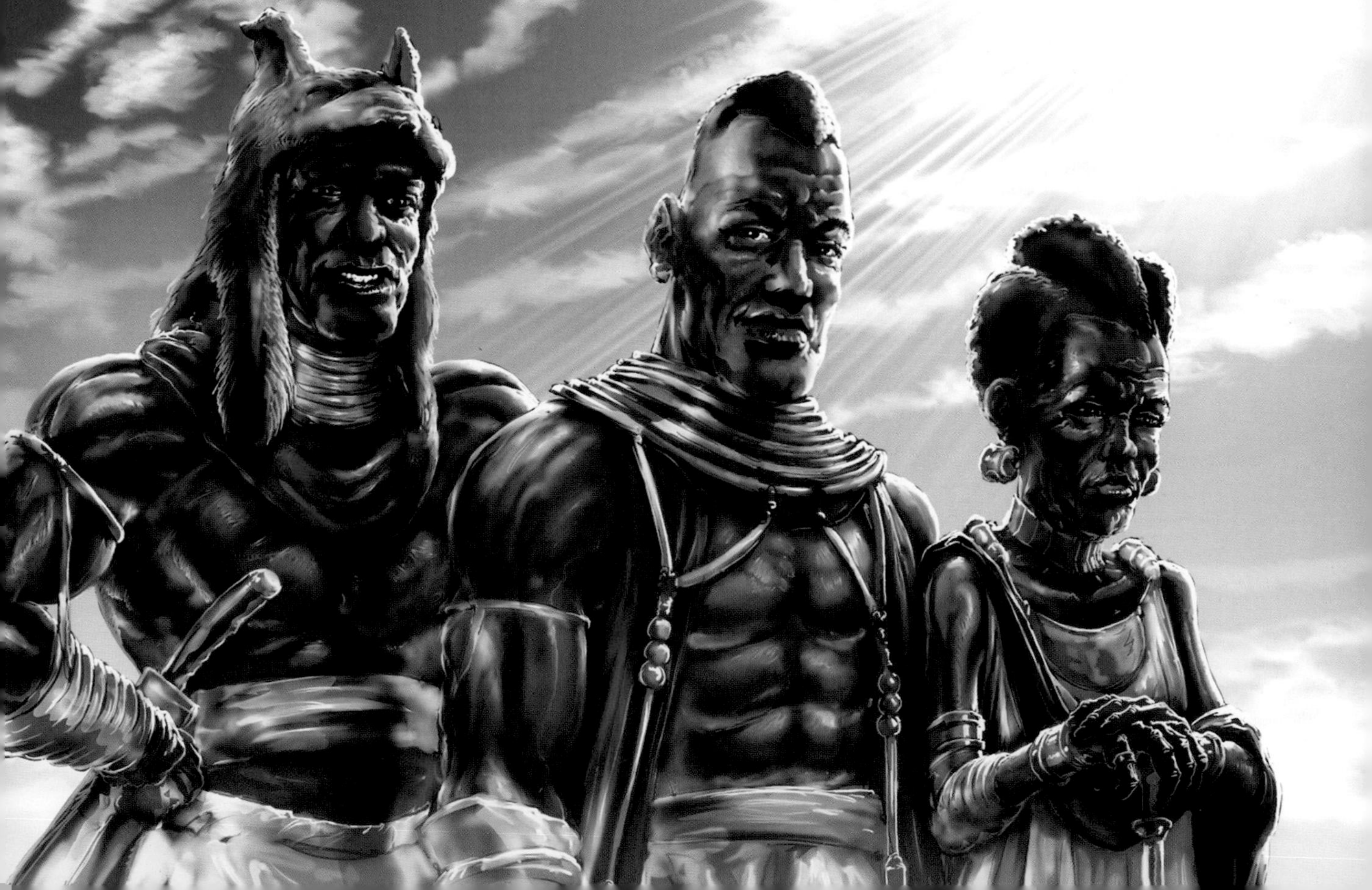

They inevitably died...the natural cycle of life. But, defying logic — the King did **NOT** age or die. The curse was **real**!

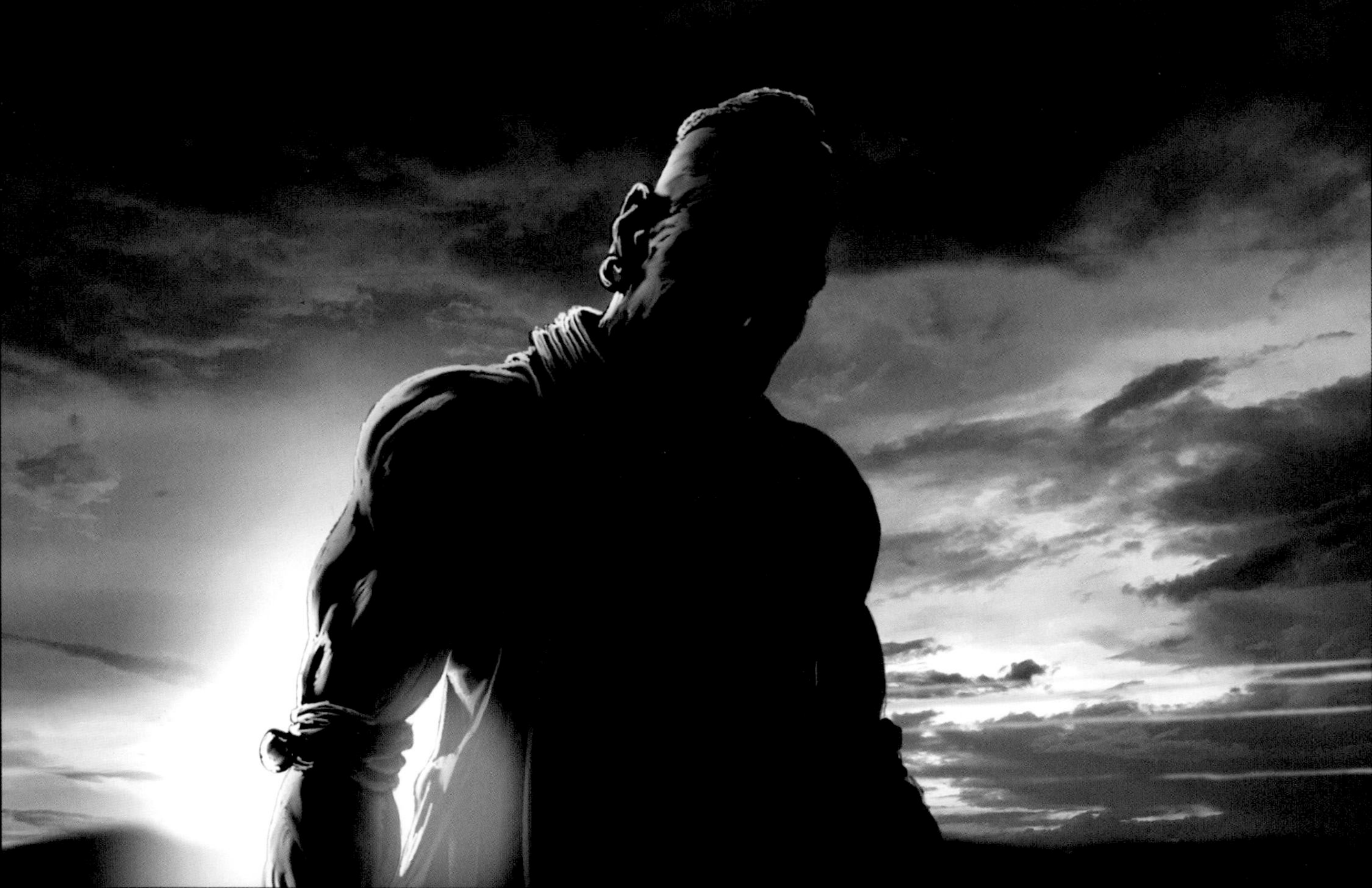

In his **mourning**, Aja Ọba became distracted. As he dwelled on the loss of Queen Lewa and his Heir, one opportunistic enemy after another brazenly **attacked the kingdom's perimeter walls**.

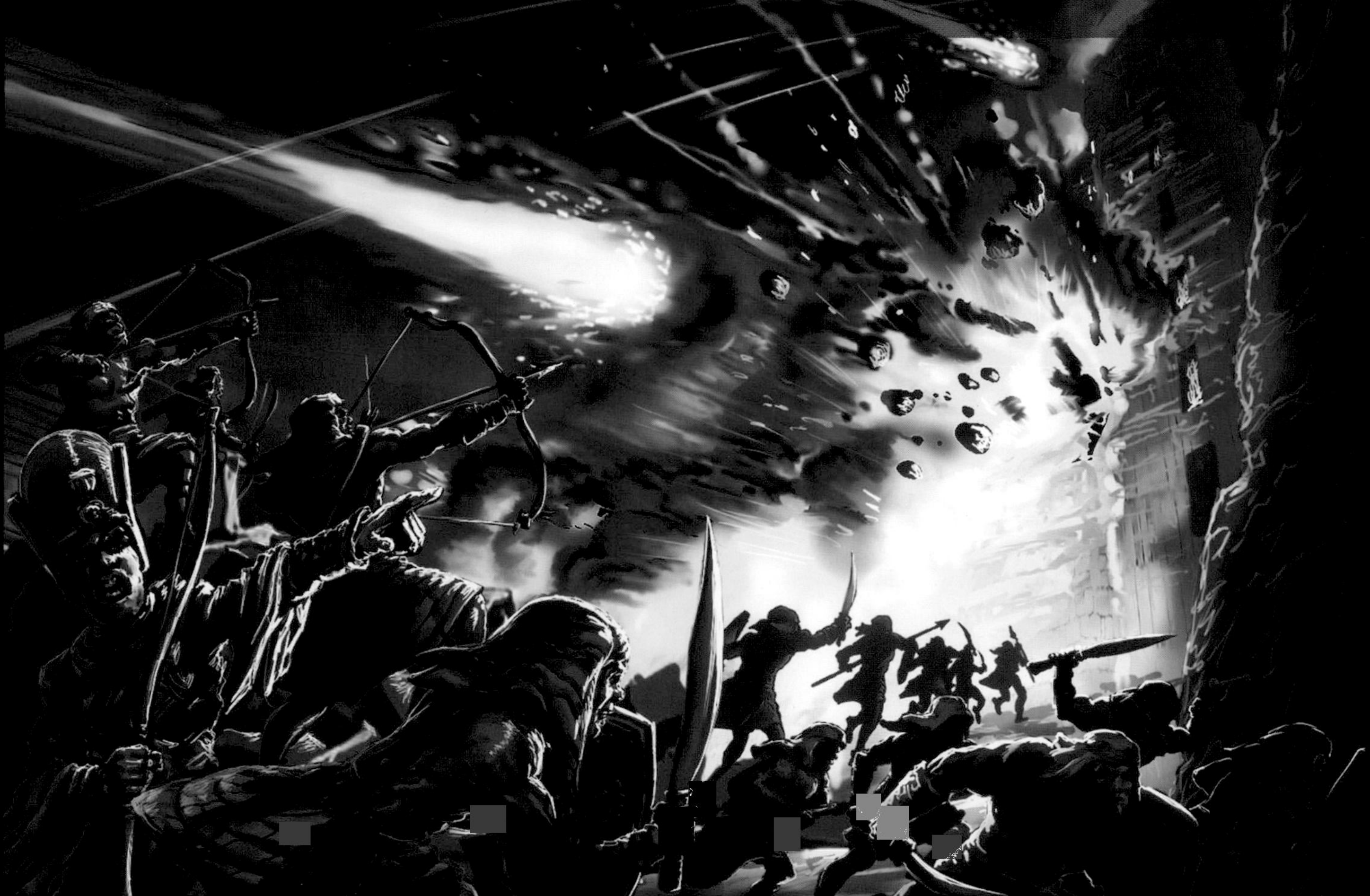

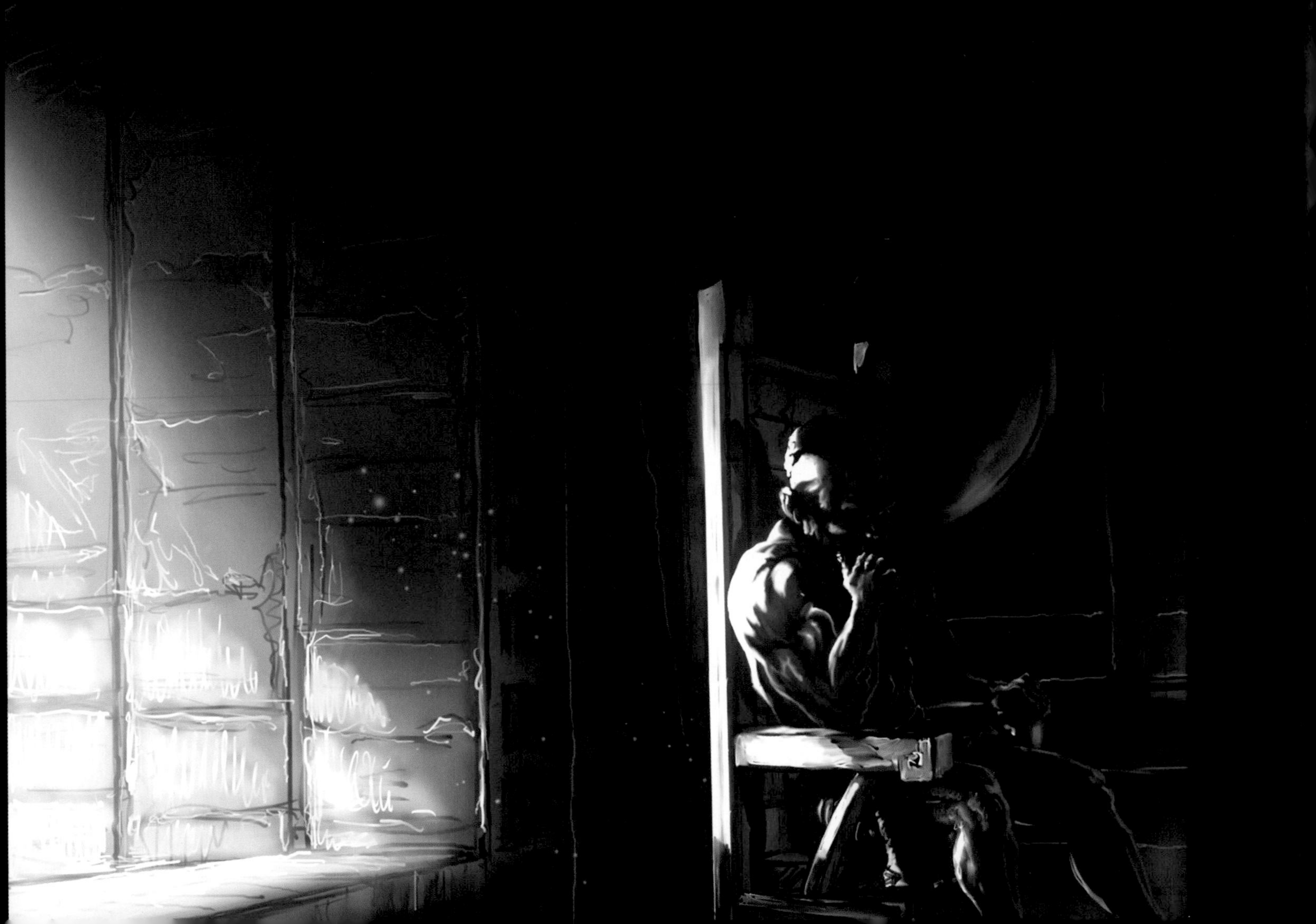

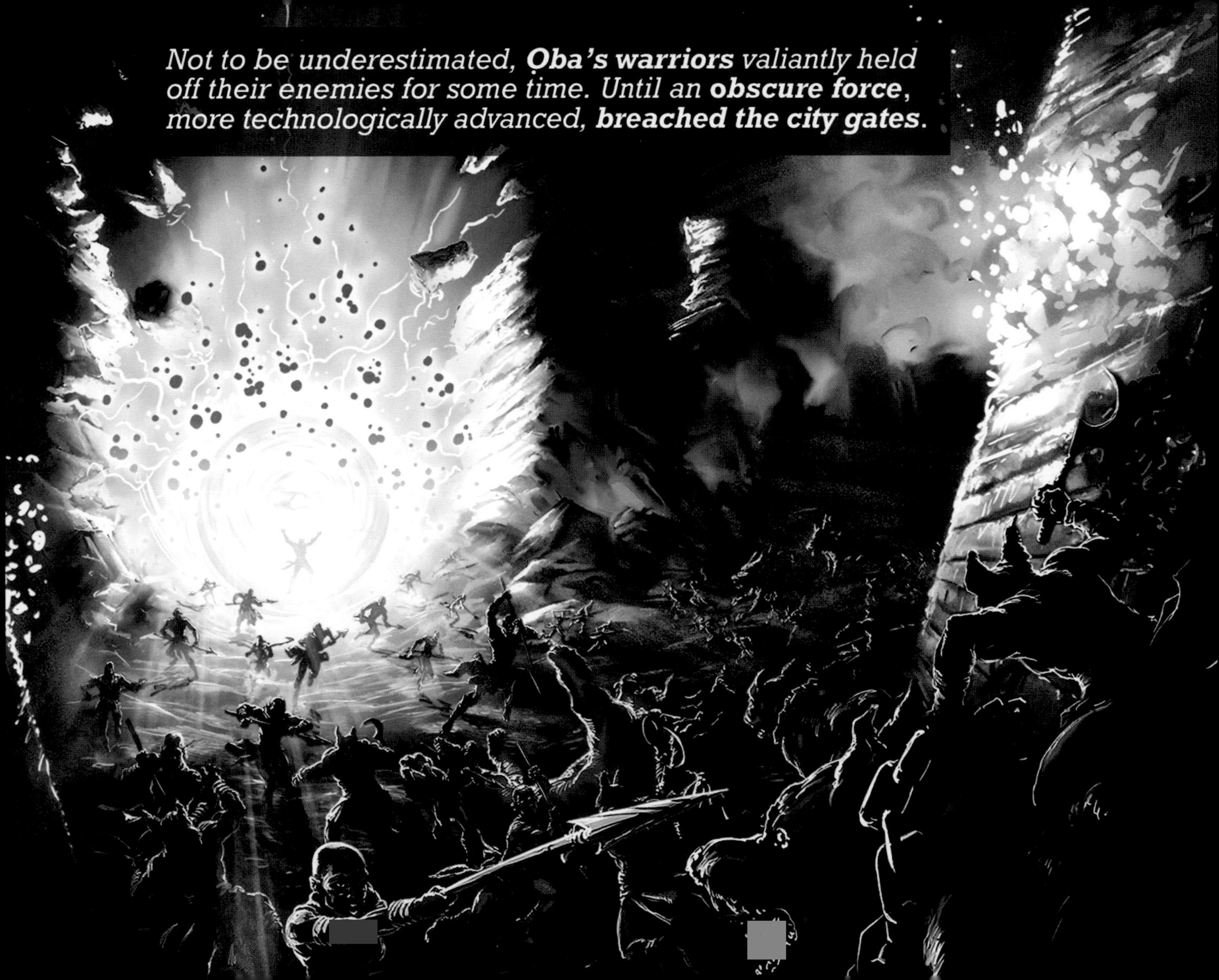
Not to be underestimated, **Oba's warriors** valiantly held off their enemies for some time. Until an **obscure force**, more technologically advanced, **breached the city gates**.

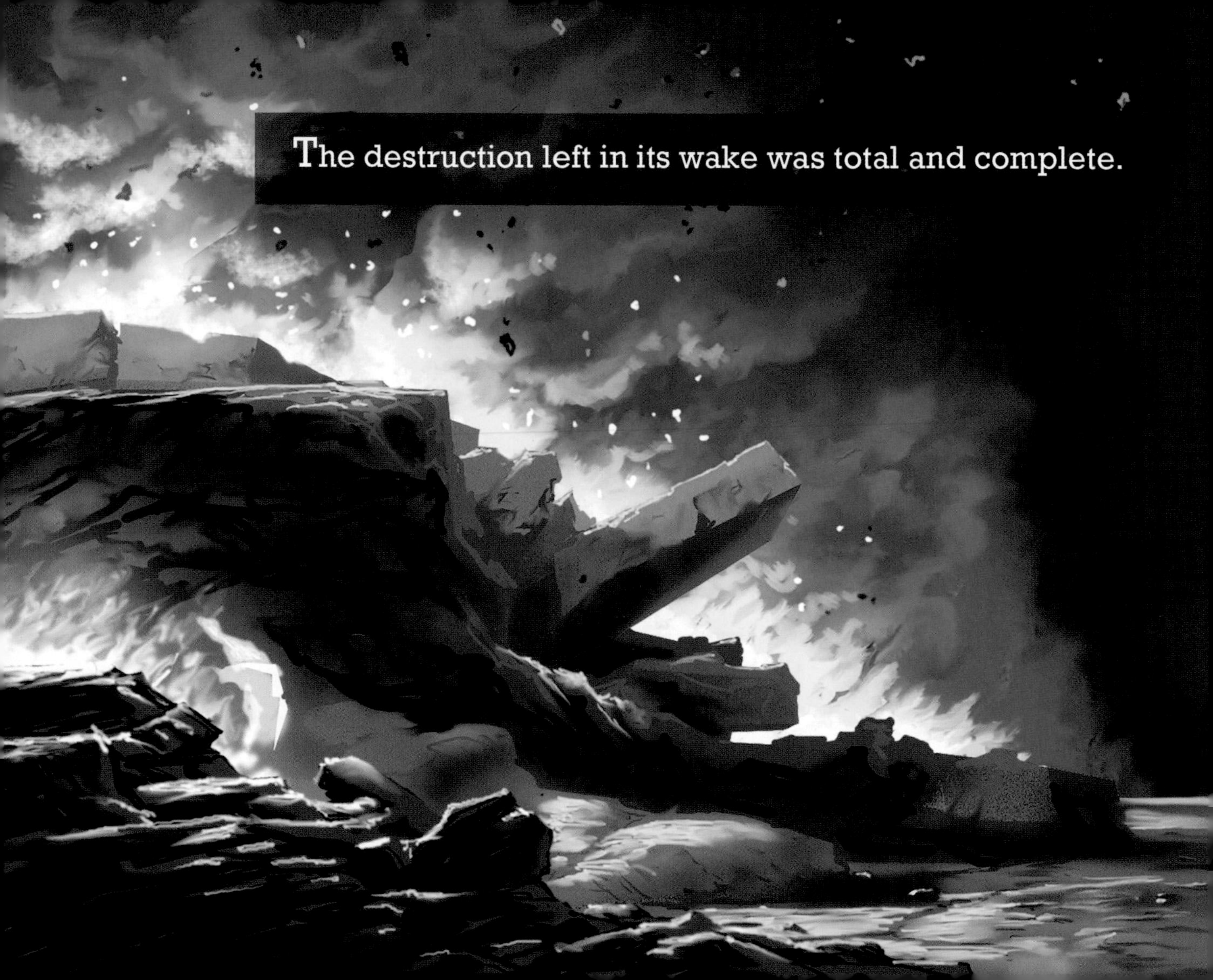
The destruction left in its wake was total and complete.

But the King did **NOT** die.

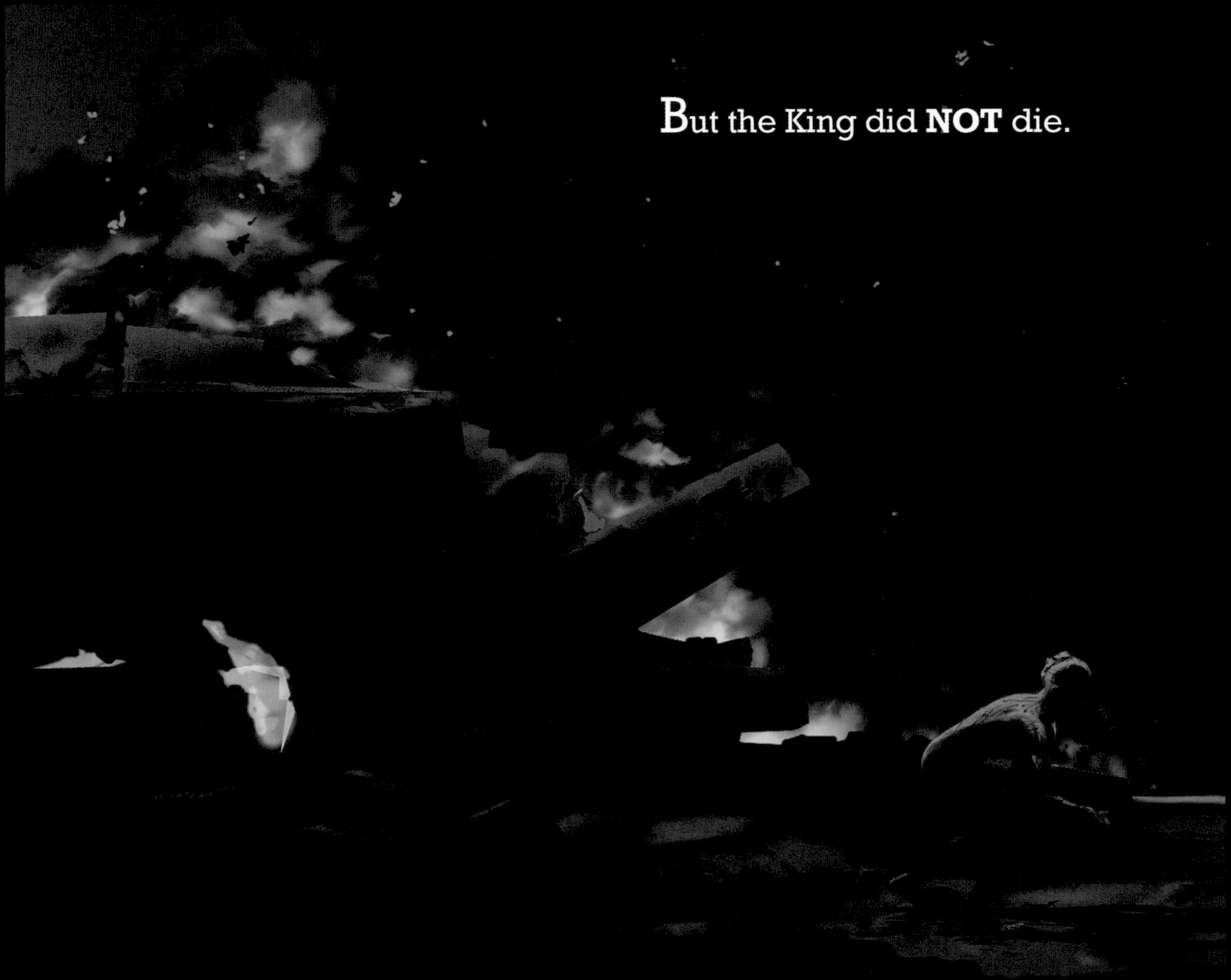

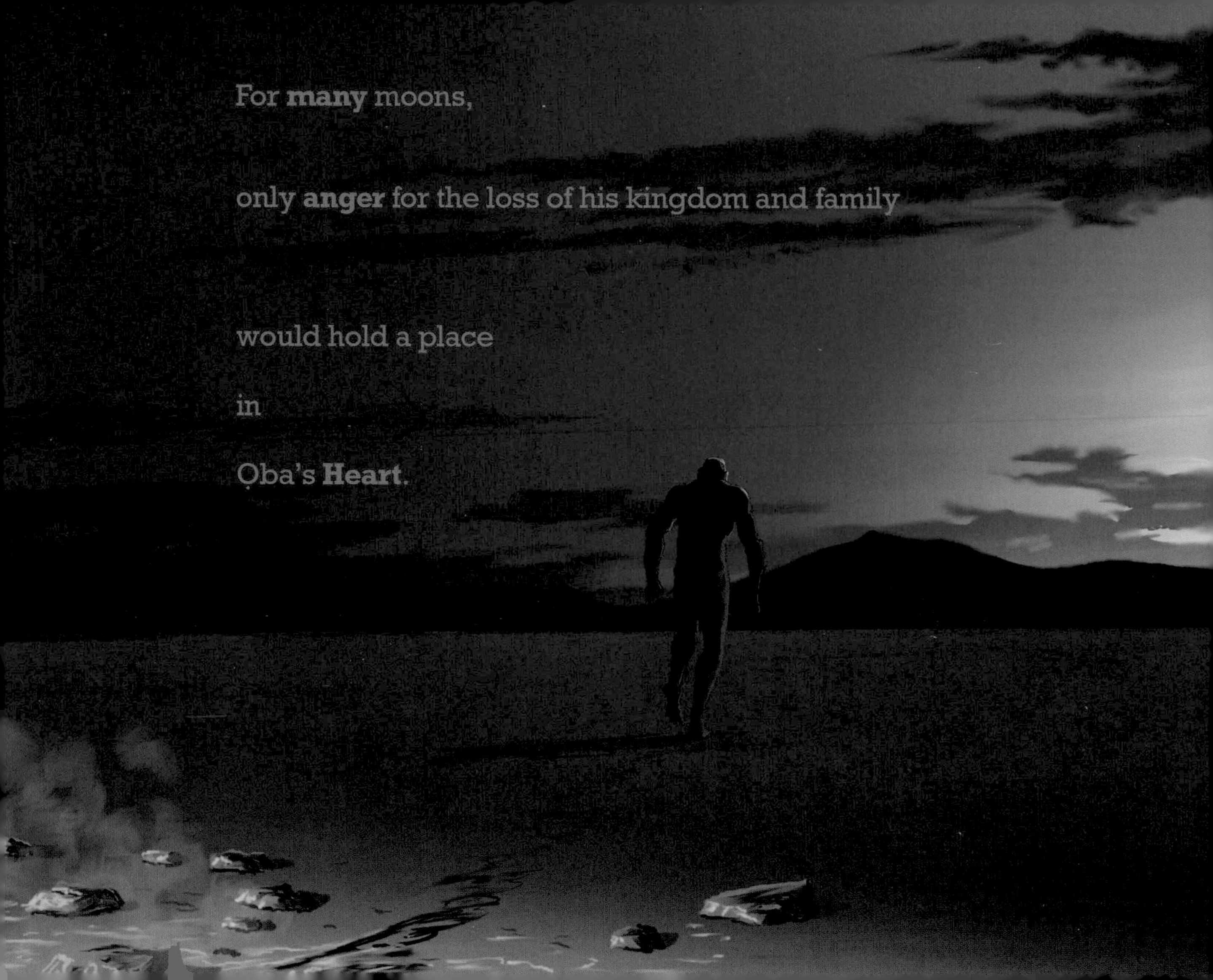

For **many** moons,

only **anger** for the loss of his kingdom and family

would hold a place

in

Ọba's **Heart**.

One of the unintended side effects of the fall of **Ọba's Kingdom**, and the eventual collapse of his competitors', was paving the way for the rise of European powers. Over **thousands of years** these armies would be led by **bloodthirsty warlords**, often presumed to be "touched" by some God. They ultimately handed over the responsibility of governance to legislative groups… or so was the intent. Using military, political, and, yes, religious power, these empires **dominated** huge swaths of humanity and territory. Ọba sought to gather fighters to strike these upstart invaders and exact revenge upon his former enemies.

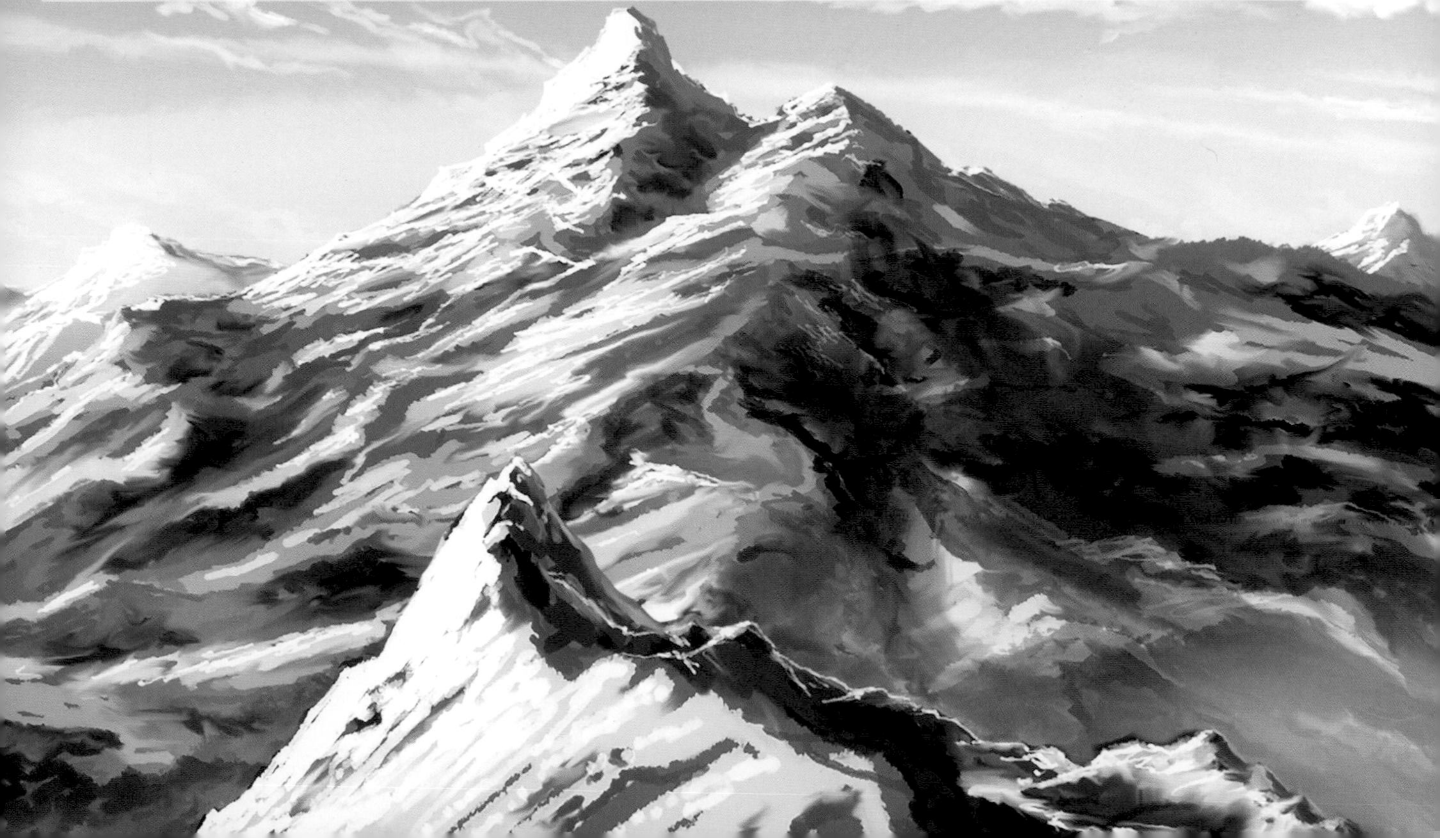

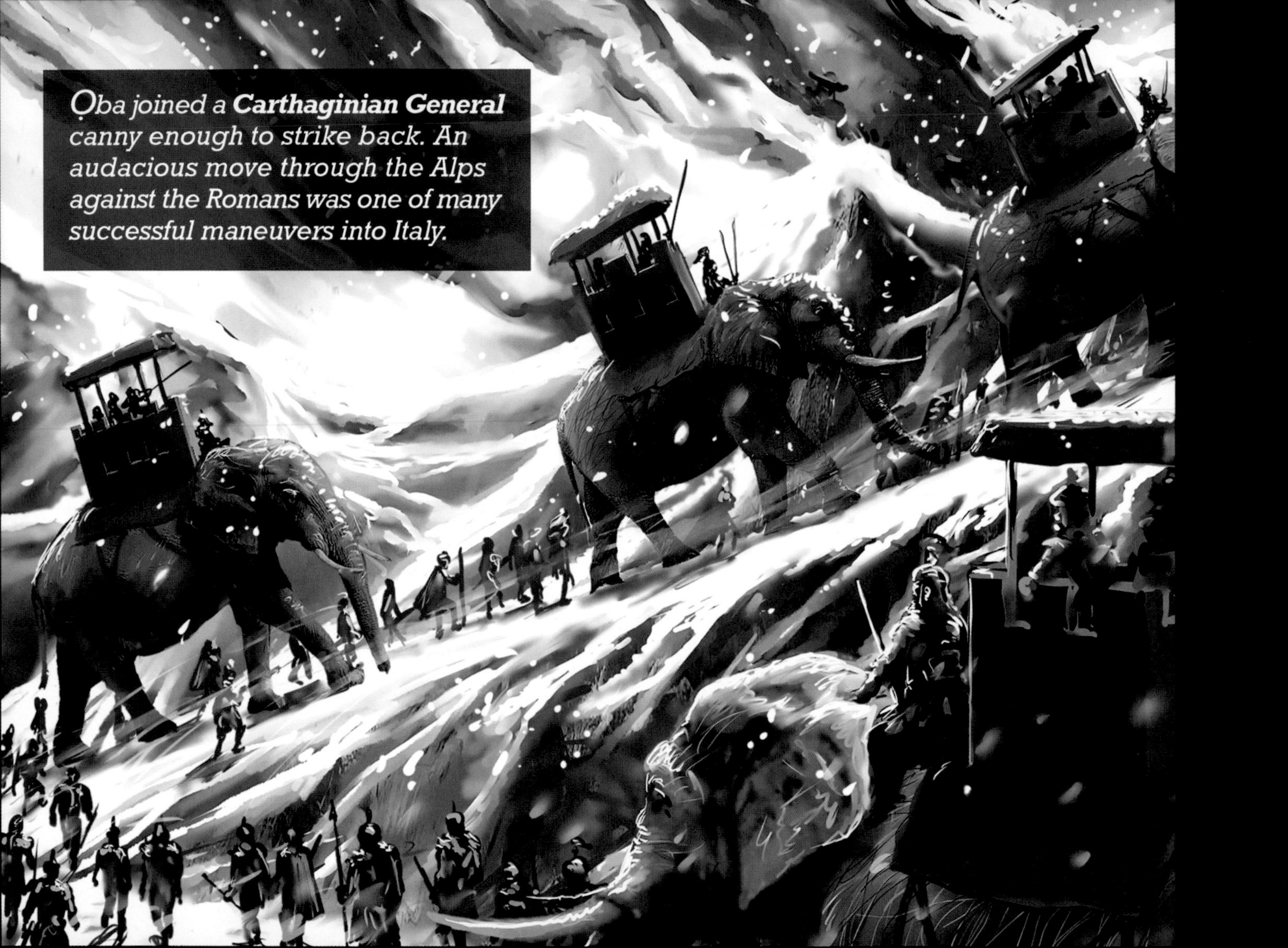
Ọba joined a **Carthaginian General** canny enough to strike back. An audacious move through the Alps against the Romans was one of many successful maneuvers into Italy.

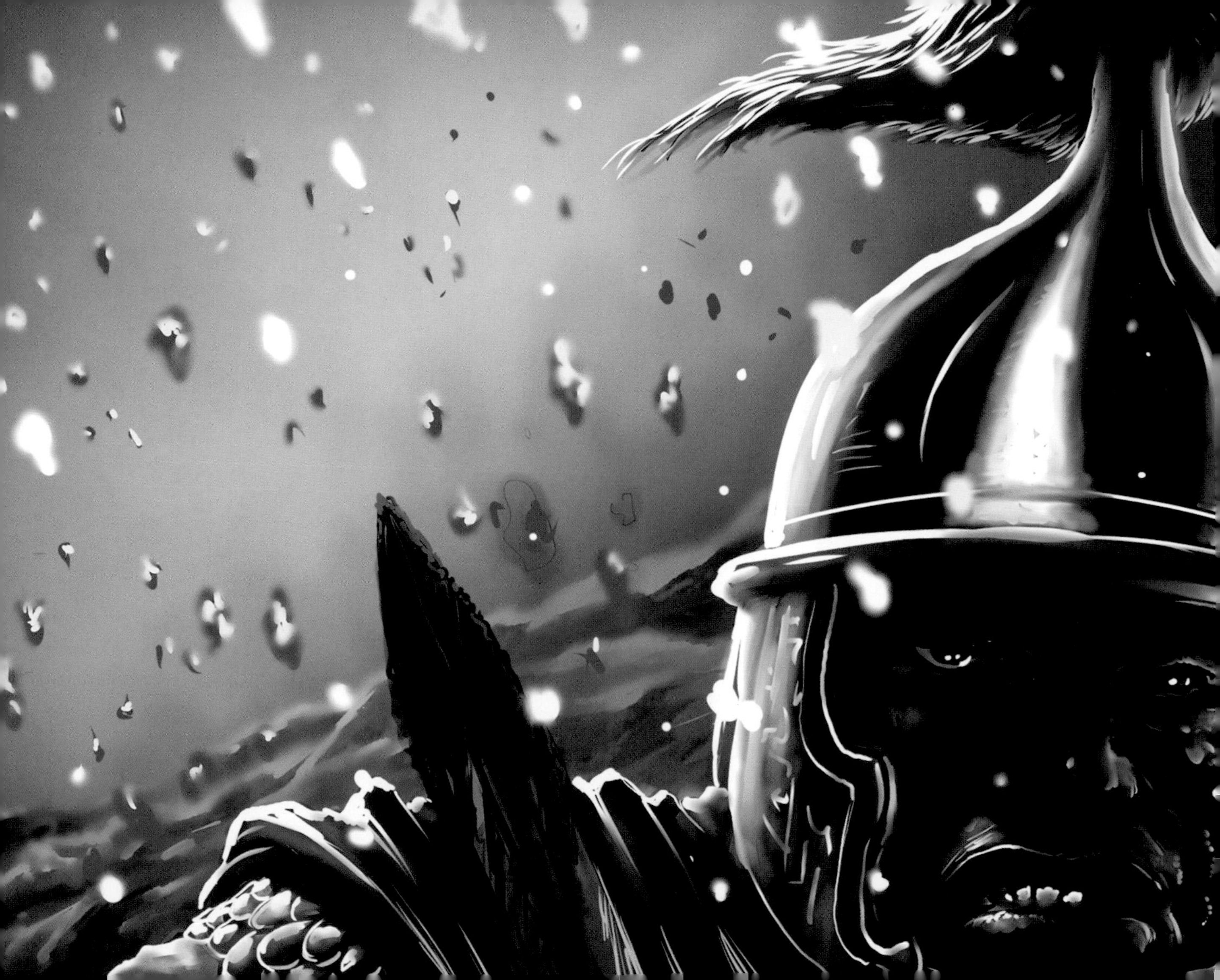

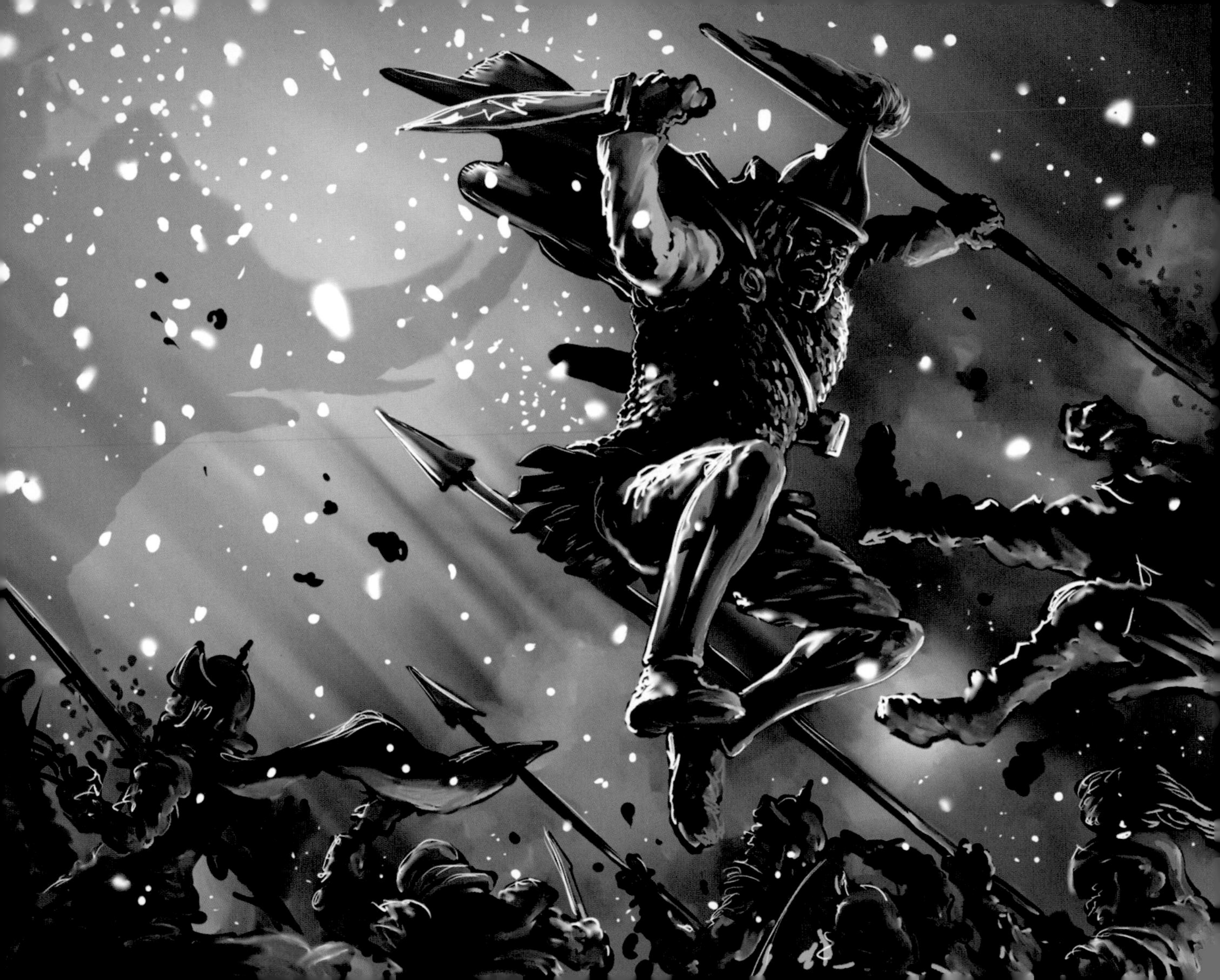

The Carthaginian Army **crushed** the **Roman Legion** in multiple battles. Despite Ọba's strong advice to seize or destroy the city of Rome, the **General** refused, wrongly thinking their work was done. Soon, Ọba was **banished** from the **inner circle**.

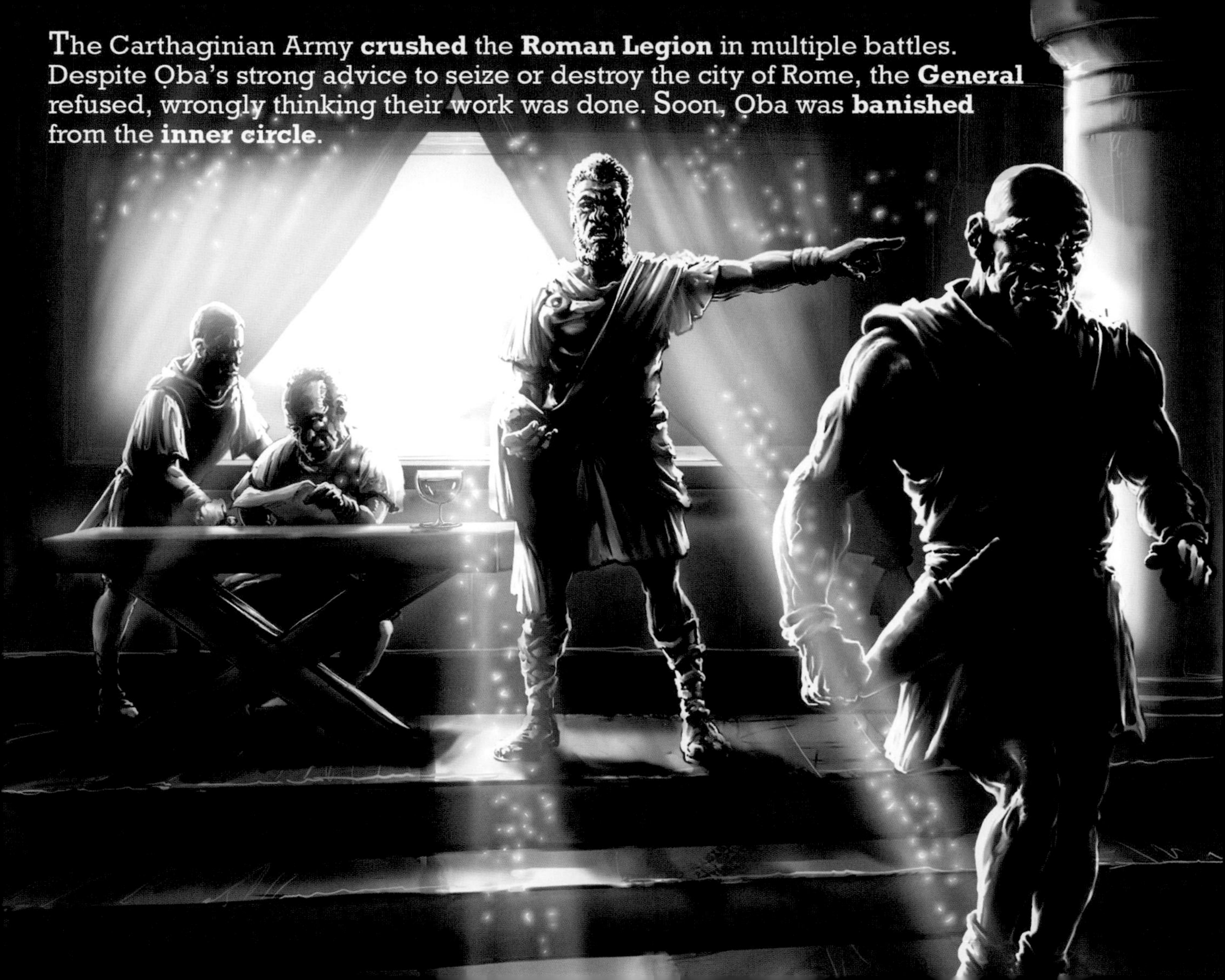

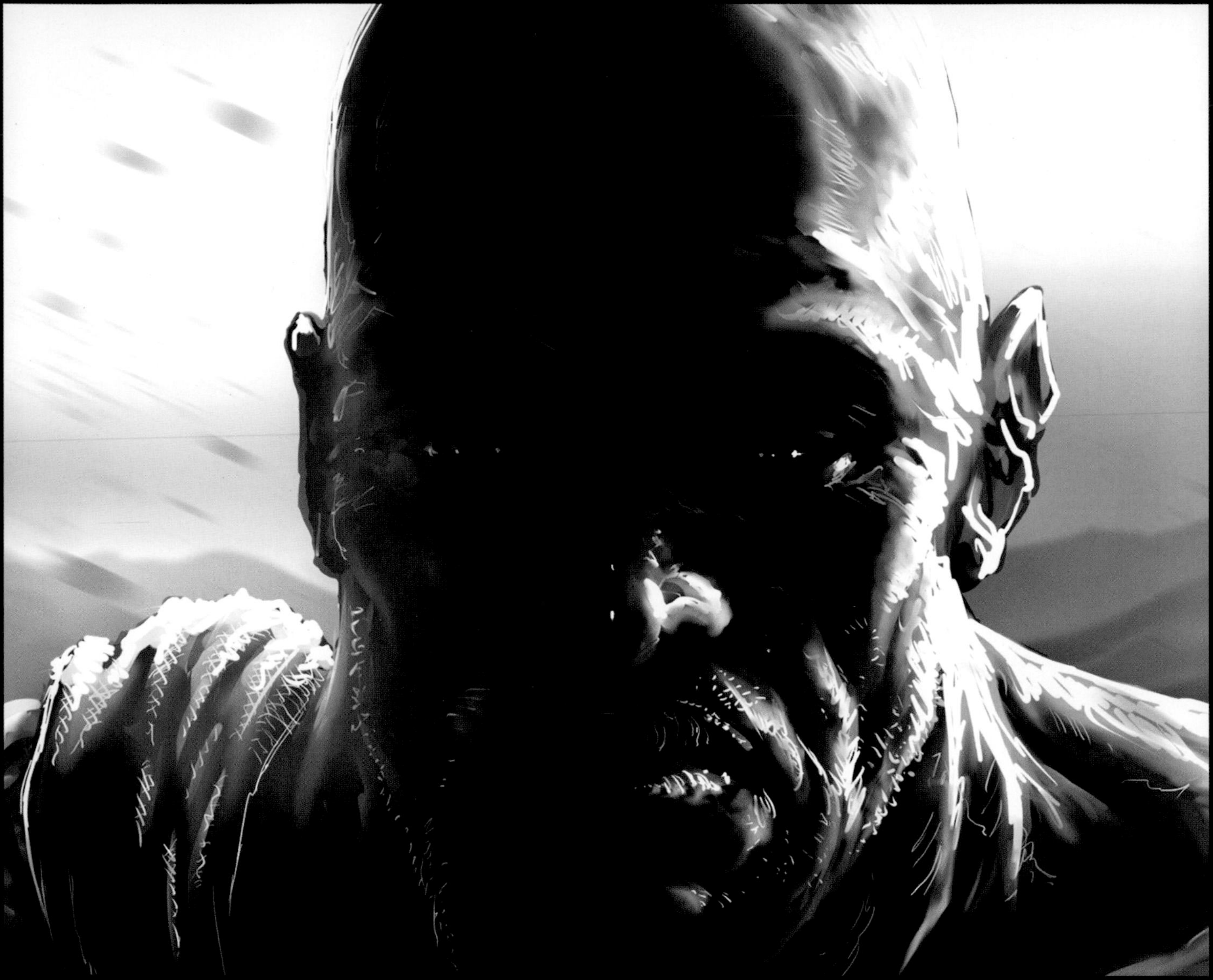

It's against my **warrior code** to take my own life – if that's even possible now. So, I've endeavored countless times to have Obinrin's miserable curse **UNDONE**.

A most obscure attempt was guided by an **Old Roots Shaman** who lived deep in the bush. He claimed that the light from his fire could not remove the shadow that marked my steps. He failed. In the end **they all failed.** Each time proving more pointless and eternally frustrating.

I am reduced to existing as an ageless animal. **I eat and shit and roam forever without rot.**

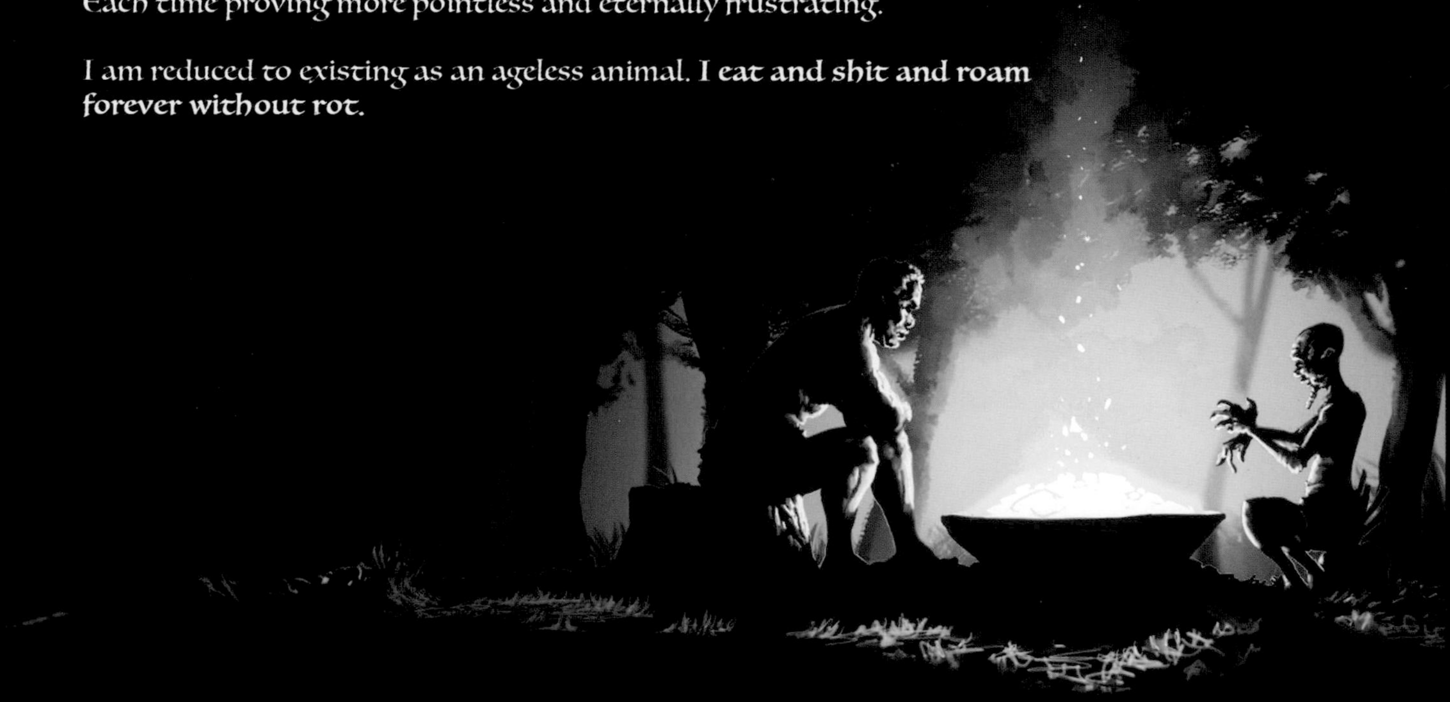

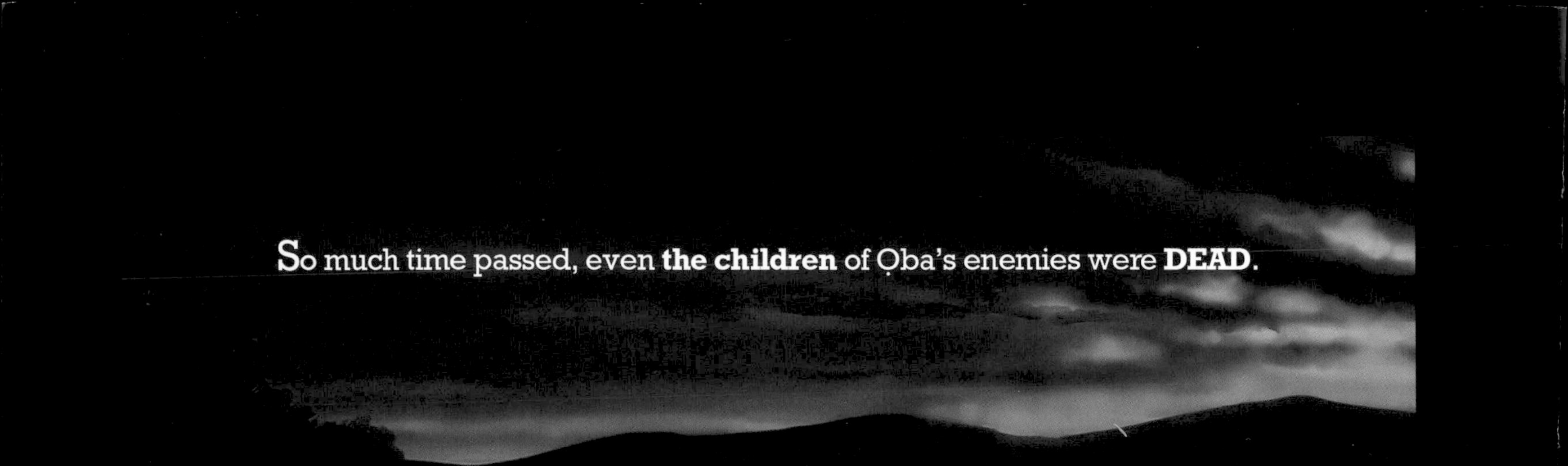

So much time passed, even **the children** of Ọba's enemies were **DEAD**.

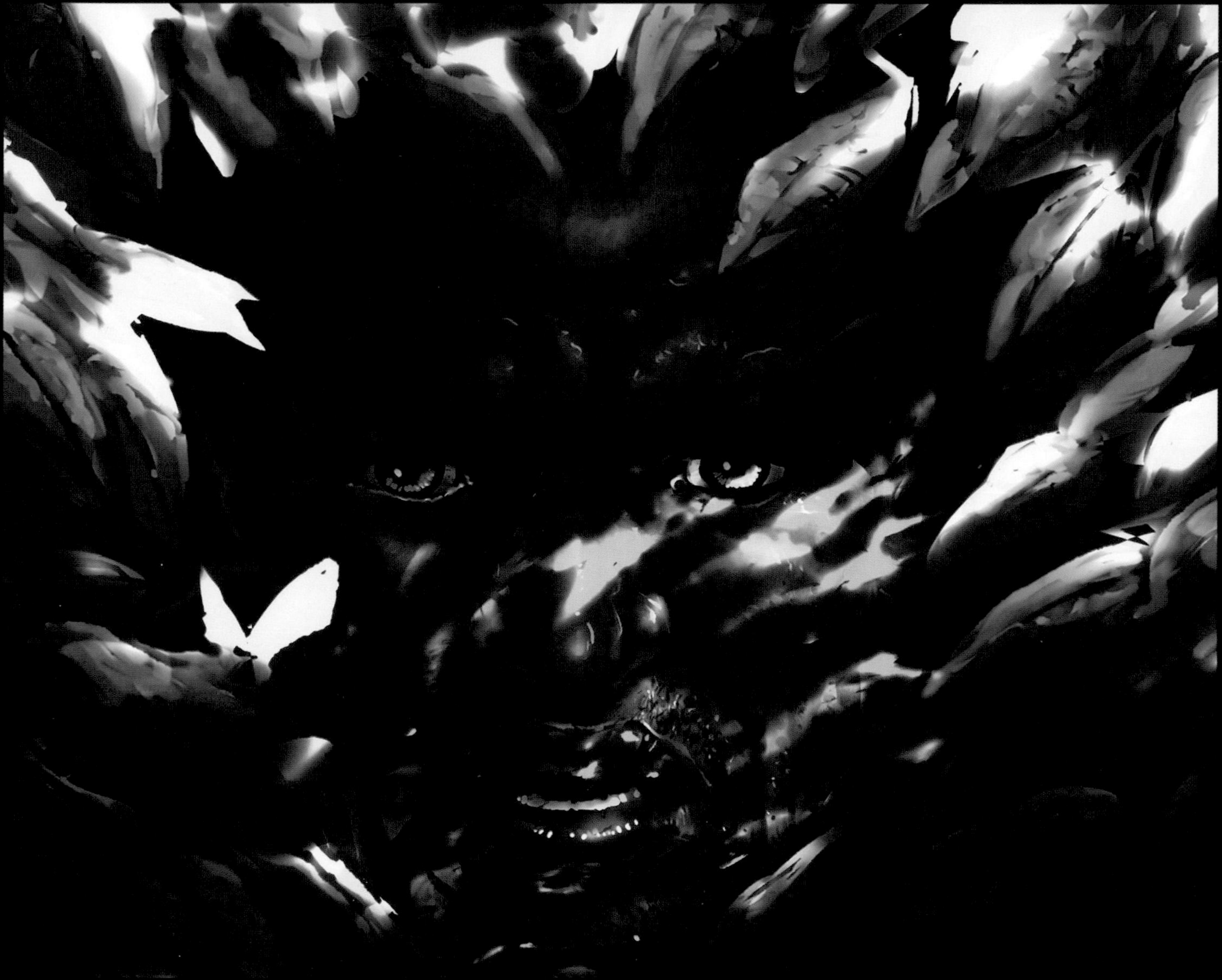

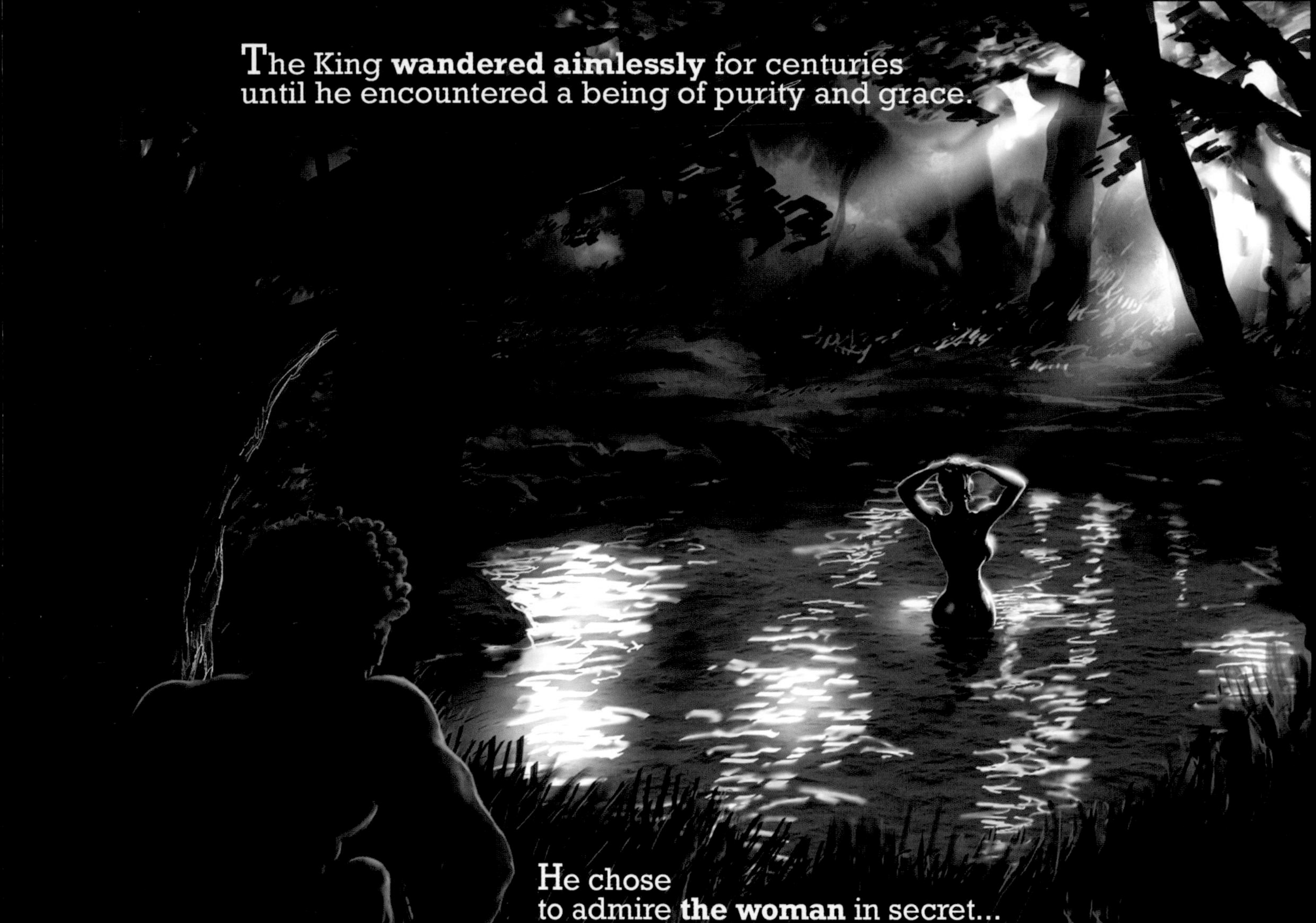
The King **wandered aimlessly** for centuries
until he encountered a being of purity and grace.
He chose
to admire **the woman** in secret...

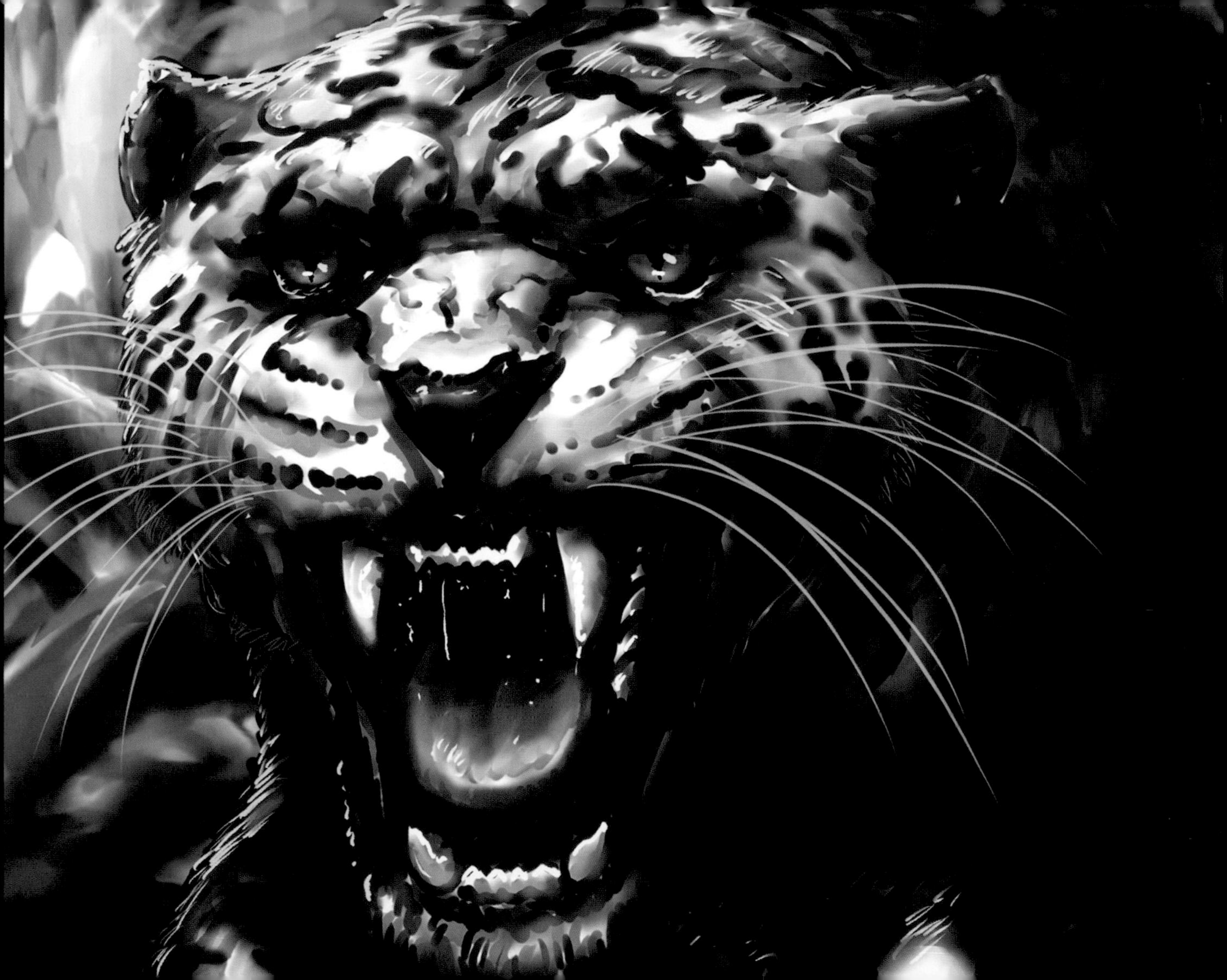

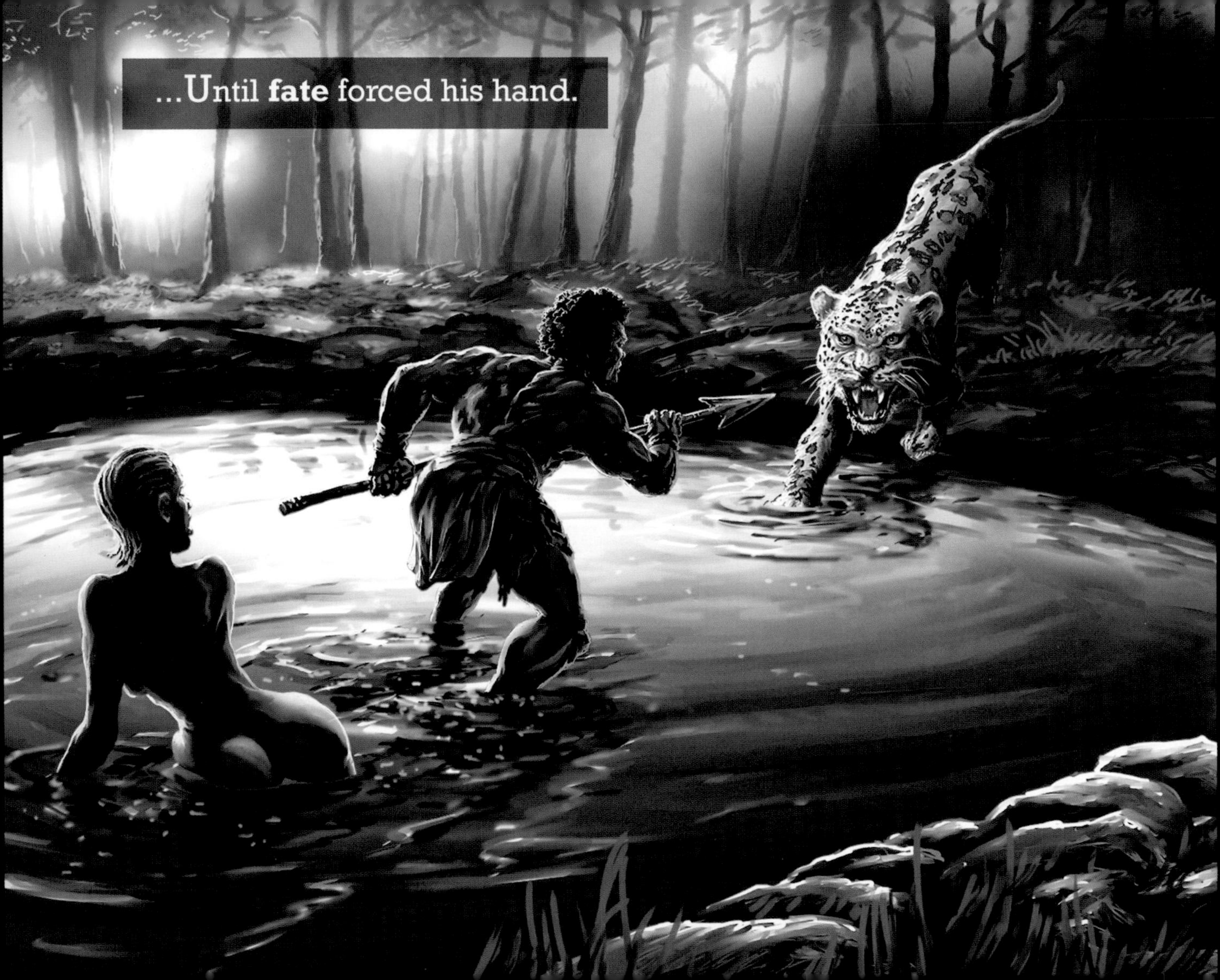
...Until **fate** forced his hand.

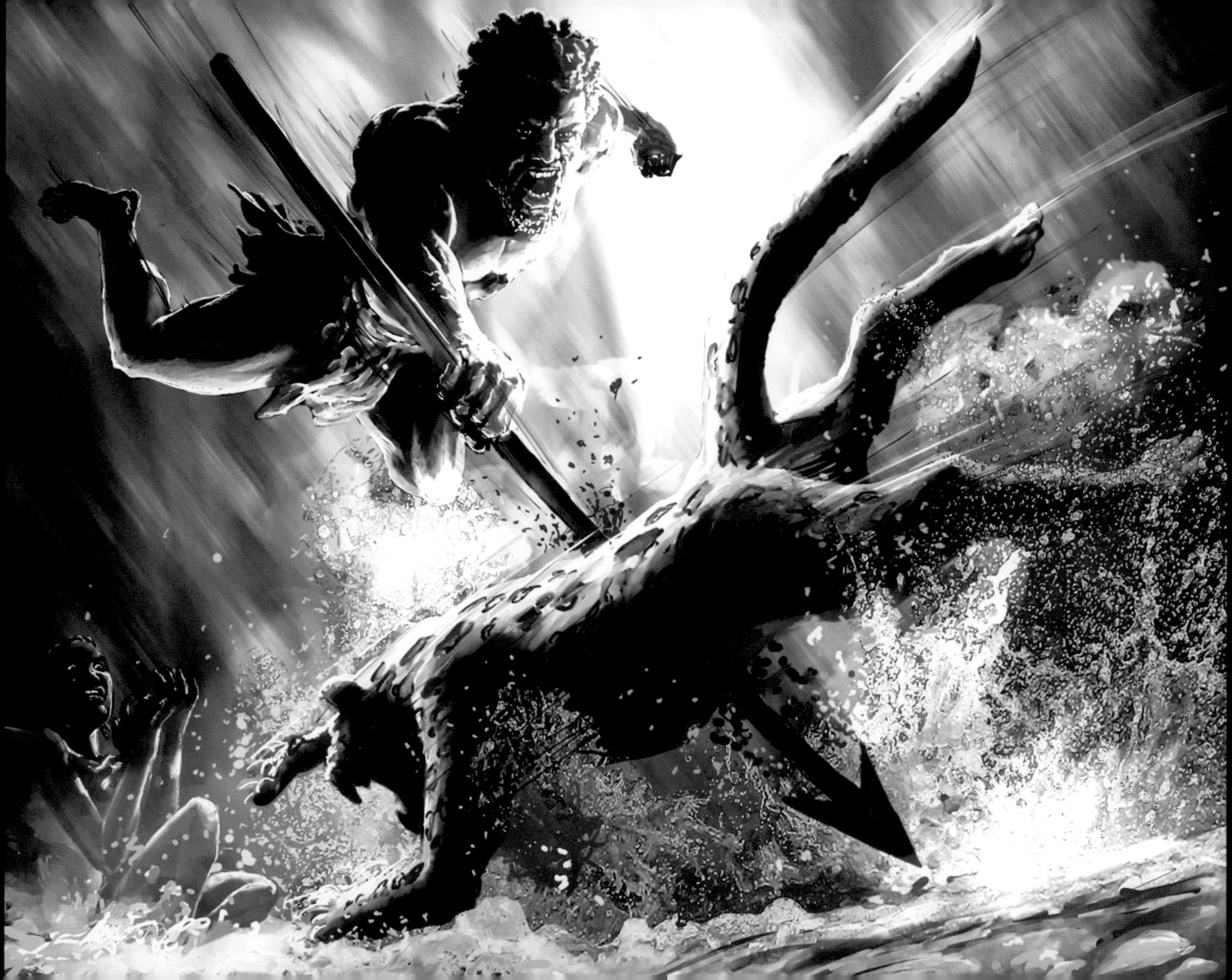

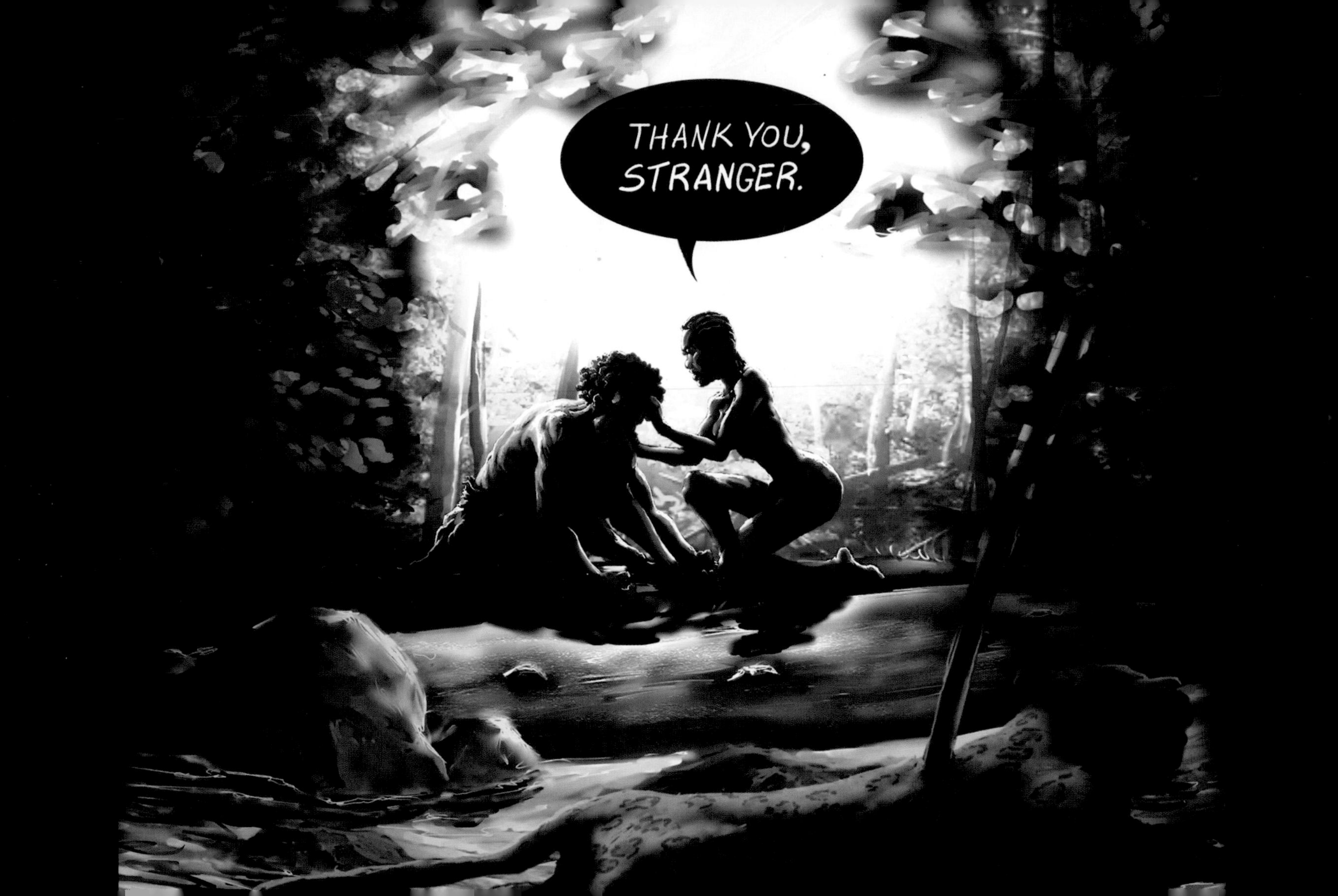
THANK YOU, STRANGER.

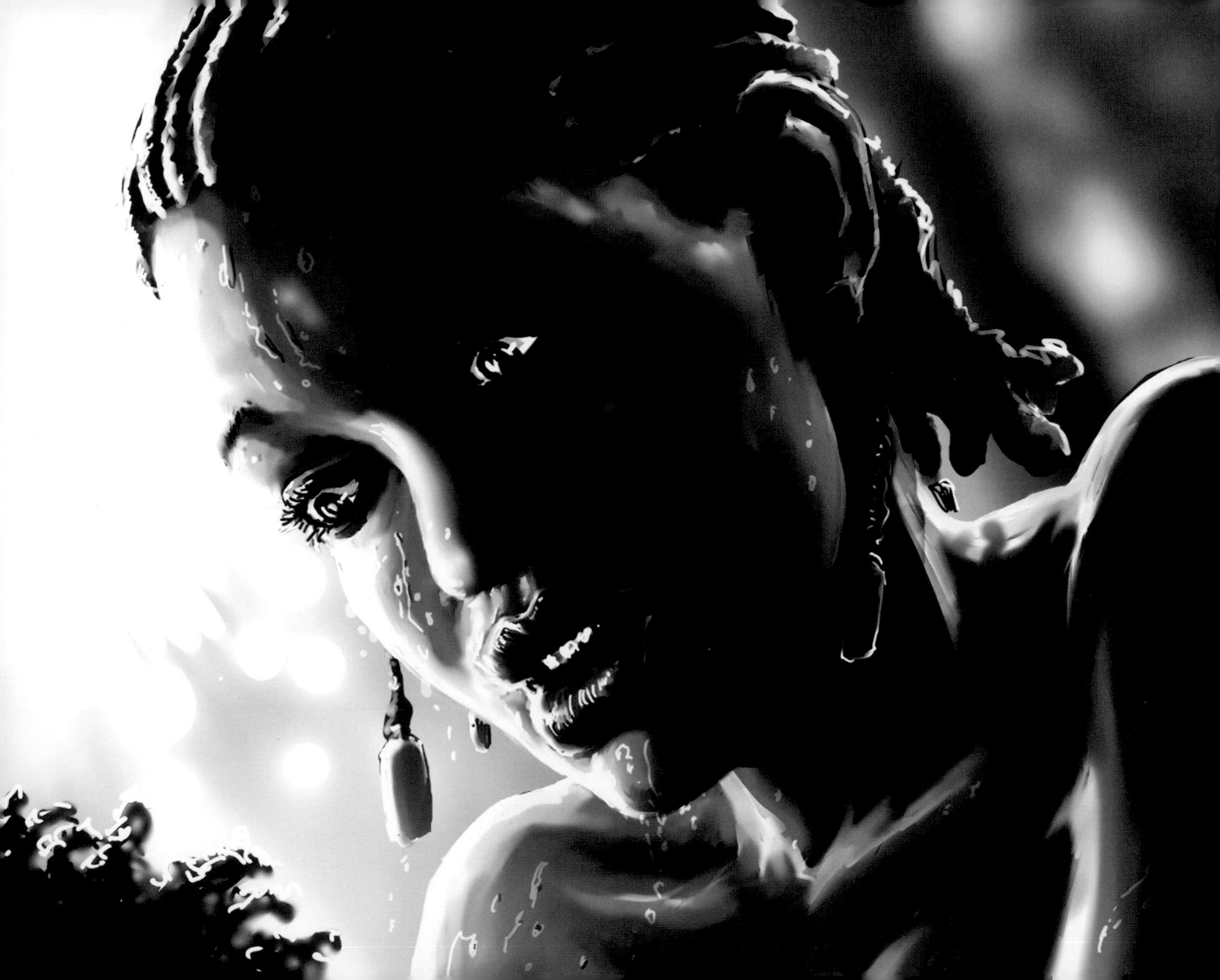

Akeyo was the most fascinating woman I've ever known. **She was a blacksmith, artist, and my truest love.** For someone so intelligent and incredibly beautiful to be immediately trusting of me – **a monster** – was miraculous and humbling.

After centuries of aimless wandering, I was staggered by **Akeyo**, a woman with a righteous soul who was capable of **bending metal** to her will – young, yet wise enough to demand better of me. Her life philosophy was to seek beauty in all things. And where she didn't find it, she felt a responsibility to create it. **Akeyo, the builder of worlds.**

If there were truly gods, **I had been shown unwarranted mercy.**

Akeyo – merciful **Akeyo** – was an escape from my past.

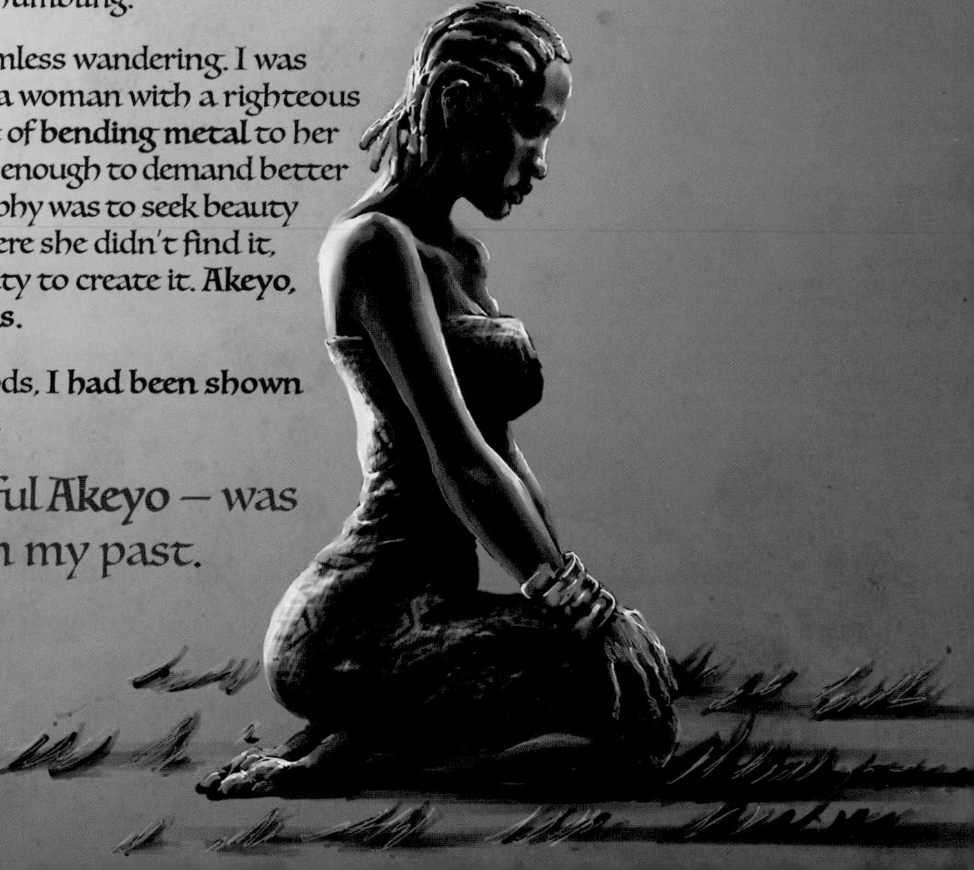

My Grandfather is the master blacksmith for our village. He has cured the tools used by our hunters and builders for three generations. After my parents died in a fire, I became self-destructive. Baba raised me, insisting that I know the discipline of metal. The village council forbade my apprenticeship because I was a girl but Grandfather would not bend to that. He cleverly claimed that I was training to be a sculptor. I'm now as highly skilled at manipulating iron and steel as the most distinguished metal artisan.

I create àrt. My expertise originally transformed basic trinkets into elegant furniture and, ultimately, into shrines. When it became known that I fabricated adornments for the village priests, my talents became accepted — even championed. But passion for creating beautiful things sometimes makes me lose sight of the others — suitors — to my Baba's chagrin.

I cherish the forests though they can be dangerous. It's foolish of me to take solitary baths but I need the quiet to dream. Today a lovely mountainous man saved me from a deadly beast. He was injured killing the animal but is healing and making himself a guest in our garden. Baba was excited to see him water and talk to our plants just like we do. The man says he loves my art. I will forge him iron in thanks.

I have to ask him his name.

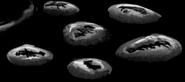

Ọba was rewarded for his bravery with **marriage to Akeyo** and a cozy house in her small village.

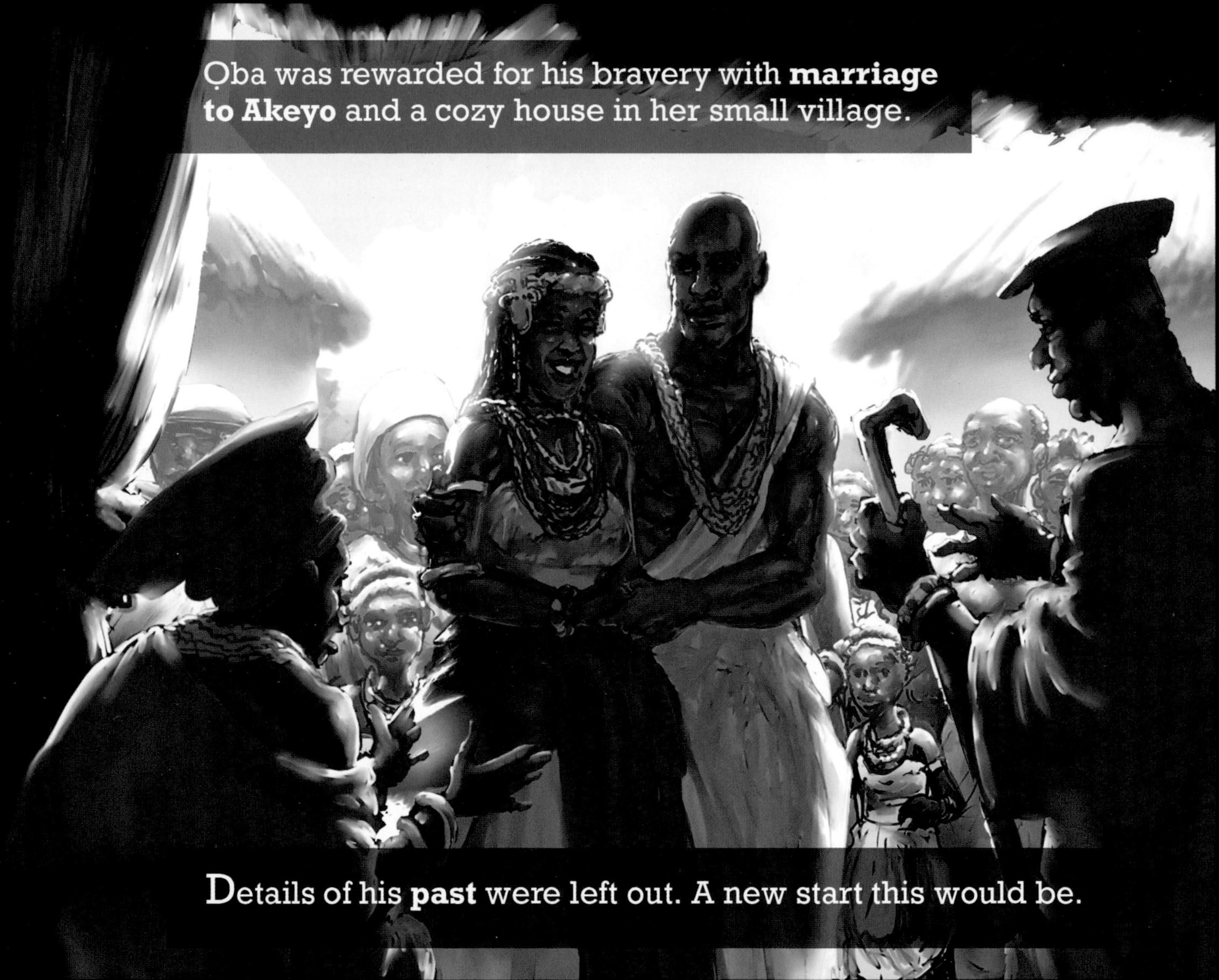

Details of his **past** were left out. A new start this would be.

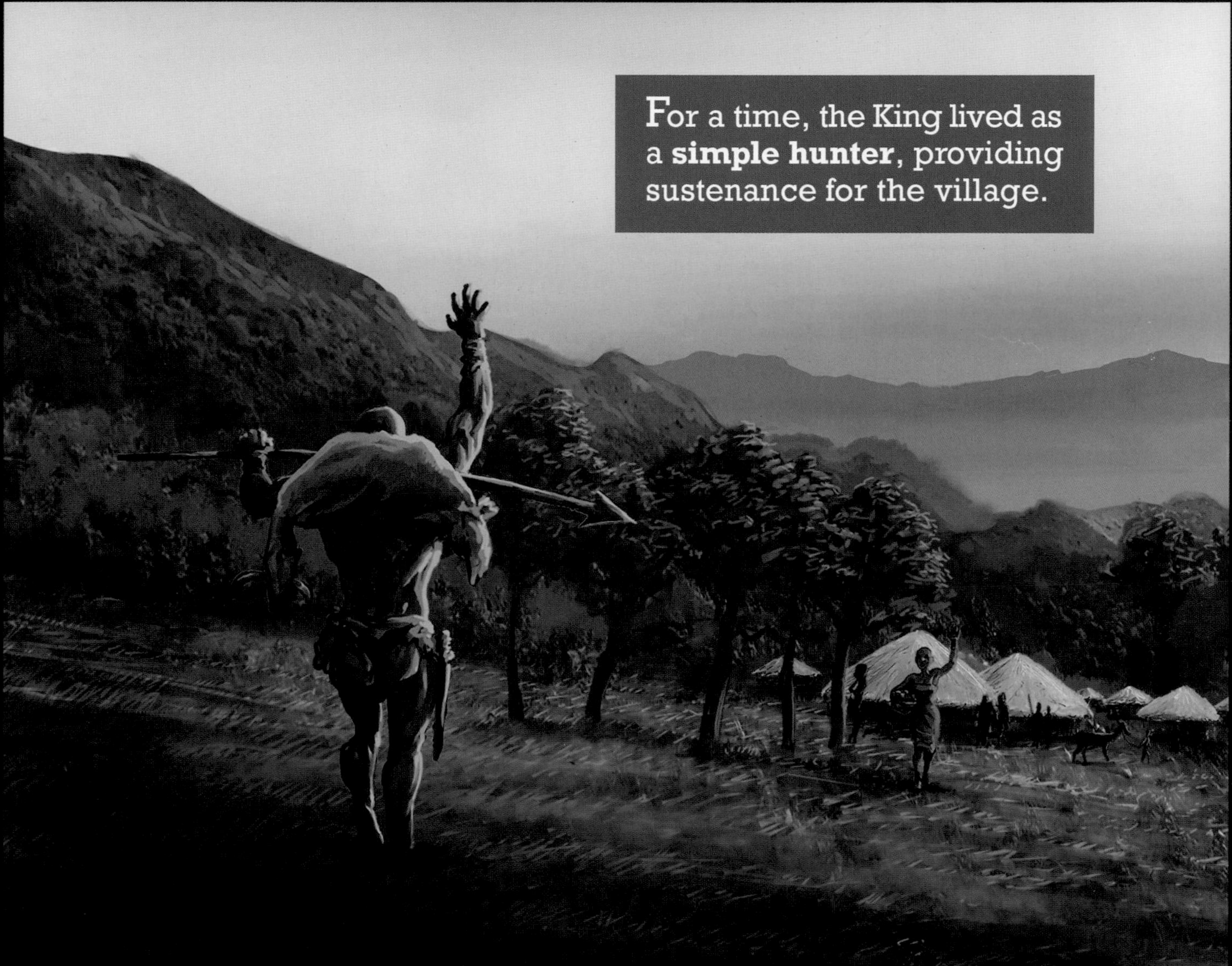

For a time, the King lived as a **simple hunter**, providing sustenance for the village.

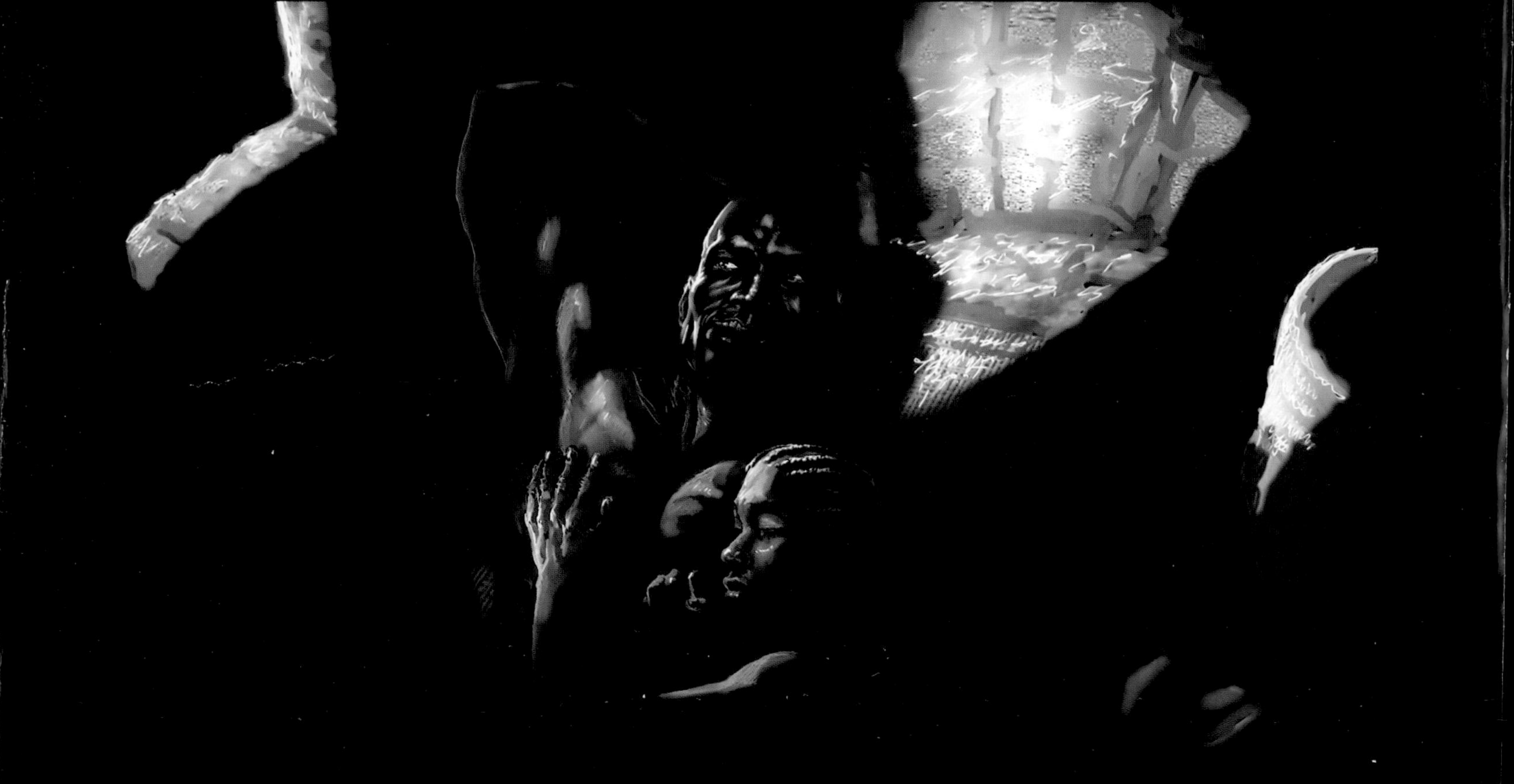

Some nights, after my duties to Akeyo and the tribe are fulfilled, **I fix my eyes on a greenish blue star.** I know instinctually that that star is an infant sun in a newly birthed galaxy. I've traveled so far across this land to now ponder my current fortunes. Resting quietly with my beautiful wife, the **Kingdom of Aja Ọba** seems like a distant complicated dream. **A vision of my long deceased parents is clear in the darkness** but my heart bleeds realizing that in this peaceful village, away from the dogs of war, **I can barely remember the sound of their voices.** I long for that wild sound **and** this possibility to start a **NEW FAMILY**.

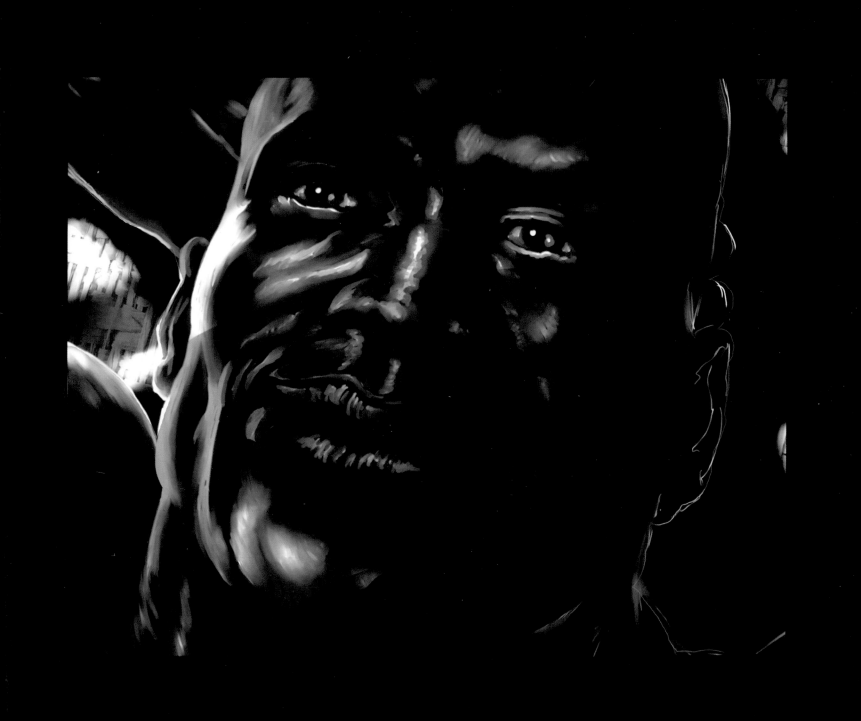

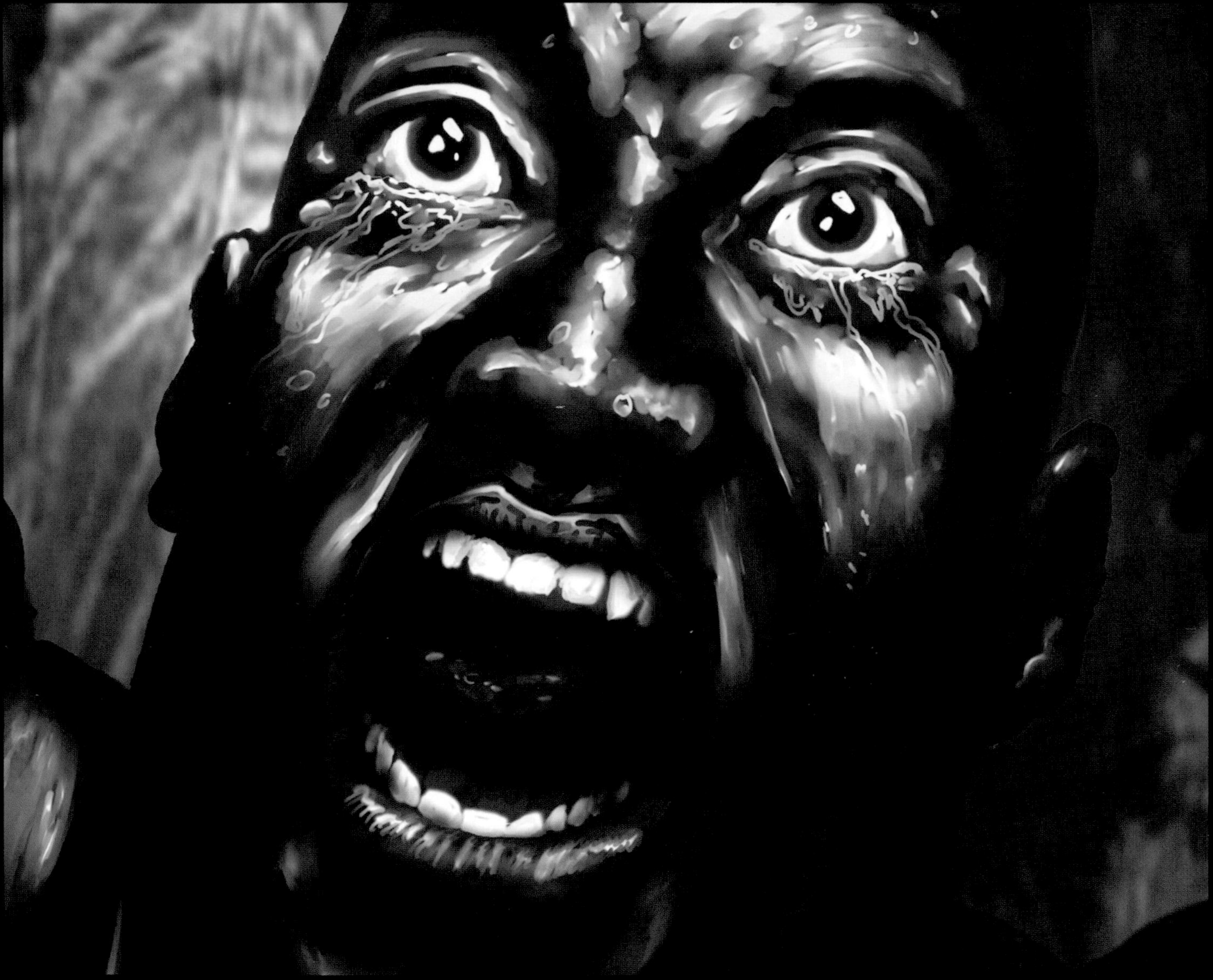

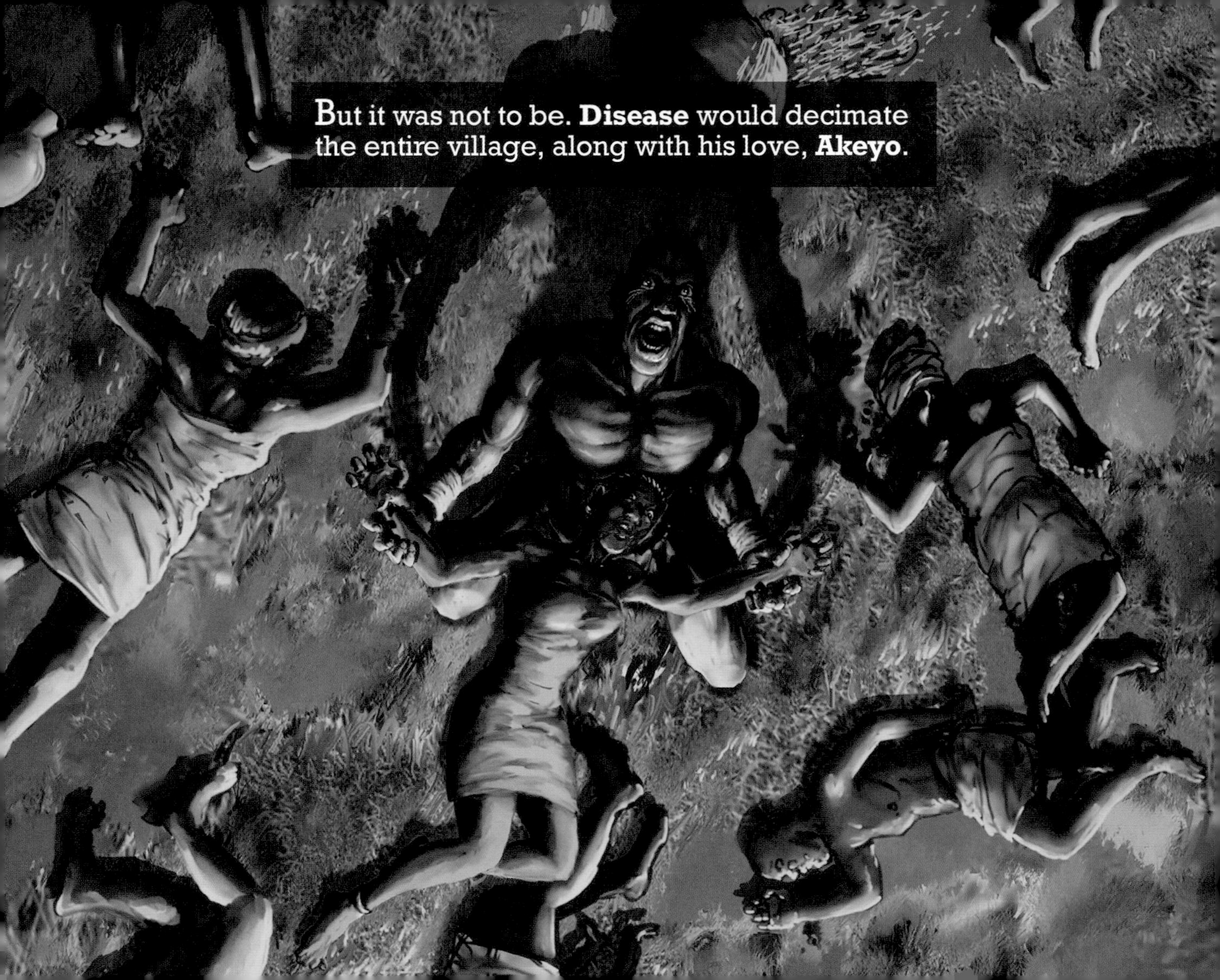
But it was not to be. **Disease** would decimate the entire village, along with his love, **Akeyo**.

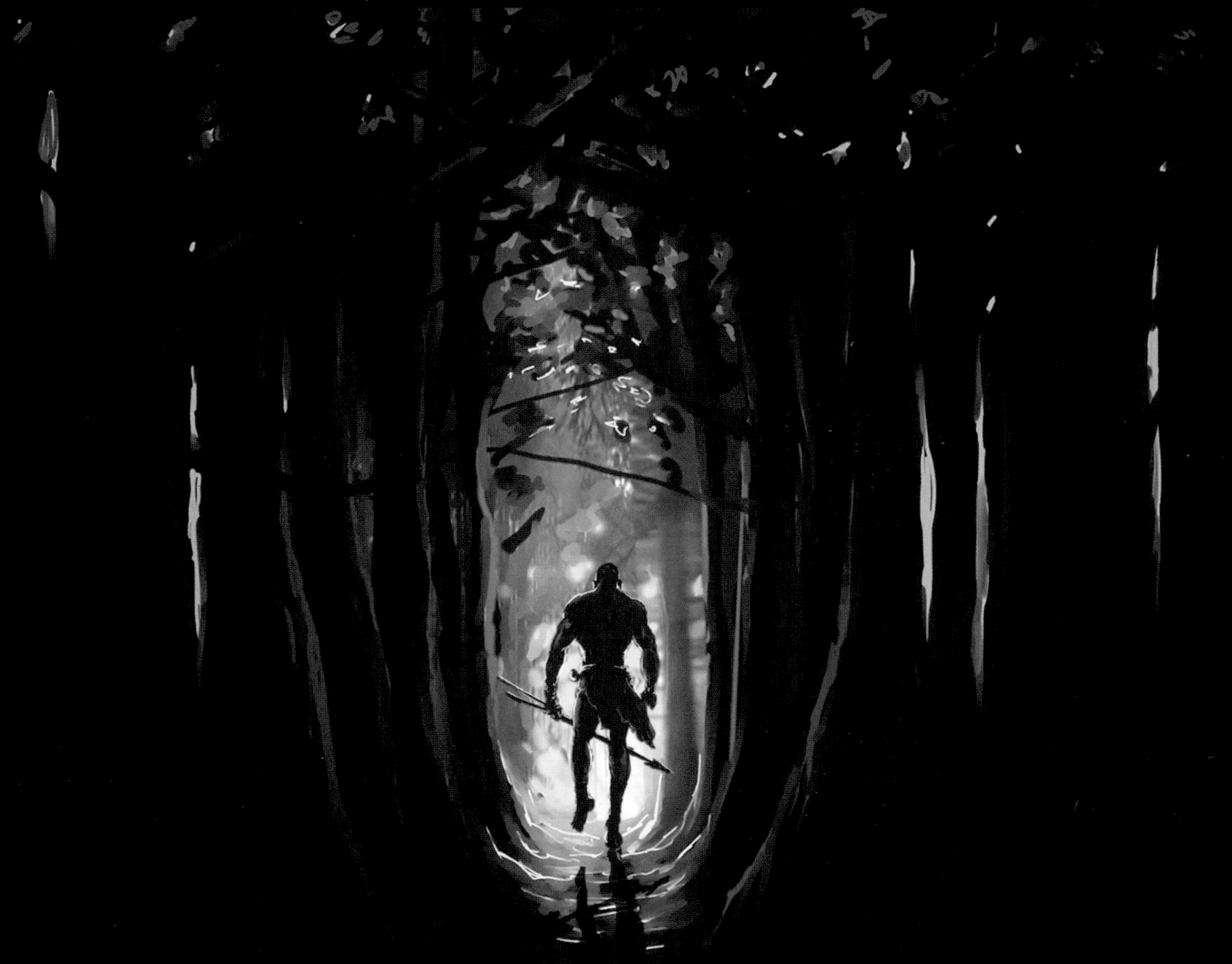

But he would go on…and on….

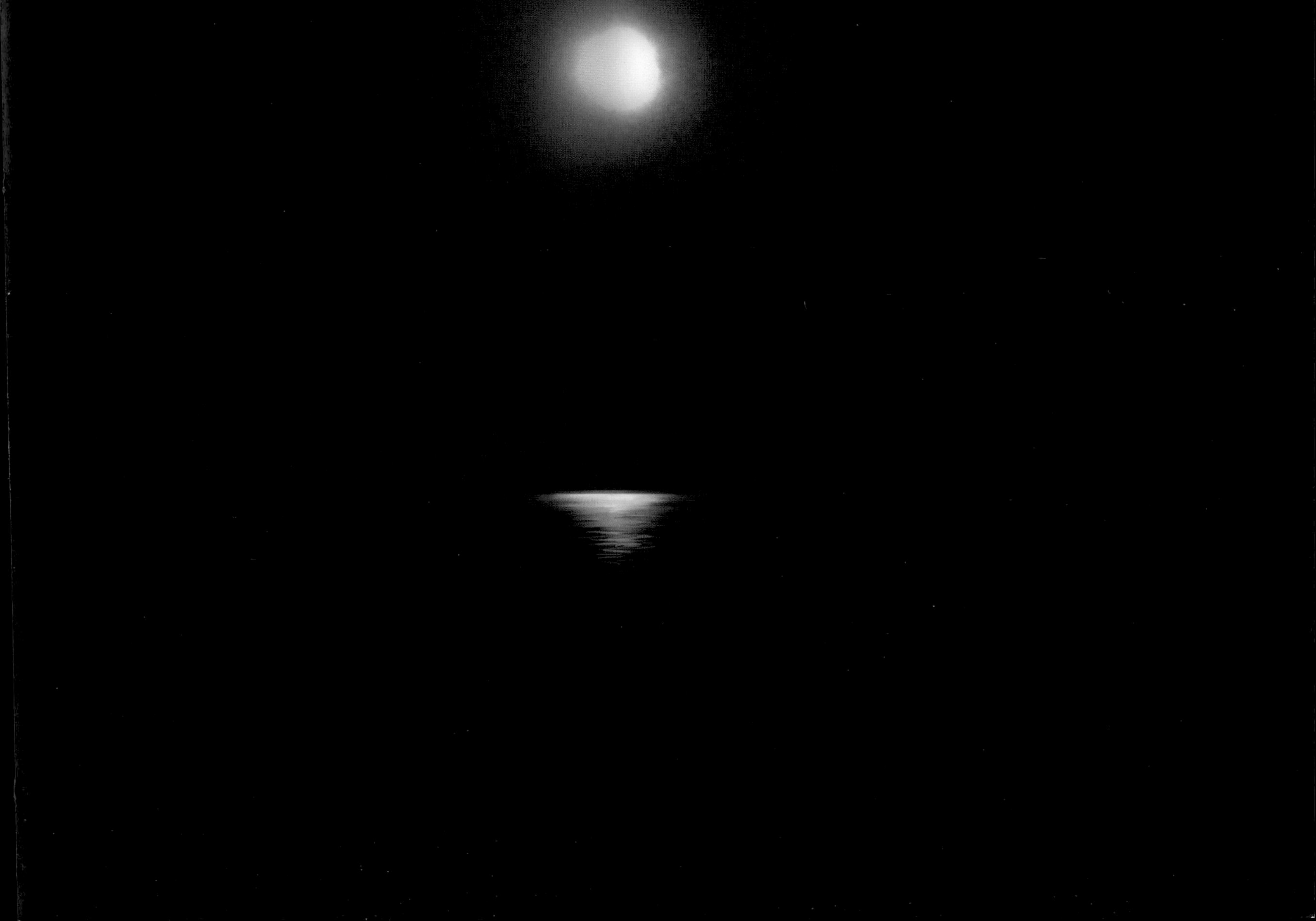

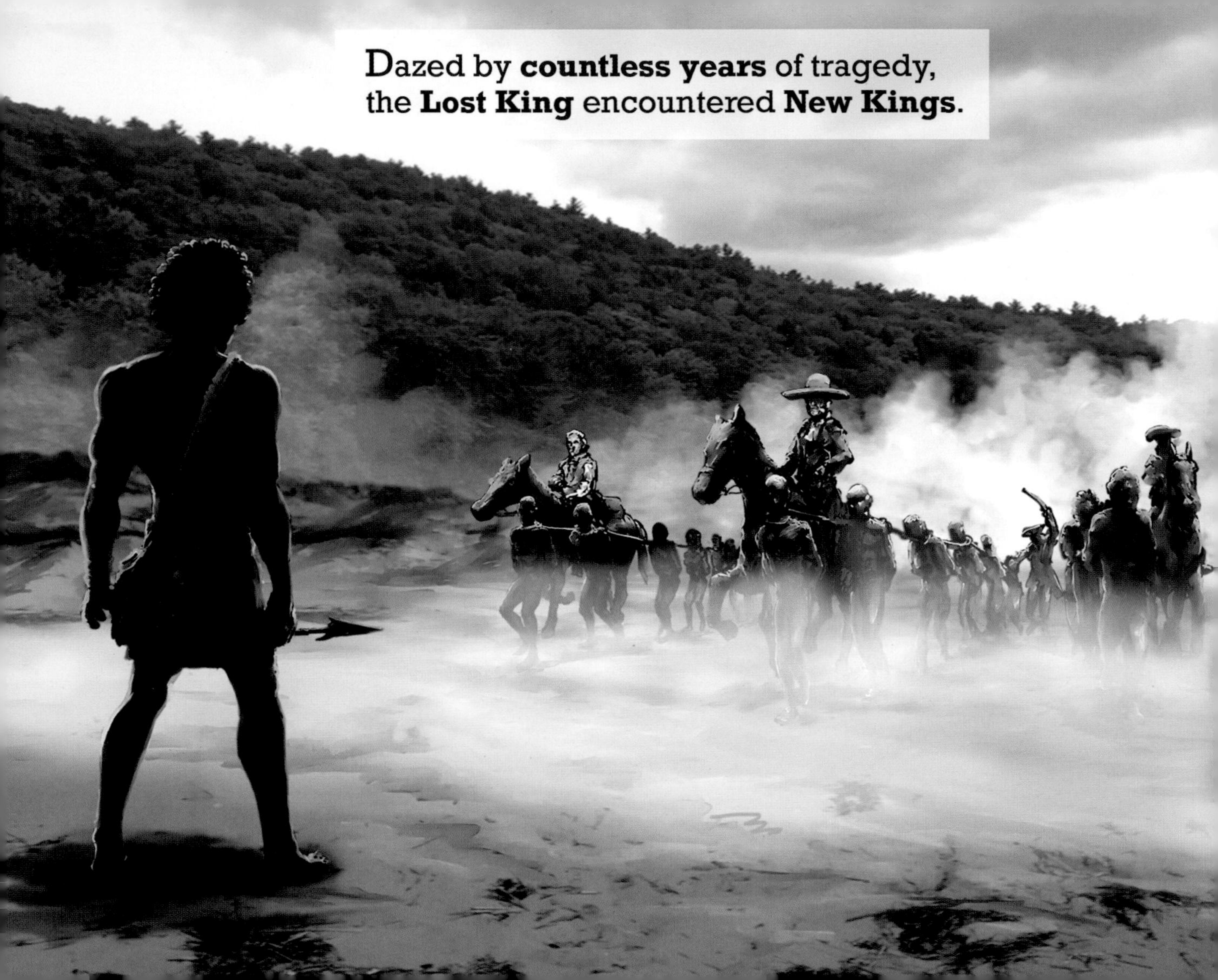
Dazed by **countless years** of tragedy,
the **Lost King** encountered **New Kings**.

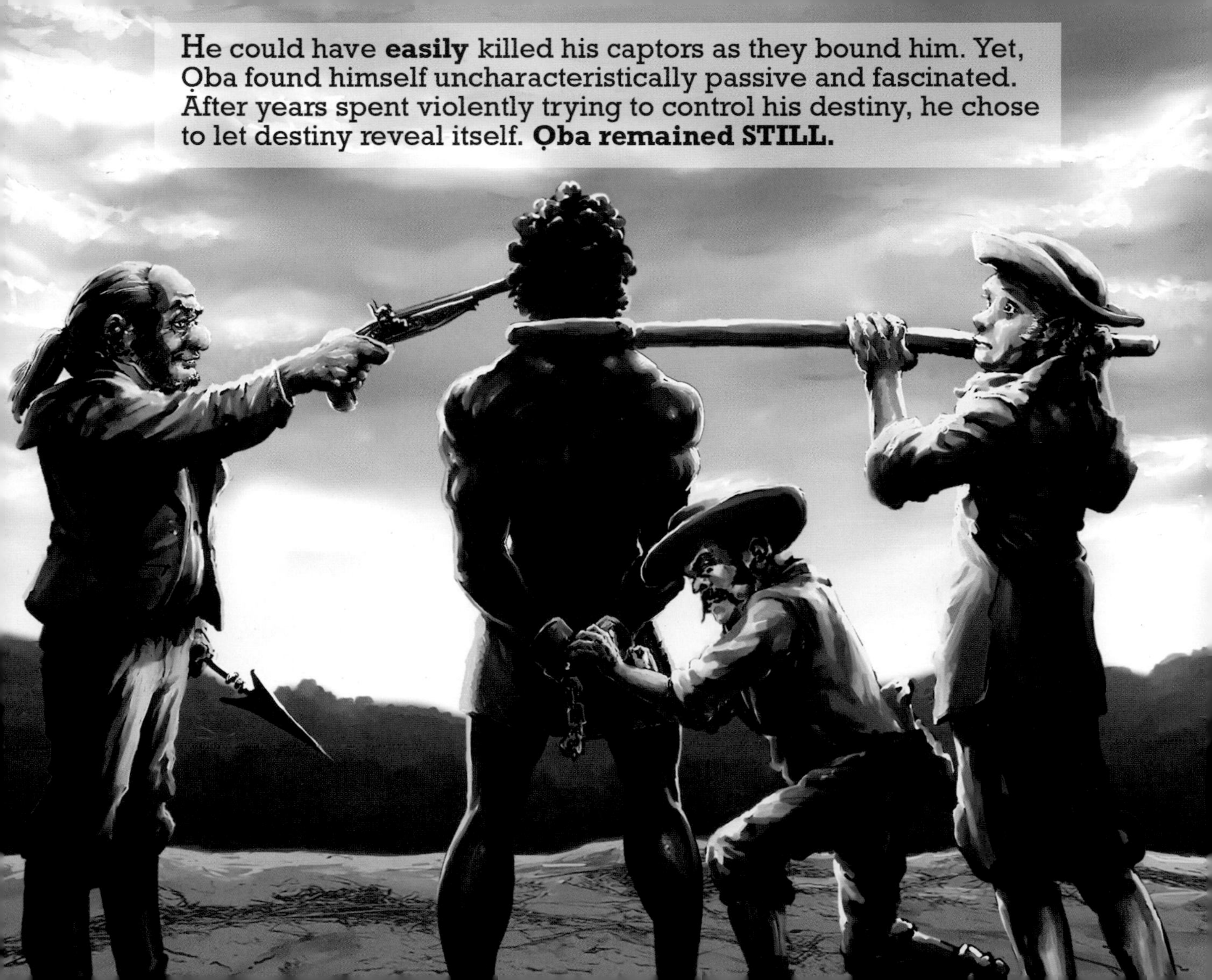
He could have **easily** killed his captors as they bound him. Yet, Ọba found himself uncharacteristically passive and fascinated. After years spent violently trying to control his destiny, he chose to let destiny reveal itself. **Ọba remained STILL.**

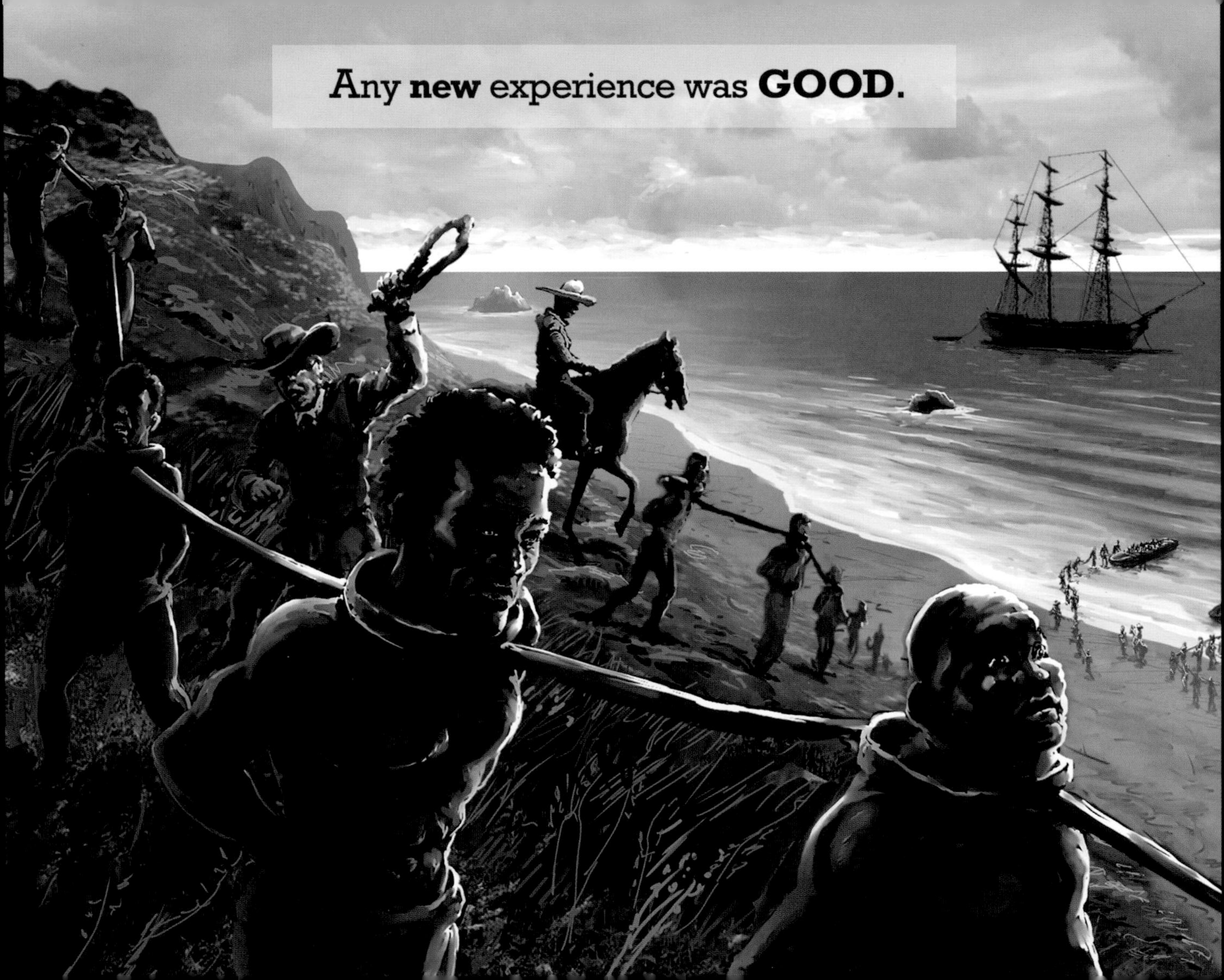
Any **new** experience was **GOOD**.

The Triangular Slave Trade was quite an insidiously ingenious system of commerce with the primary product being shackled and bloodied Black bodies. What was later called The Middle Passage served as a thoroughfare to transport 13 million human beings while culling cultures. In effect, the cruel ordeal stripped away the individuality of each captive for one purpose:

Working In Chattel Slavery Until Death.

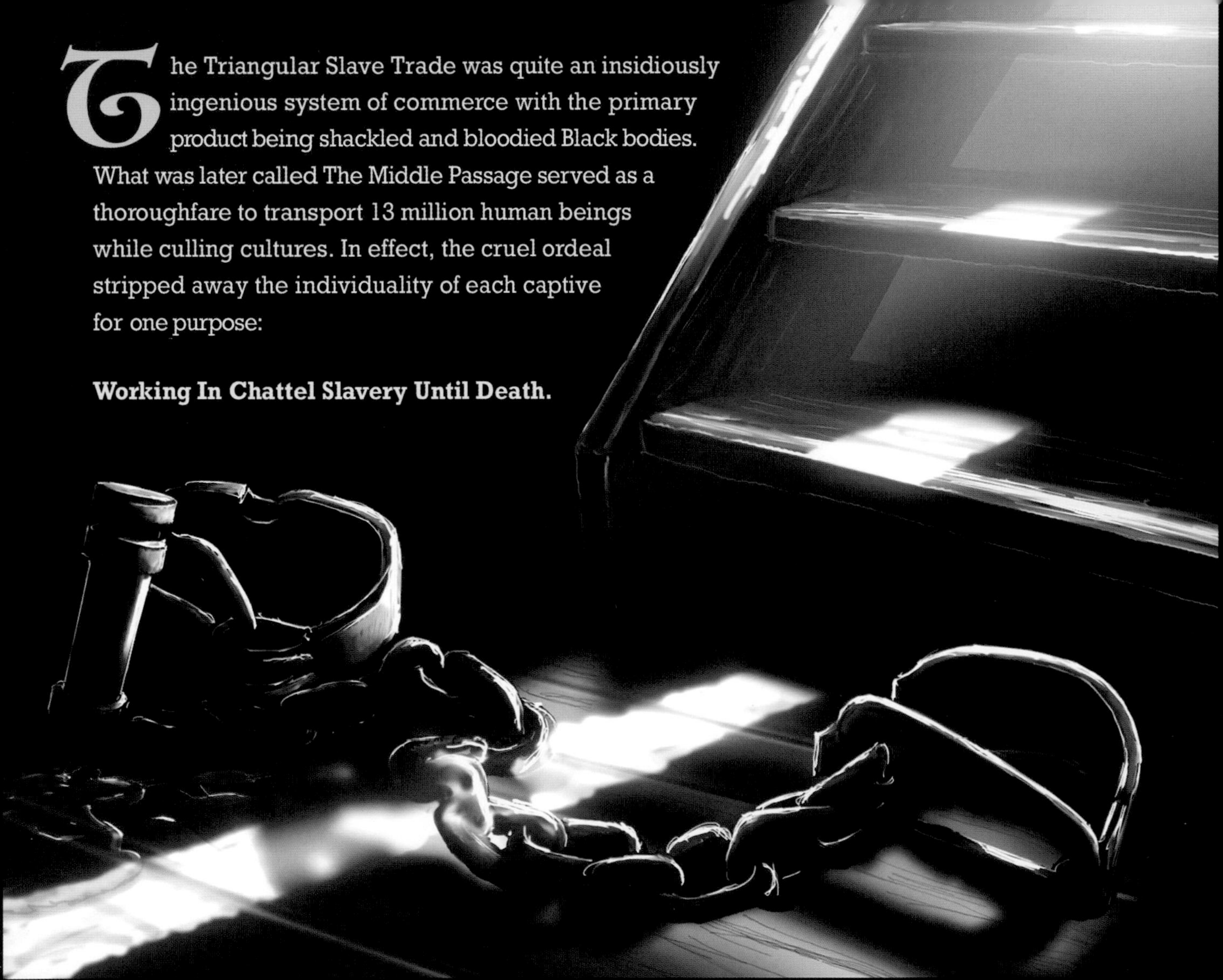

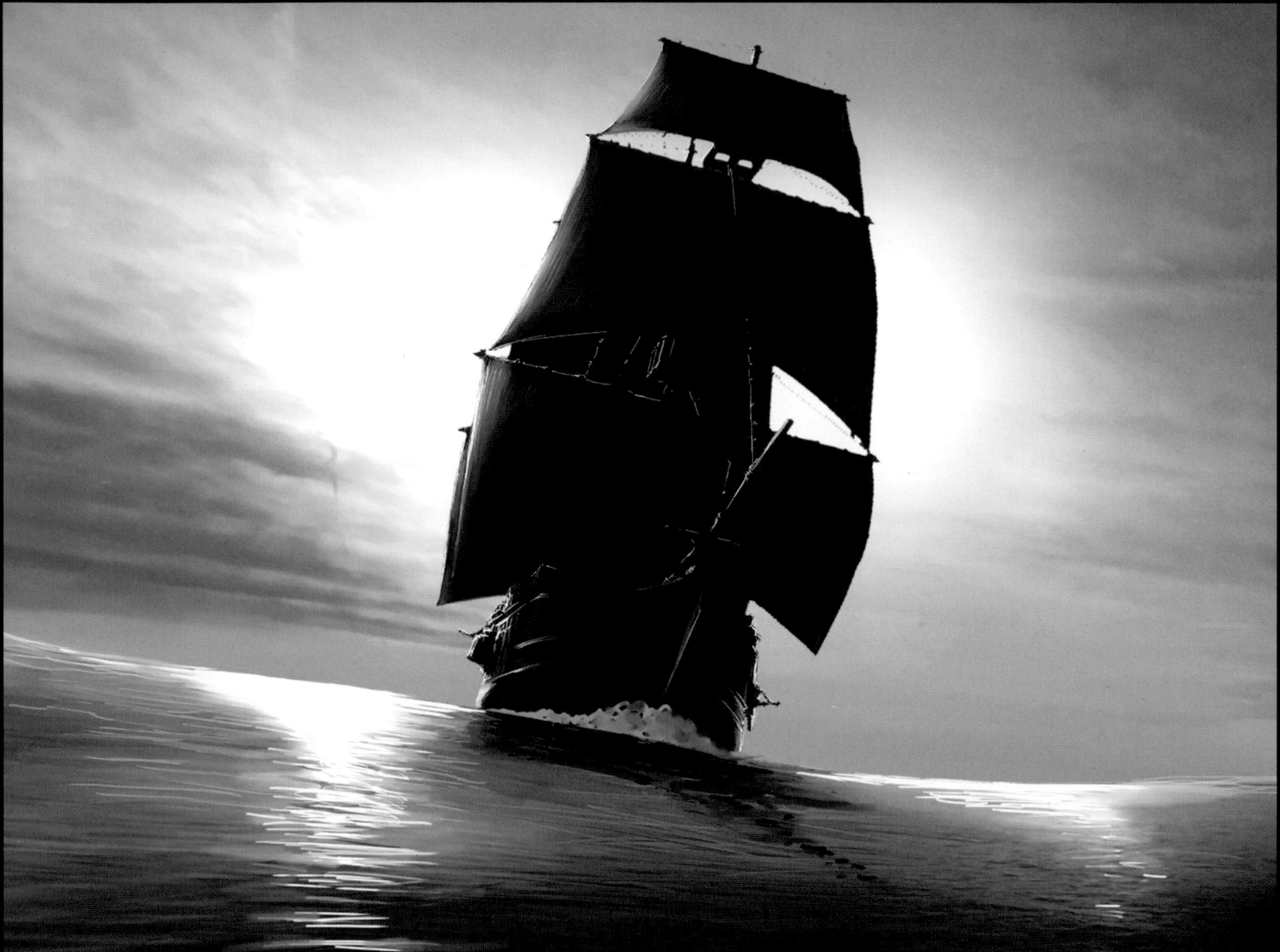

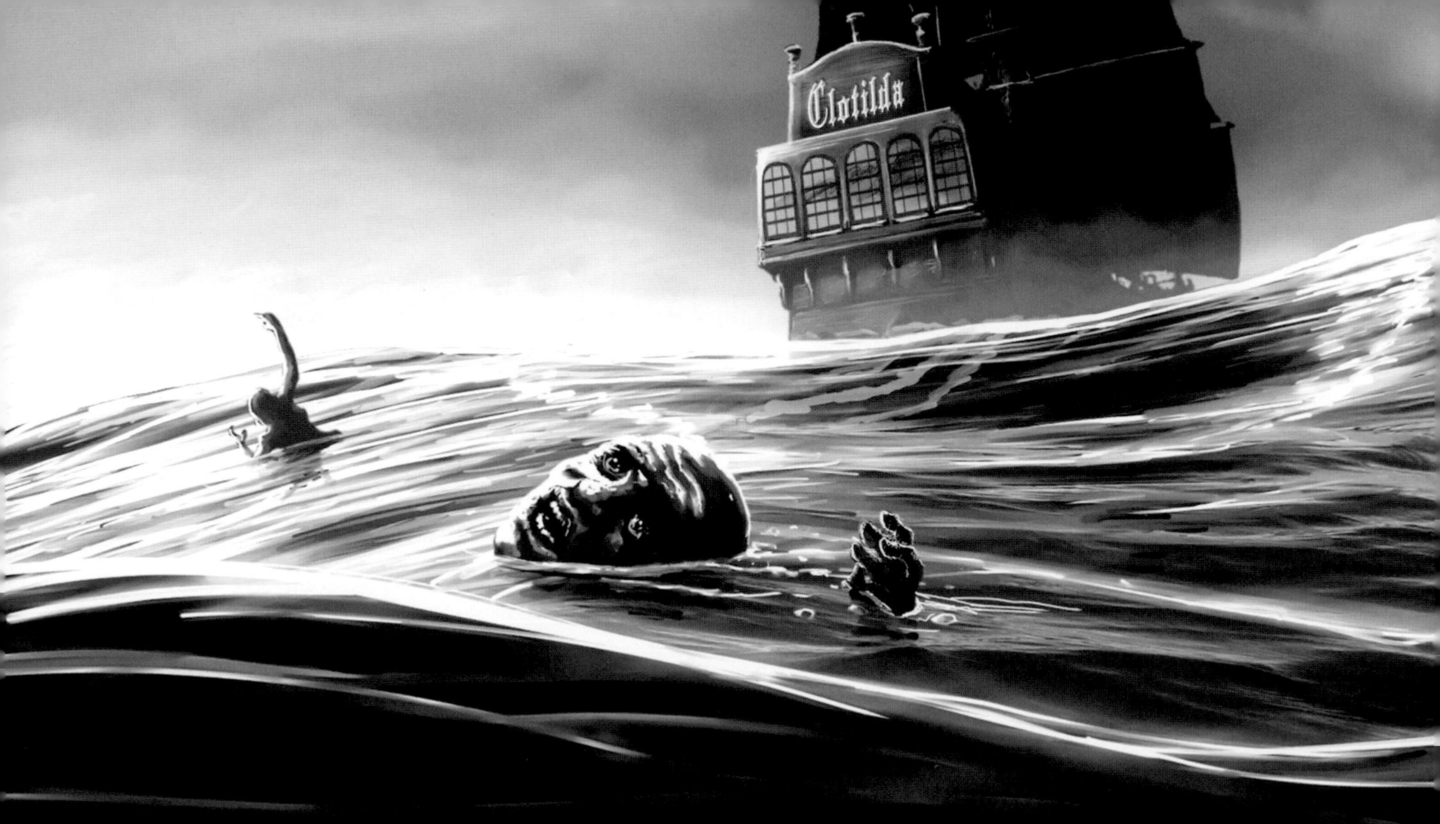
Clotilda

Captives — **adults and children** — who did not accept or adapt to the **brutal system** either revolted, were murdered, or chose to end their own lives in the **ocean depths**.

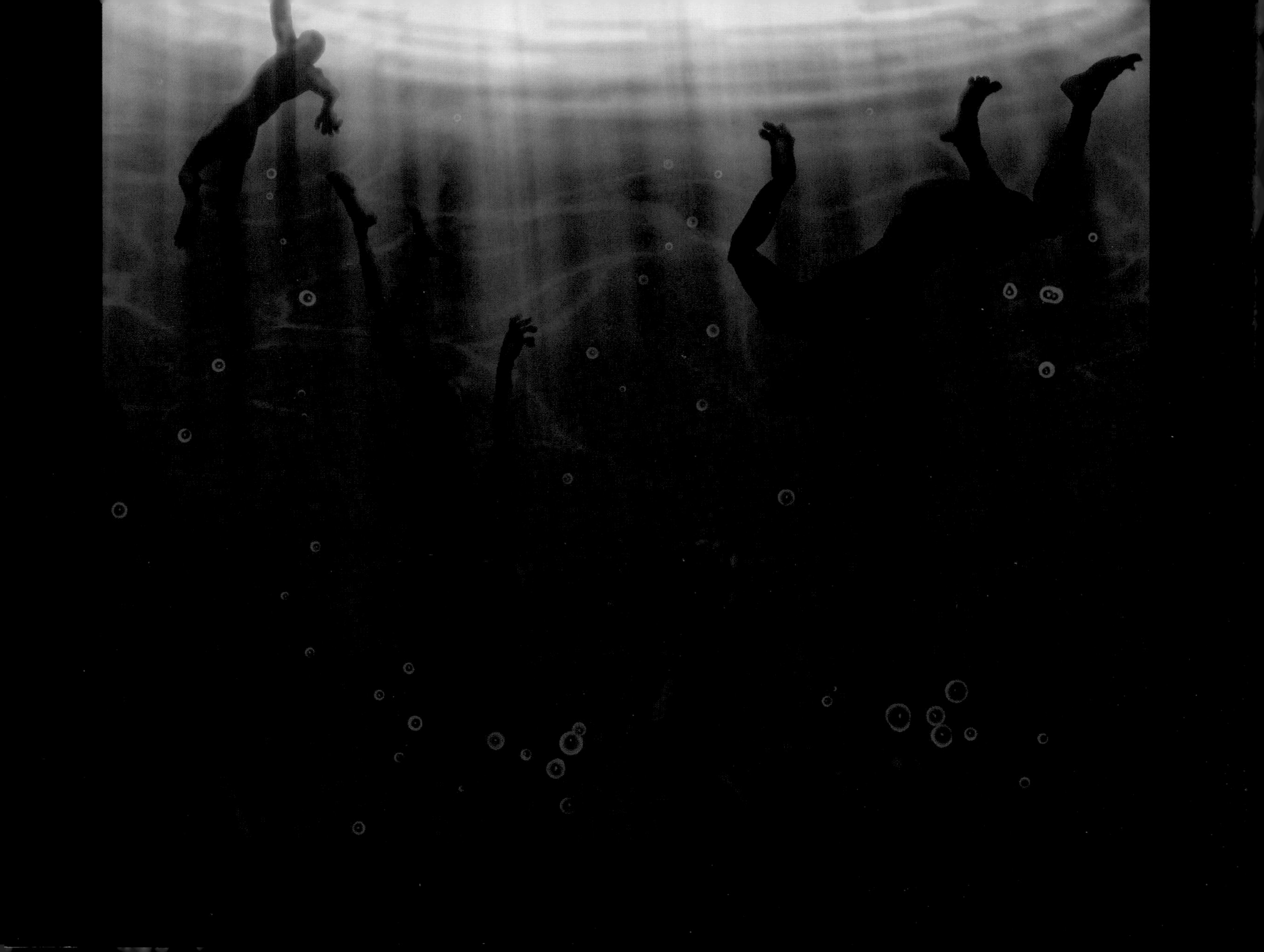

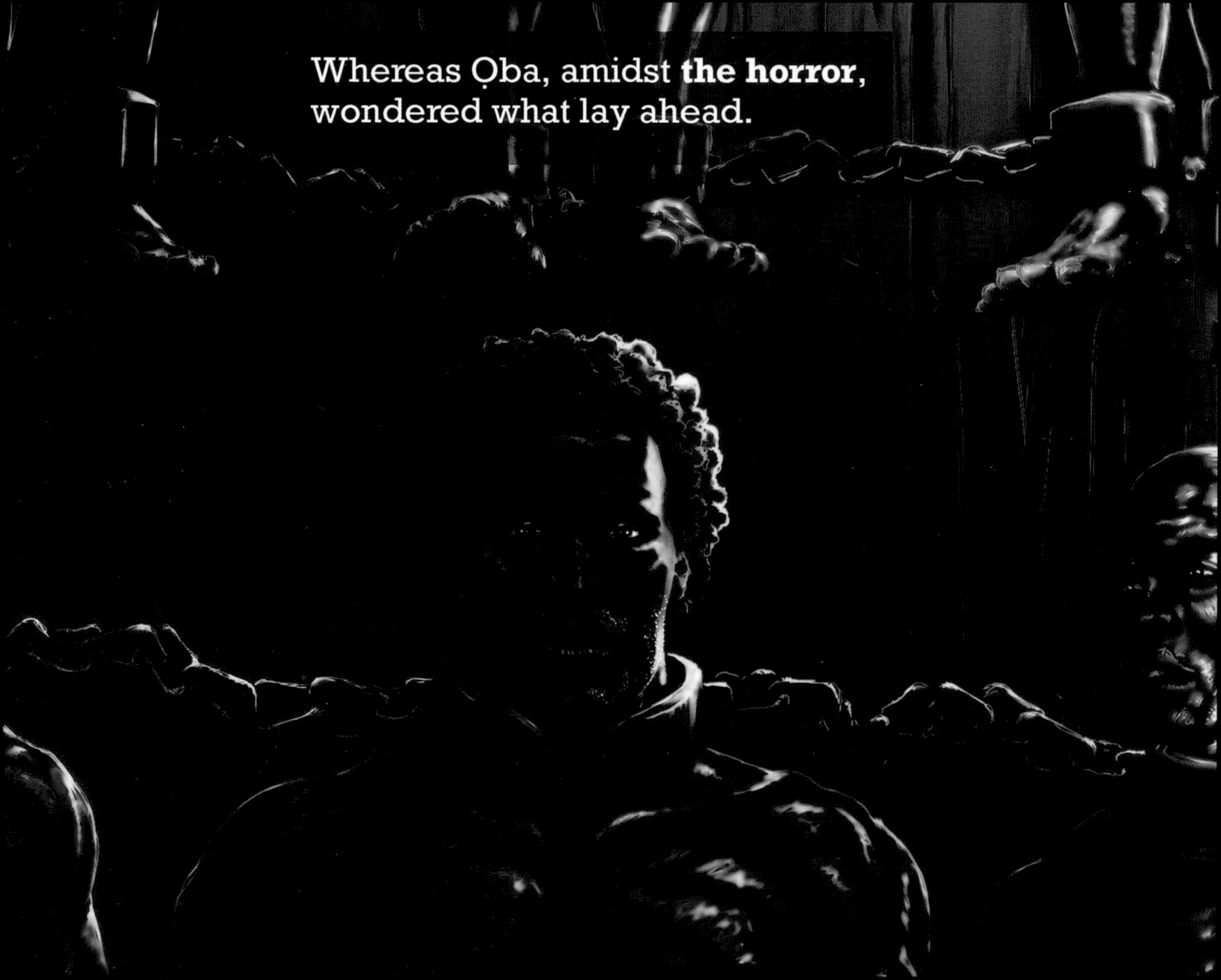

Whereas Ọba, amidst **the horror**,
wondered what lay ahead.

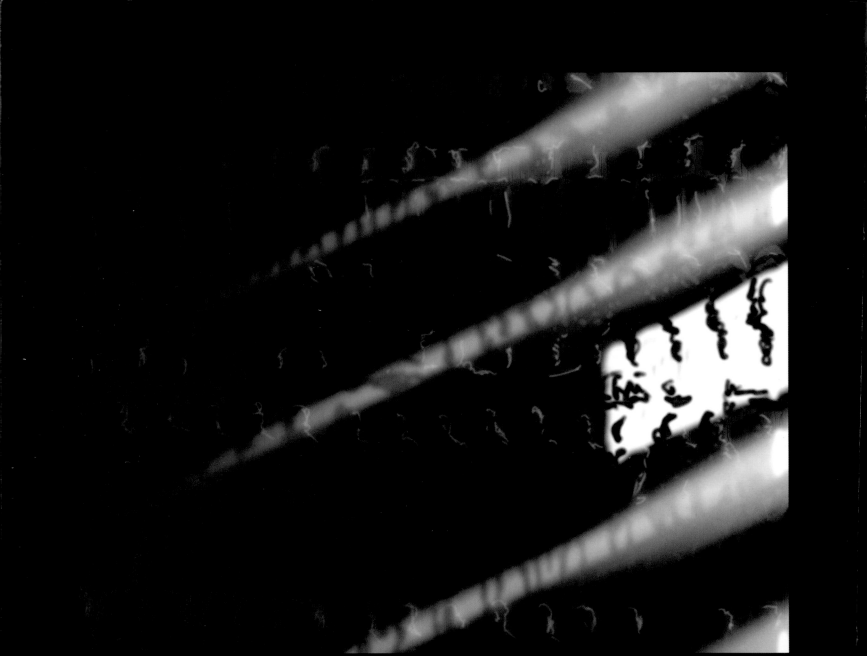

He found that in this “**New World**,” as one of the enslaved, he could become someone else. Ọba was given the name “***John***.”

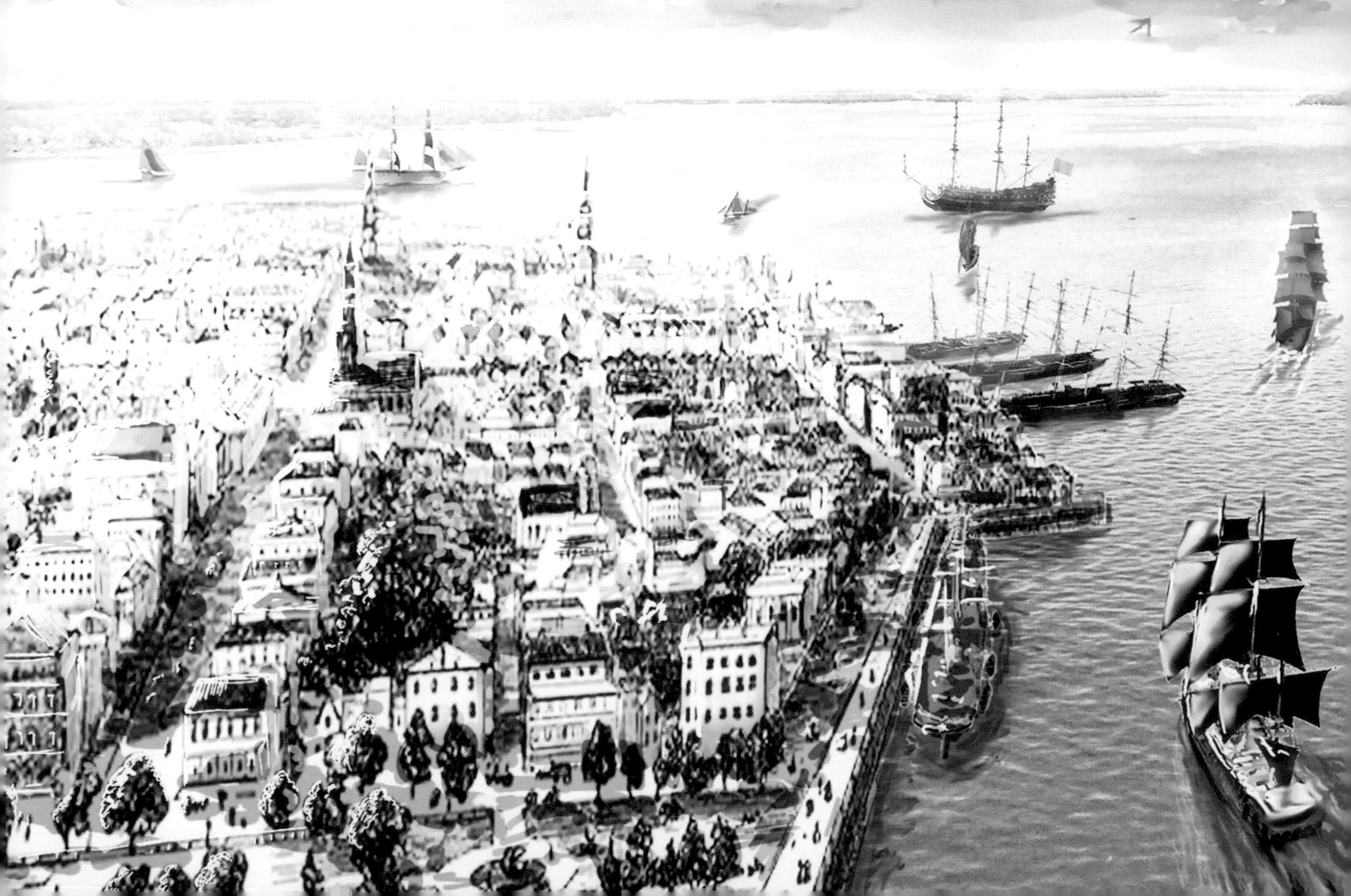

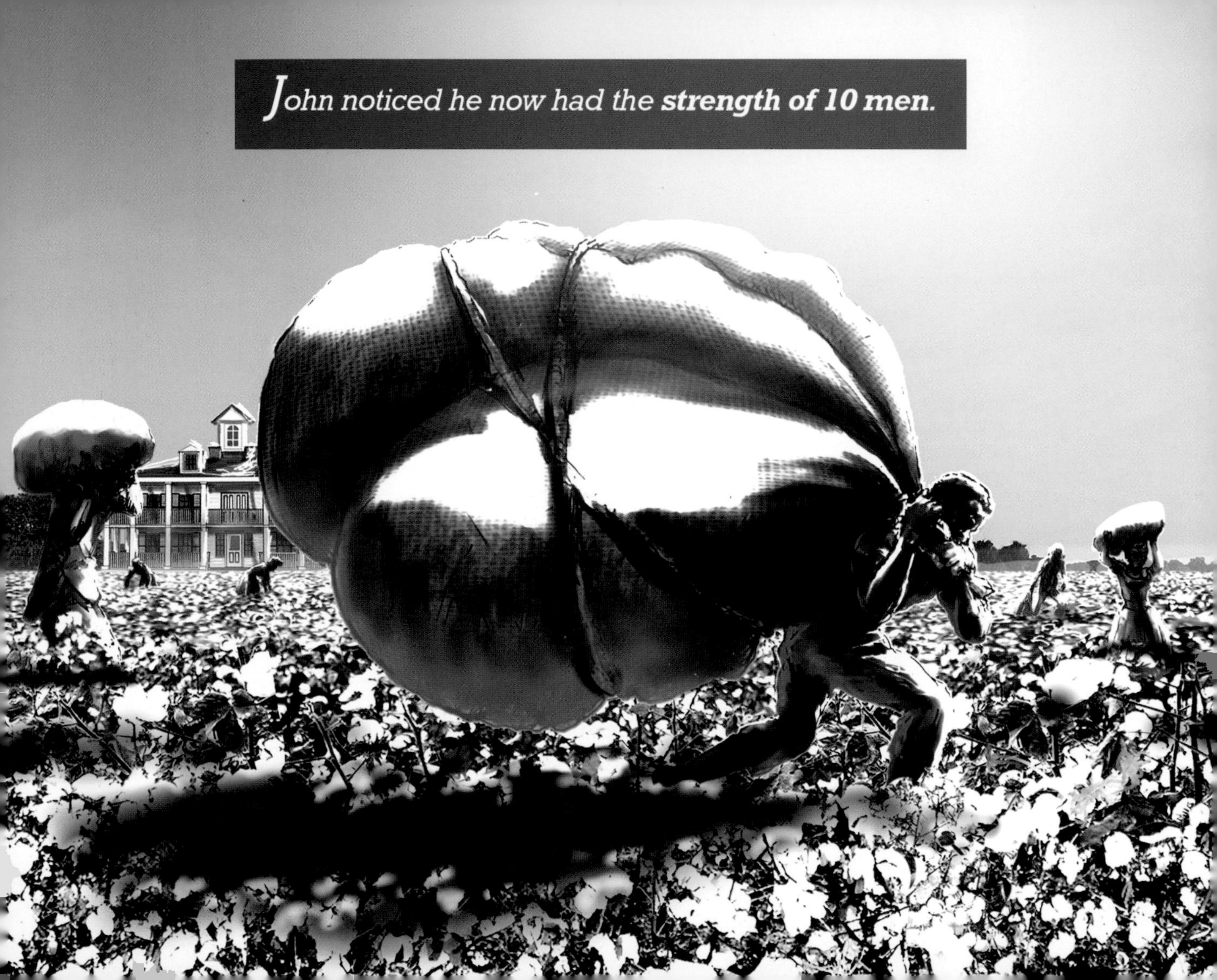
John noticed he now had the **strength of 10 men.**

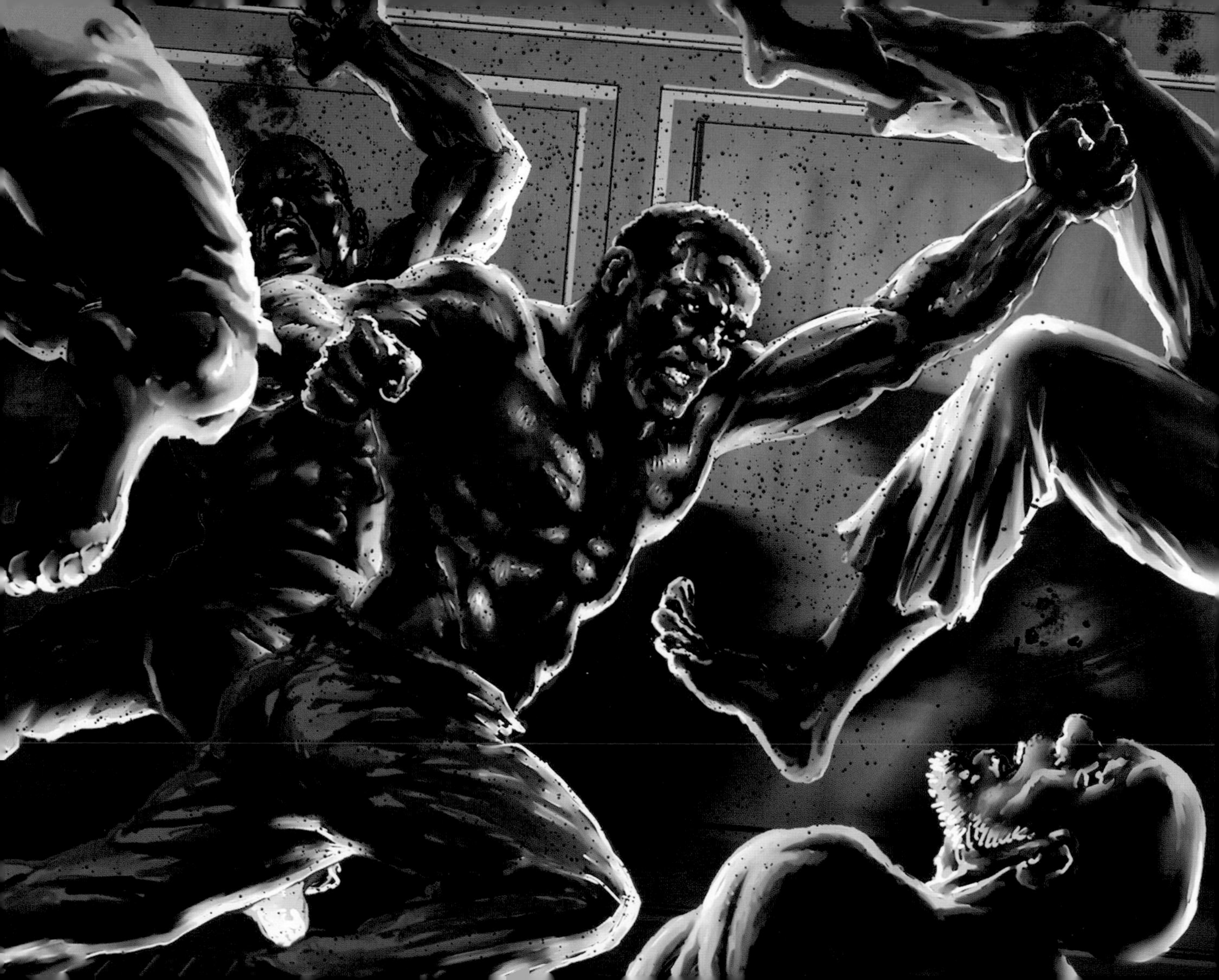

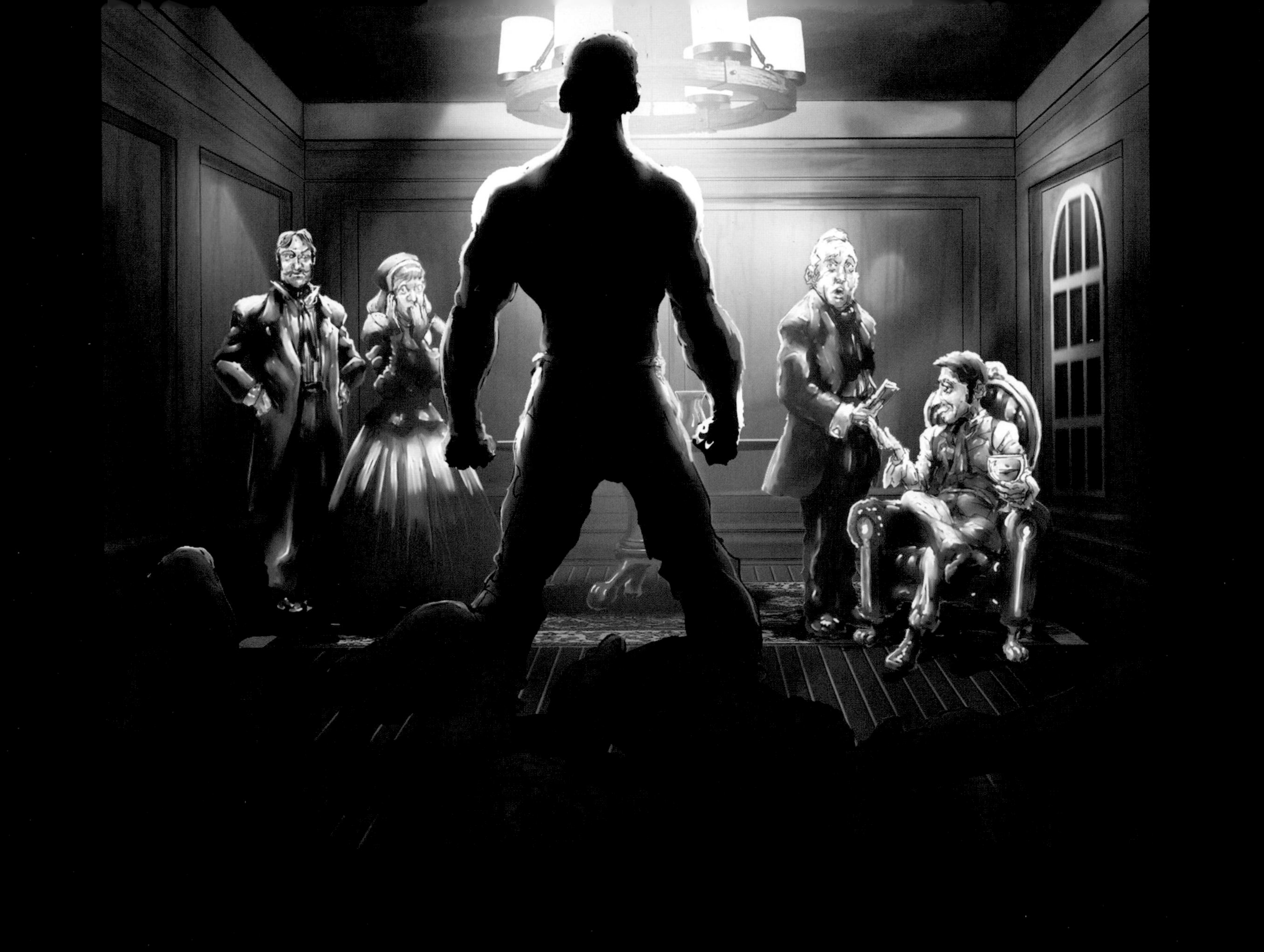

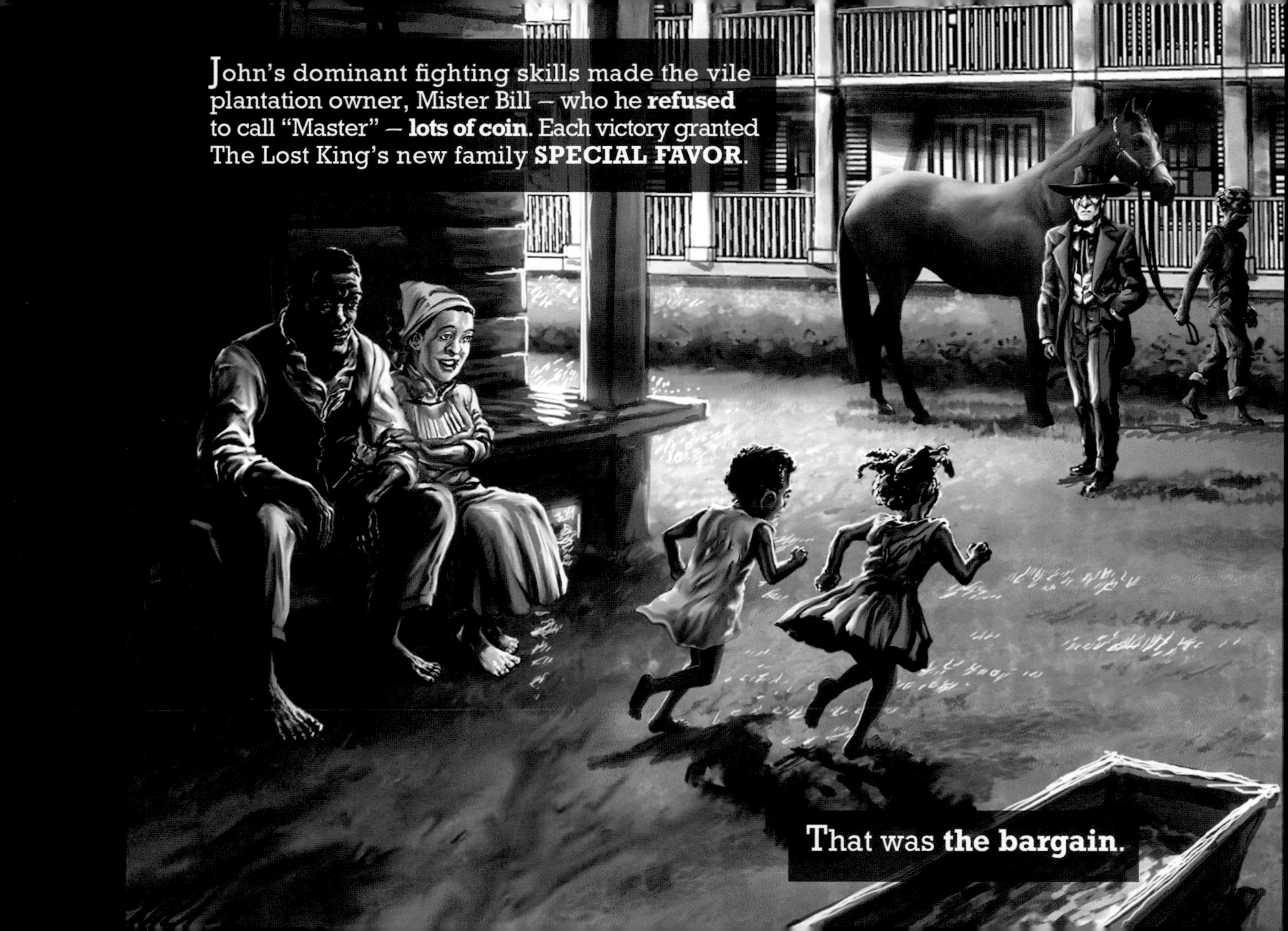
John's dominant fighting skills made the vile plantation owner, Mister Bill – who he **refused** to call "Master" – **lots of coin.** Each victory granted The Lost King's new family **SPECIAL FAVOR**.
That was **the bargain.**

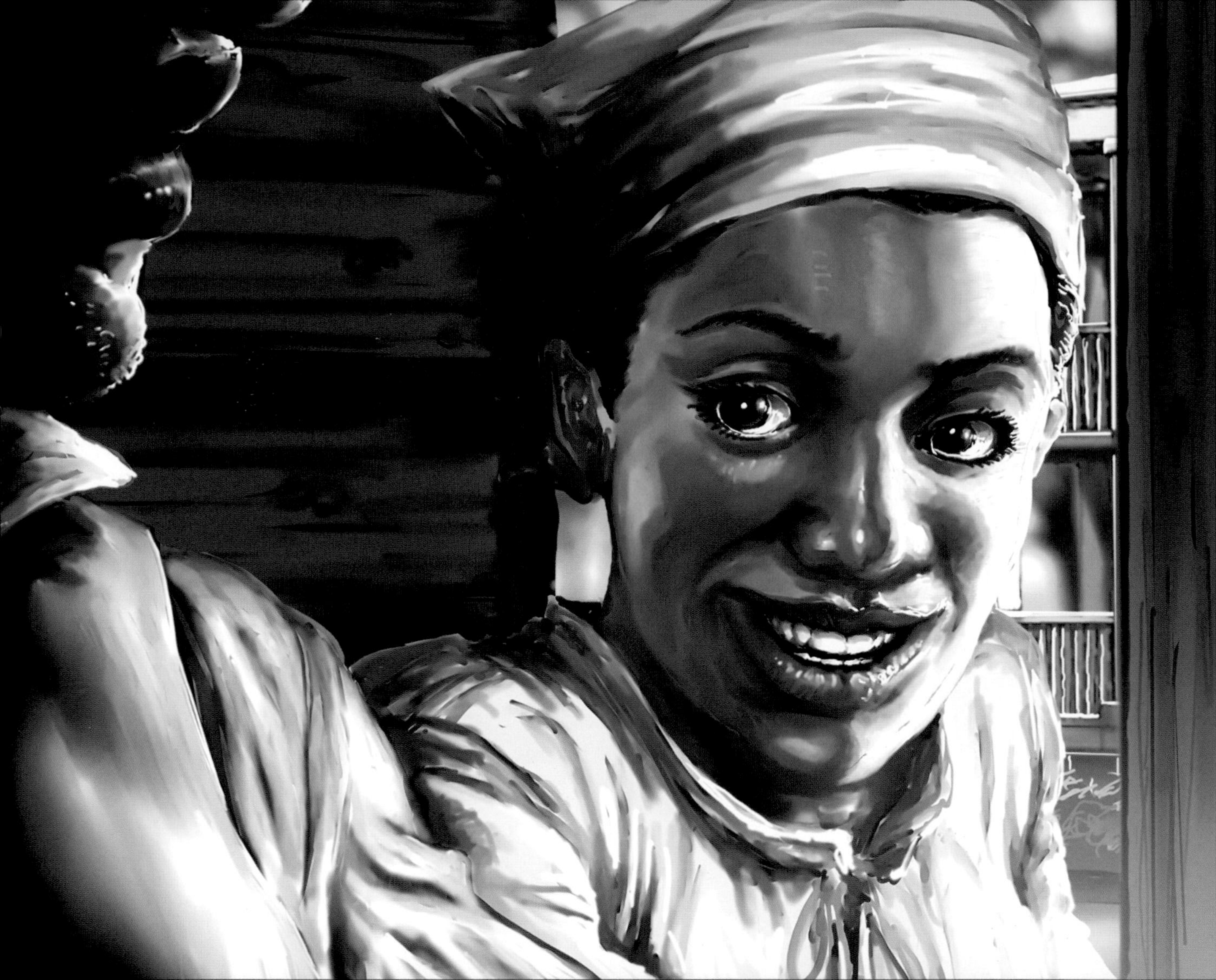

I was labeled a "field nigger." But my capabilities helped win the hand of **Ambermae Smith**, a young woman who'd shown me unending kindness. The general rule said she was the daughter of a so-called "house nigger" named **Jediah**.

But whispers said **Ambermae** was the **5th child of slaveholder, Bill Smith.** He'd never claim her as his offspring when she had more value to him as one of the enslaved.

Ambermae's spiritual fire cast light onto my life. She birthed me **a son and daughter.** I allowed myself to love this family as well.

I should have known better.

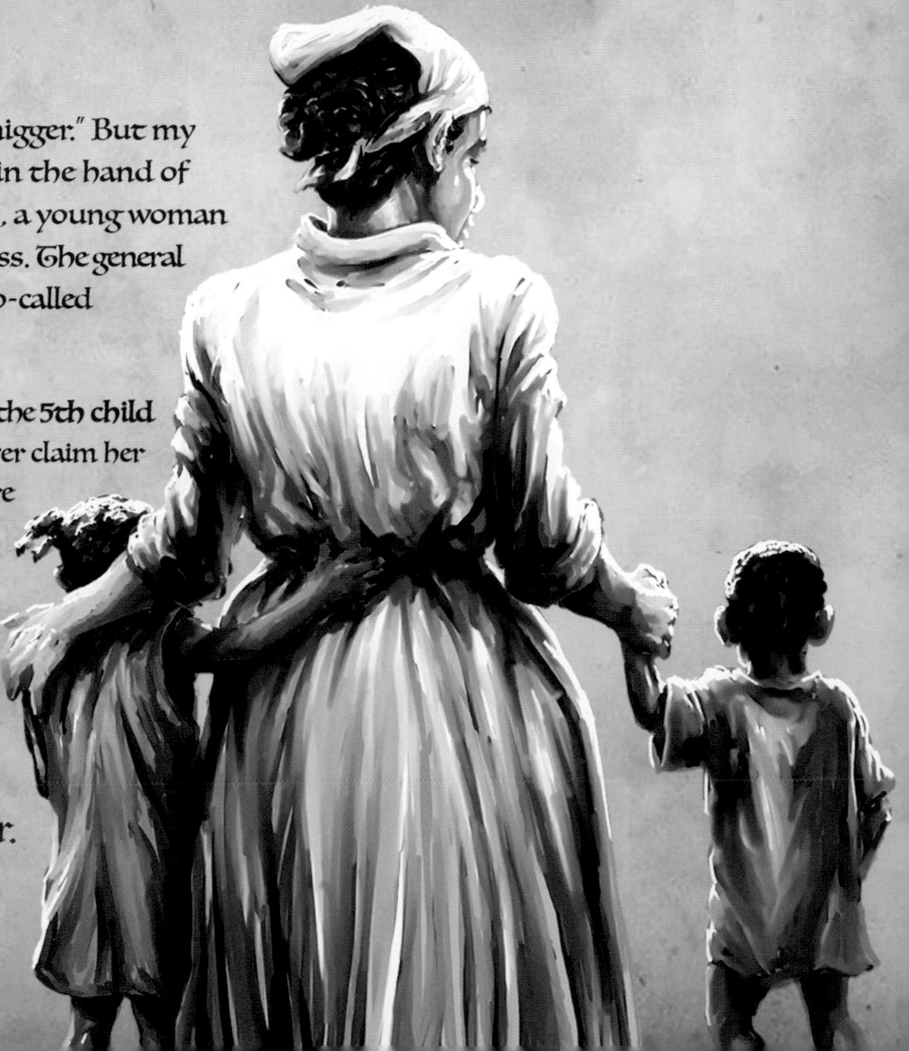

A m b e r m a e

I thank the good Lord every day for my blessings. Lucky to be a servant in Master Bill's house — cooking, cleaning, and watching the children on the plantation. Folks working the fields be jealous of me but my tasks start before sun up and run 'til sundown. I be bone tired most'a the time. Sunday's devoted to rest and worship for most of us — just as it's been since I was a little one.

Johnny's a fallen angel. He stronger than a bull and don't say too much, which mostly keeps messy folk and the bosses away. Sometimes I clean 'im up after he and Master return from trips over yonder. He come back covered in dried blood…and reckons to kill Master Bill. I tells 'im "No, this my home, Johnny. Leave it be." No man could stop 'im if he chose to walk off into the woods. So I read scripture and sing softly to calm his spirit. Don't want 'im to go.

He bring me flowers and candy. Even scooped me 'cross the lake in his arms a few times. When Johnny said he wanted to jump the broom with me, good Lord, I got so scared I run off into the woods crying. What a strapping man like that see in a lil yellow gal like me?

We made two beautiful Christian babies — Mary and Adam. We talks mostly after they's put to bed — 'bout Africa, witches, and a king. He even point in the Bible to where that king was s'posed to live. As God is my witness, Johnny reads better than any white man I ever seen. He learned me to read a little bit. Reading makes me feel like they's a future for us — but no one can know or there'll be trouble.

We don't want no trouble.

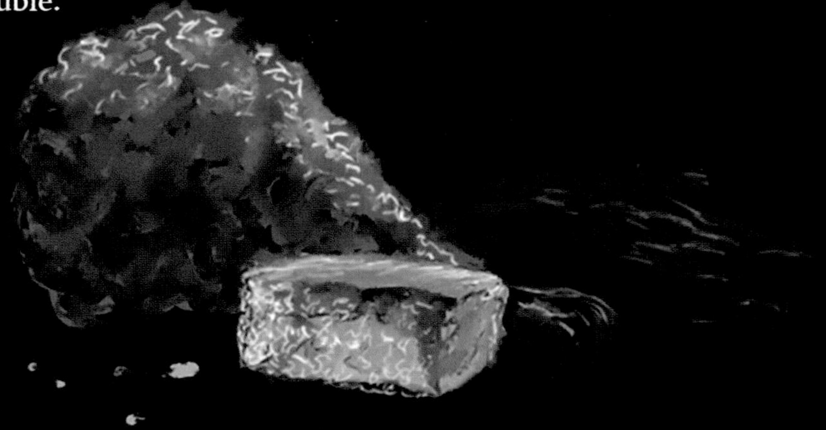

Exploiting his privileged position, John would from time to time help those less fortunate **escape** their plantations.

He enjoyed exchanging pleasantries and military strategy with their **Guide** to freedom — a woman called "**MOSES,**" who was perhaps the most **free person** he had ever known.

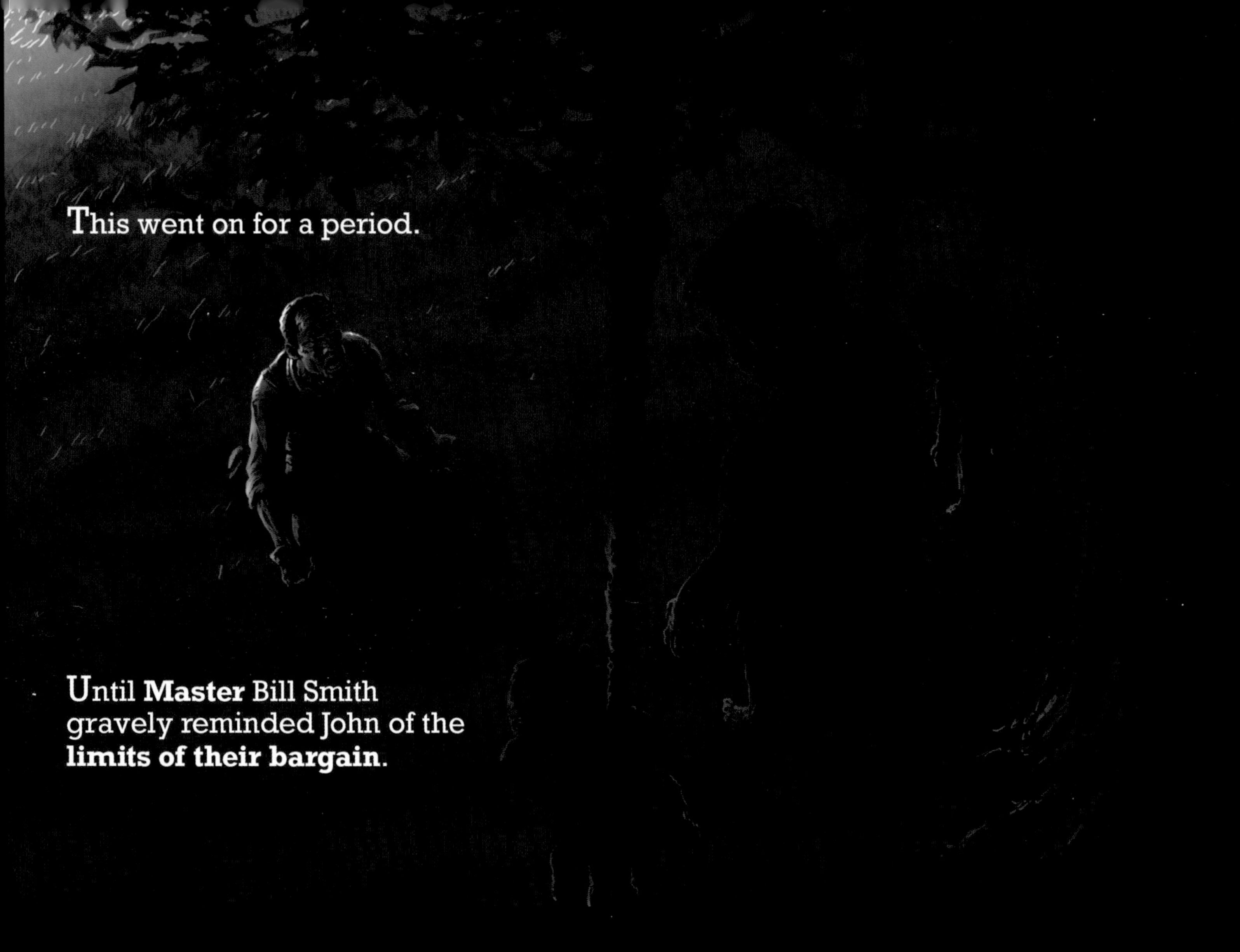

This went on for a period.

Until **Master** Bill Smith gravely reminded John of the **limits of their bargain**.

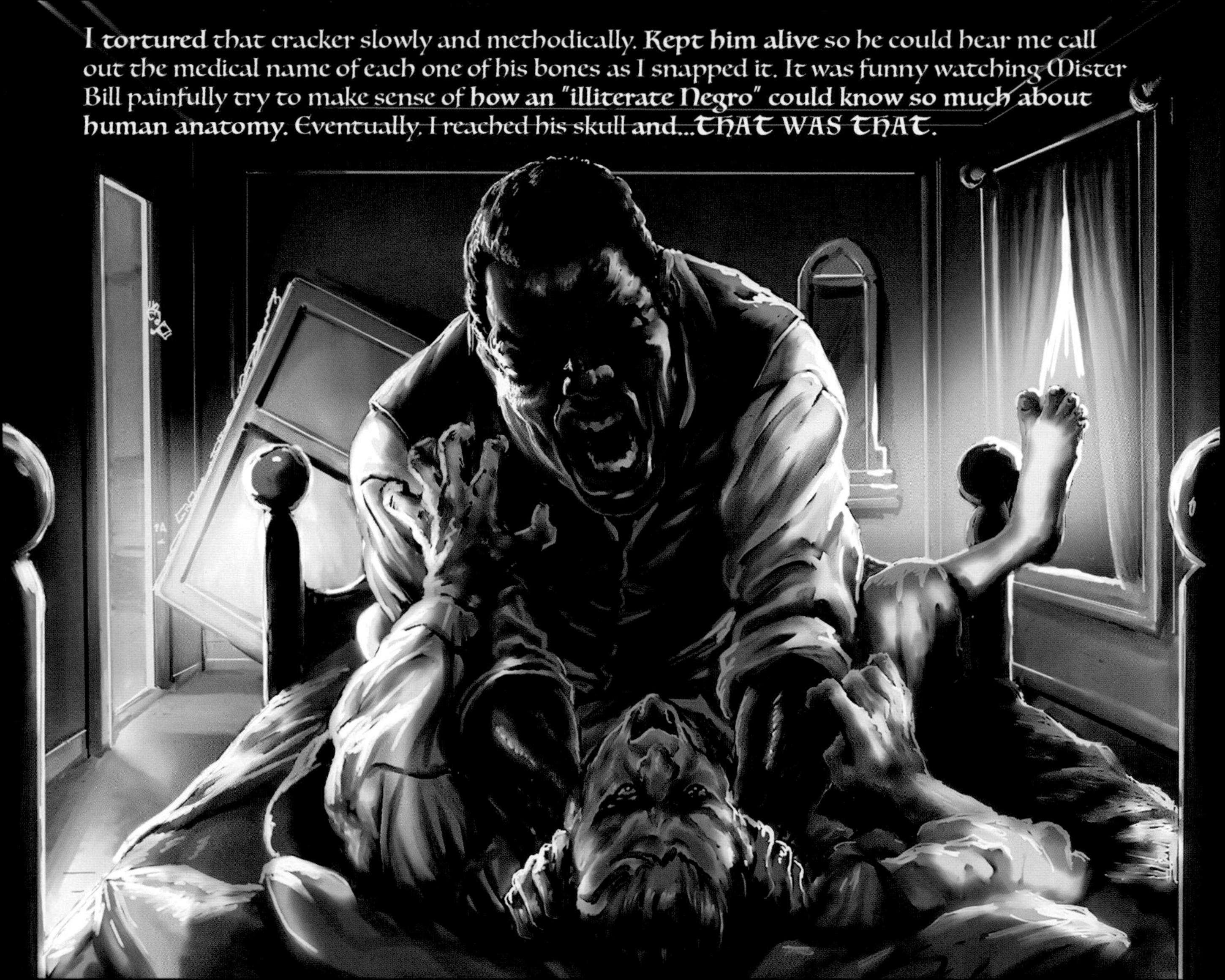
I tortured that cracker slowly and methodically. Kept him alive so he could hear me call out the medical name of each one of his bones as I snapped it. It was funny watching Mister Bill painfully try to make sense of how an "illiterate Negro" could know so much about human anatomy. Eventually, I reached his skull and...THAT WAS THAT.

John took **revenge** and **repeated the act** on several nearby plantations, signifying that only he was the **true MASTER**.

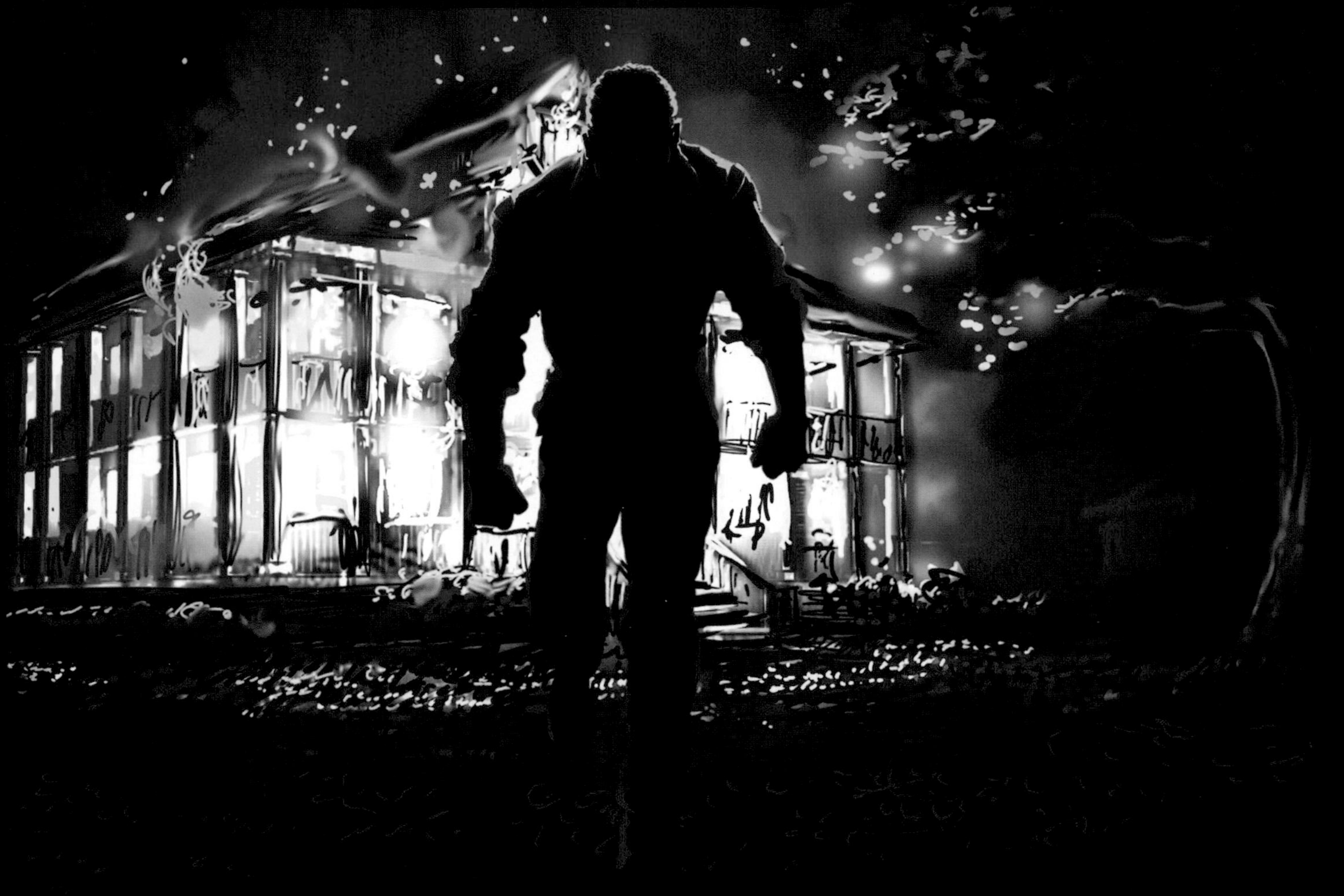

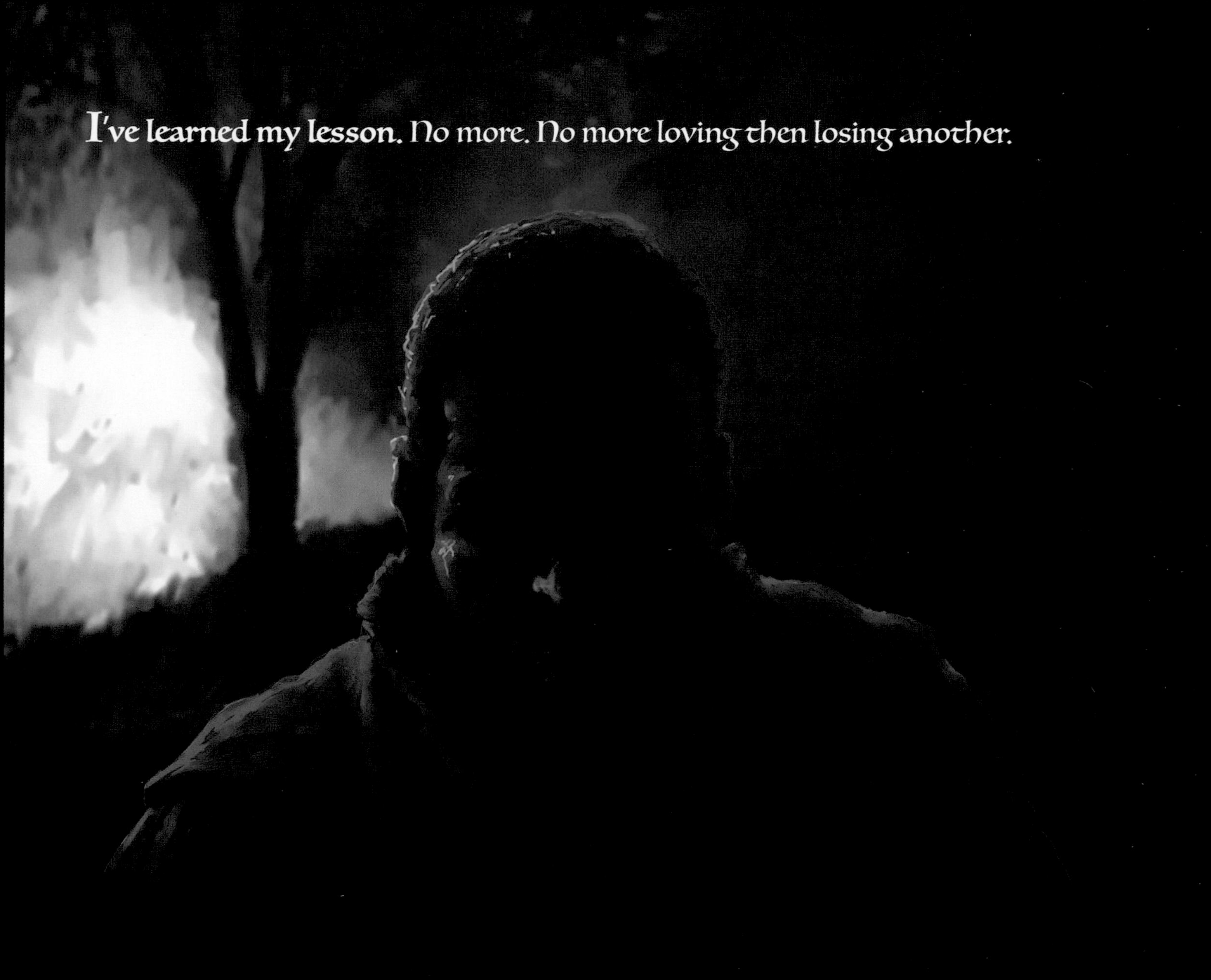
I've learned my lesson. No more. No more loving then losing another.

John hacked his way through the American South and beyond. Notably, he came upon an area he'd visited **thousands of years before** when his kingdom had been focused on seafaring, exploration, and trade. He had been quite popular with **the Olmec people**.

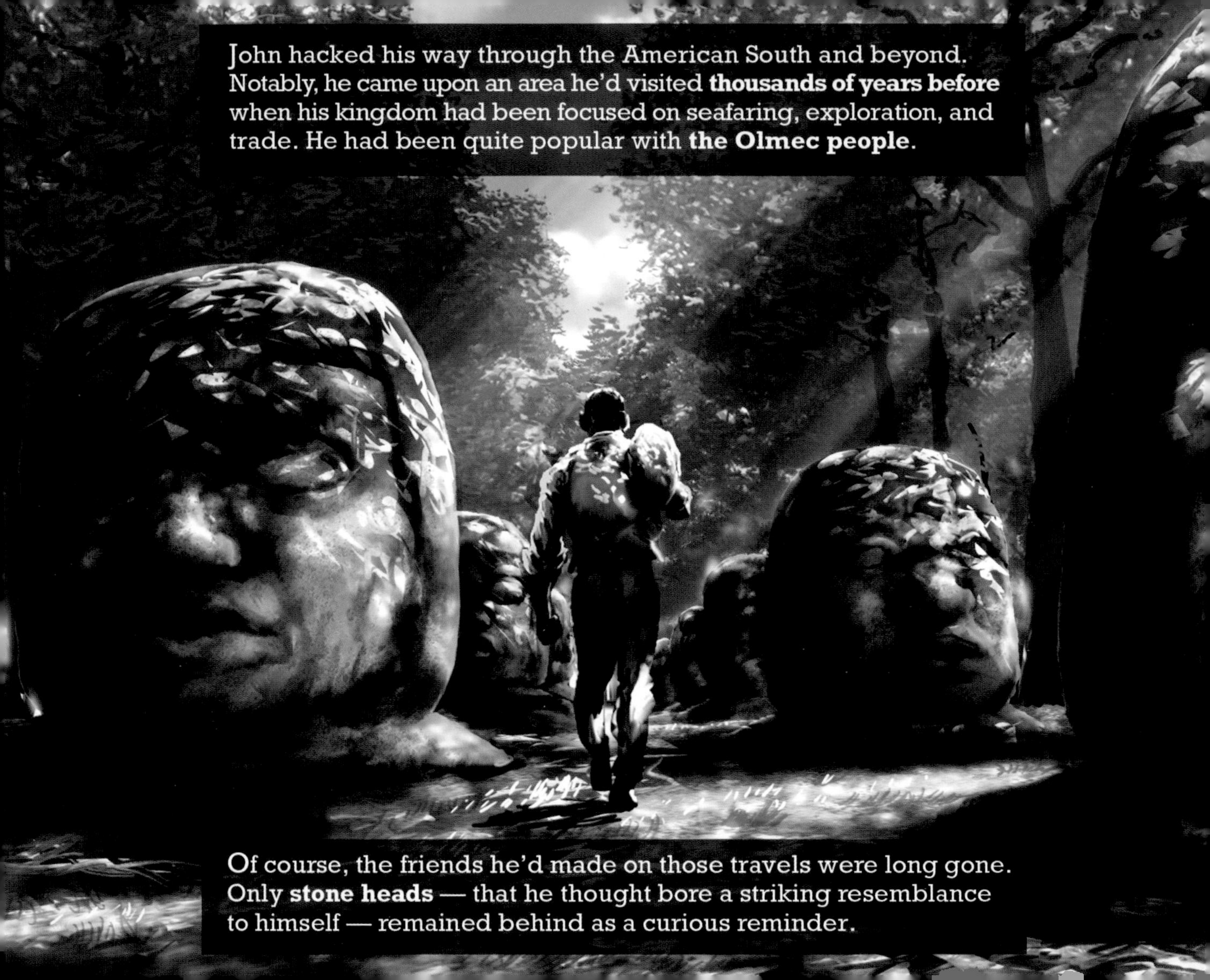

Of course, the friends he'd made on those travels were long gone. Only **stone heads** — that he thought bore a striking resemblance to himself — remained behind as a curious reminder.

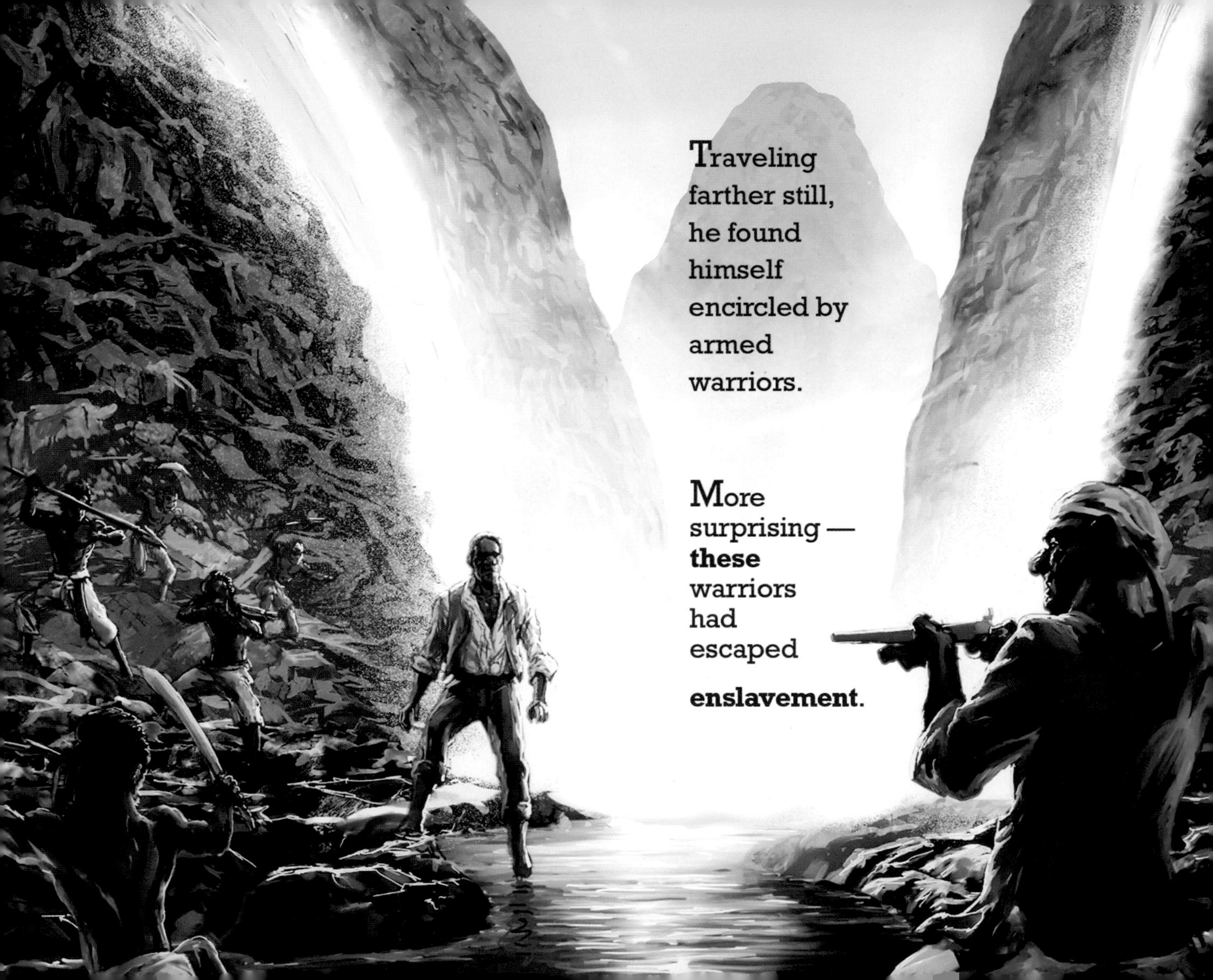

Traveling farther still, he found himself encircled by armed warriors.

More surprising — **these** warriors had escaped **enslavement**.

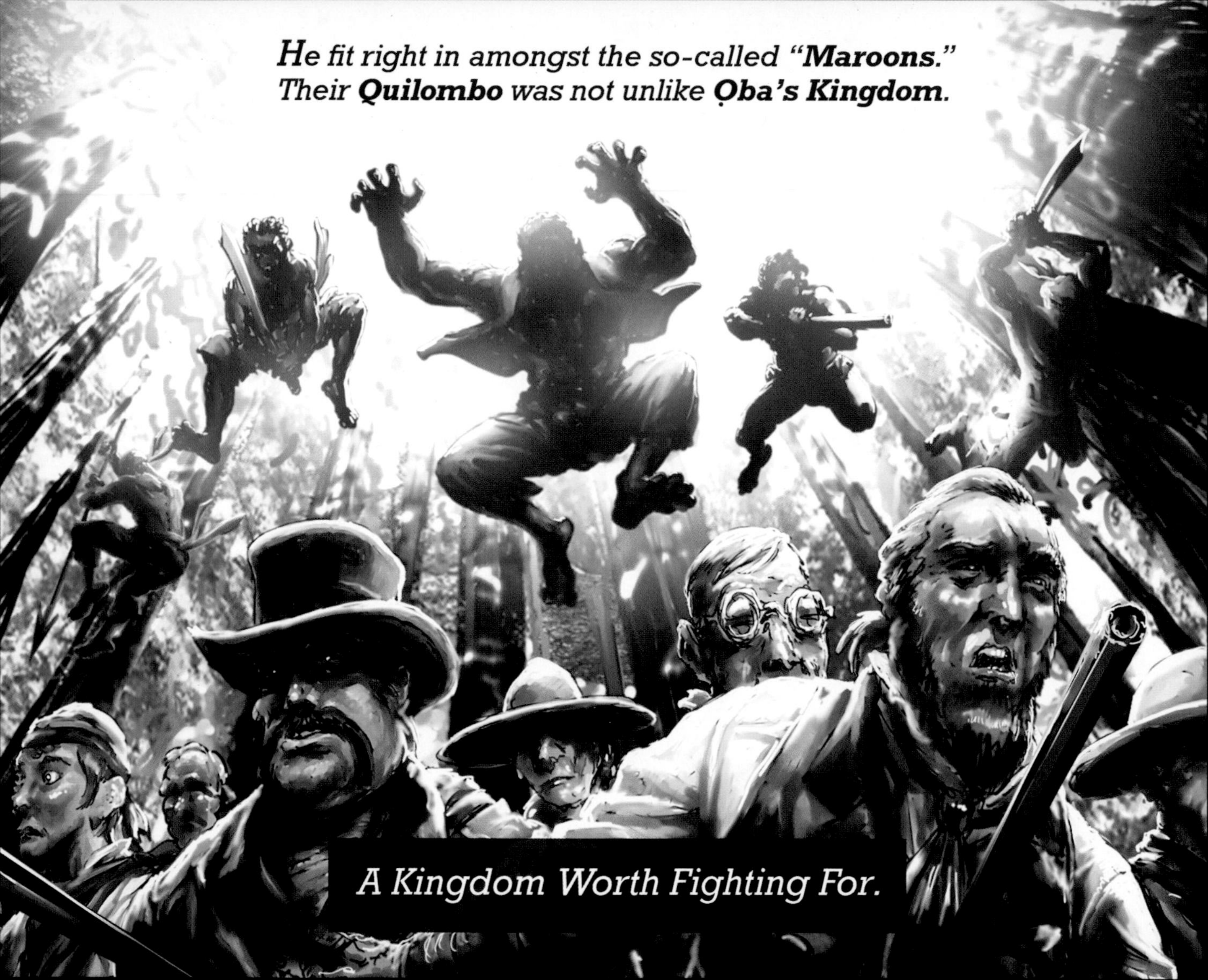
He fit right in amongst the so-called "Maroons." Their Quilombo was not unlike Ọba's Kingdom.
A Kingdom Worth Fighting For.

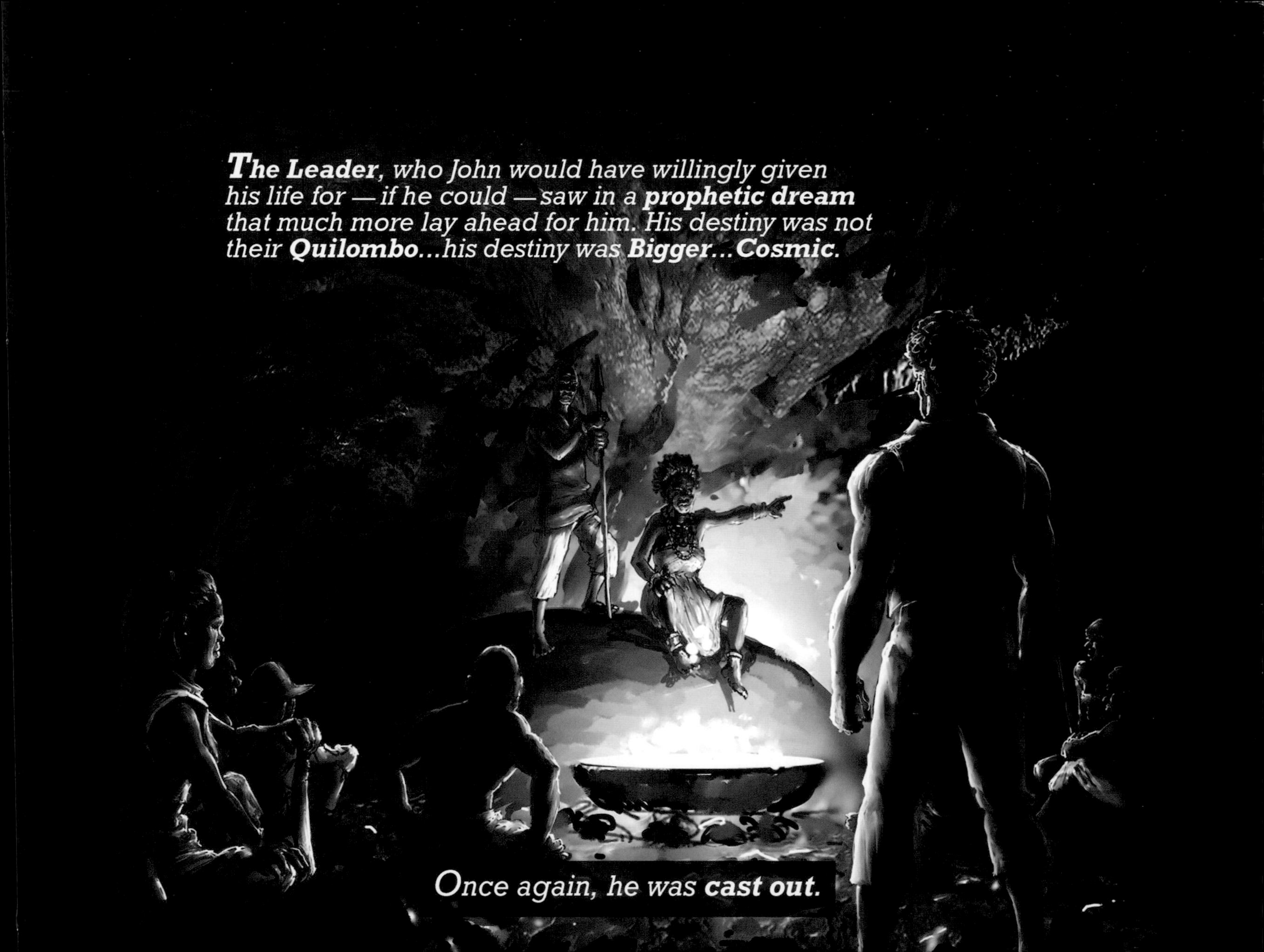
The Leader, who John would have willingly given his life for — if he could — saw in a prophetic dream that much more lay ahead for him. His destiny was not their Quilombo...his destiny was Bigger...Cosmic.
Once again, he was cast out.

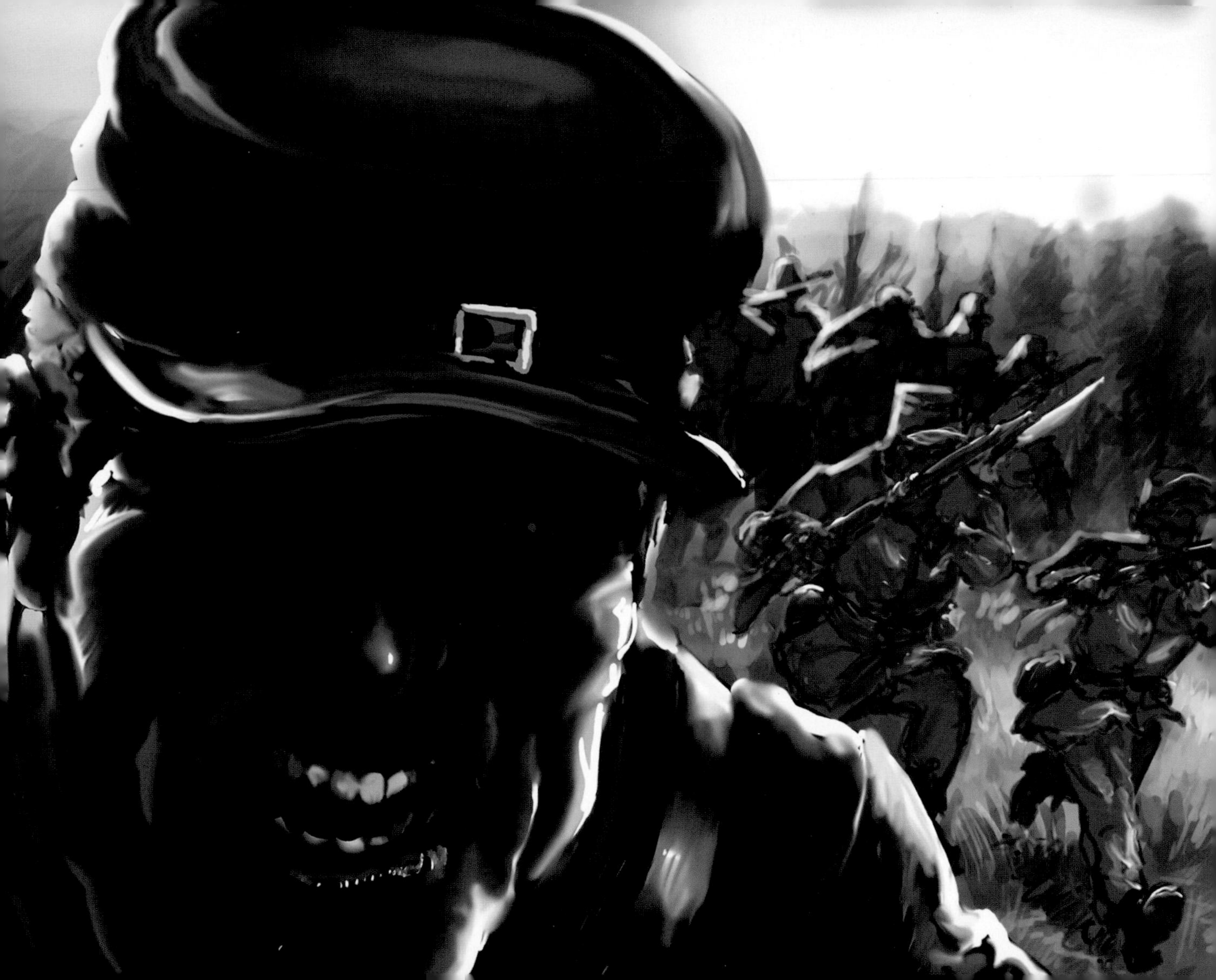

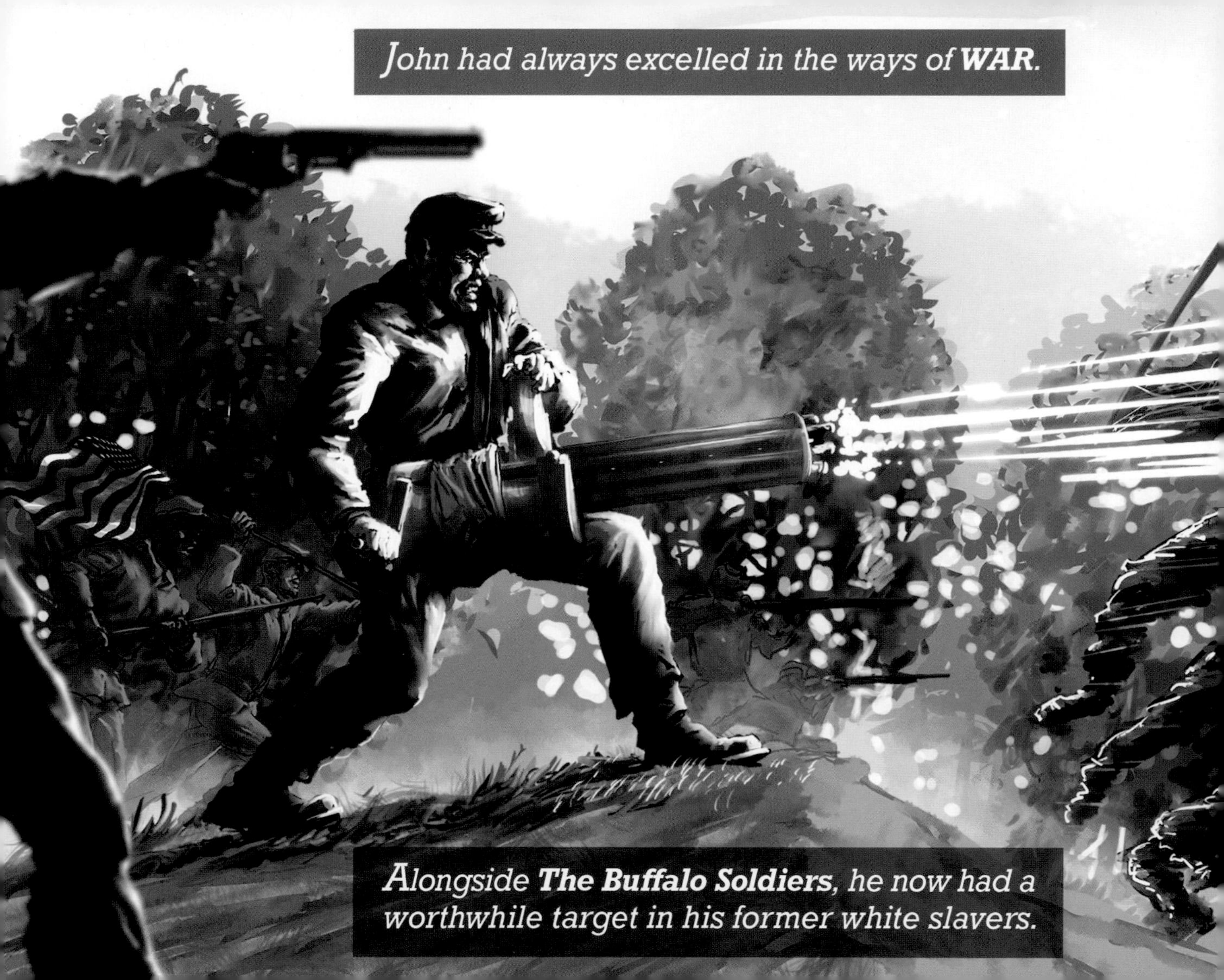
John had always excelled in the ways of **WAR**.
Alongside **The Buffalo Soldiers**, he now had a worthwhile target in his former white slavers.

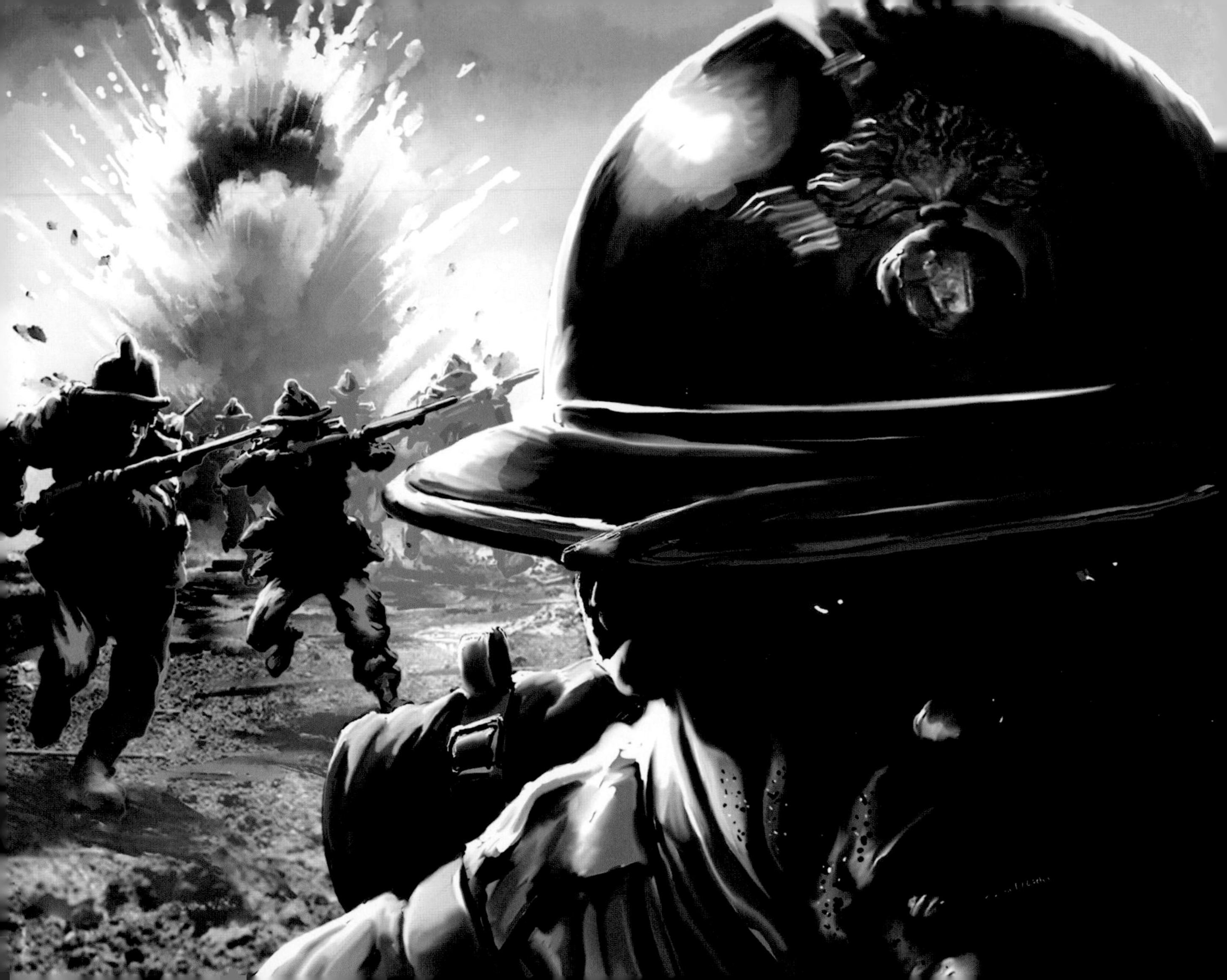

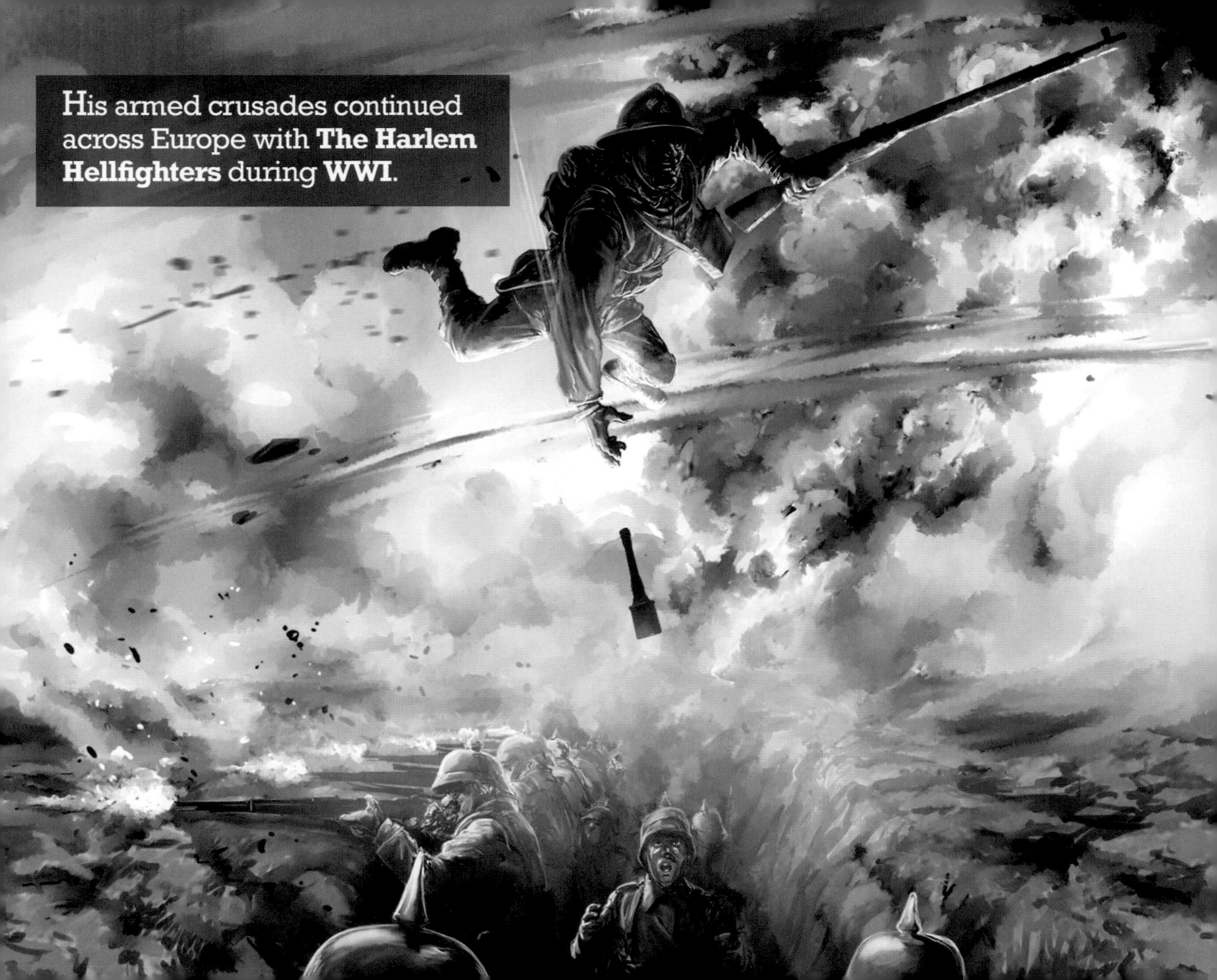
His armed crusades continued across Europe with **The Harlem Hellfighters** during **WWI**.

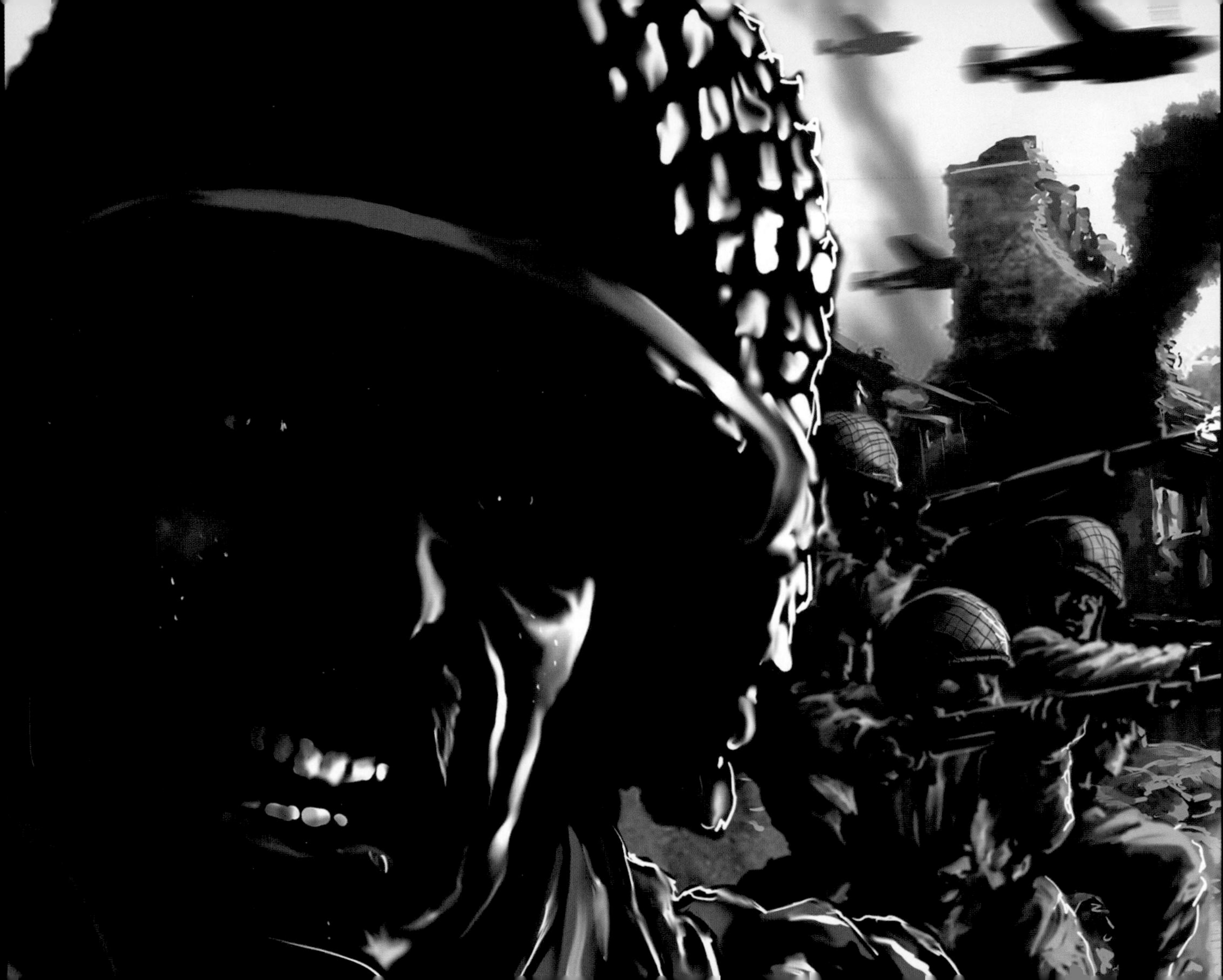

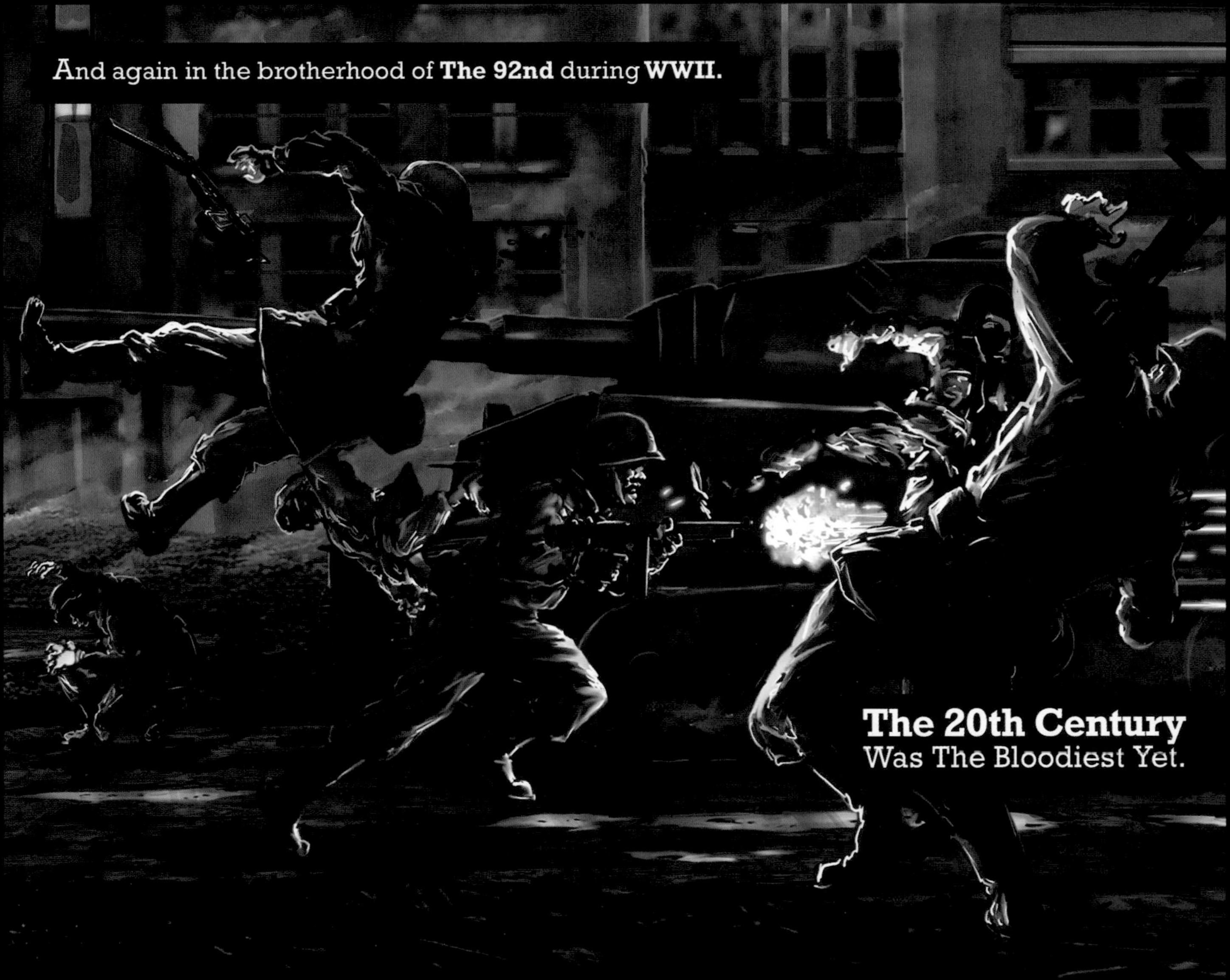
And again in the brotherhood of **The 92nd** during **WWII.**
The 20th Century
Was The Bloodiest Yet.

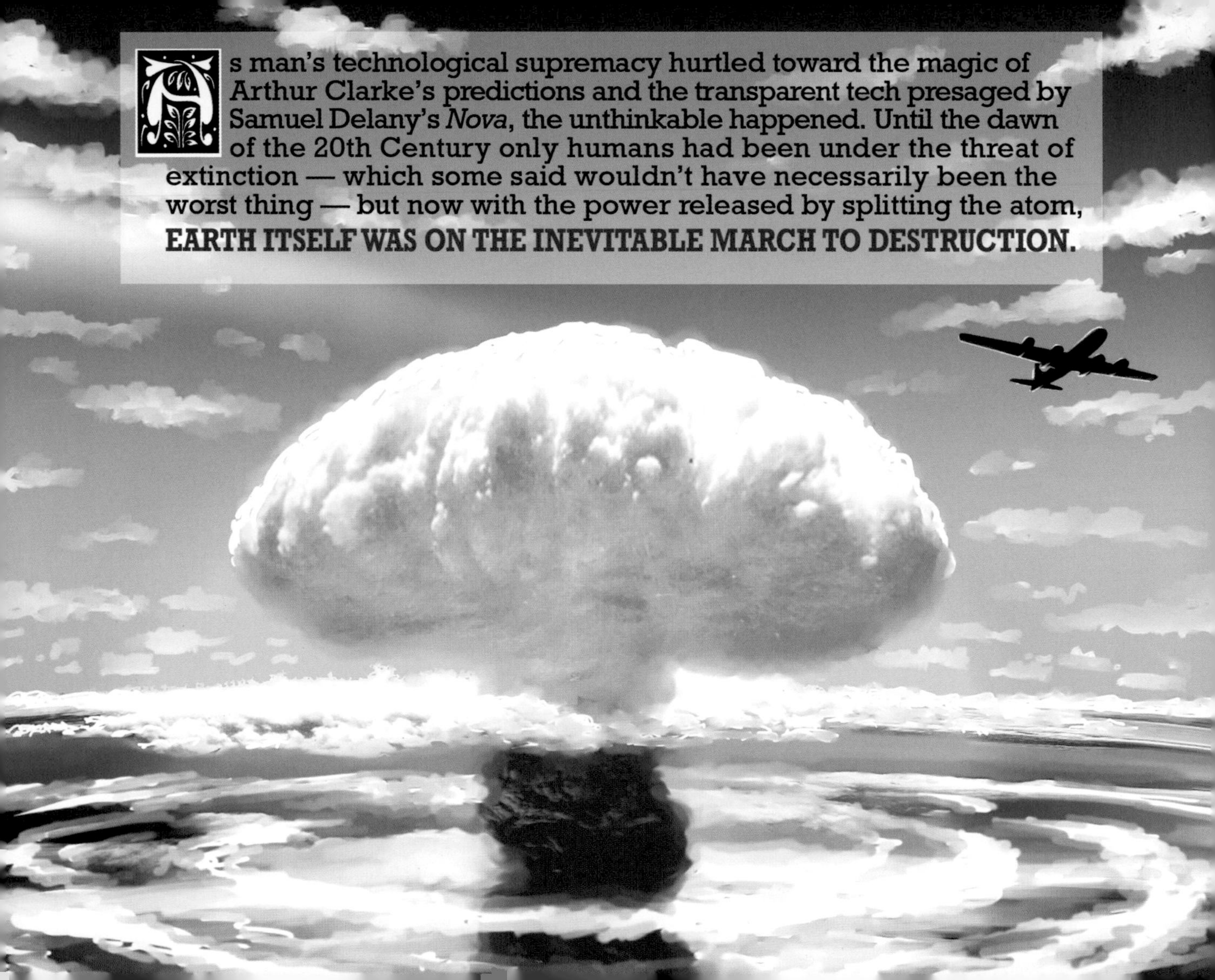
As man's technological supremacy hurtled toward the magic of Arthur Clarke's predictions and the transparent tech presaged by Samuel Delany's *Nova*, the unthinkable happened. Until the dawn of the 20th Century only humans had been under the threat of extinction — which some said wouldn't have necessarily been the worst thing — but now with the power released by splitting the atom,
EARTH ITSELF WAS ON THE INEVITABLE MARCH TO DESTRUCTION.

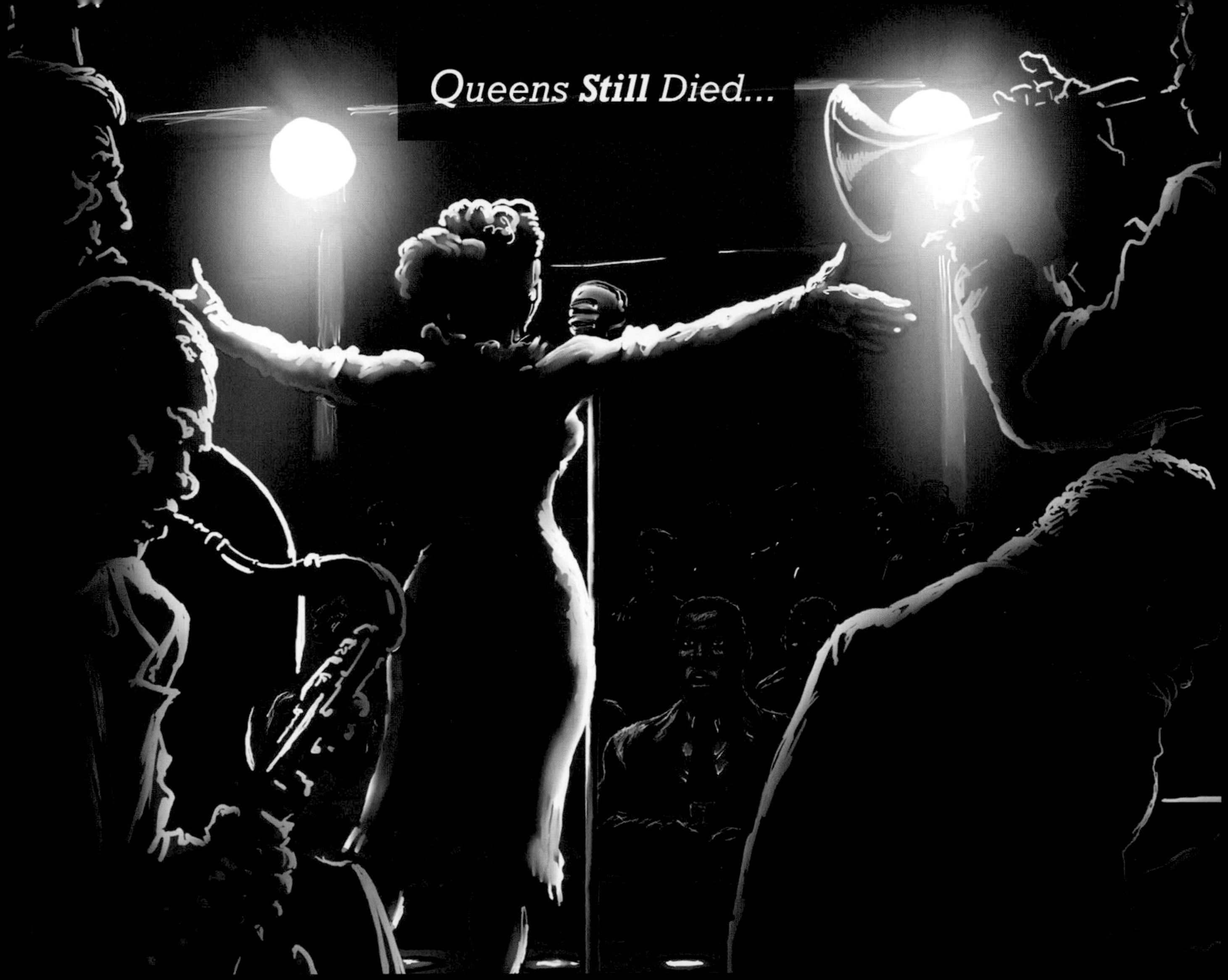
Queens **Still** Died...

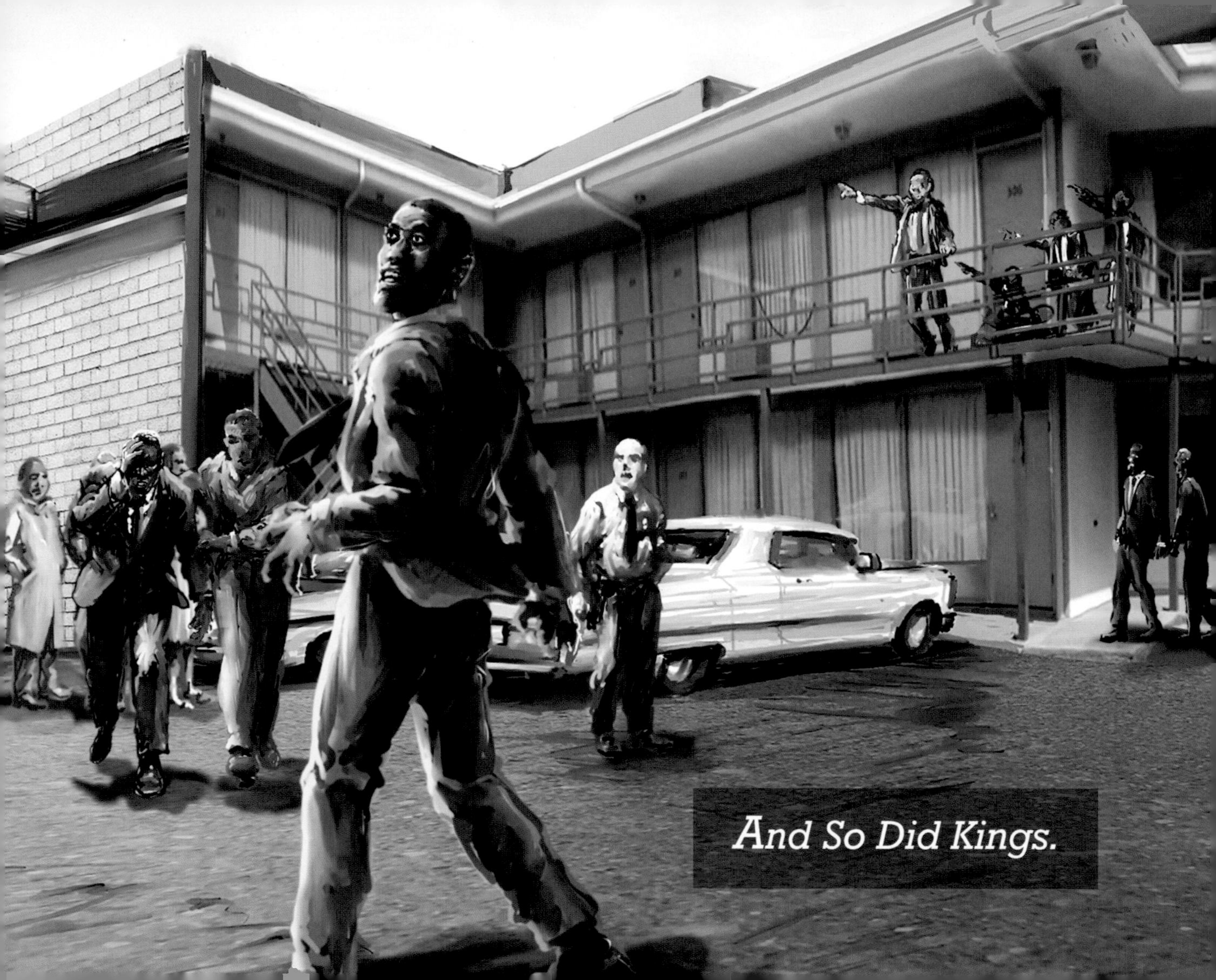
And So Did Kings.

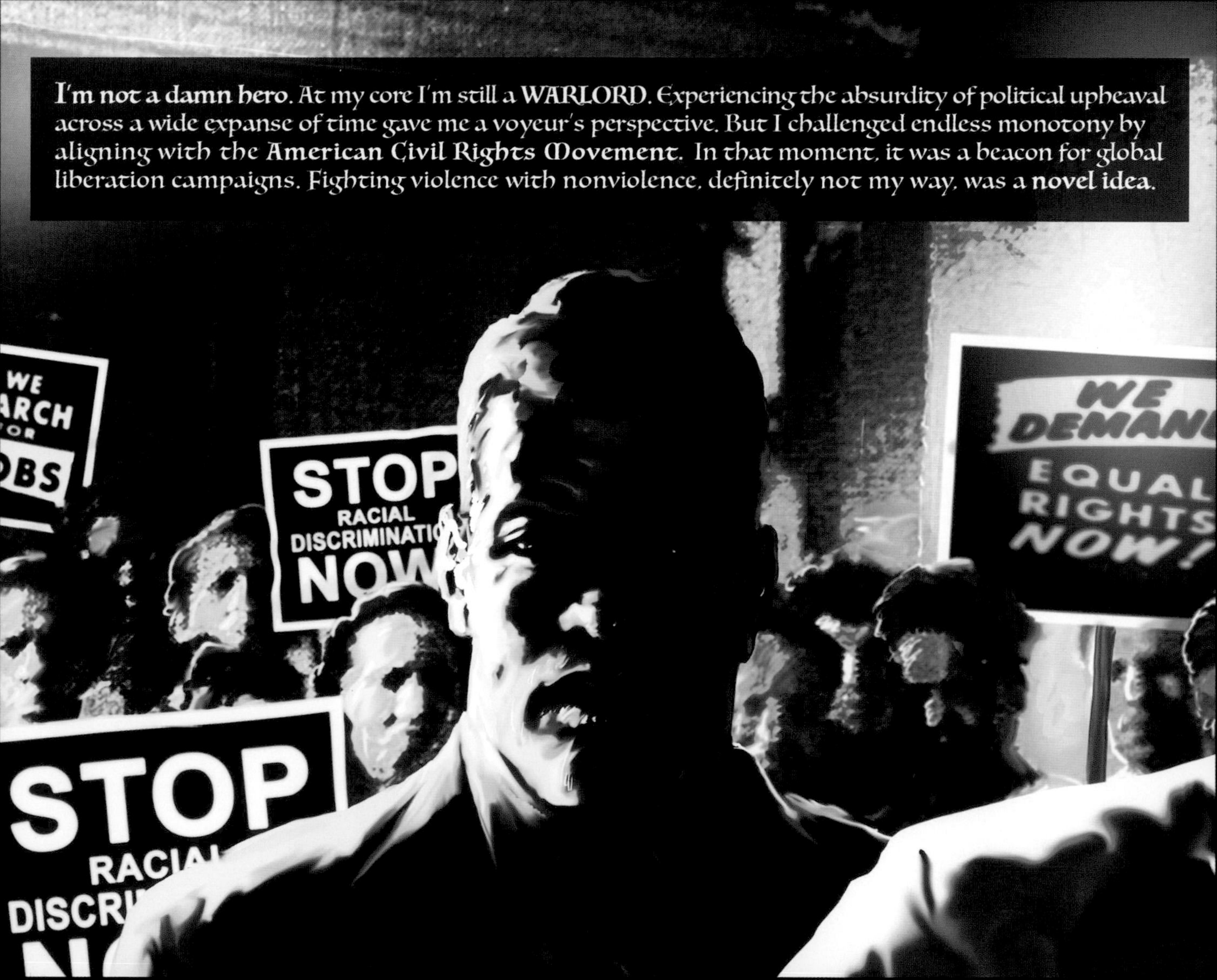
I'm not a damn hero. At my core I'm still a WARLORD. Experiencing the absurdity of political upheaval across a wide expanse of time gave me a voyeur's perspective. But I challenged endless monotony by aligning with the American Civil Rights Movement. In that moment, it was a beacon for global liberation campaigns. Fighting violence with nonviolence, definitely not my way, was a novel idea.
WE
STOP
RACIAL
EQUAL
NOW!
STOP

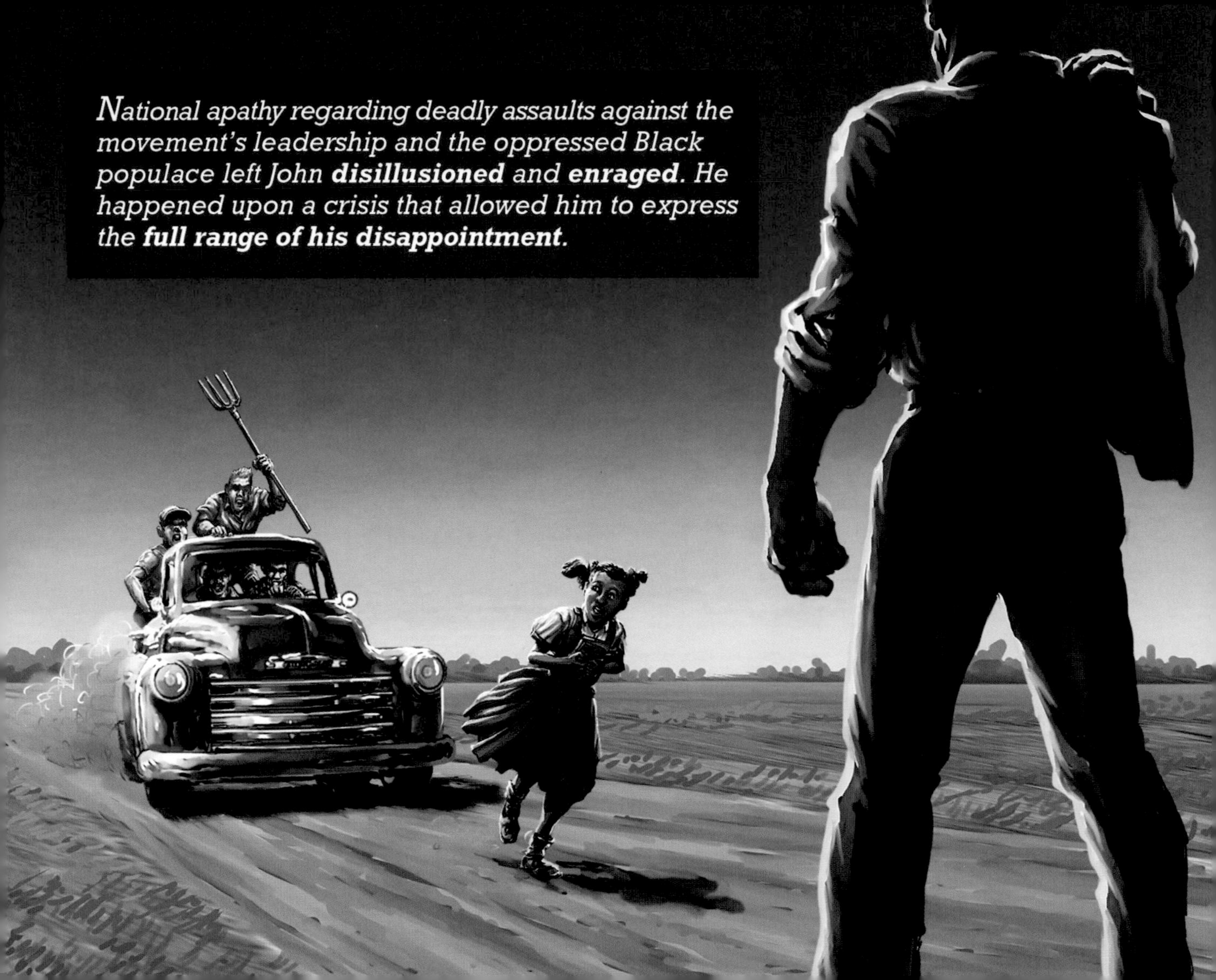

National apathy regarding deadly assaults against the movement's leadership and the oppressed Black populace left John ***disillusioned*** *and* ***enraged****. He happened upon a crisis that allowed him to express the* ***full range of his disappointment****.*

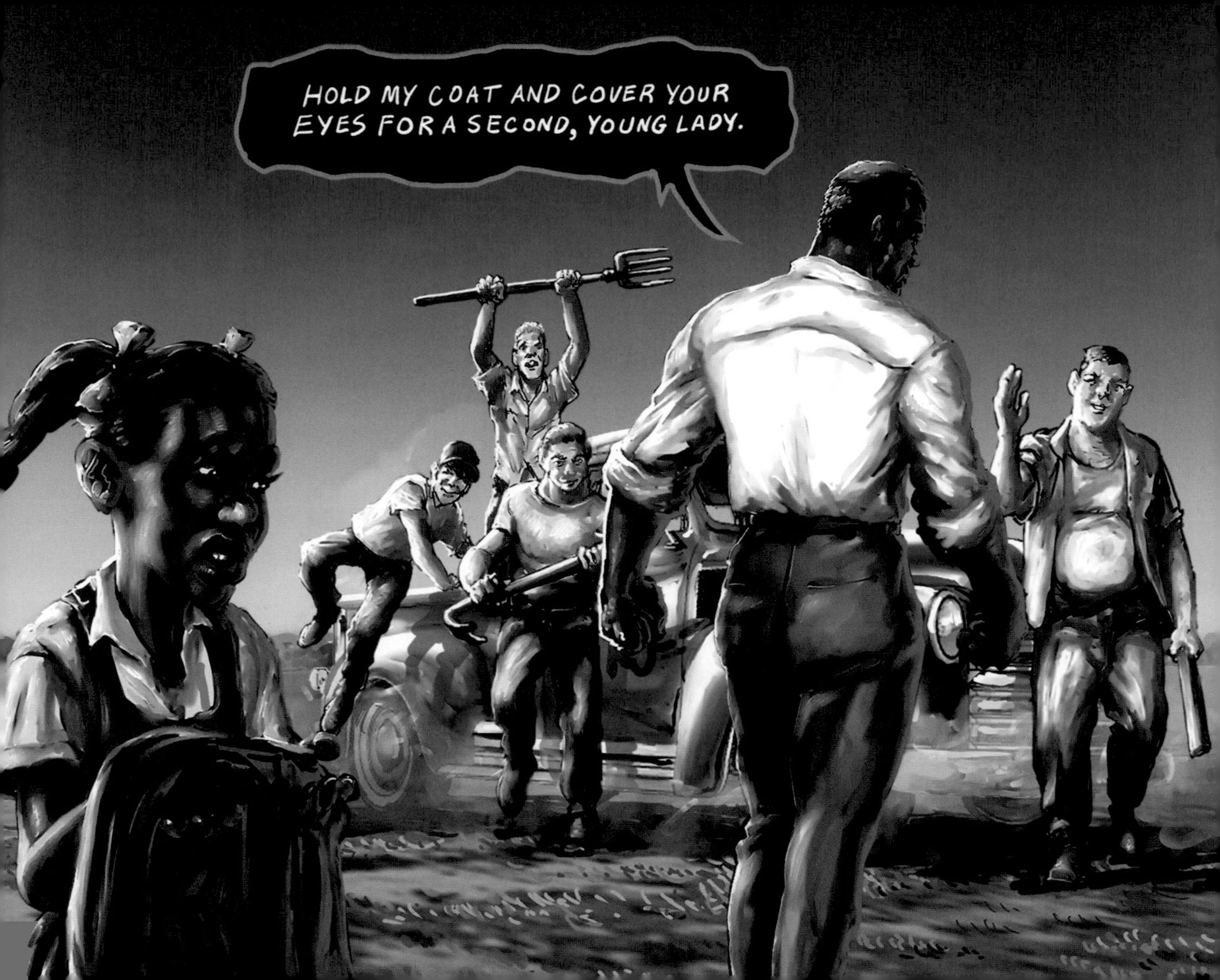
HOLD MY COAT AND COVER YOUR EYES FOR A SECOND, YOUNG LADY.

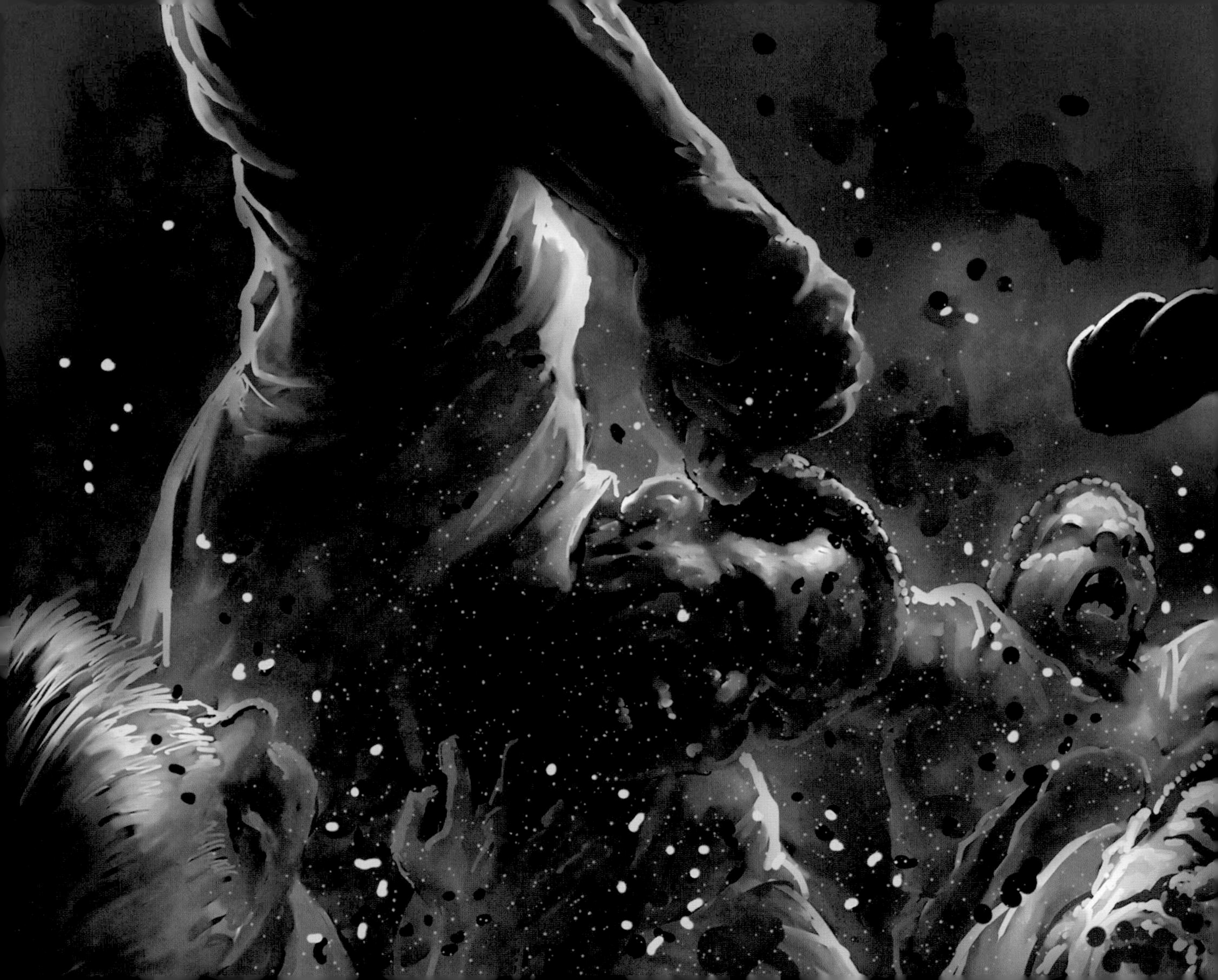

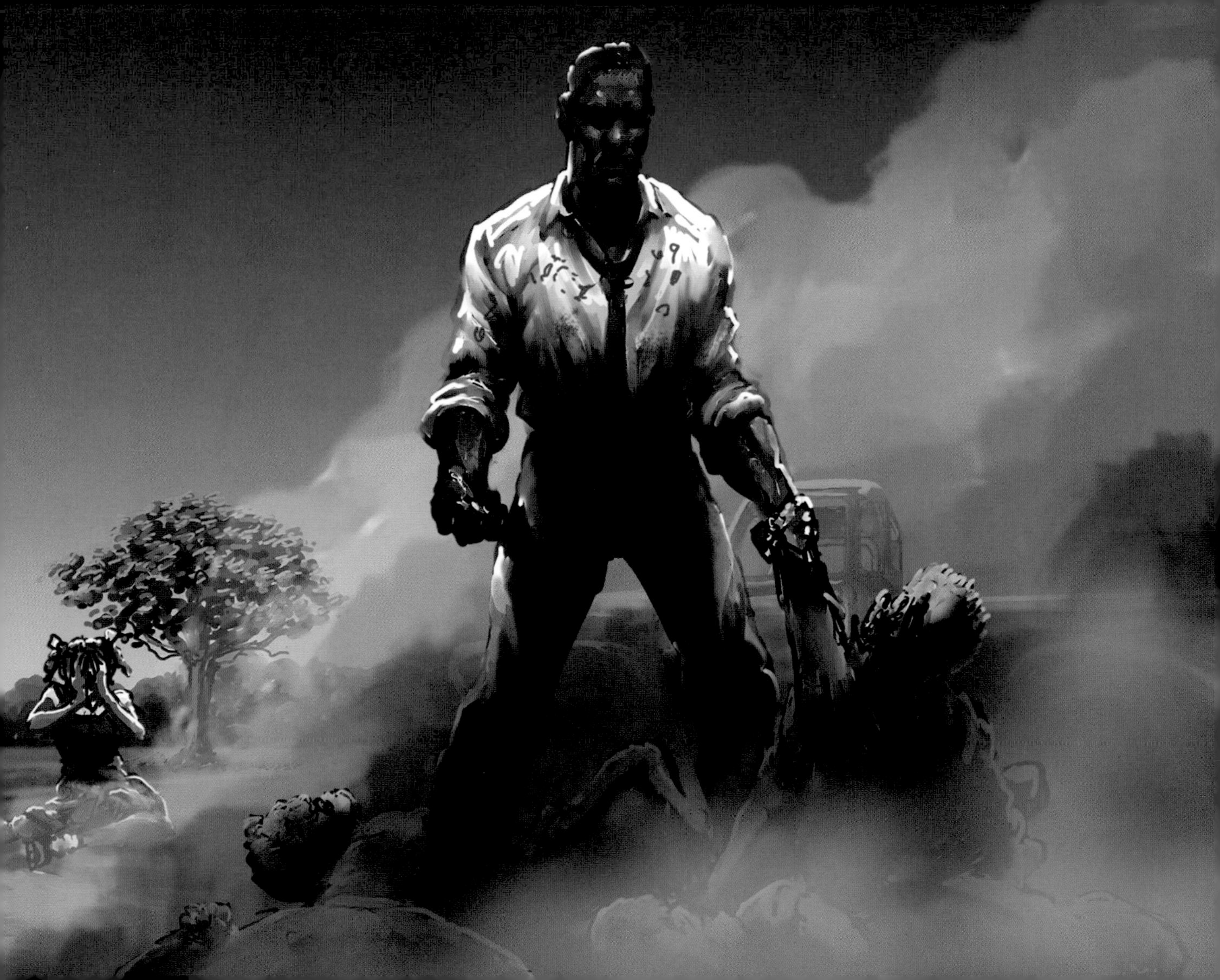

After "**acquiring**" transportation, John needed an immediate change of scenery.

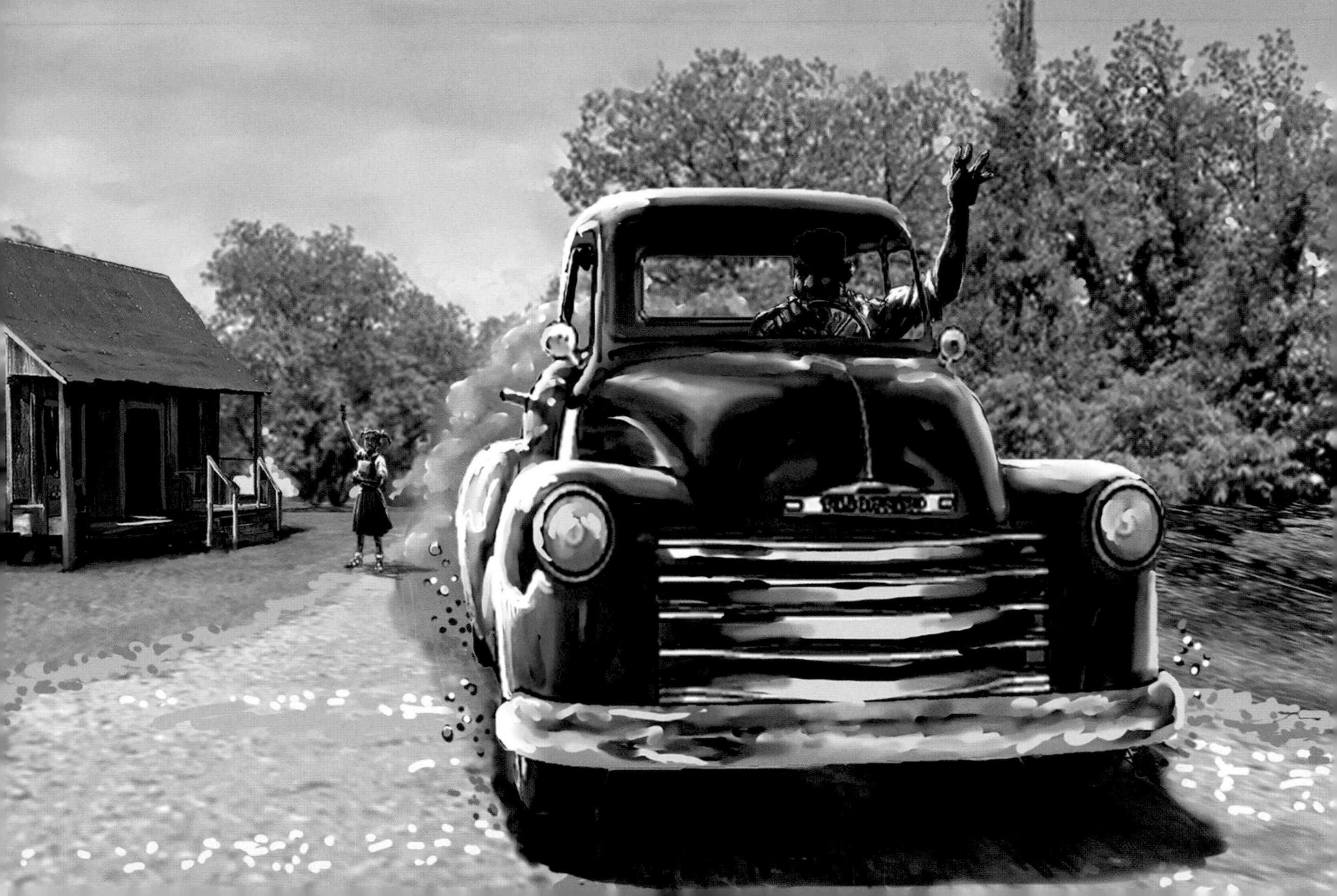

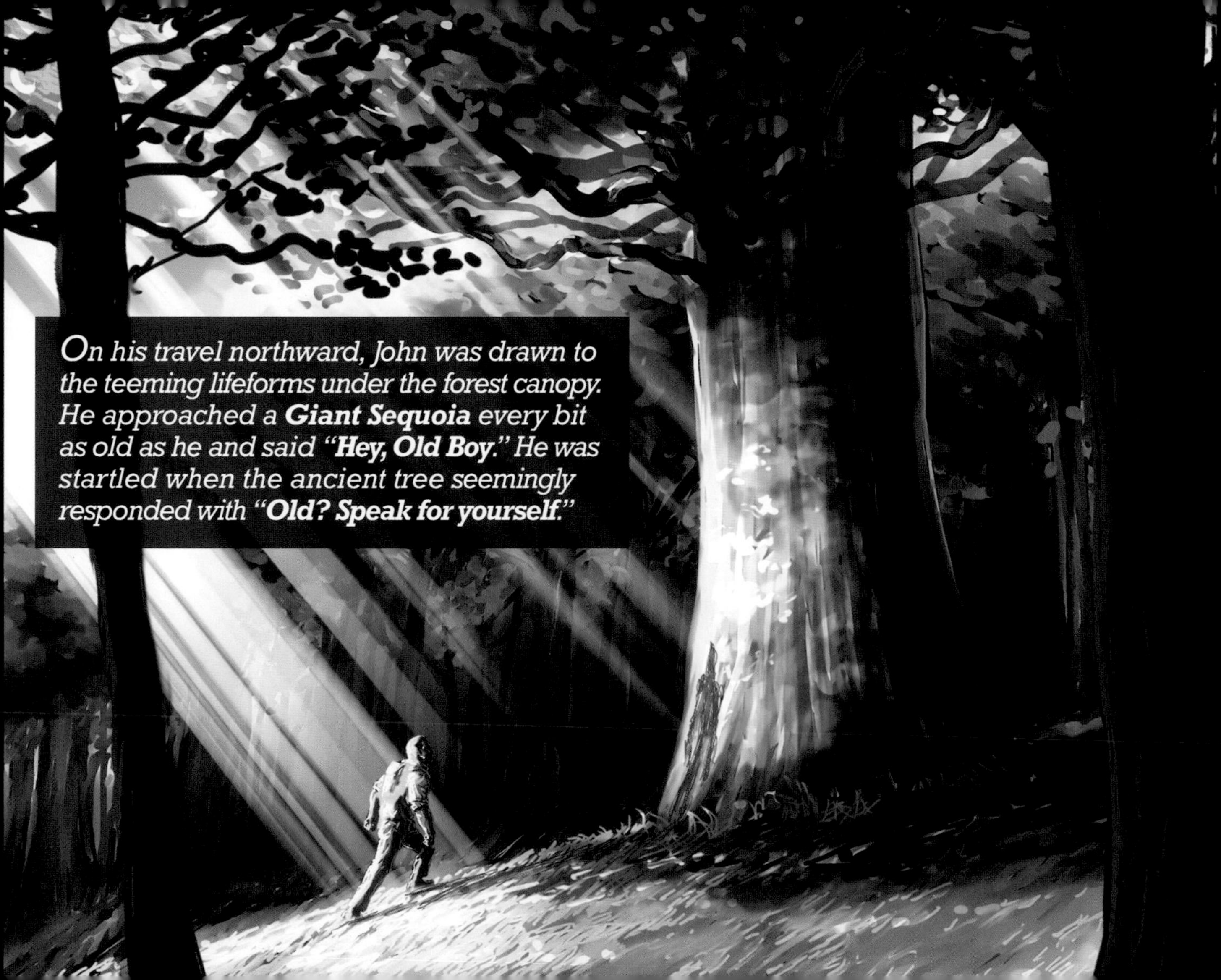
On his travel northward, John was drawn to the teeming lifeforms under the forest canopy. He approached a **Giant Sequoia** every bit as old as he and said "**Hey, Old Boy**." He was startled when the ancient tree seemingly responded with "**Old? Speak for yourself**."

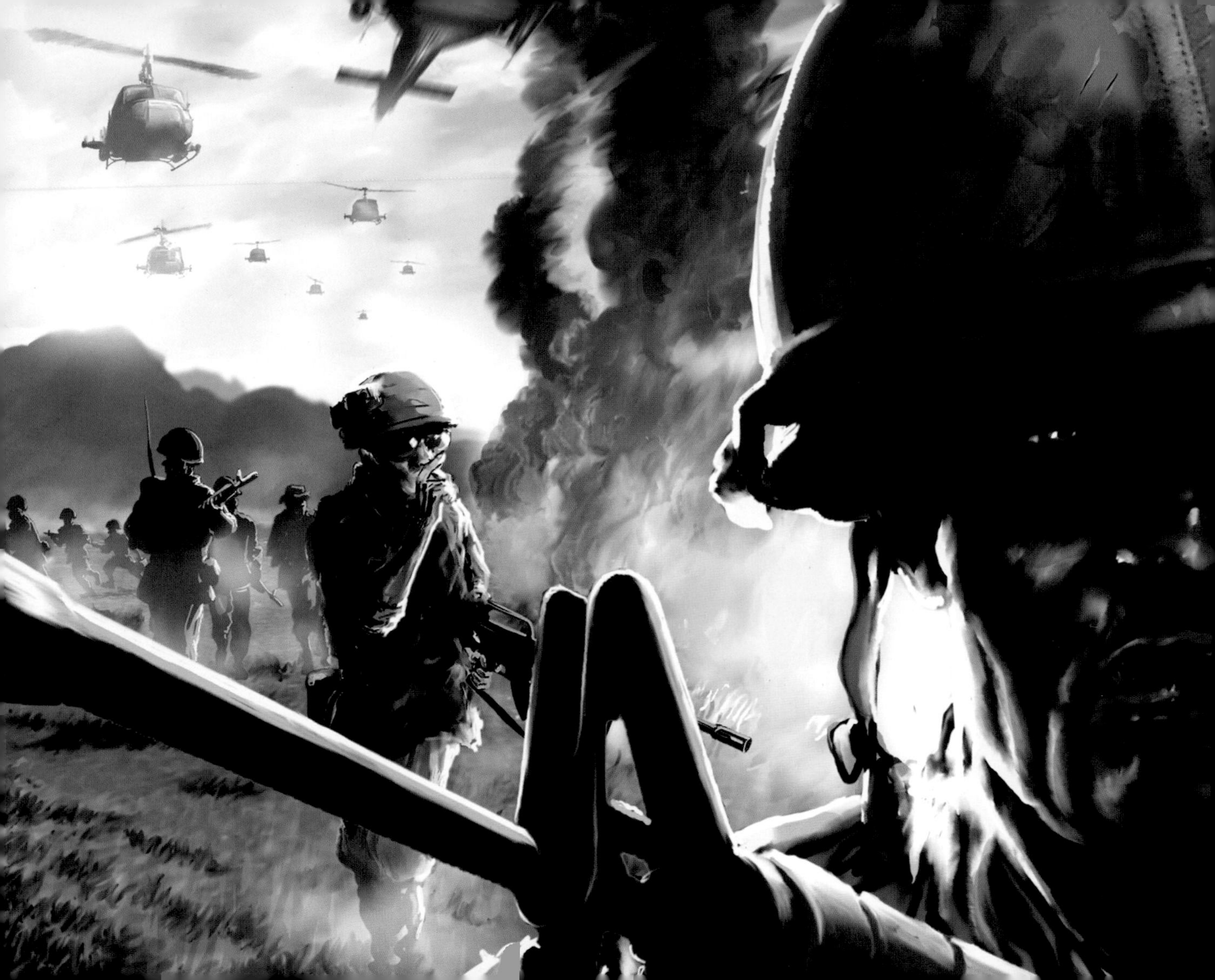

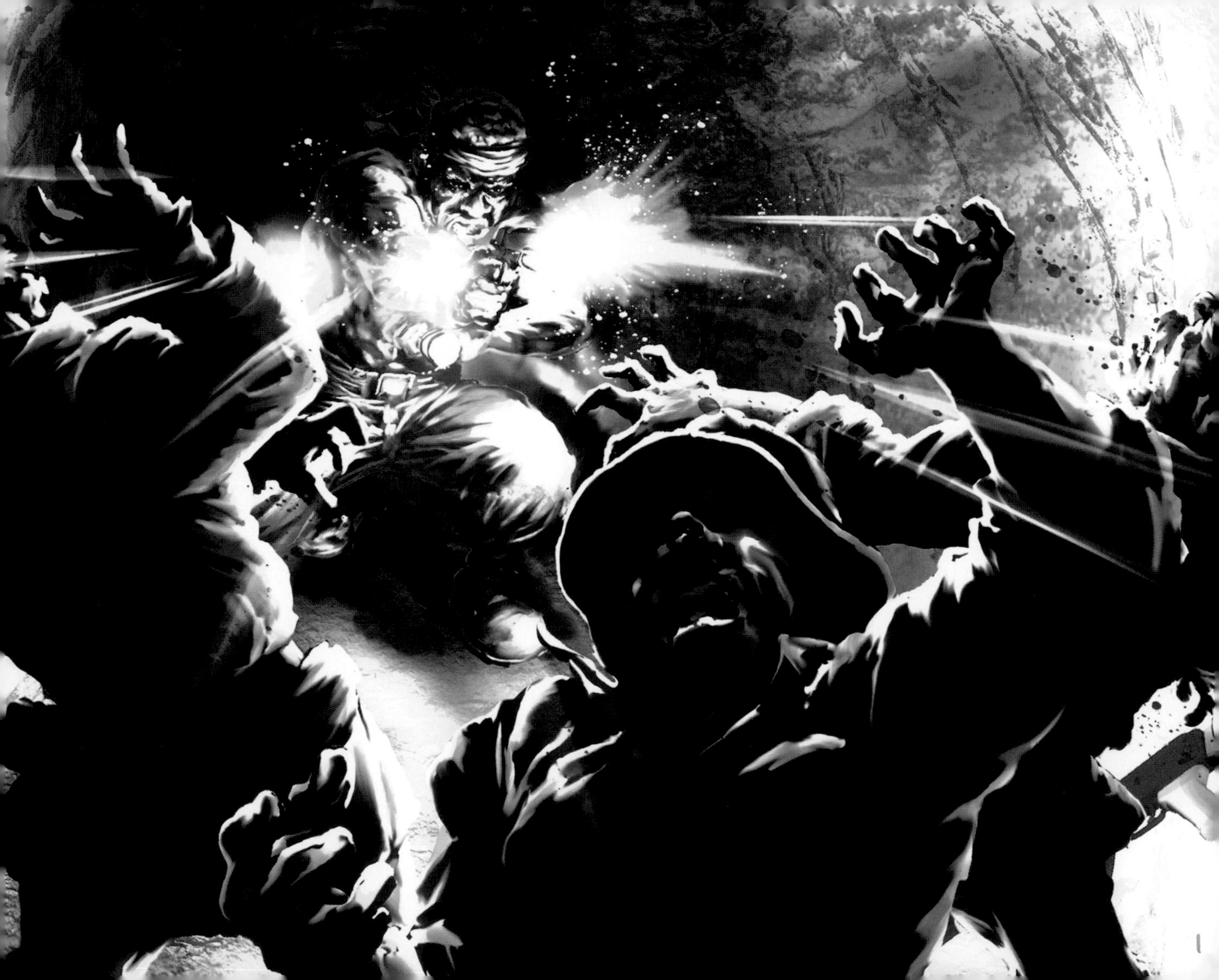

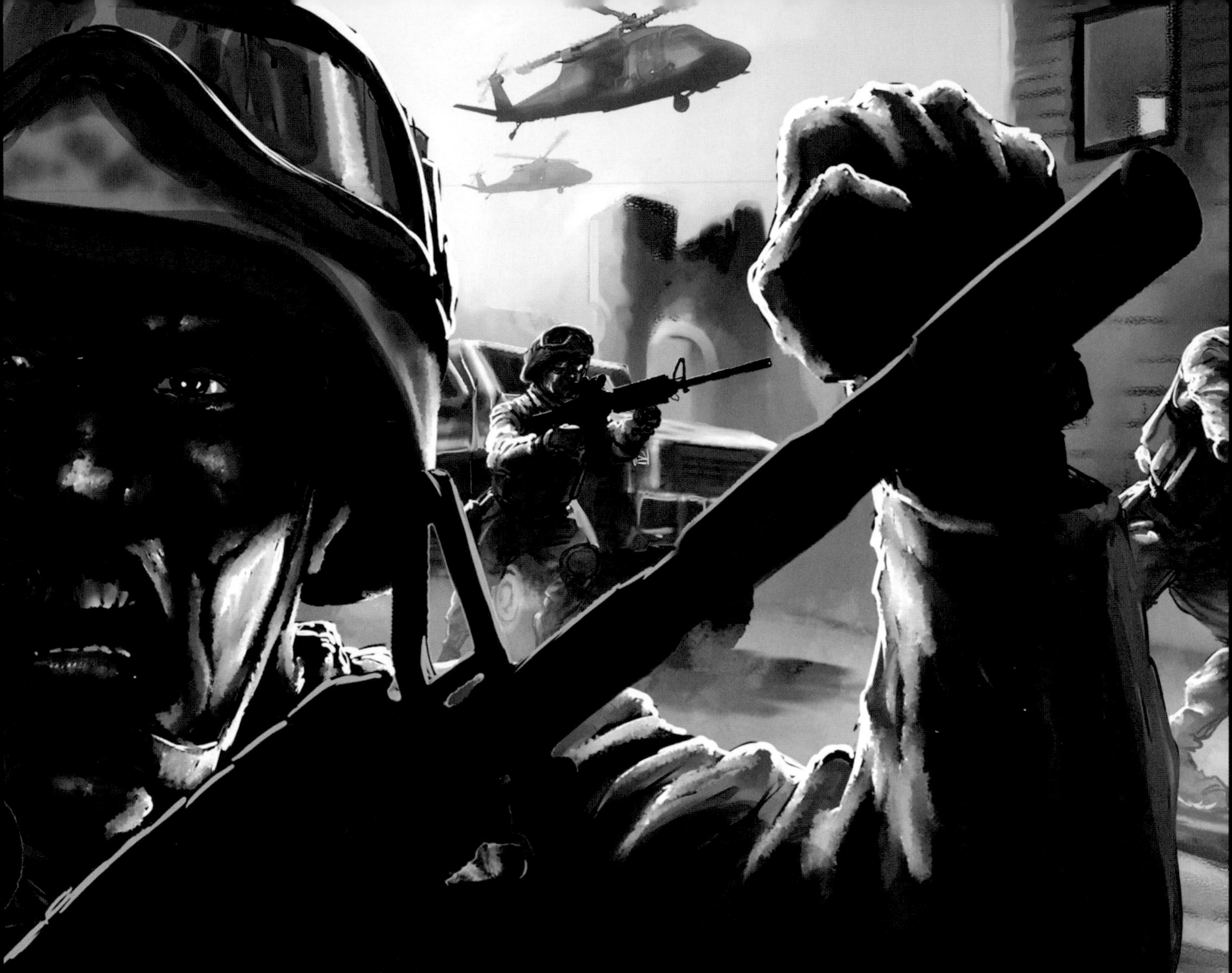

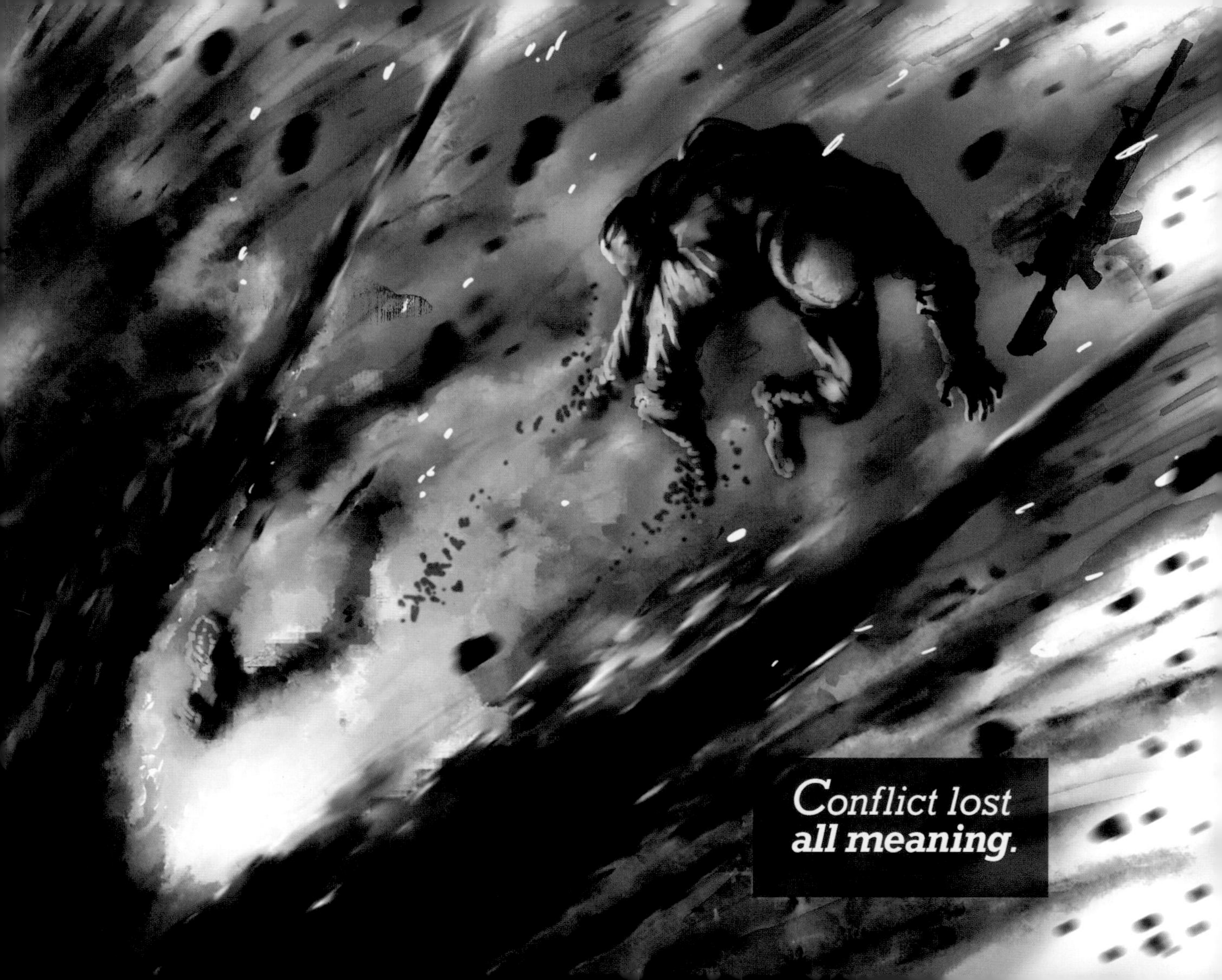
Conflict lost all meaning.

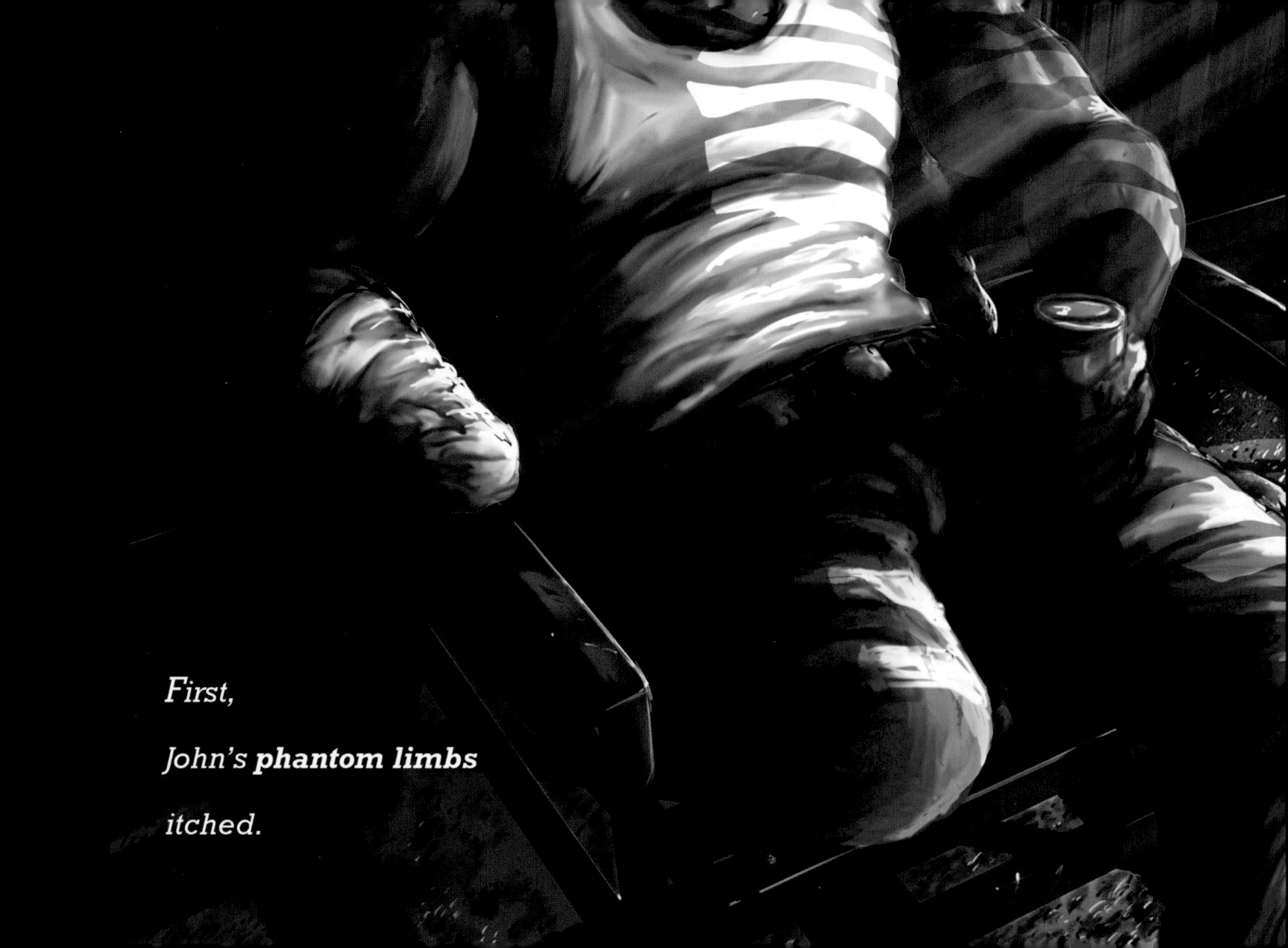

First,

John's ***phantom limbs***

itched.

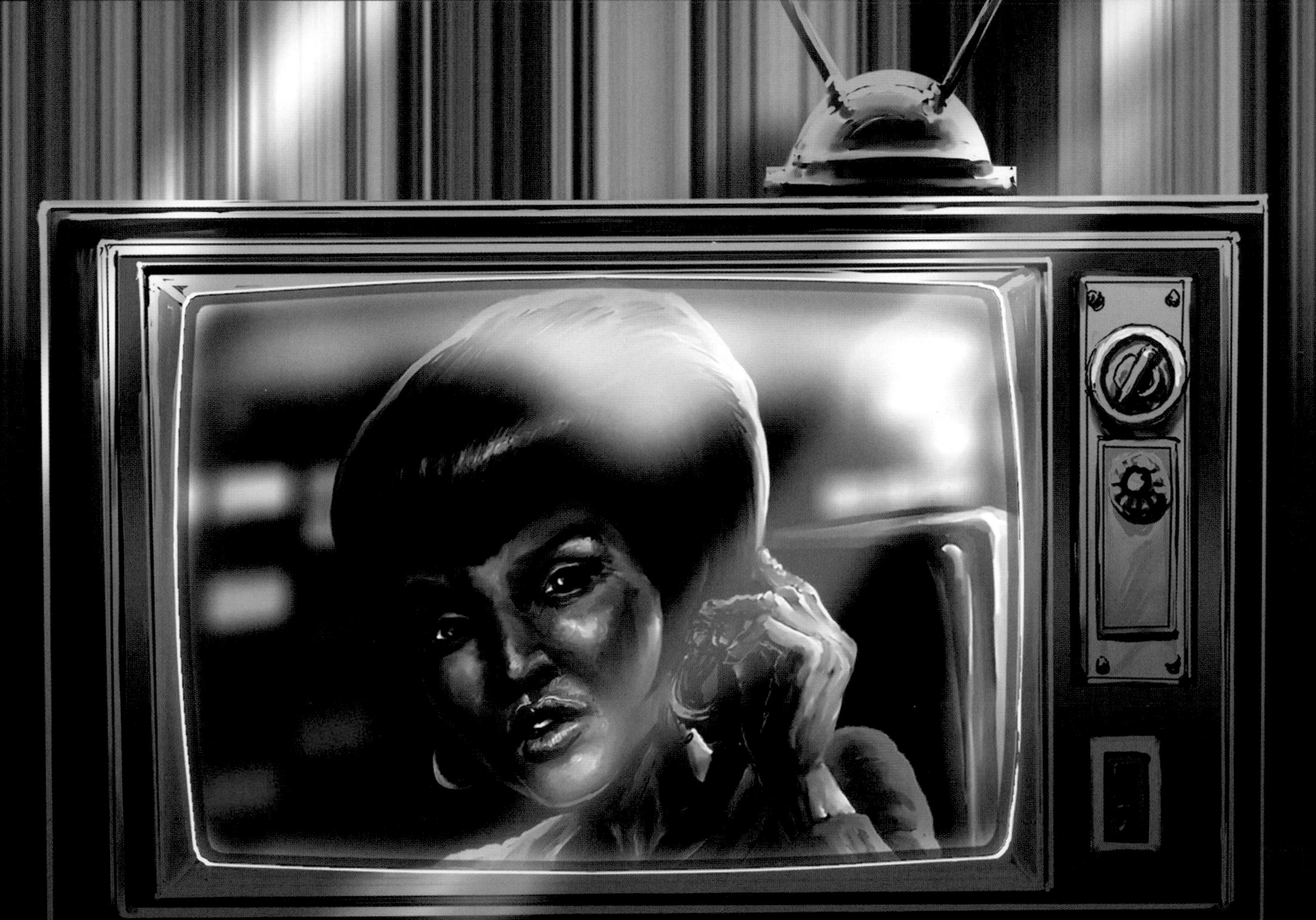

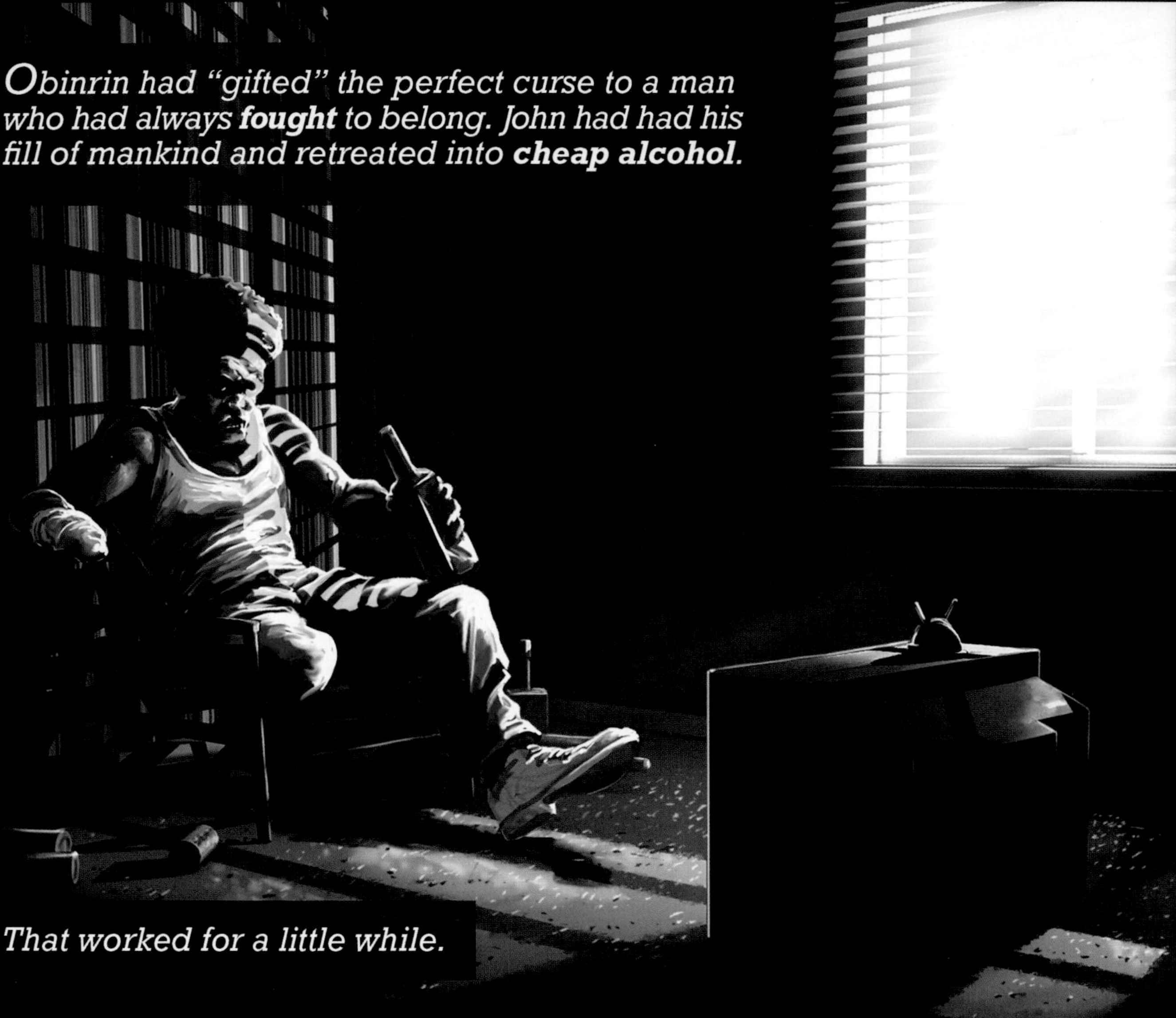
*Obinrin had "gifted" the perfect curse to a man who had always **fought** to belong. John had had his fill of mankind and retreated into **cheap alcohol**.*
That worked for a little while.

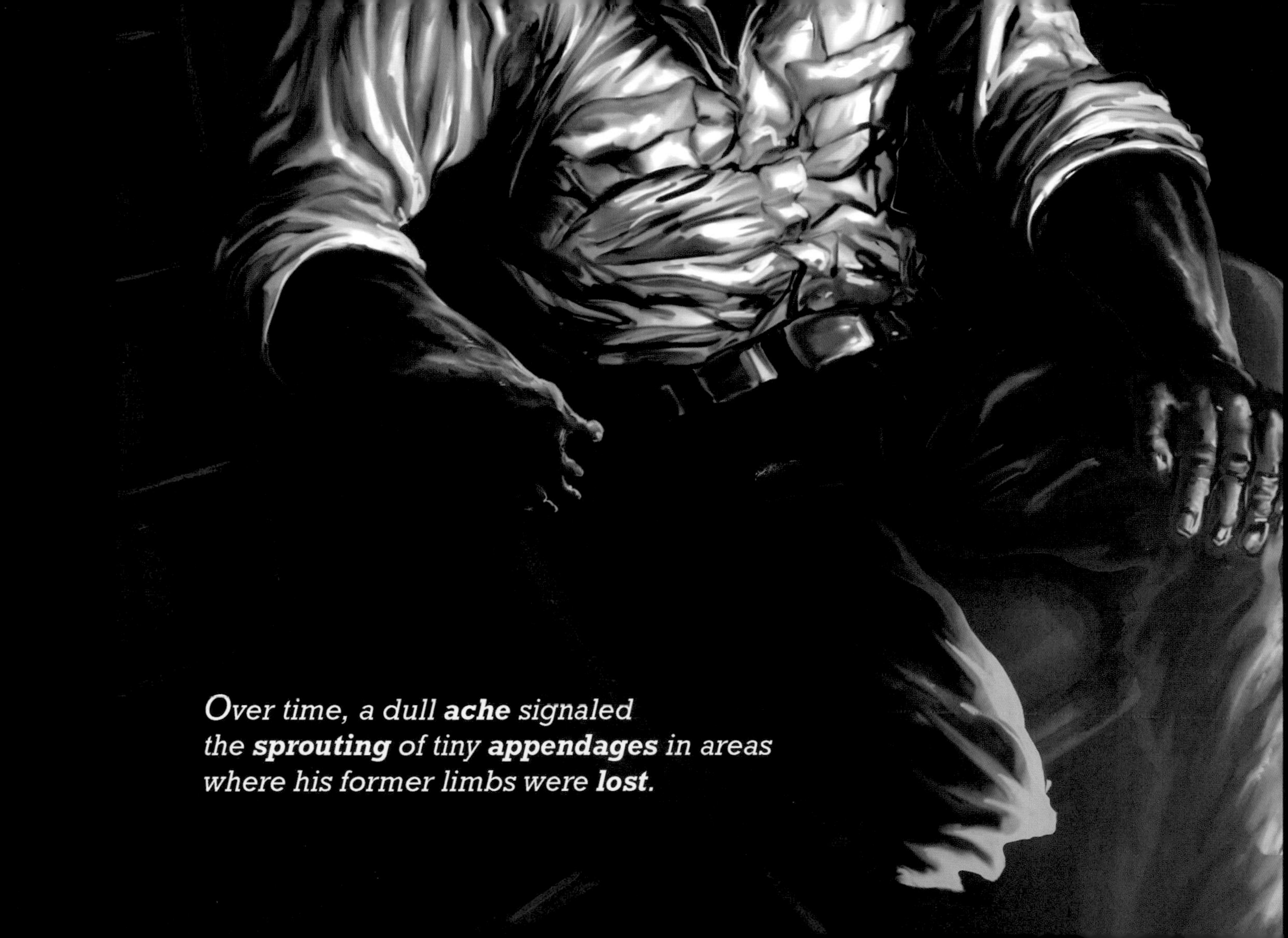

Over time, a dull ***ache*** *signaled the* ***sprouting*** *of tiny* ***appendages*** *in areas where his former limbs were* ***lost****.*

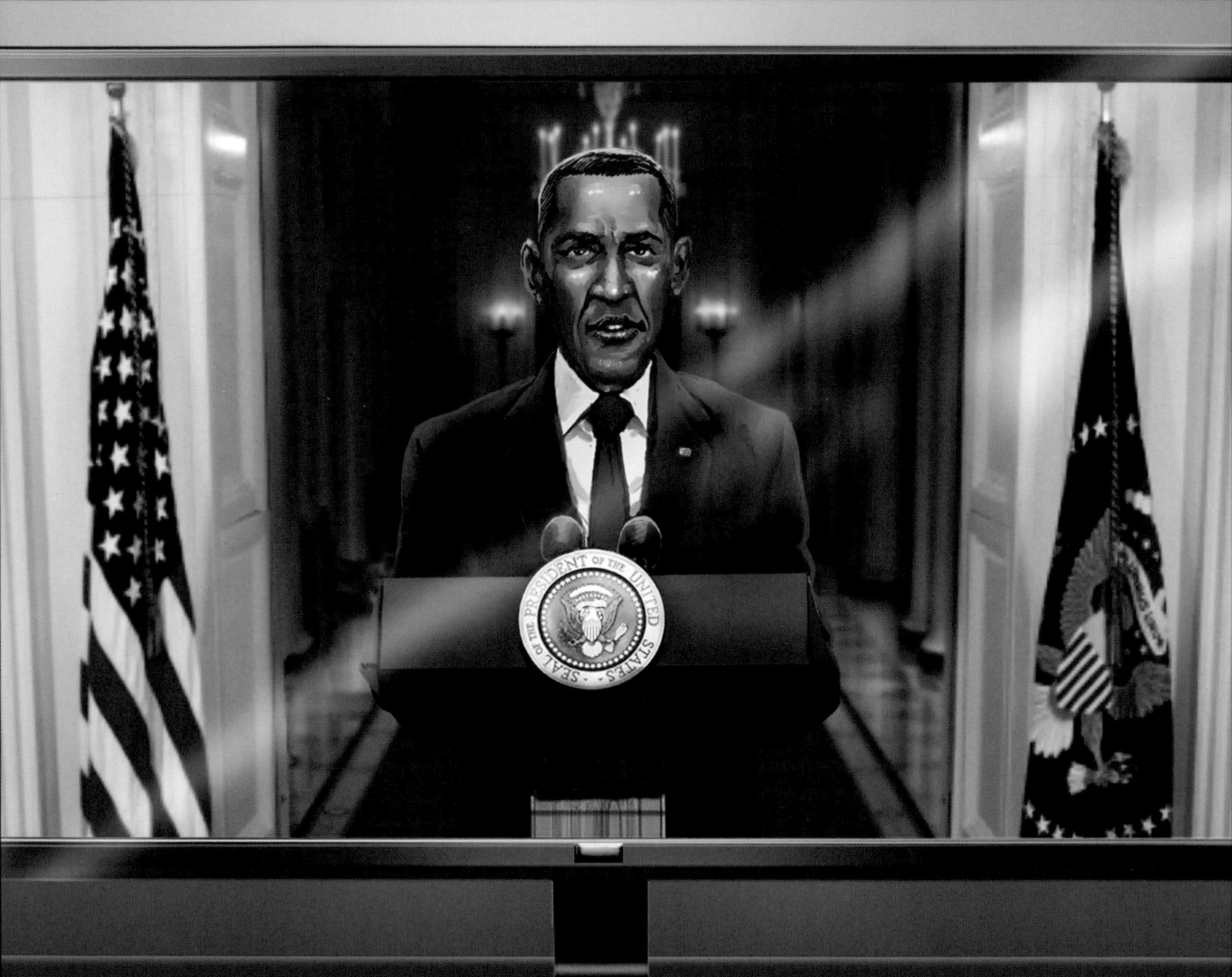
SEAL OF THE PRESIDENT OF THE UNITED STATES

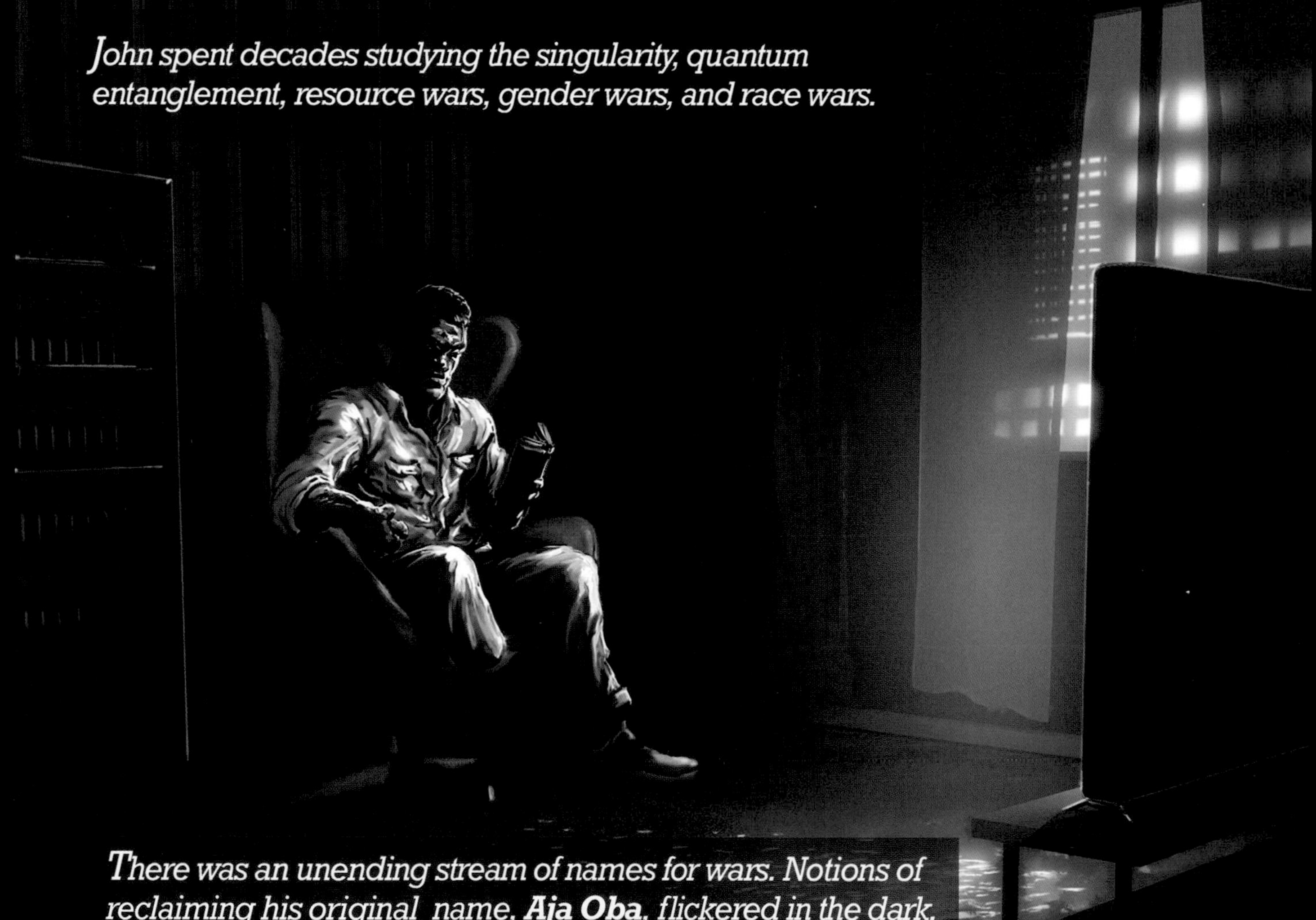
John spent decades studying the singularity, quantum entanglement, resource wars, gender wars, and race wars.
There was an unending stream of names for wars. Notions of reclaiming his original name, **Aja Oba**, flickered in the dark.

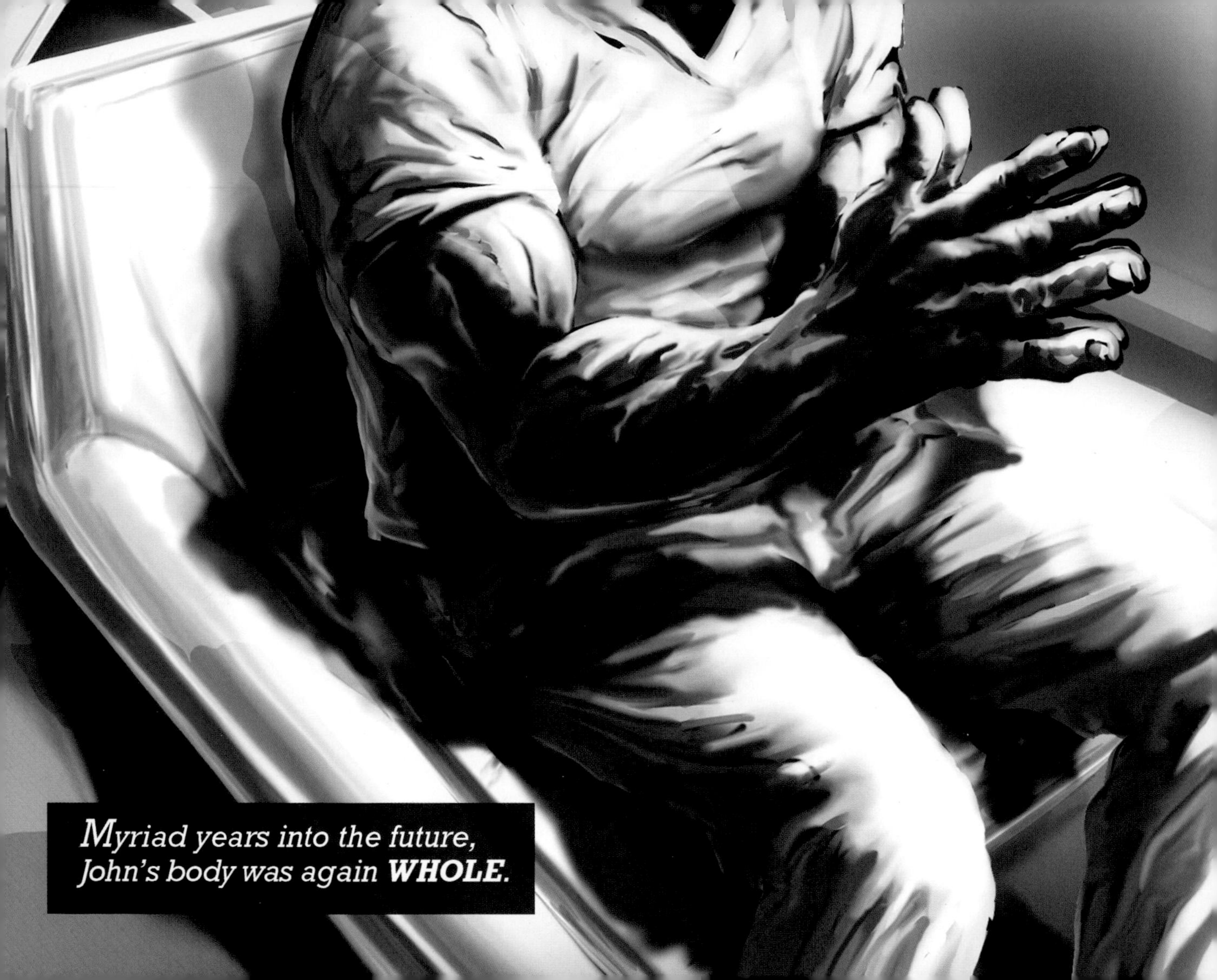
Myriad years into the future, John's body was again WHOLE.

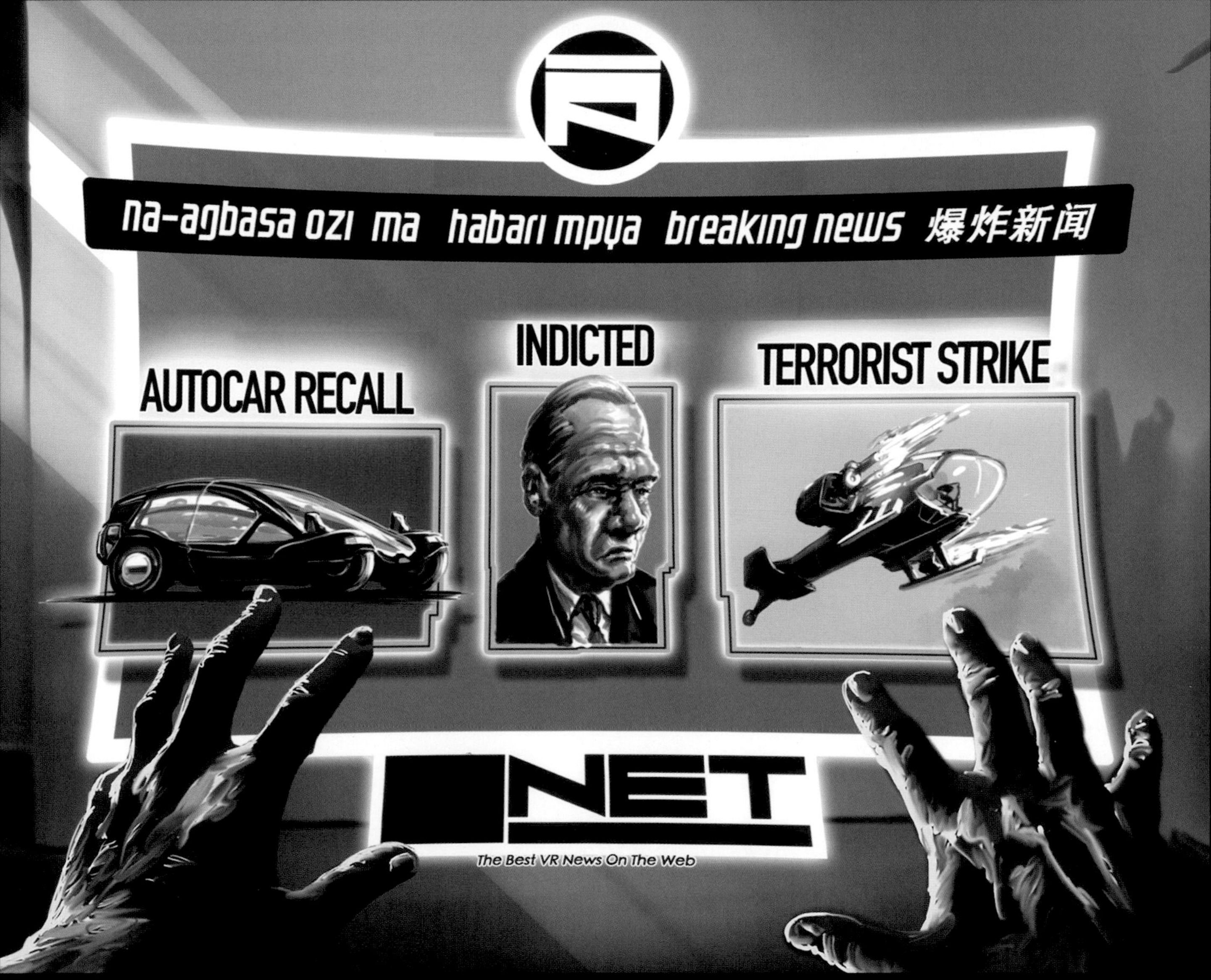
na-agbasa ozi ma
habari mpya
breaking news
爆炸新闻
AUTOCAR RECALL
INDICTED
TERRORIST STRIKE
NET
The Best VR News On The Web

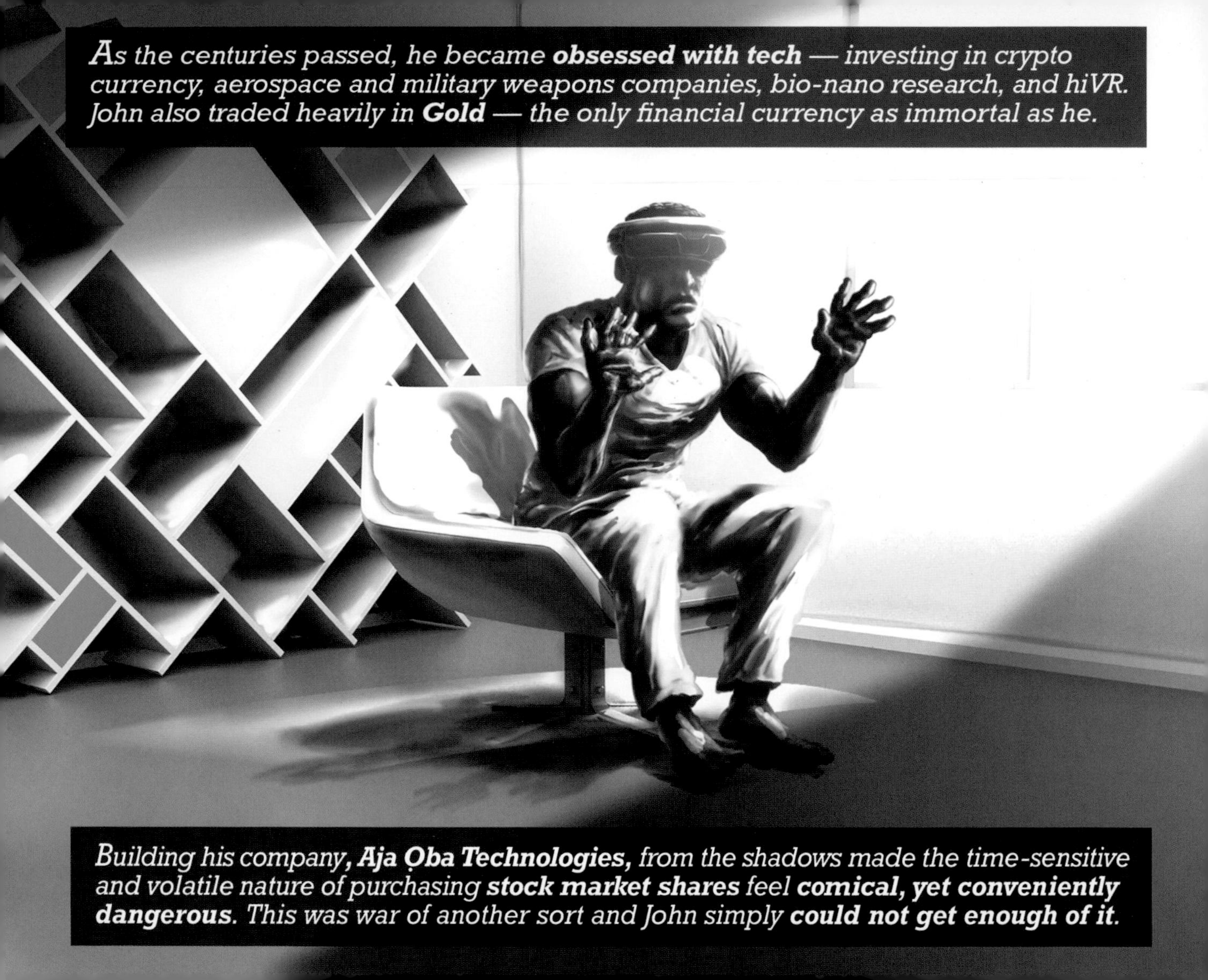
As the centuries passed, he became obsessed with tech — investing in crypto currency, aerospace and military weapons companies, bio-nano research, and hiVR. John also traded heavily in Gold — the only financial currency as immortal as he.
Building his company, Aja Ọba Technologies, from the shadows made the time-sensitive and volatile nature of purchasing stock market shares feel comical, yet conveniently dangerous. This was war of another sort and John simply could not get enough of it.

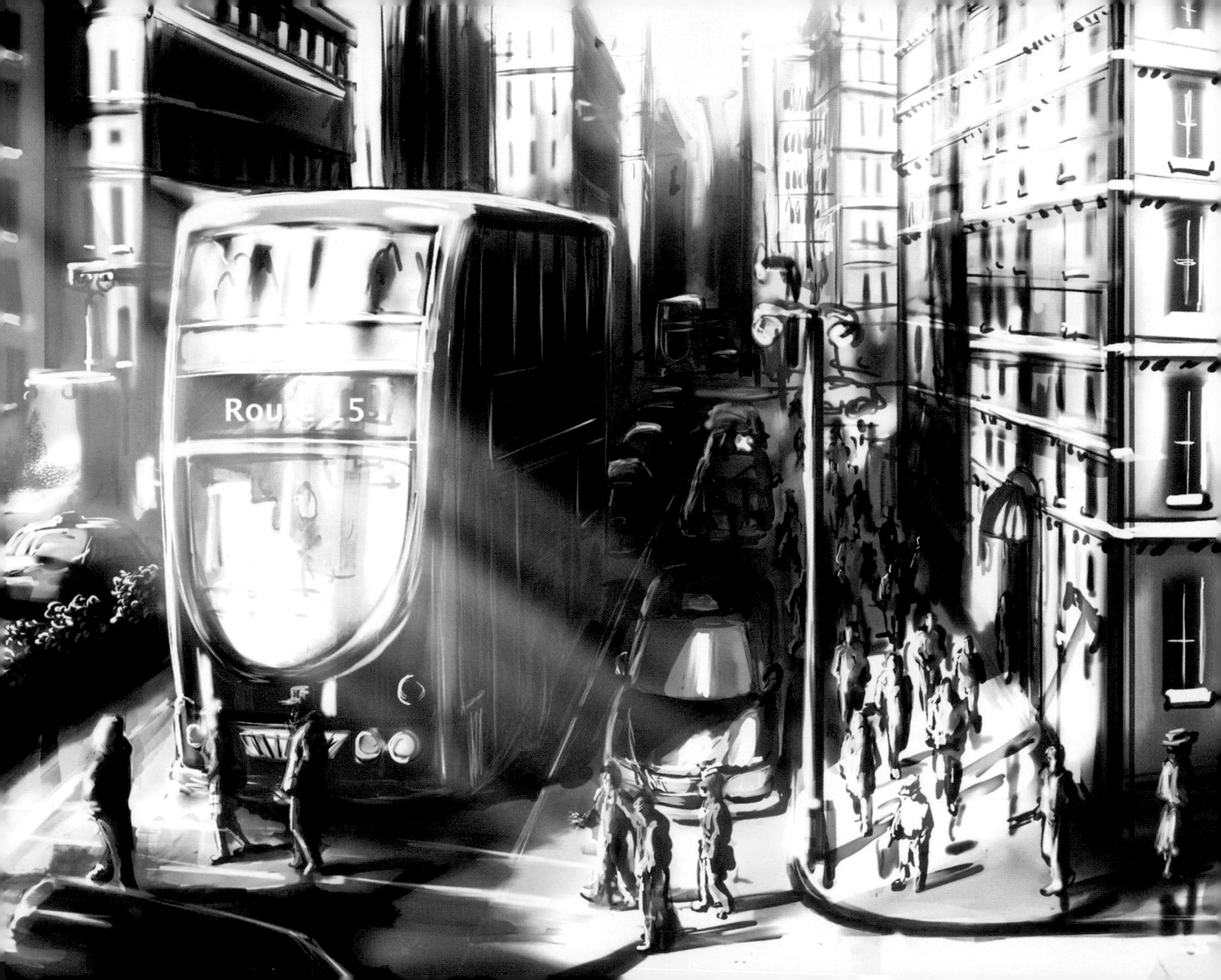
Route 15

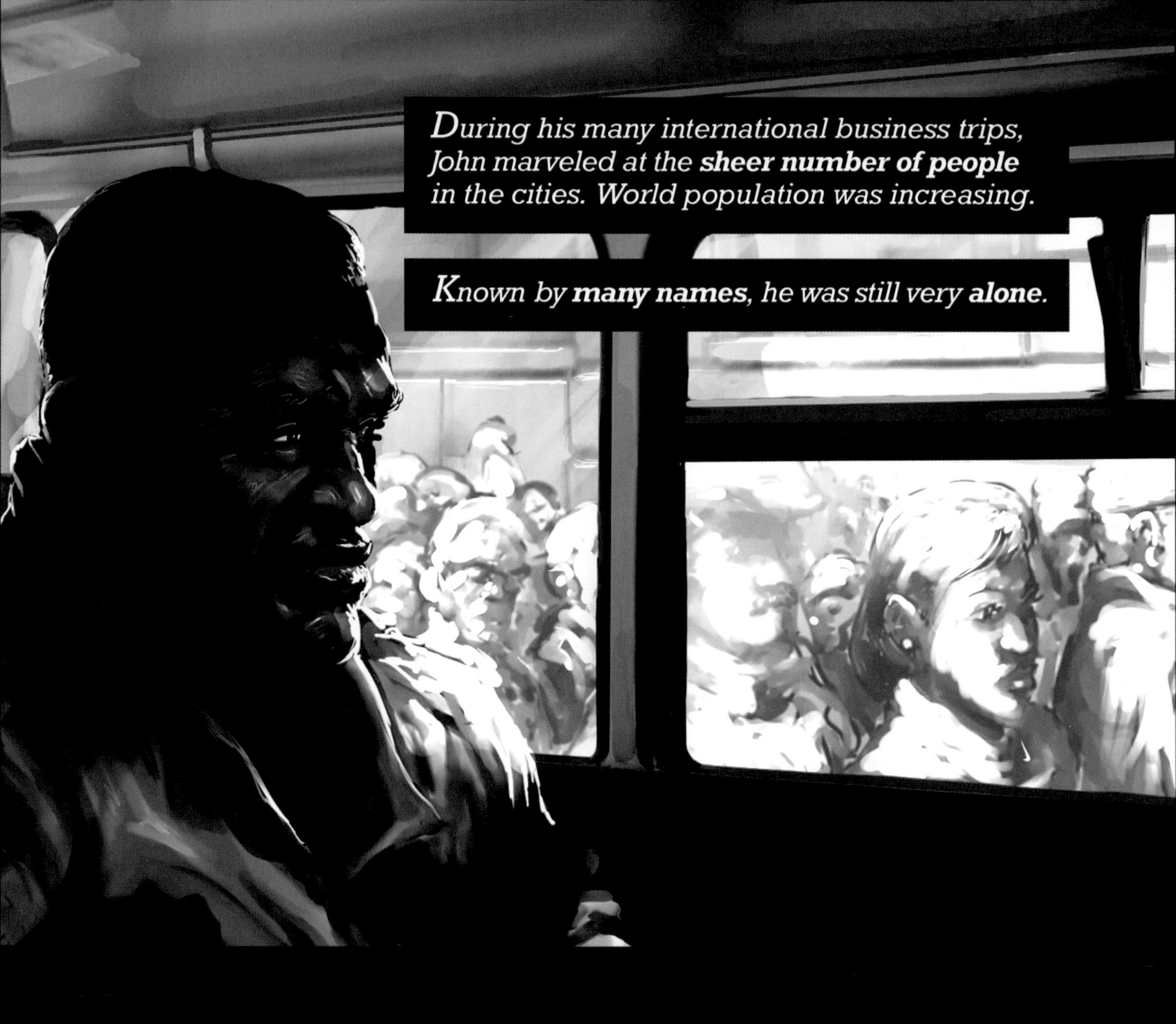
During his many international business trips, John marveled at the **sheer number of people** in the cities. World population was increasing.
Known by **many names**, he was still very **alone**.

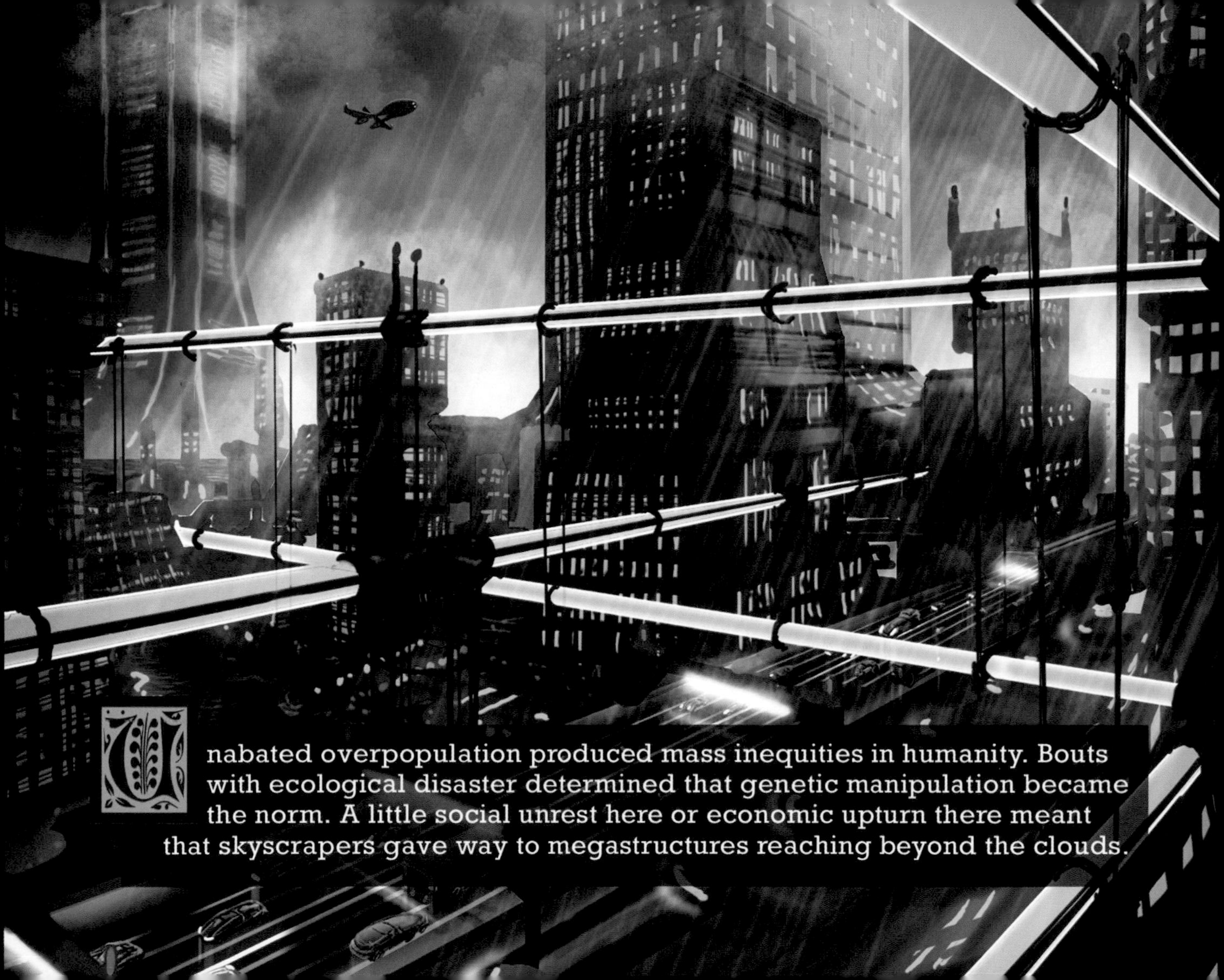

Unabated overpopulation produced mass inequities in humanity. Bouts with ecological disaster determined that genetic manipulation became the norm. A little social unrest here or economic upturn there meant that skyscrapers gave way to megastructures reaching beyond the clouds.

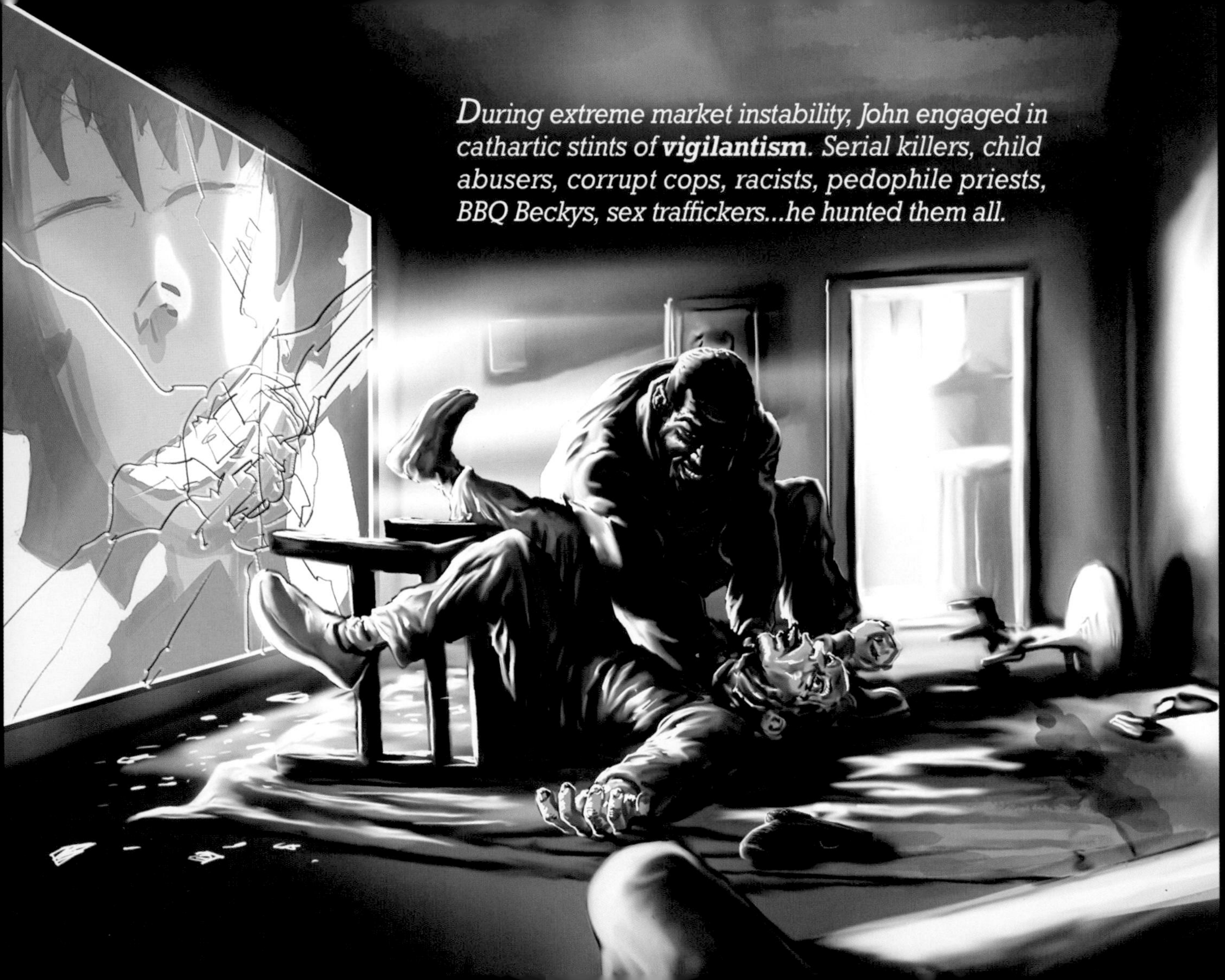
*During extreme market instability, John engaged in cathartic stints of **vigilantism**. Serial killers, child abusers, corrupt cops, racists, pedophile priests, BBQ Beckys, sex traffickers...he hunted them all.*

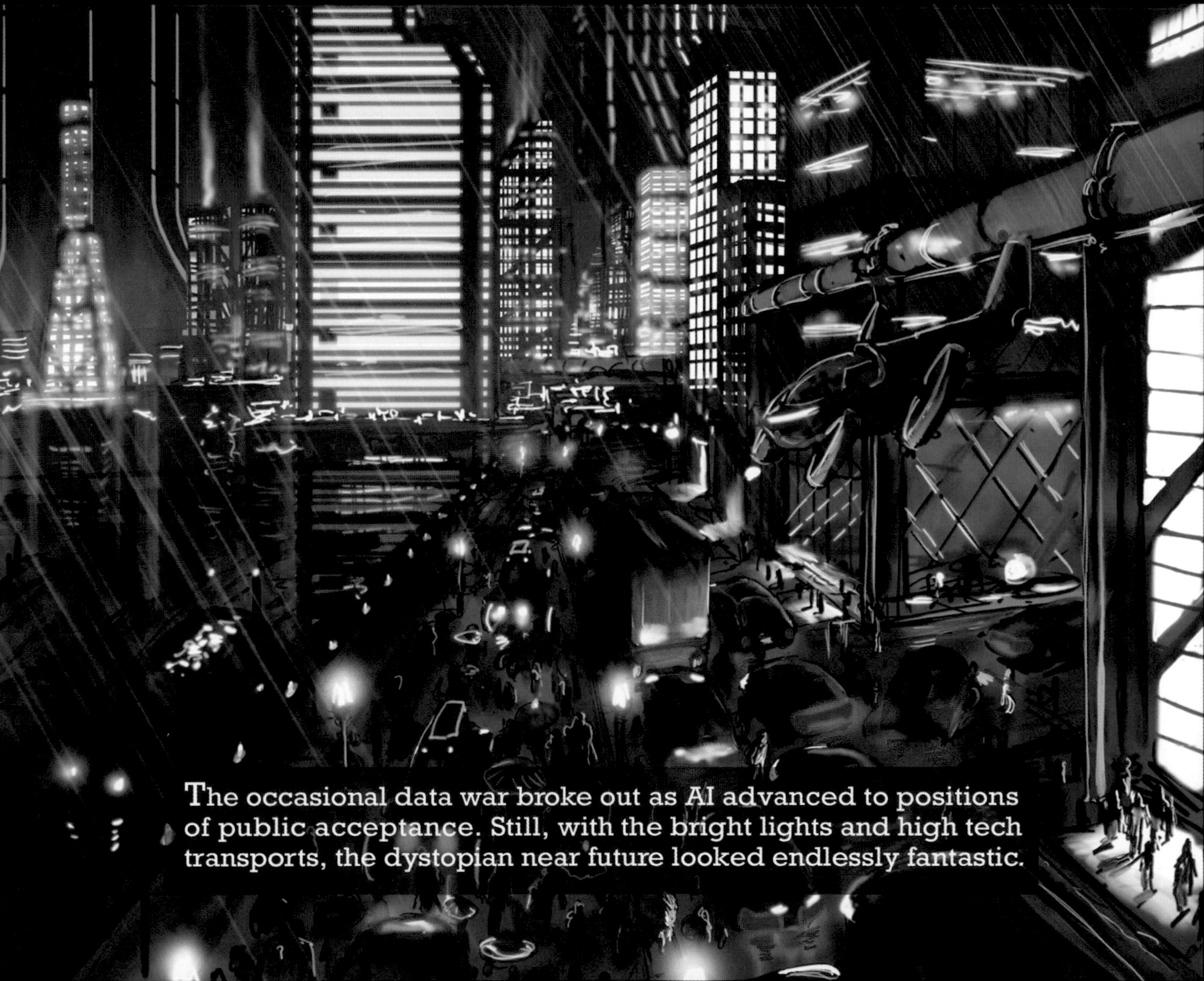

The occasional data war broke out as AI advanced to positions of public acceptance. Still, with the bright lights and high tech transports, the dystopian near future looked endlessly fantastic.

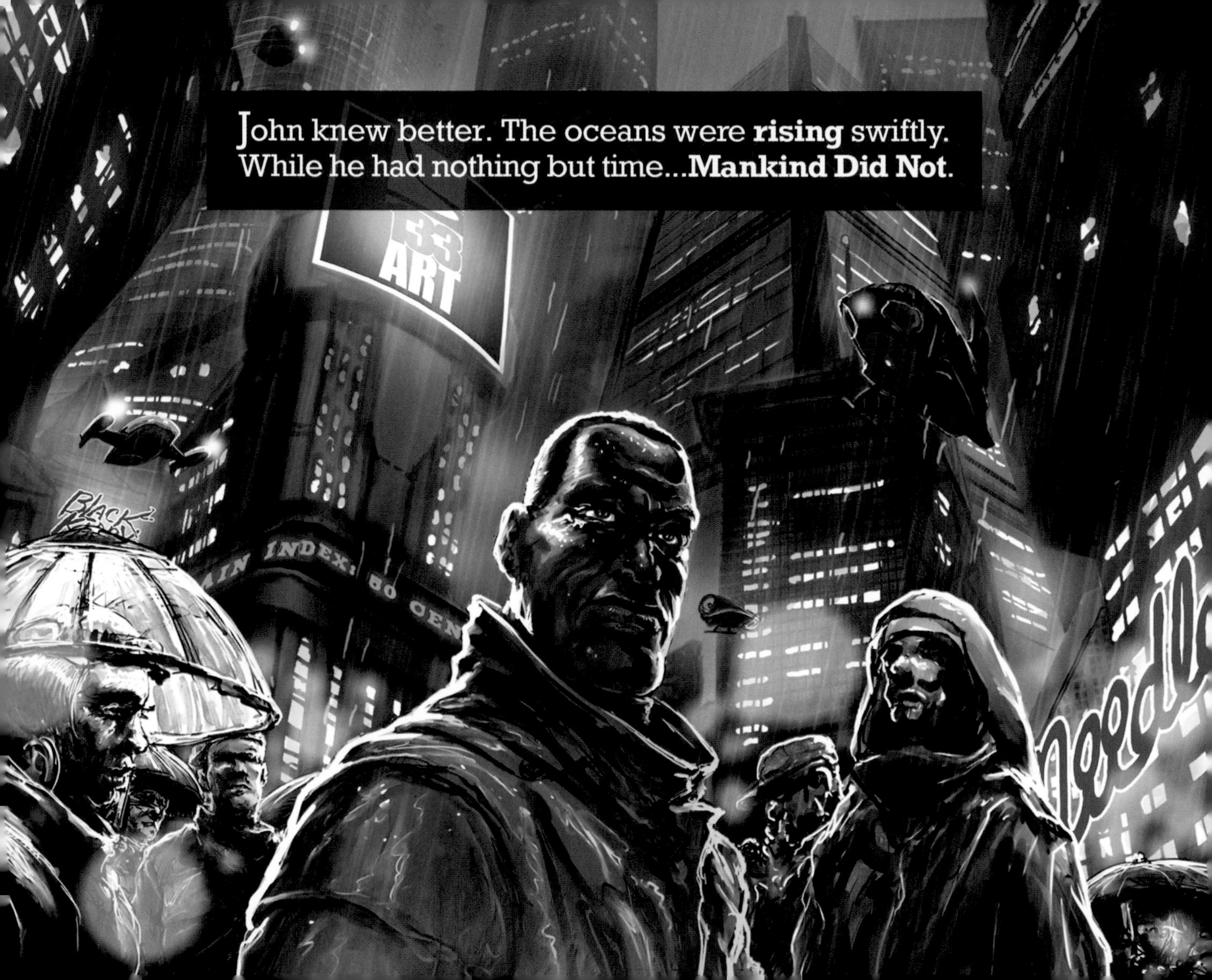
John knew better. The oceans were **rising** swiftly.
While he had nothing but time...**Mankind Did Not**.
ART
INDEX

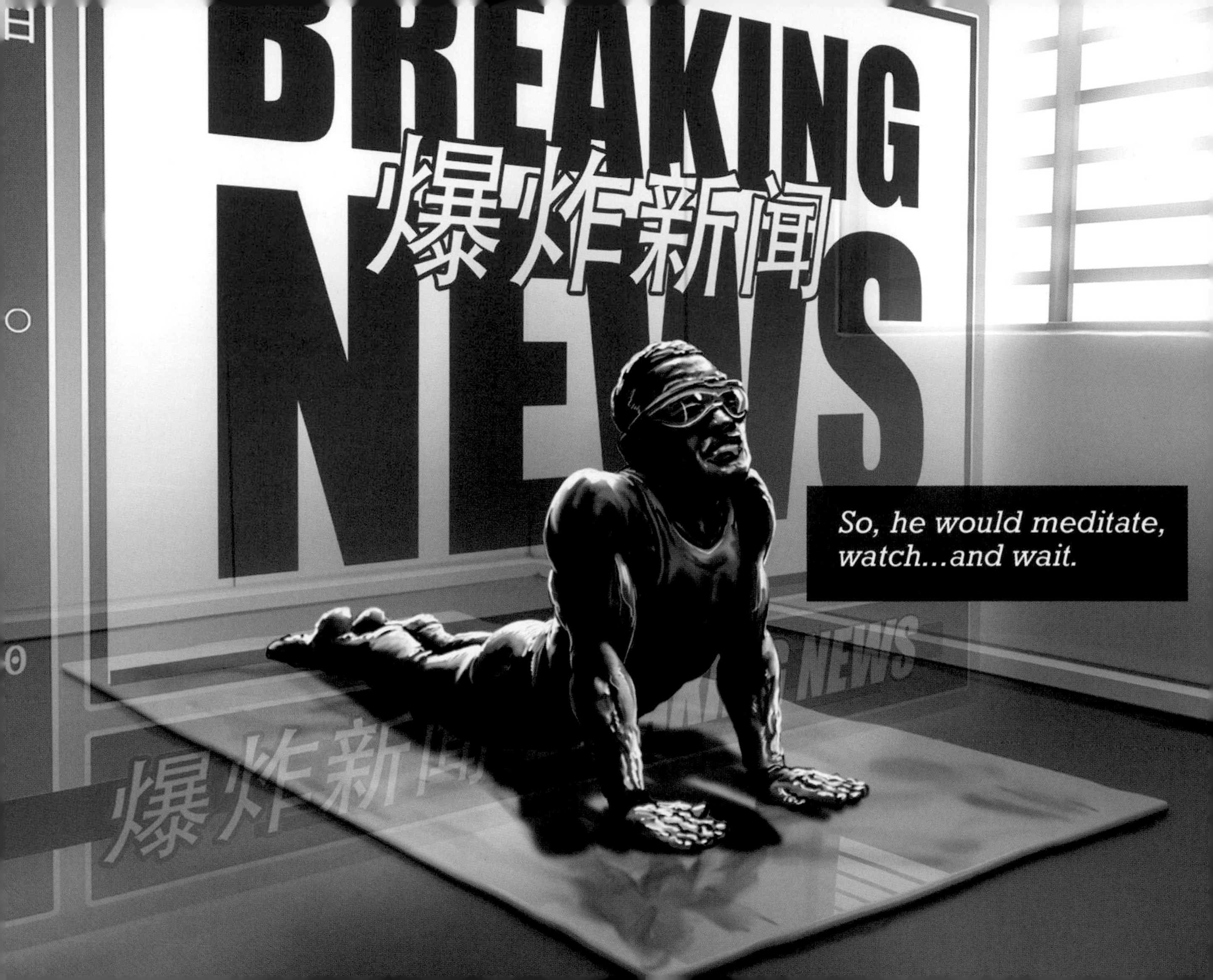
BREAKING NEWS
爆炸新闻
So, he would meditate, watch...and wait.
爆炸新闻
NEWS

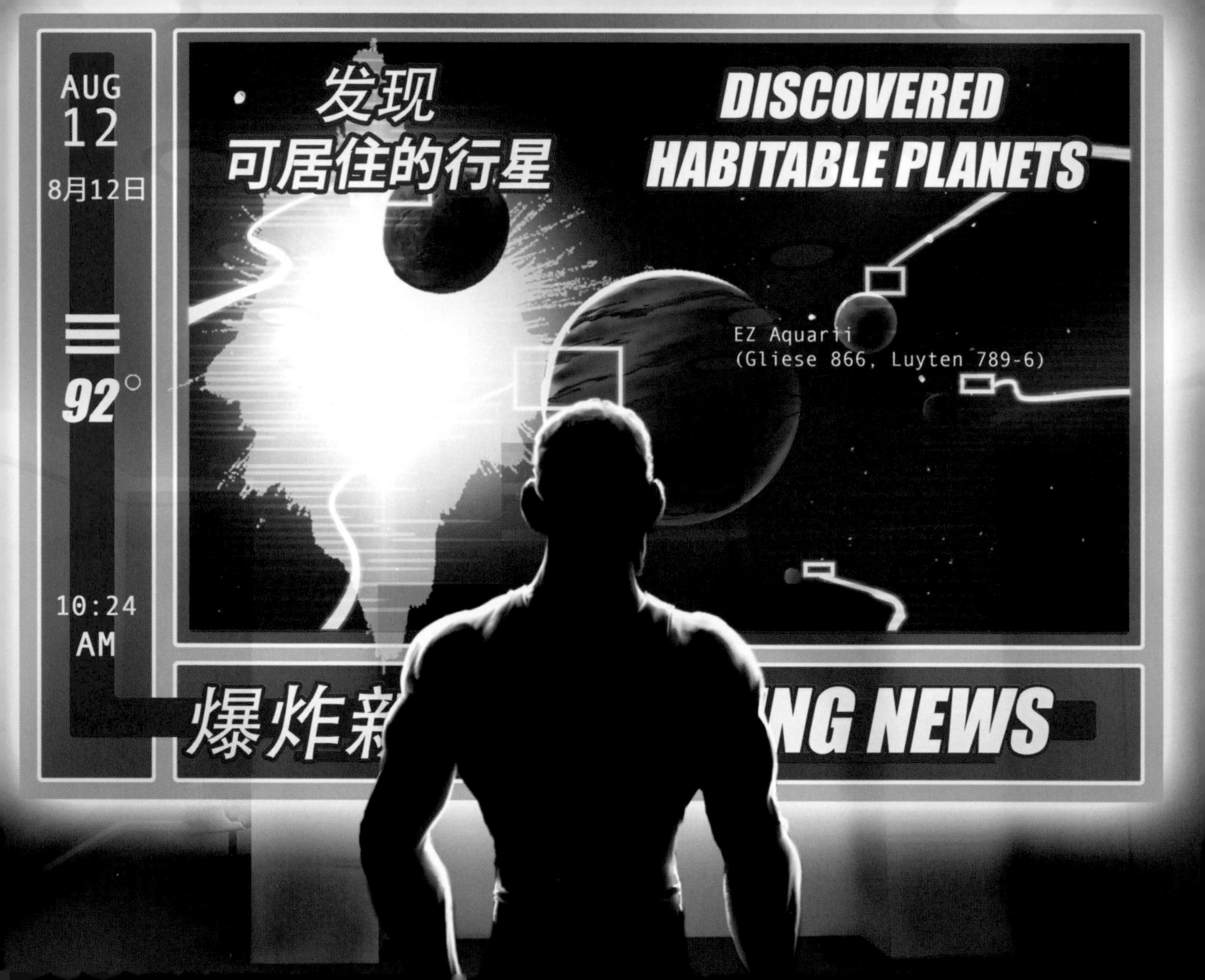
AUG
12
8月12日
92°
10:24
AM
发现
可居住的行星
DISCOVERED
HABITABLE PLANETS
EZ Aquarii
(Gliese 866, Luyten 789-6)
爆炸新
NG NEWS

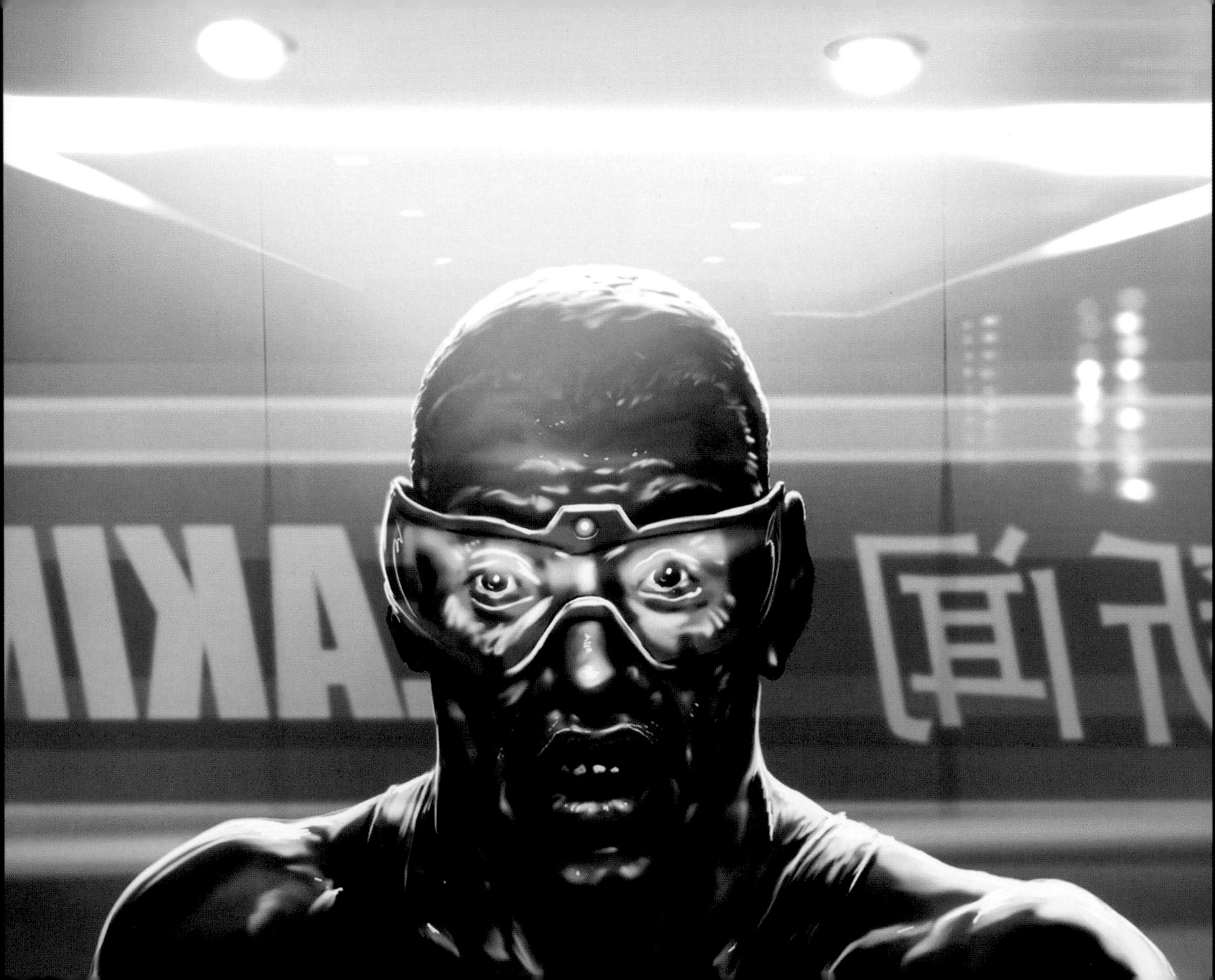

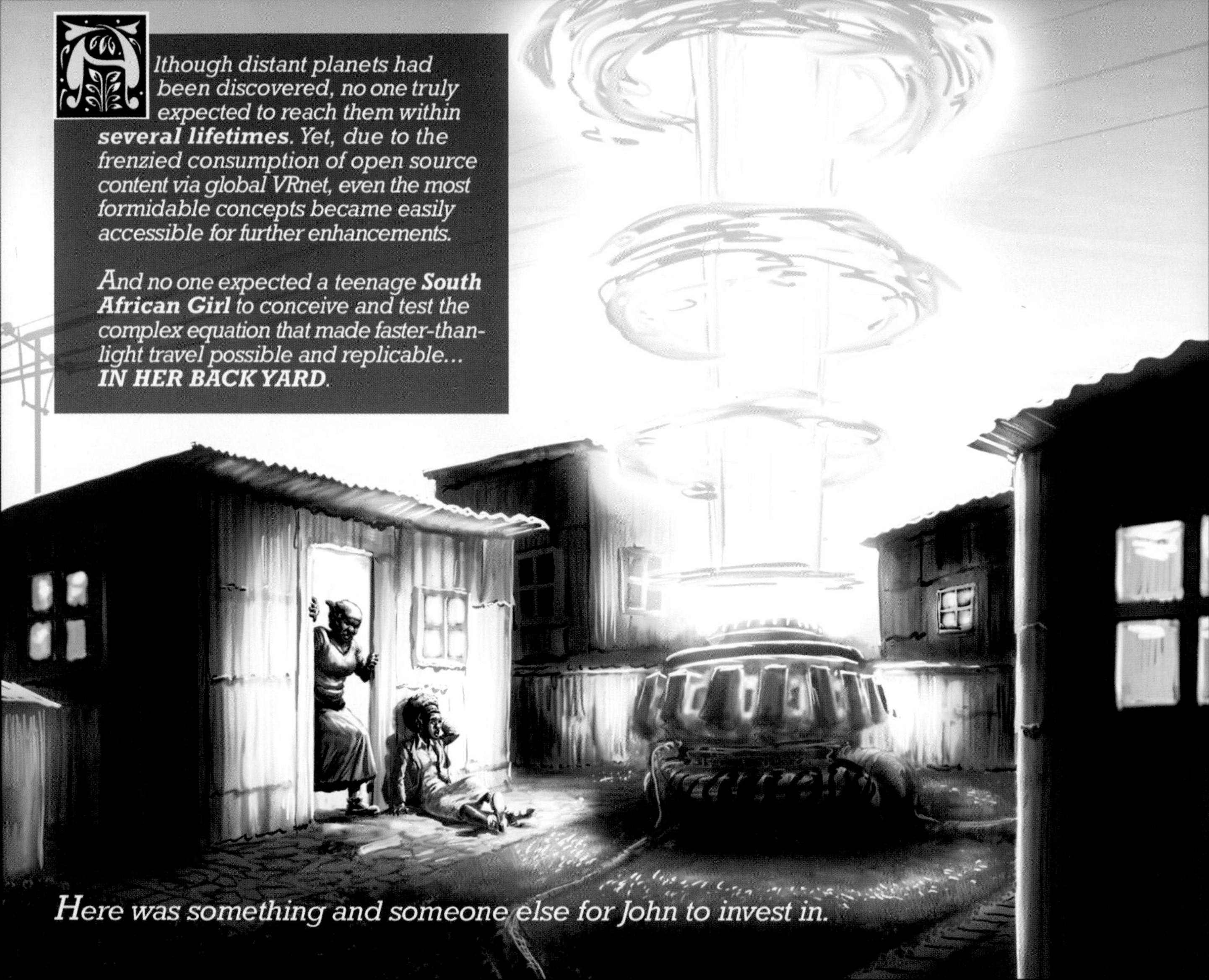
Although distant planets had been discovered, no one truly expected to reach them within **several lifetimes**. Yet, due to the frenzied consumption of open source content via global VRnet, even the most formidable concepts became easily accessible for further enhancements.
And no one expected a teenage **South African Girl** to conceive and test the complex equation that made faster-than-light travel possible and replicable... **IN HER BACK YARD**.
Here was something and someone else for John to invest in.

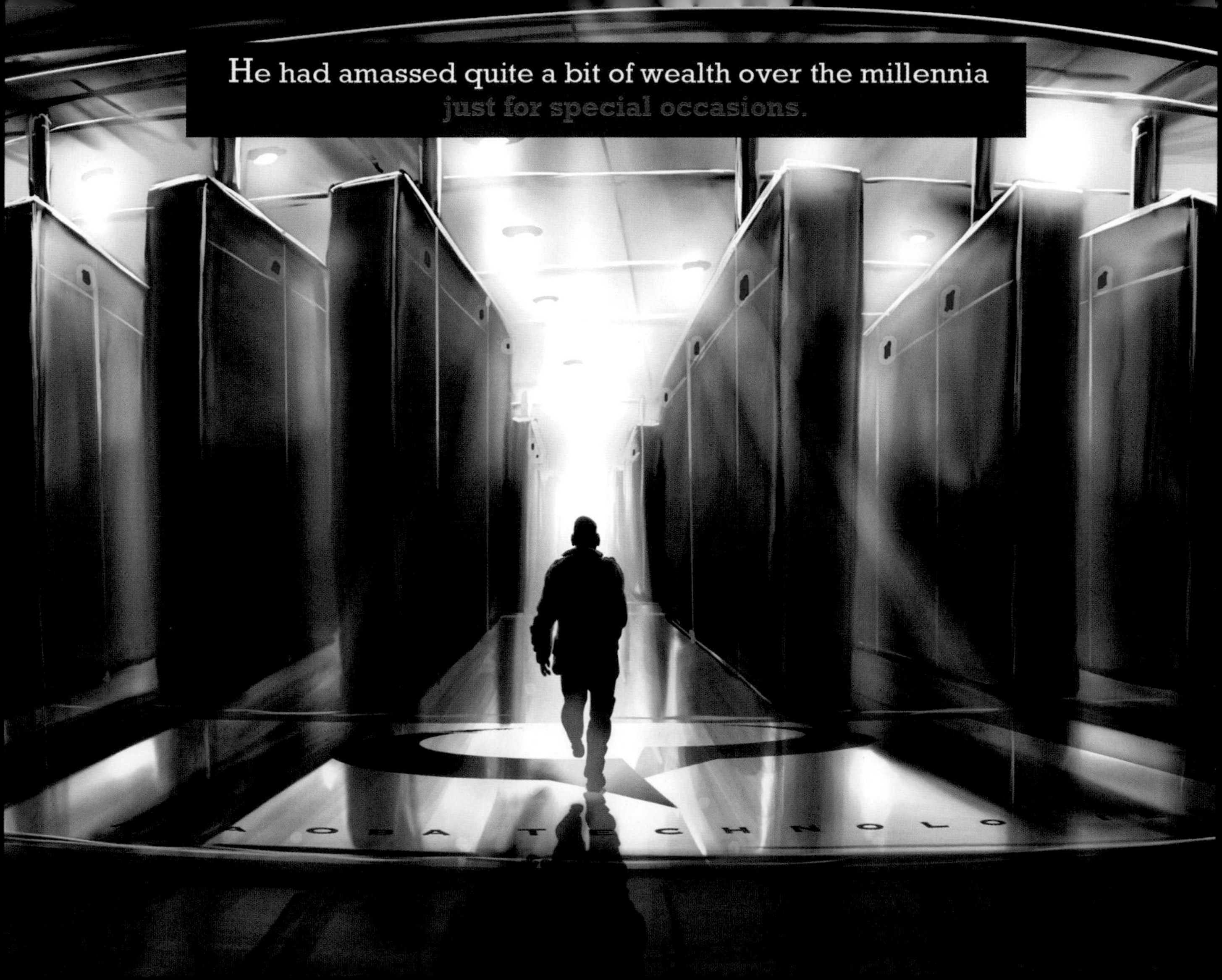
He had amassed quite a bit of wealth over the millennia
just for special occasions.

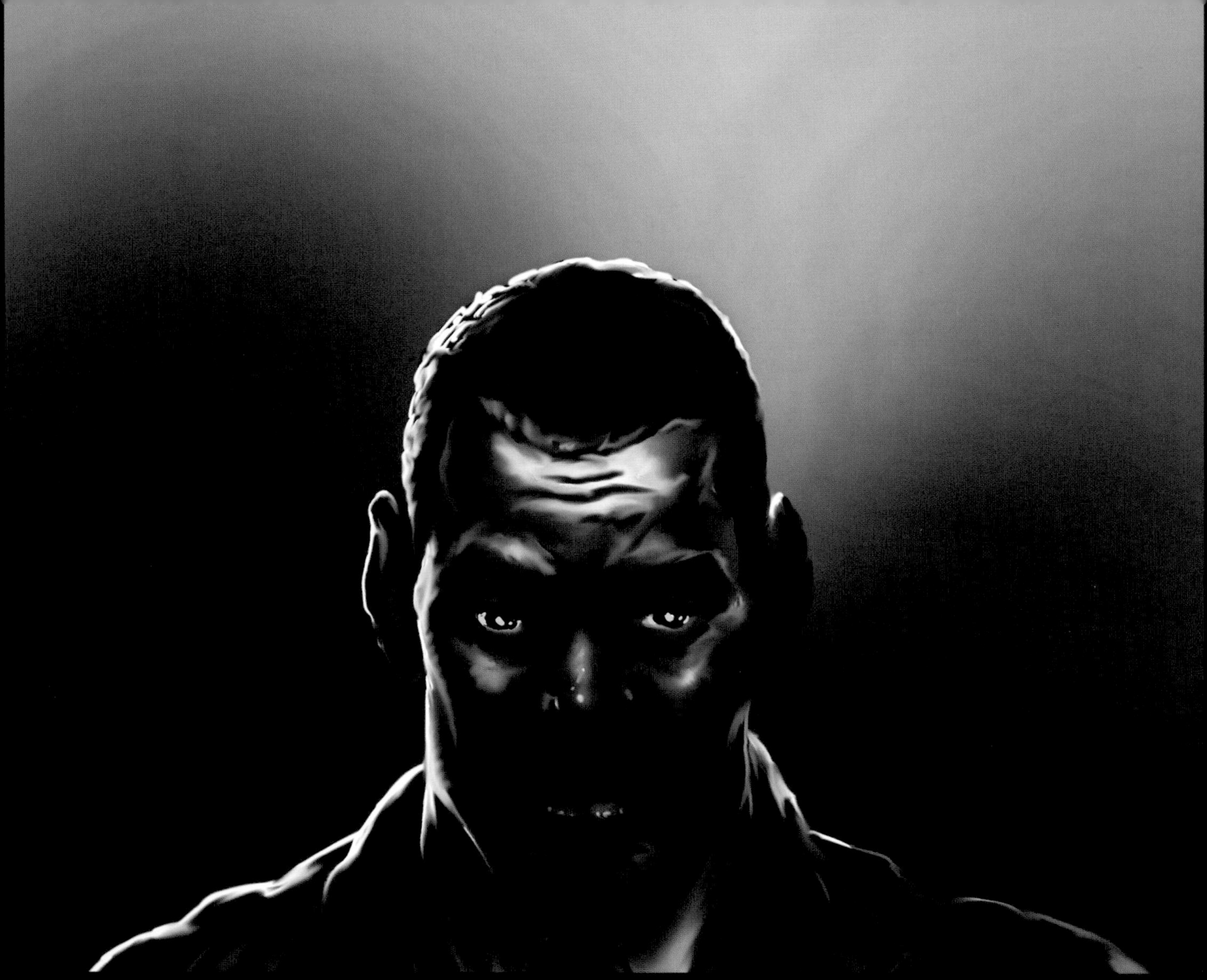

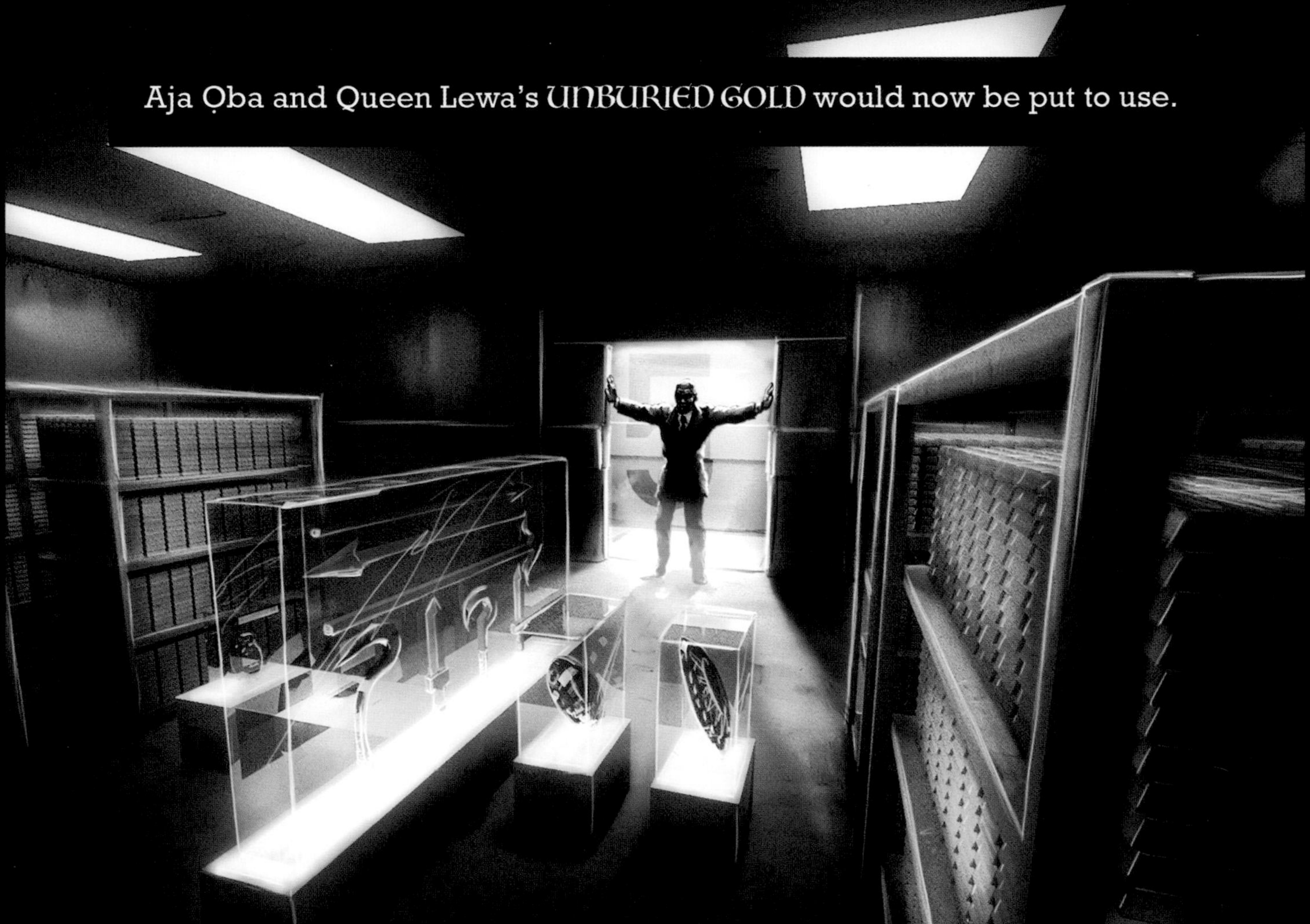
Aja Ọba and Queen Lewa's UNBURIED GOLD would now be put to use.

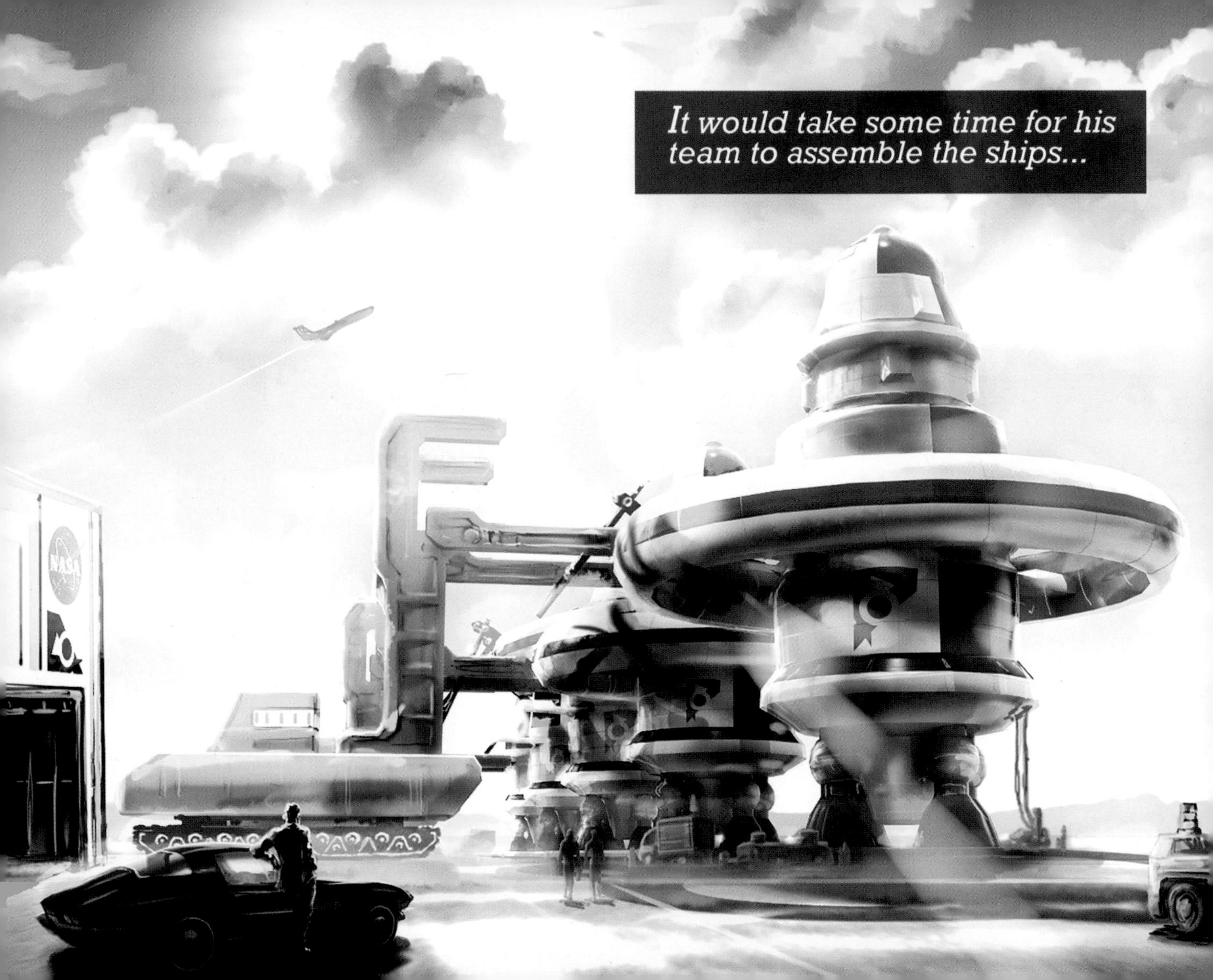
It would take some time for his team to assemble the ships...
NASA

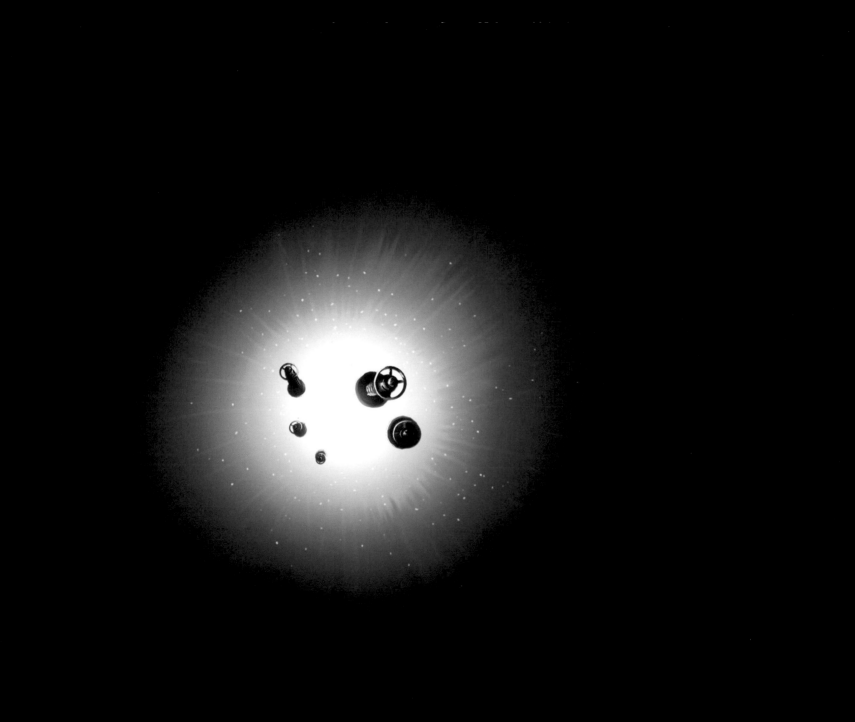

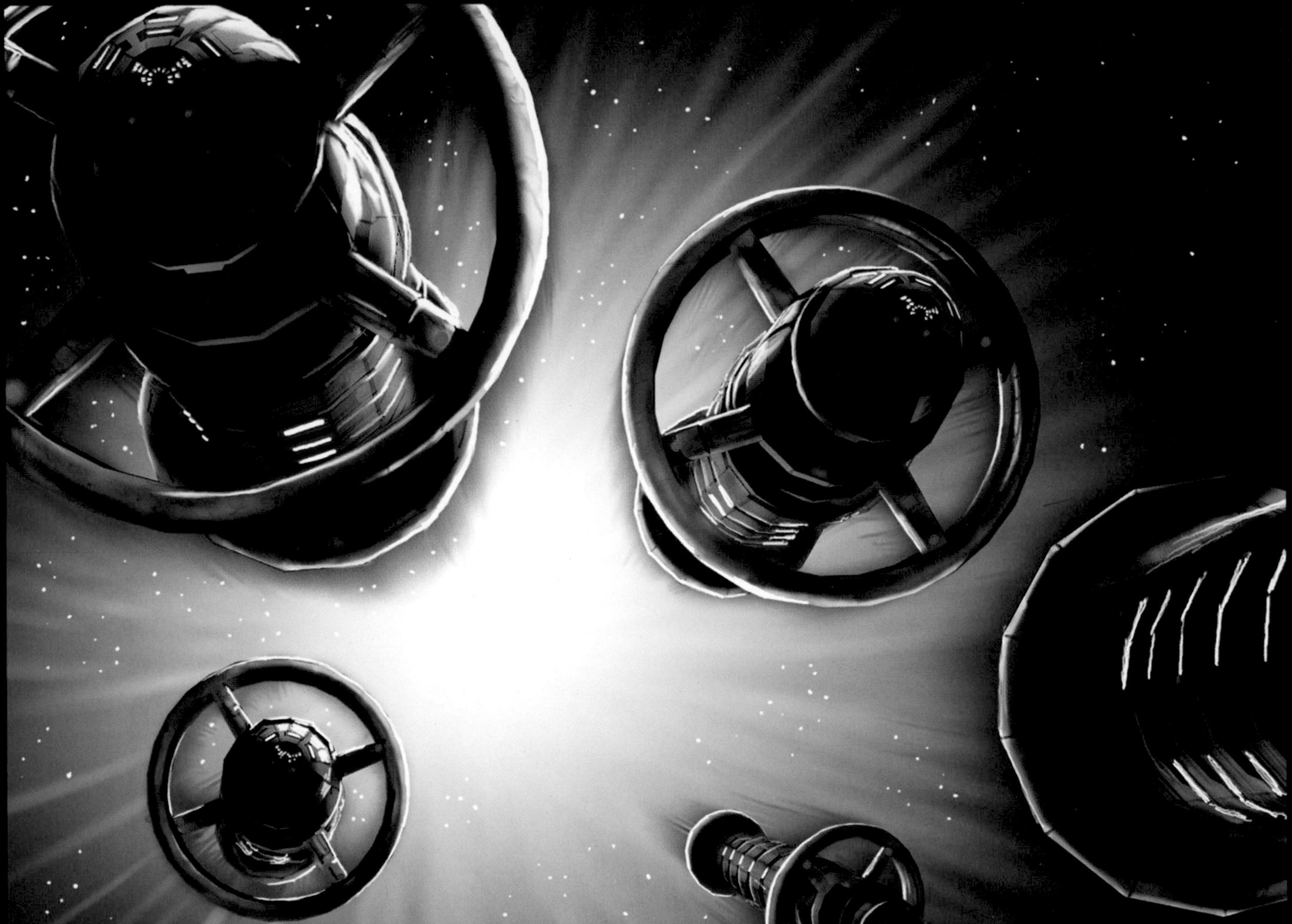

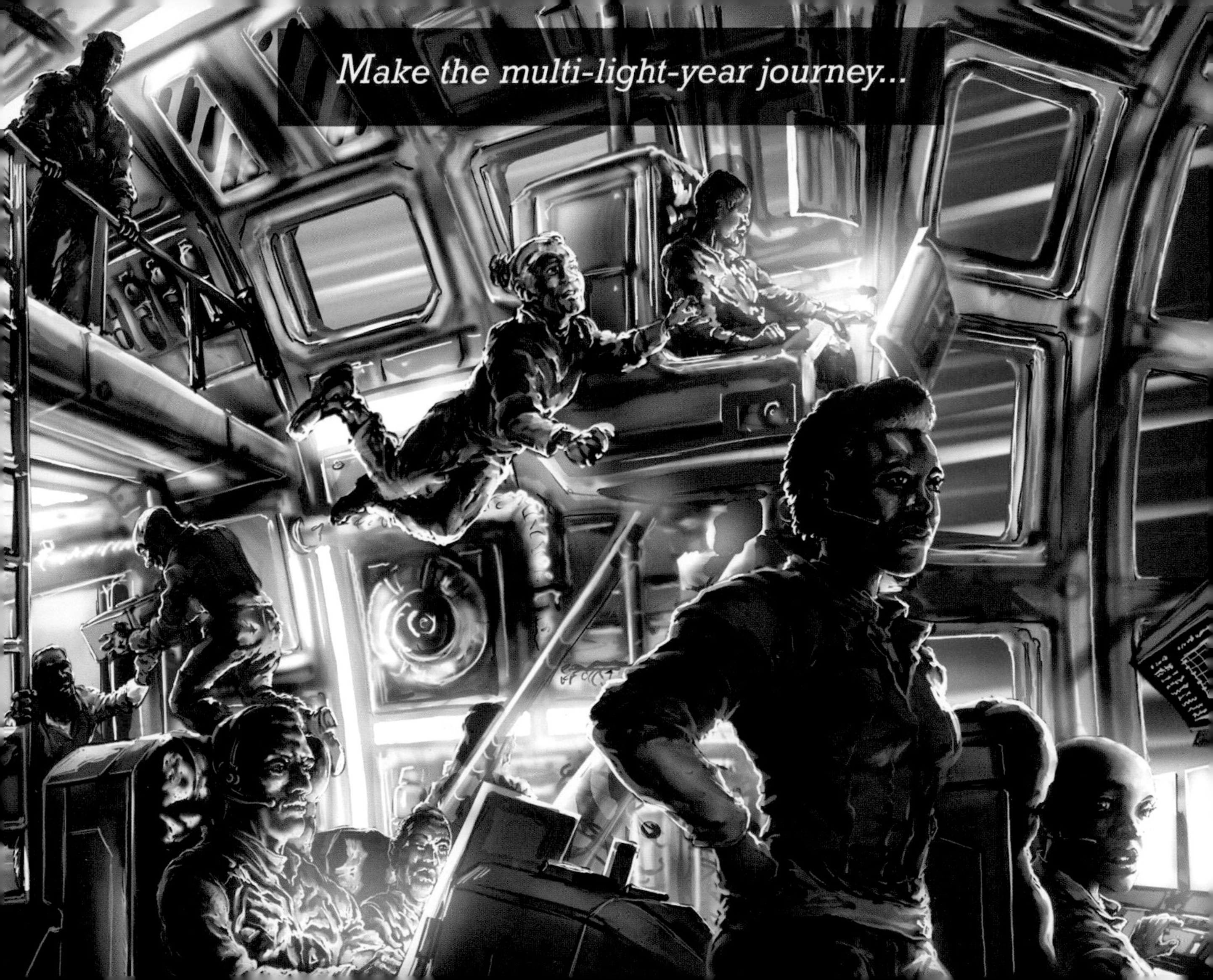
Make the multi-light-year journey...

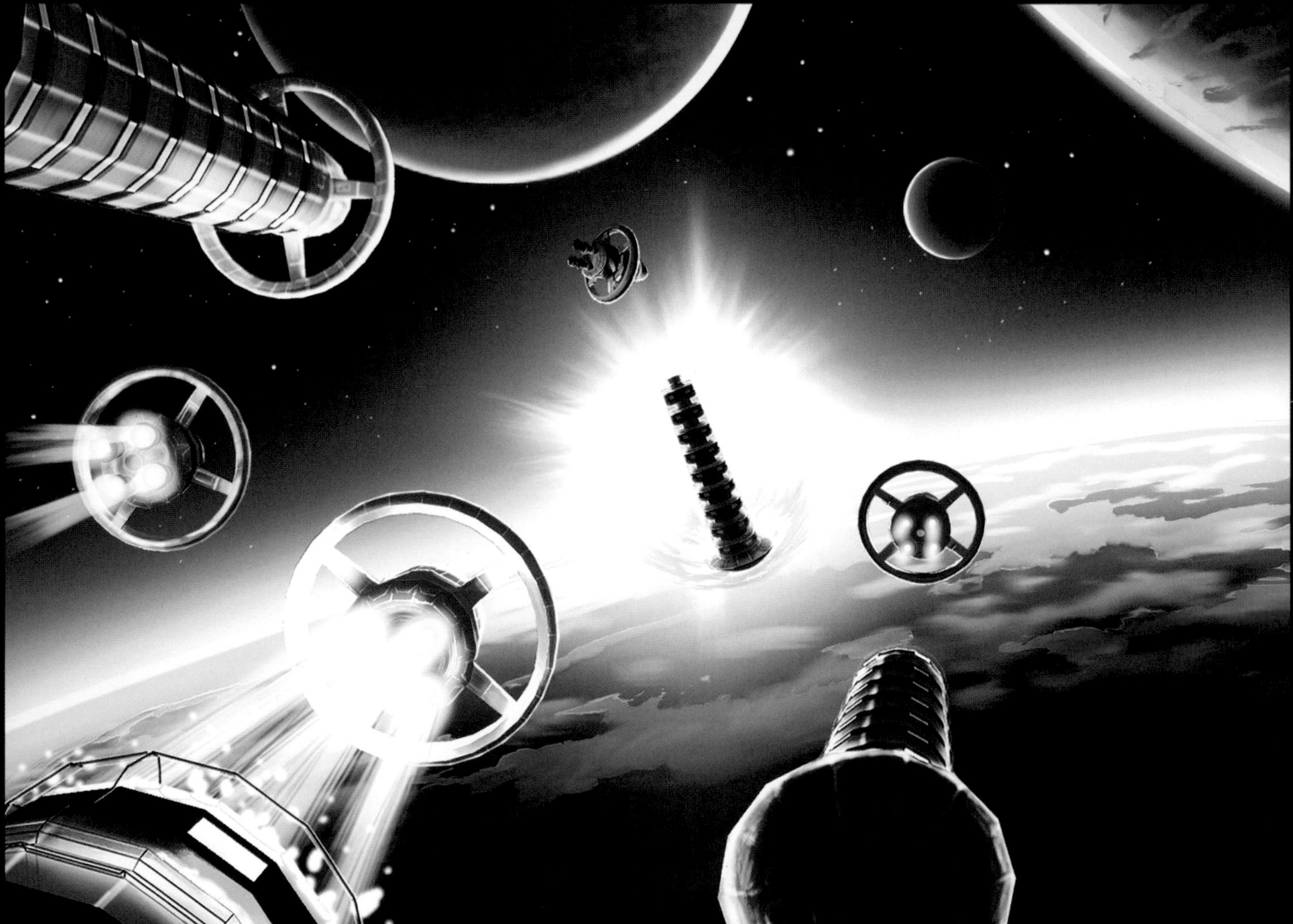

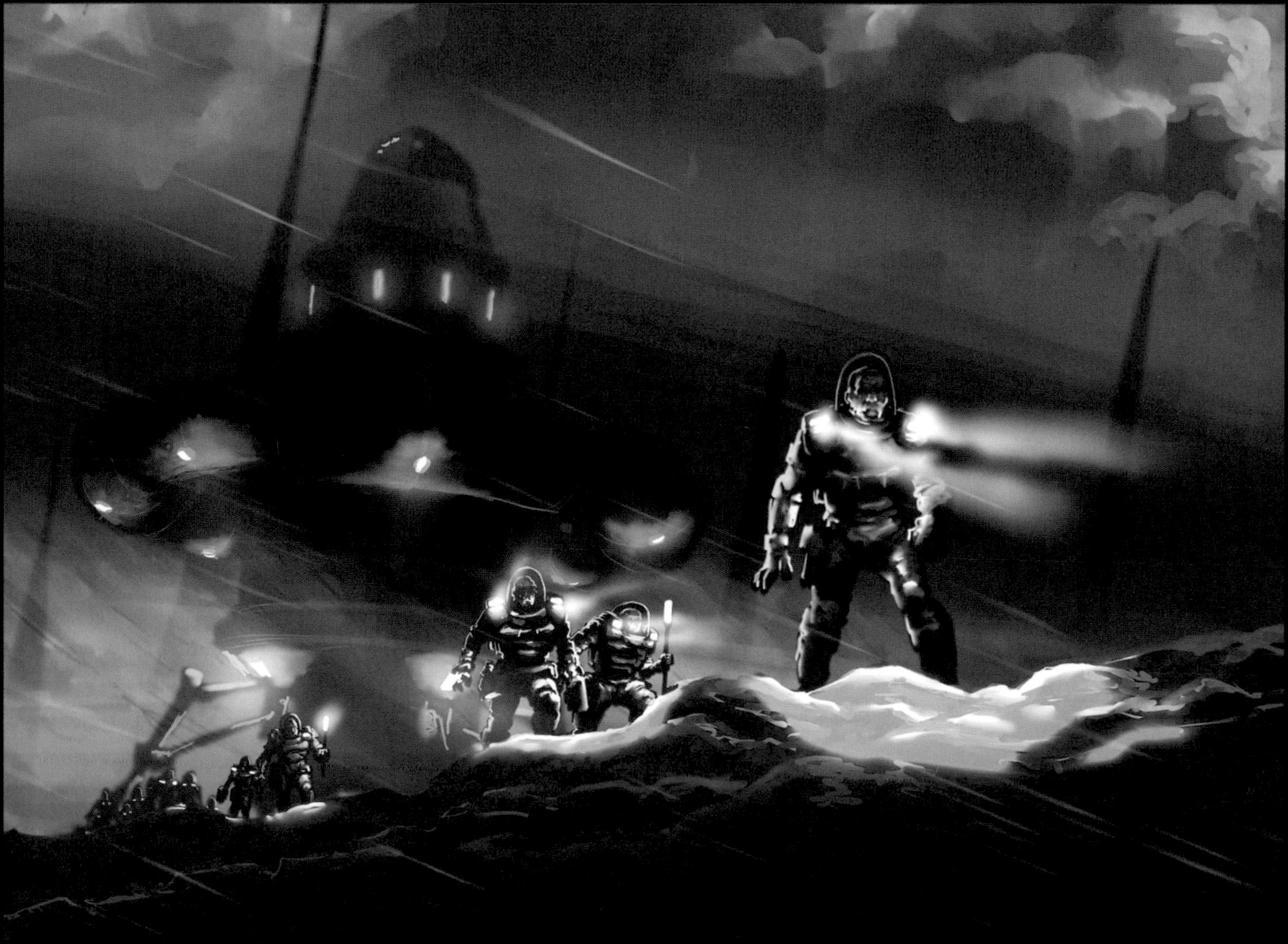

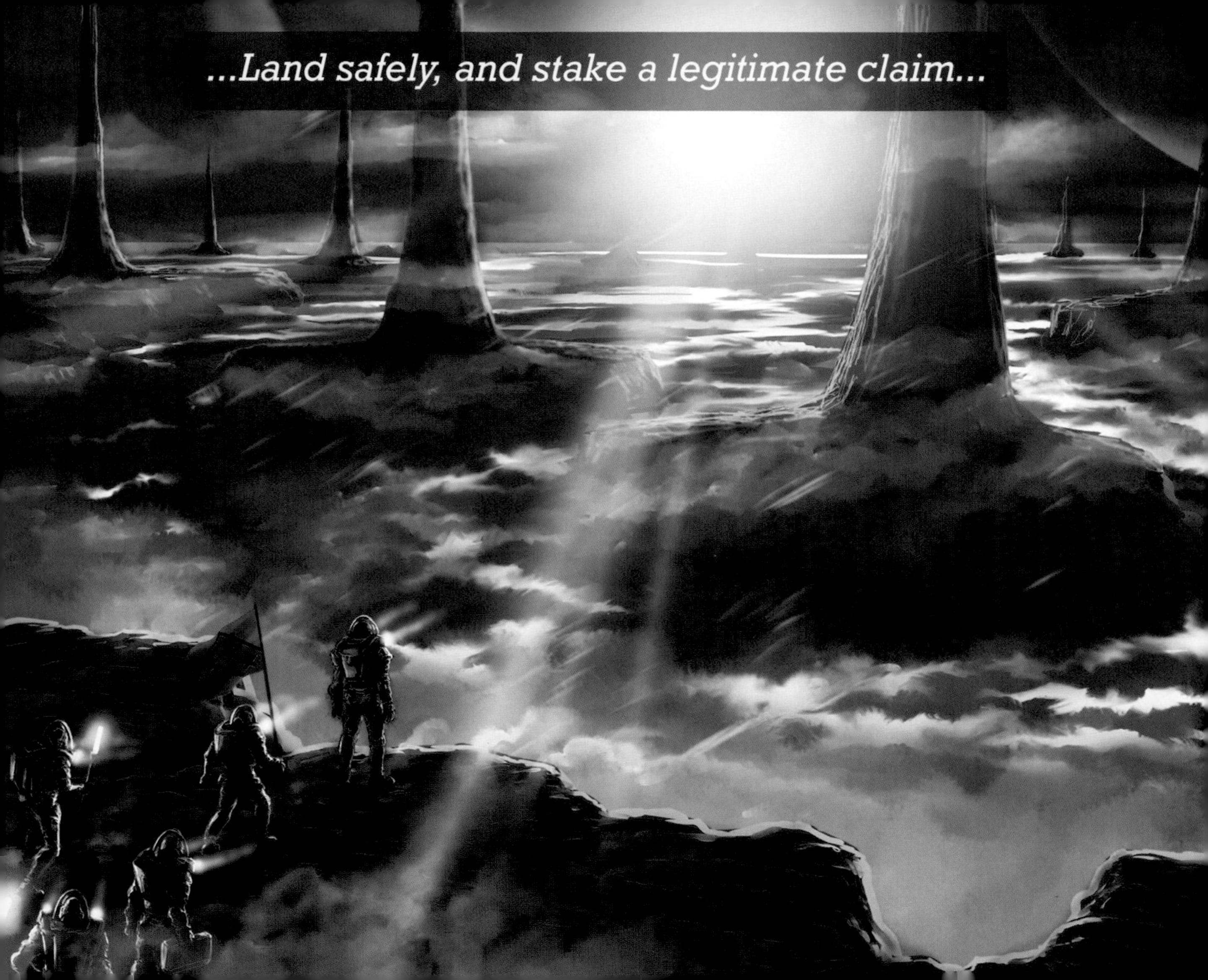
...Land safely, and stake a legitimate claim...

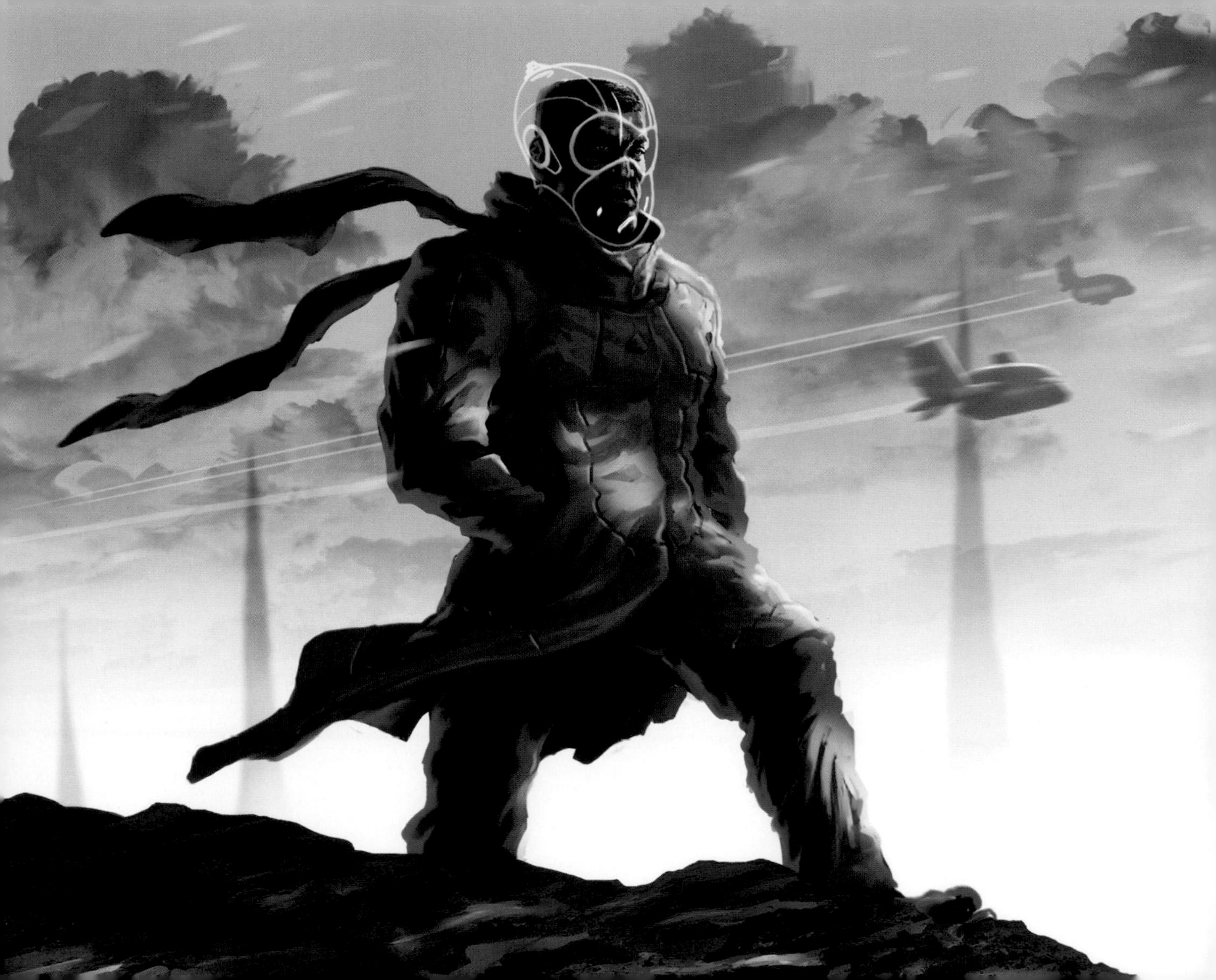

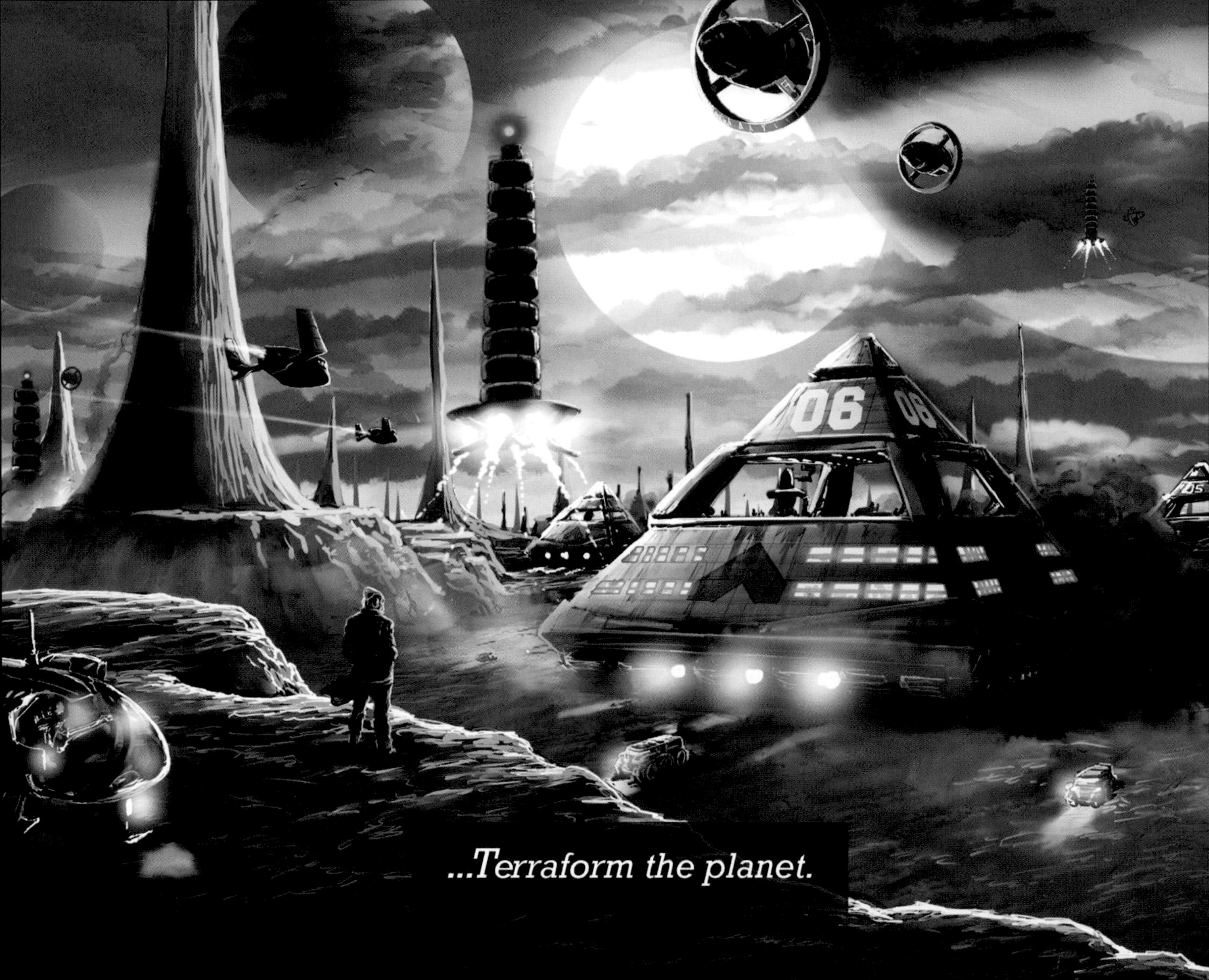
...Terraform the planet.

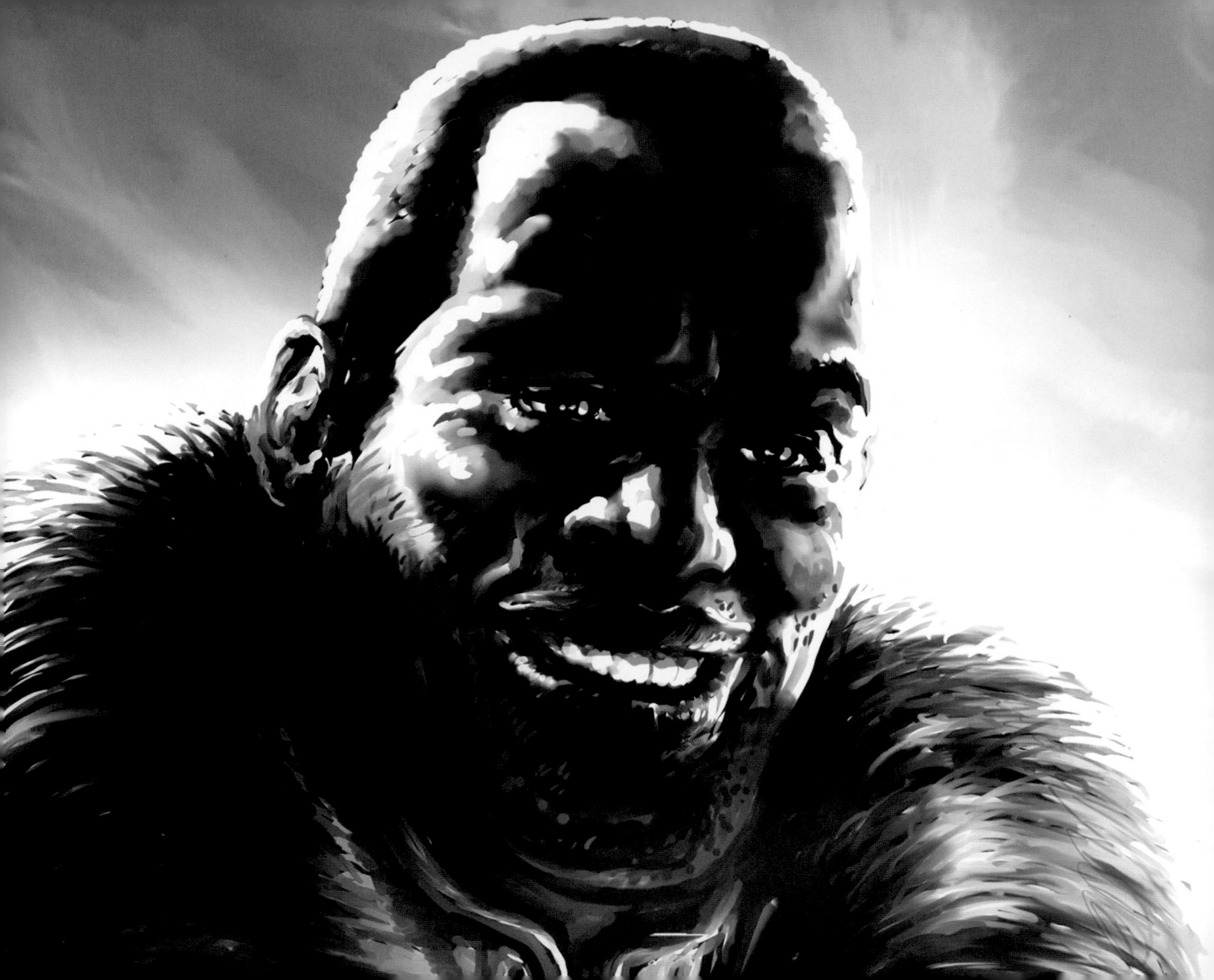

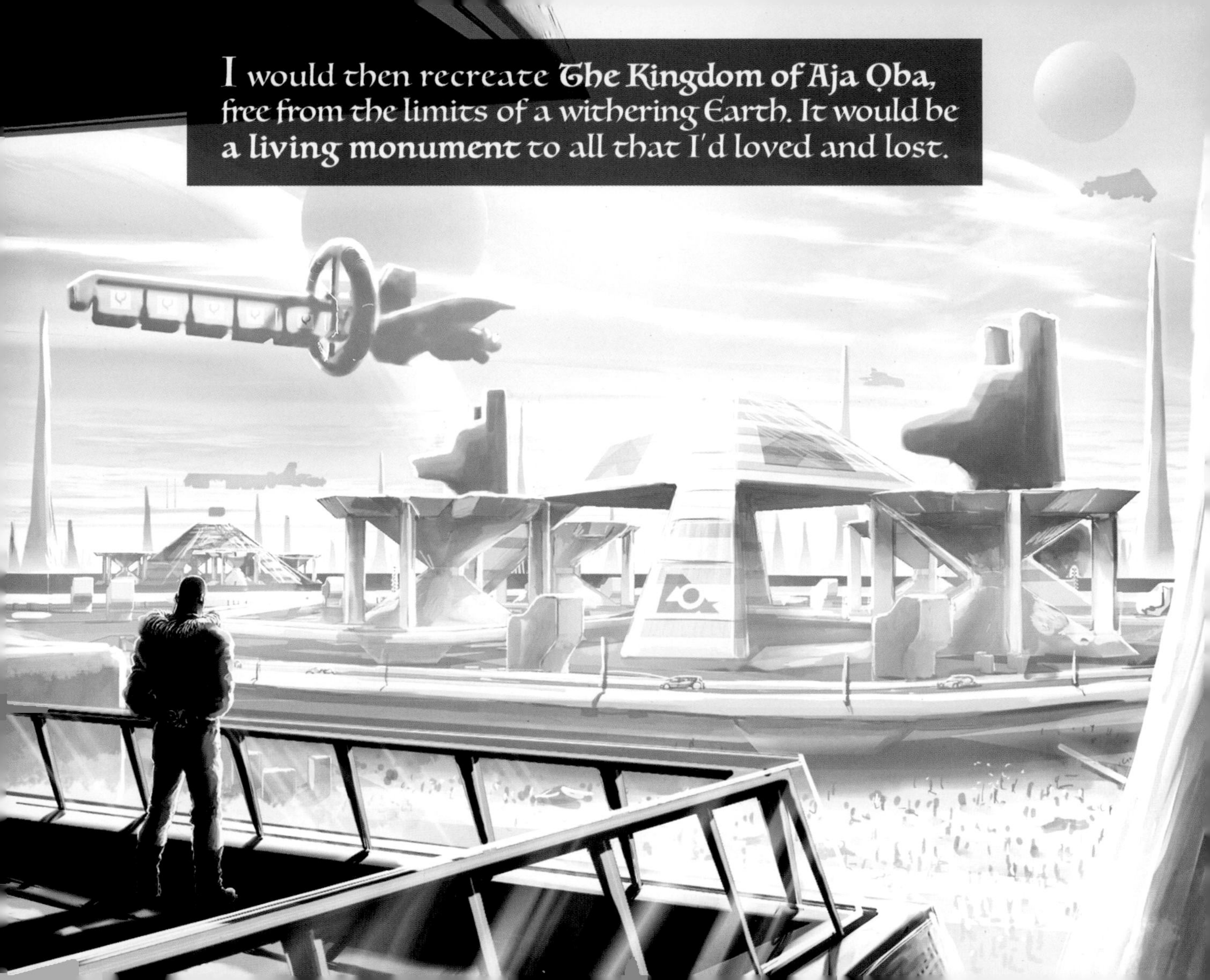
I would then recreate **The Kingdom of Aja Ọba,** free from the limits of a withering Earth. It would be **a living monument** to all that I'd loved and lost.

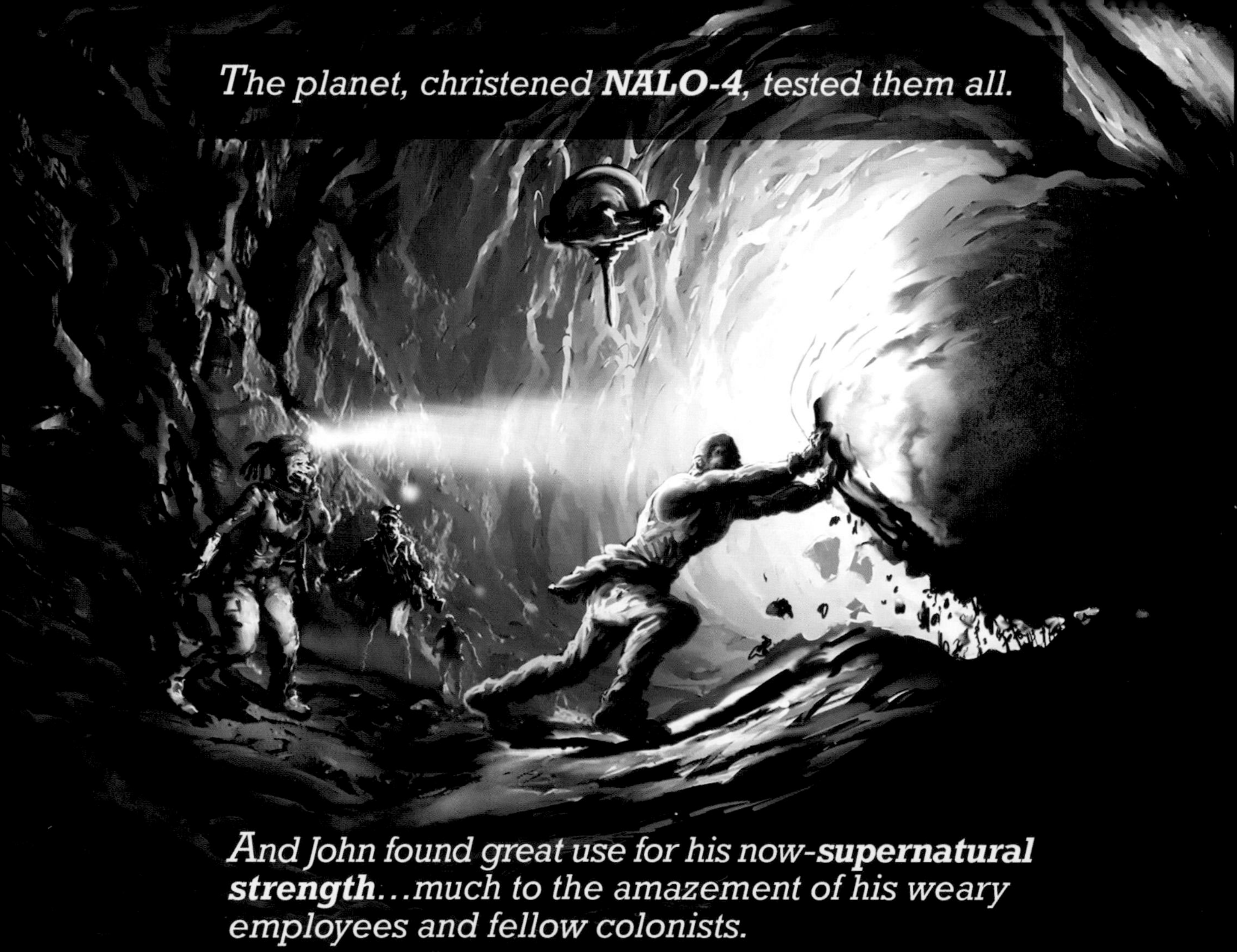
The planet, christened **NALO-4**, tested them all.
And John found great use for his now-**supernatural strength**…much to the amazement of his weary employees and fellow colonists.

This was a **new life**.

John even took a **lover**.

Something he **swore**
he'd never do again.

Jason José Diaz appeared quite unexpectedly out of my blind spot. He was a botanist and a bit of an idealist. I was transfixed by him in every way.

The process of transforming the atmosphere and ecosystem of **Nalo-4** to one suitable for human life would be a massive undertaking. **Jason** wooed me with his intellect and work ethic.

Long ago, I'd shut off the part of myself that envisioned love. There was simply too much pain from the loss of loved ones... and Obinrin's tormenting words echoing in my ears. But **Jason** listened patiently to me and held my secrets. After so many millennia, here I was very happy...

Complete.

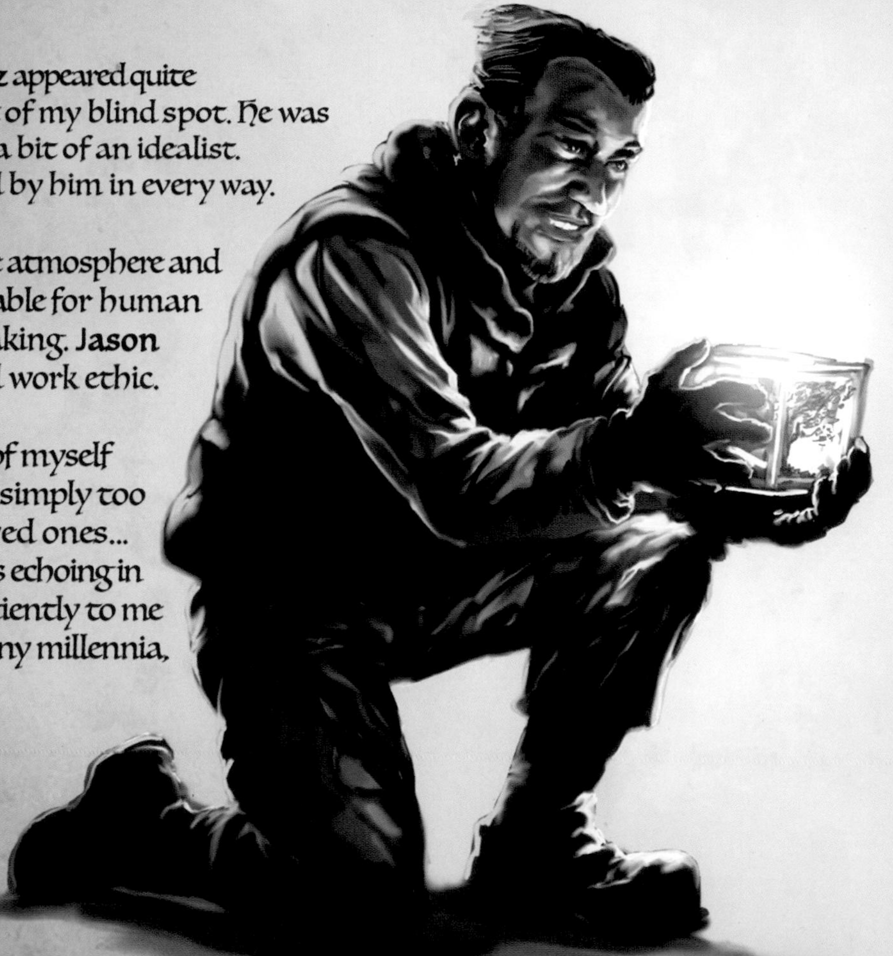

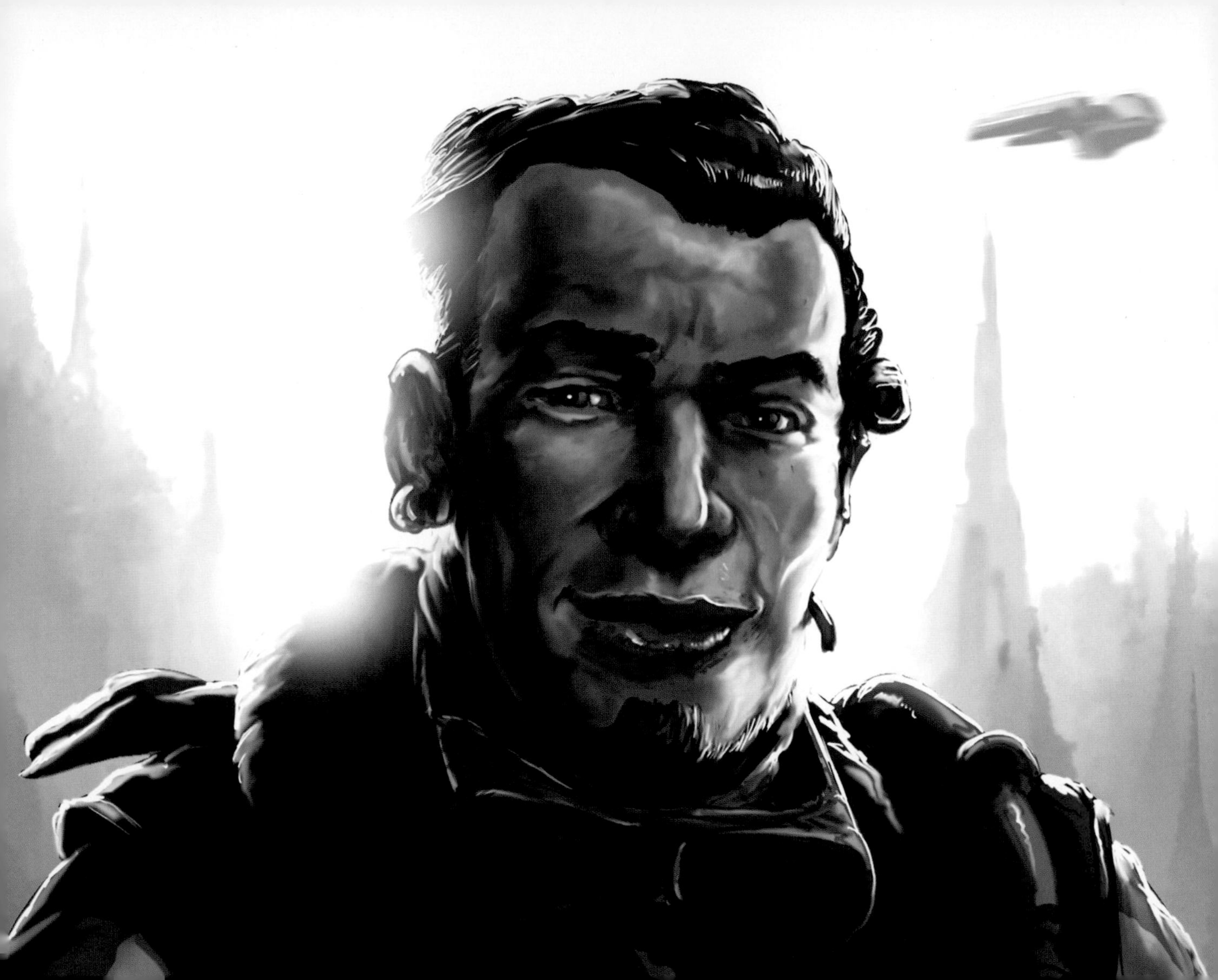

met John on a dare. I'd made a good living as a botanist in the vertical farming cooperatives on the new coasts. But my mother, ever the forward thinker, encouraged me to answer the stellar colonization job boards. I nailed a virtual interview and eventually found myself in an in-person meeting with John. I won't lie, I was intimidated. He was a pioneer in faster-than-light drives, biosemiosis, and other emerging organic tech fields. But after passing four radical written and physical exams, I had signed up with Aja Ọba Technologies.

Exobotany was a field that mostly existed in science fiction. But John's resources made cultivating edible crops in alien soil seem possible. After a truly historic FTL jump, our migration team set up base camp on the target planet, Nalo-4. Bit by bit, despite the occasional setback, my work bore fruit...literally.

On the planet, John began exhibiting mega physical strength, so I was assigned to collect data from his daily activities. We were inseparable. I'd kept my adoration of him quiet so imagine my shock when he revealed his love for me — and that he'd lived thousands of years under a curse. I laughed. He spoke of Einstein's "spooky" theorems, ghosts, and the regerminative genius of saltwater invertebrates. Were his expanding abilities random or connected to some measurable stimuli? He had no answer. His power clearly disrupted the laws of physics. But I just couldn't accept his irrational fables.

I still don't.

I listen because I care. I'm afraid for John...for us.

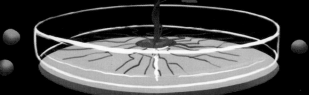

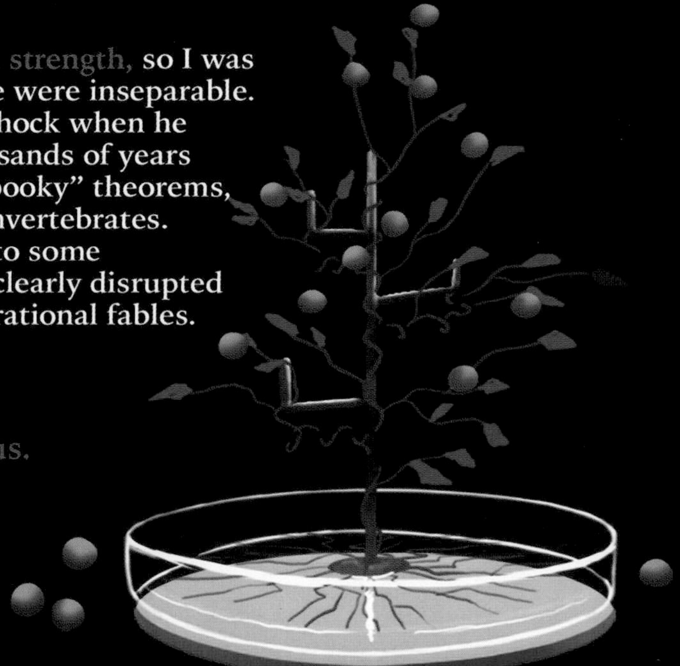

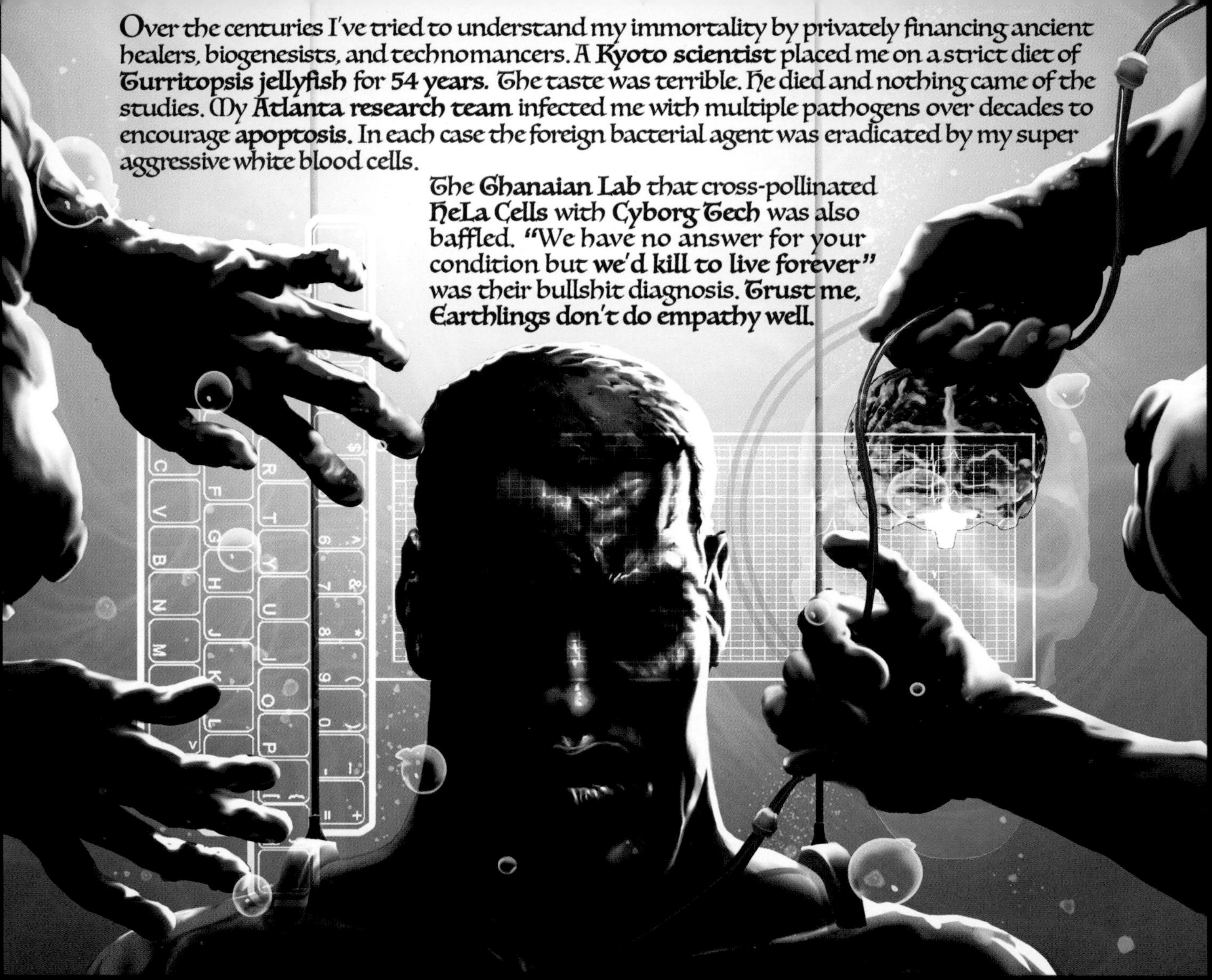
Over the centuries I've tried to understand my immortality by privately financing ancient healers, biogenesists, and technomancers. A **Kyoto scientist** placed me on a strict diet of **Turritopsis jellyfish** for **54 years.** The taste was terrible. He died and nothing came of the studies. My **Atlanta research team** infected me with multiple pathogens over decades to encourage **apoptosis.** In each case the foreign bacterial agent was eradicated by my super aggressive white blood cells.
The **Ghanaian Lab** that cross-pollinated **HeLa Cells** with **Cyborg Tech** was also baffled. "We have no answer for your condition but **we'd kill to live forever"** was their bullshit diagnosis. **Trust me, Earthlings don't do empathy well.**

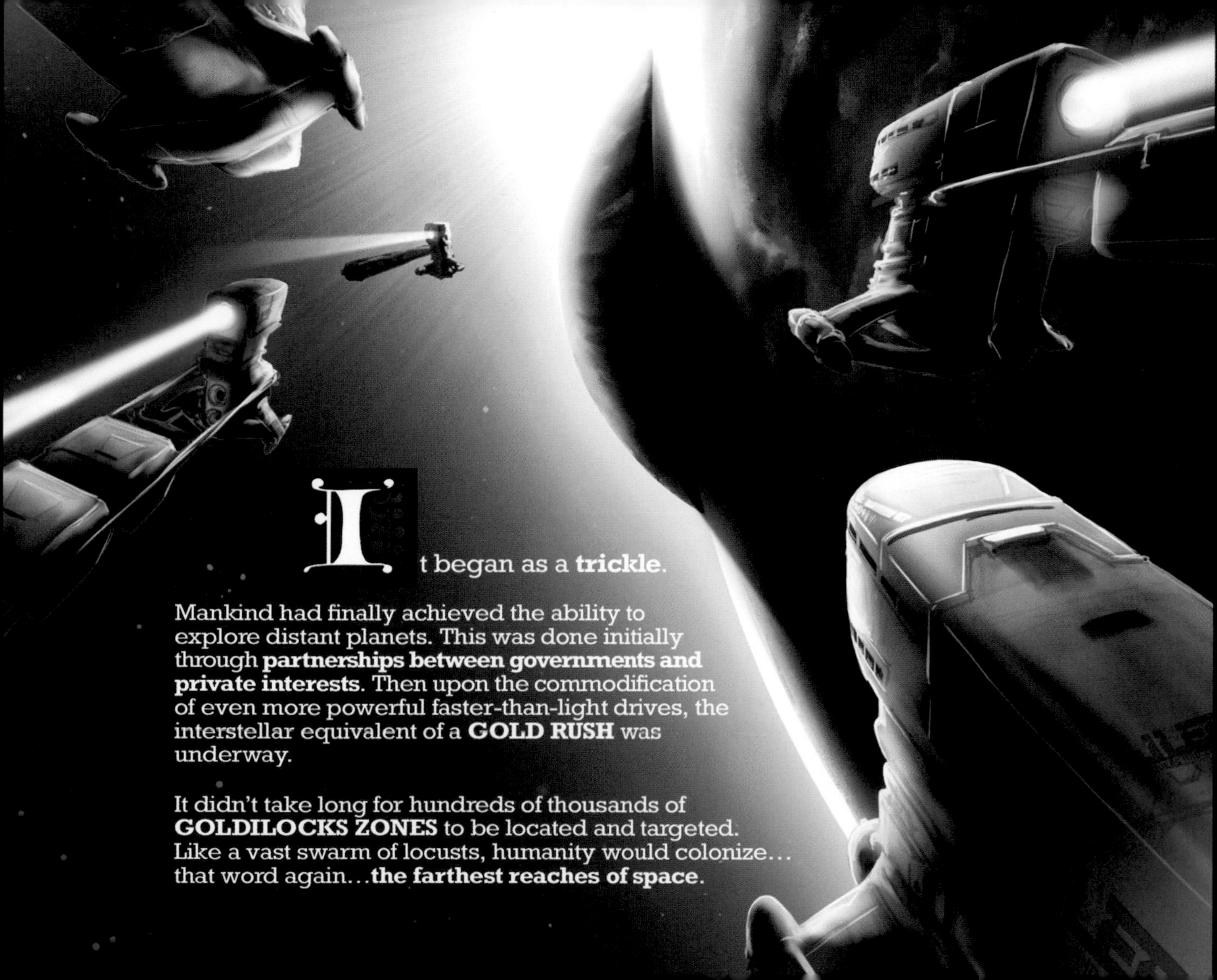

It began as a **trickle**.

Mankind had finally achieved the ability to explore distant planets. This was done initially through **partnerships between governments and private interests.** Then upon the commodification of even more powerful faster-than-light drives, the interstellar equivalent of a **GOLD RUSH** was underway.

It didn't take long for hundreds of thousands of **GOLDILOCKS ZONES** to be located and targeted. Like a vast swarm of locusts, humanity would colonize… that word again…**the farthest reaches of space**.

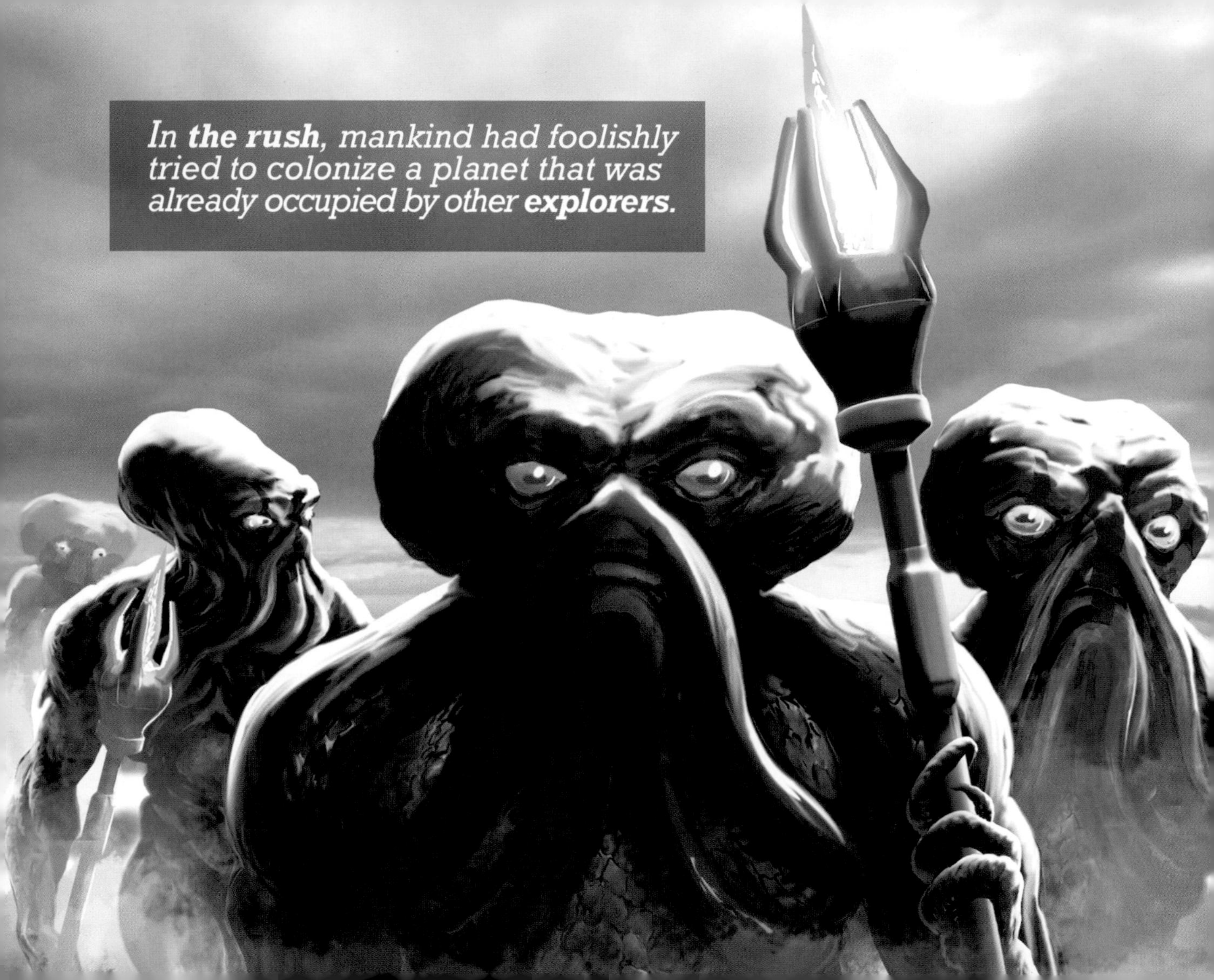
In **the rush**, mankind had foolishly tried to colonize a planet that was already occupied by other **explorers**.

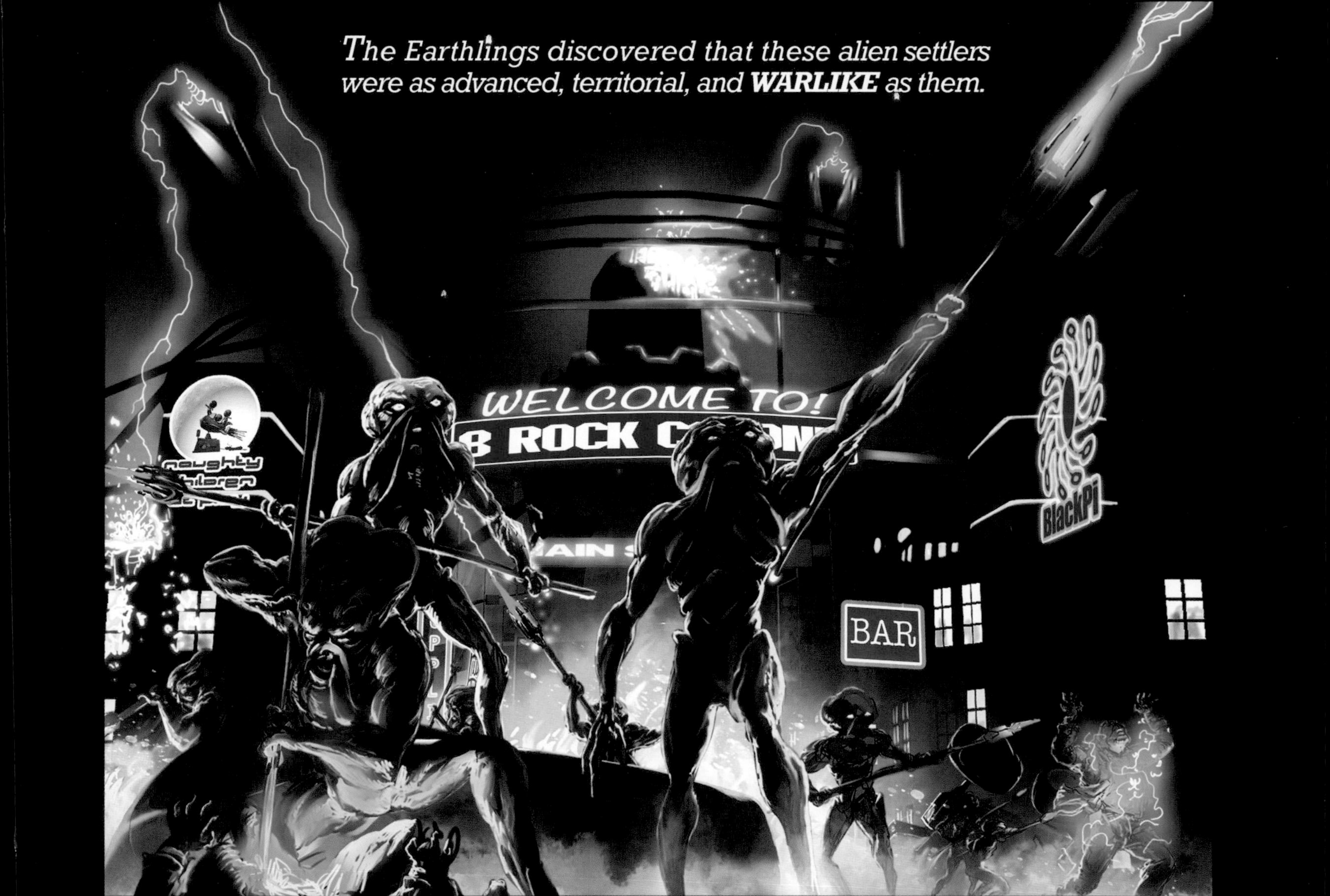
The Earthlings discovered that these alien settlers were as advanced, territorial, and **WARLIKE** as them.
WELCOME TO!
BAR
BlackPi

John wasn't surprised when ***Intergalactic War*** *broke out shortly thereafter.*

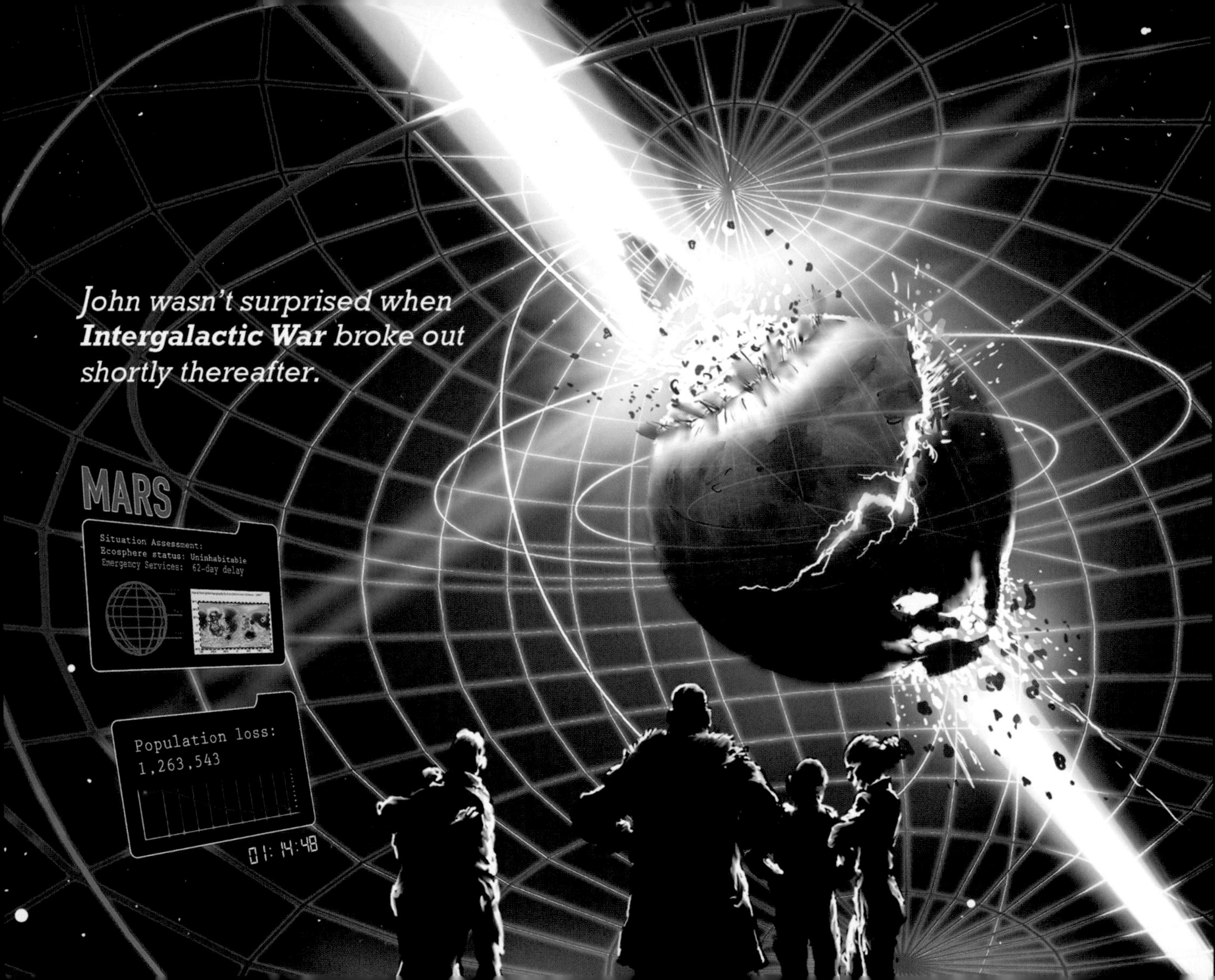
MARS
Situation Assessment:
Ecosphere status: Uninhabitable
Emergency Services: 62-day delay
Population loss:
1,263,543
01:14:48

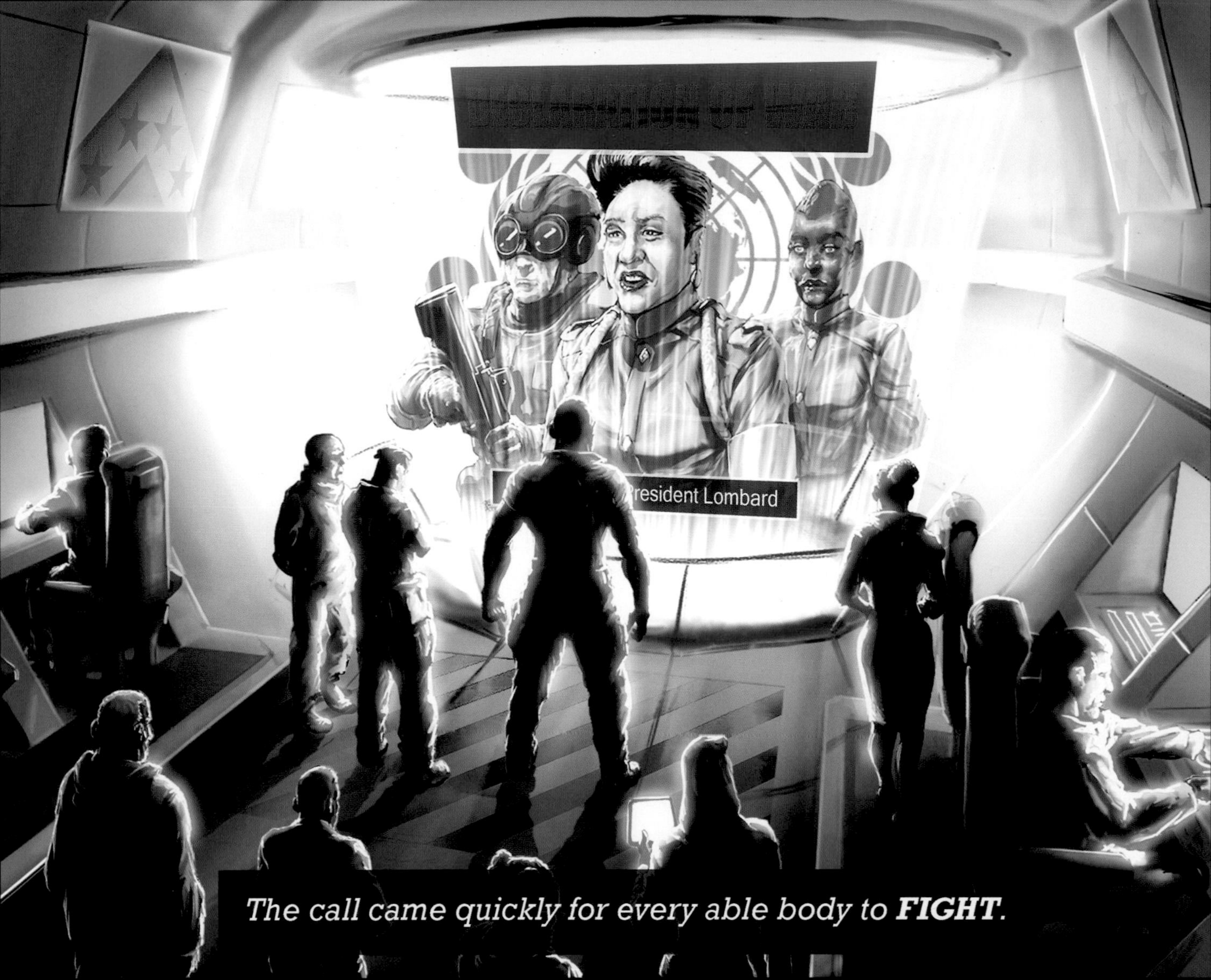
President Lombard
The call came quickly for every able body to **FIGHT**.

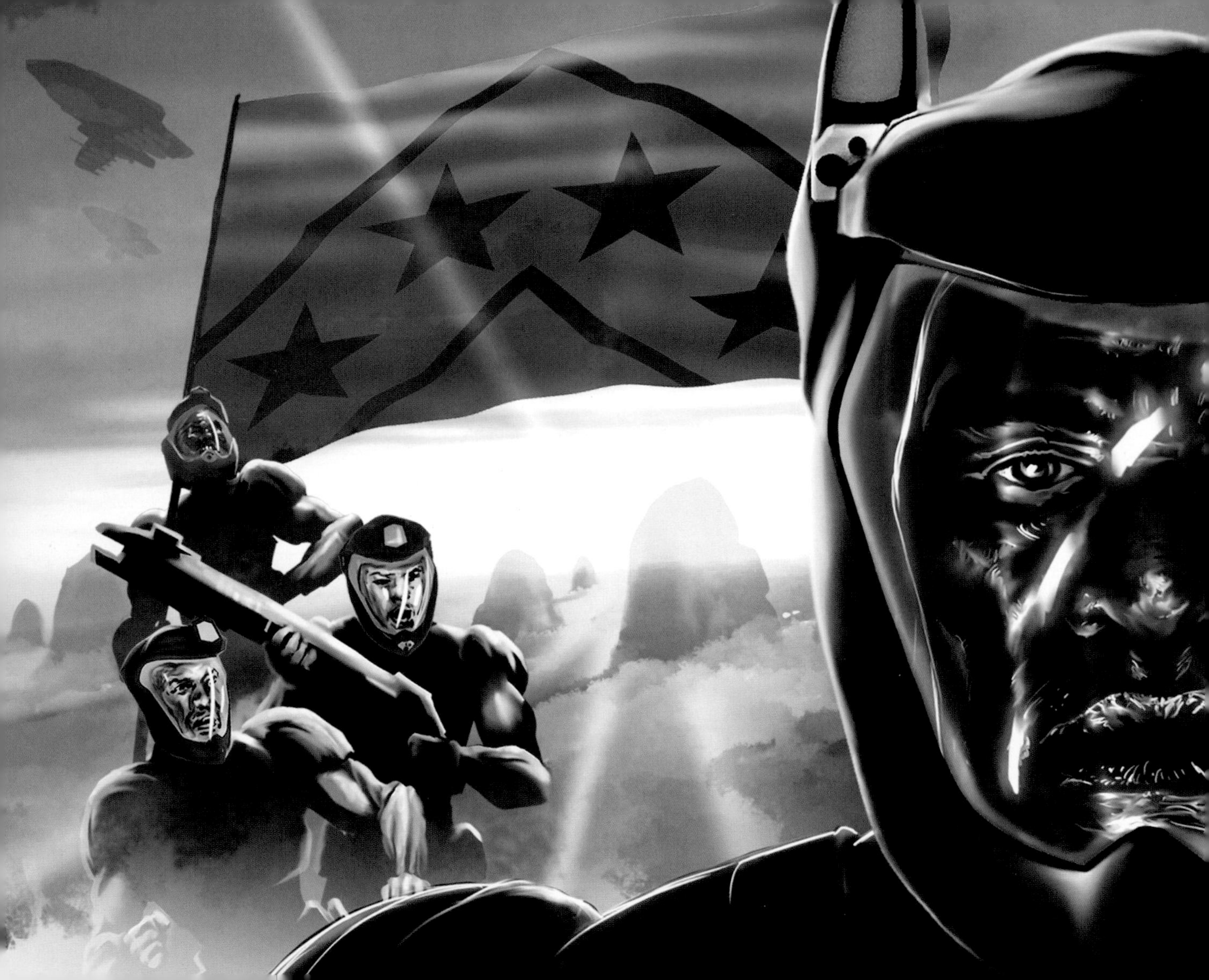

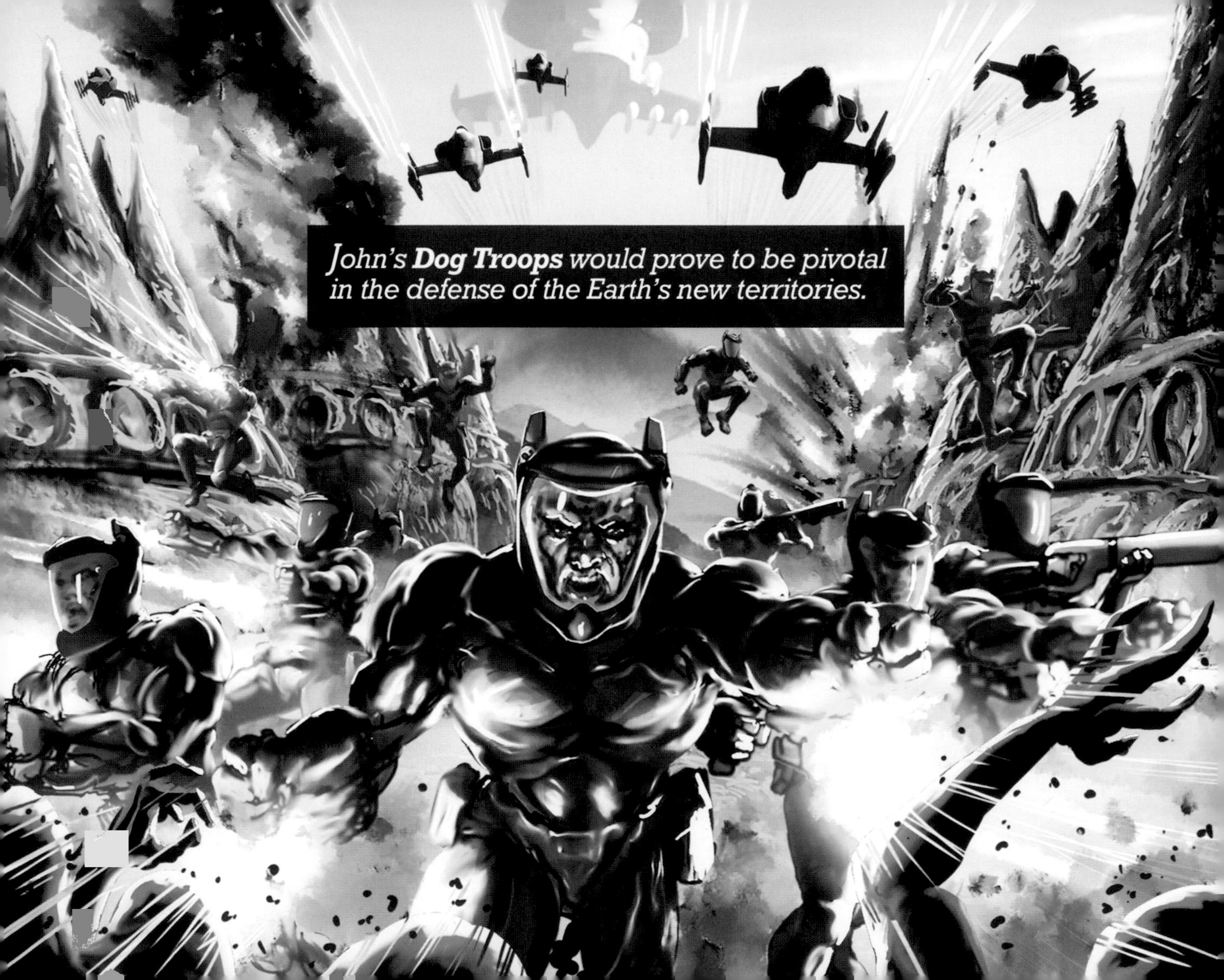
John's **Dog Troops** would prove to be pivotal in the defense of the Earth's new territories.

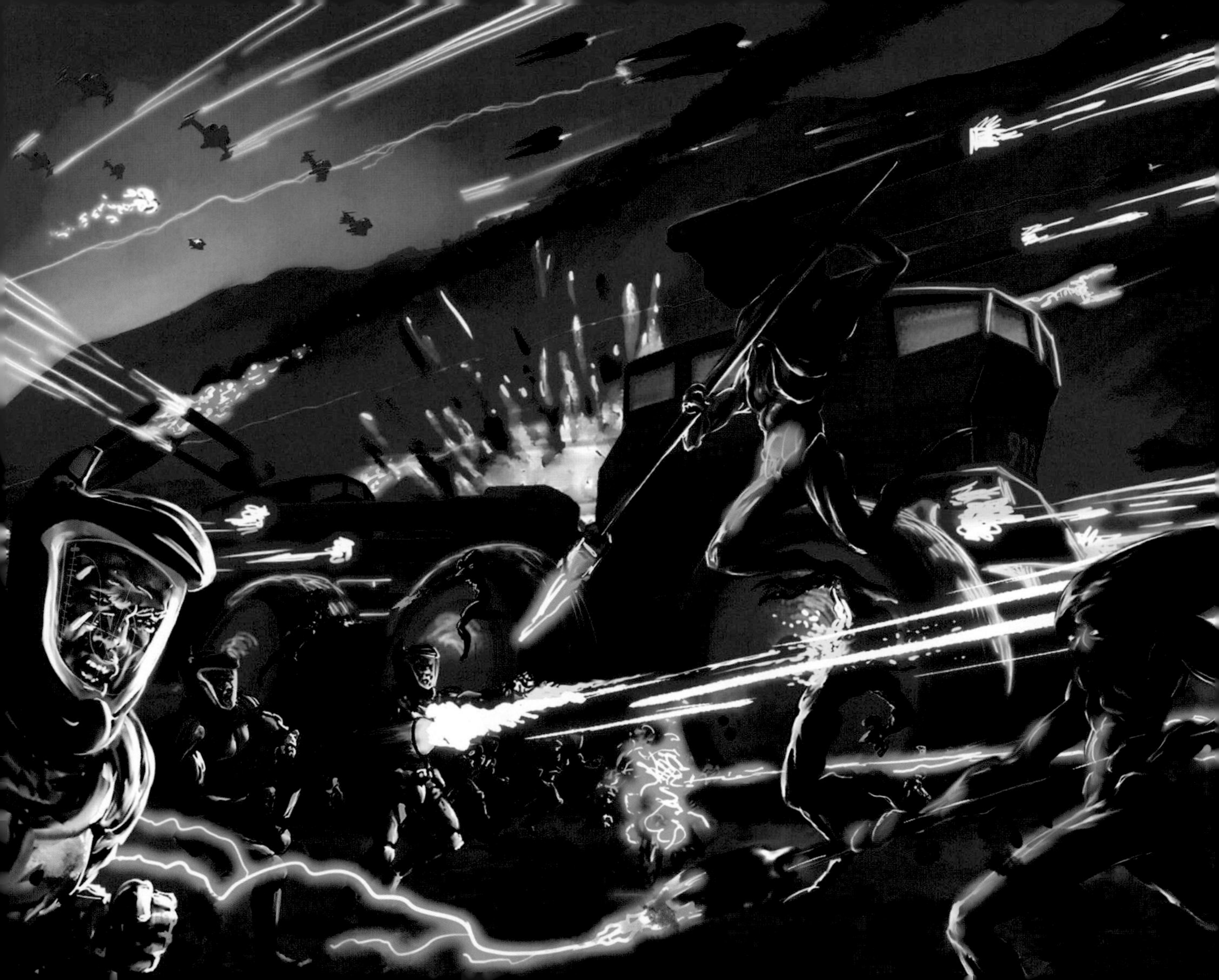

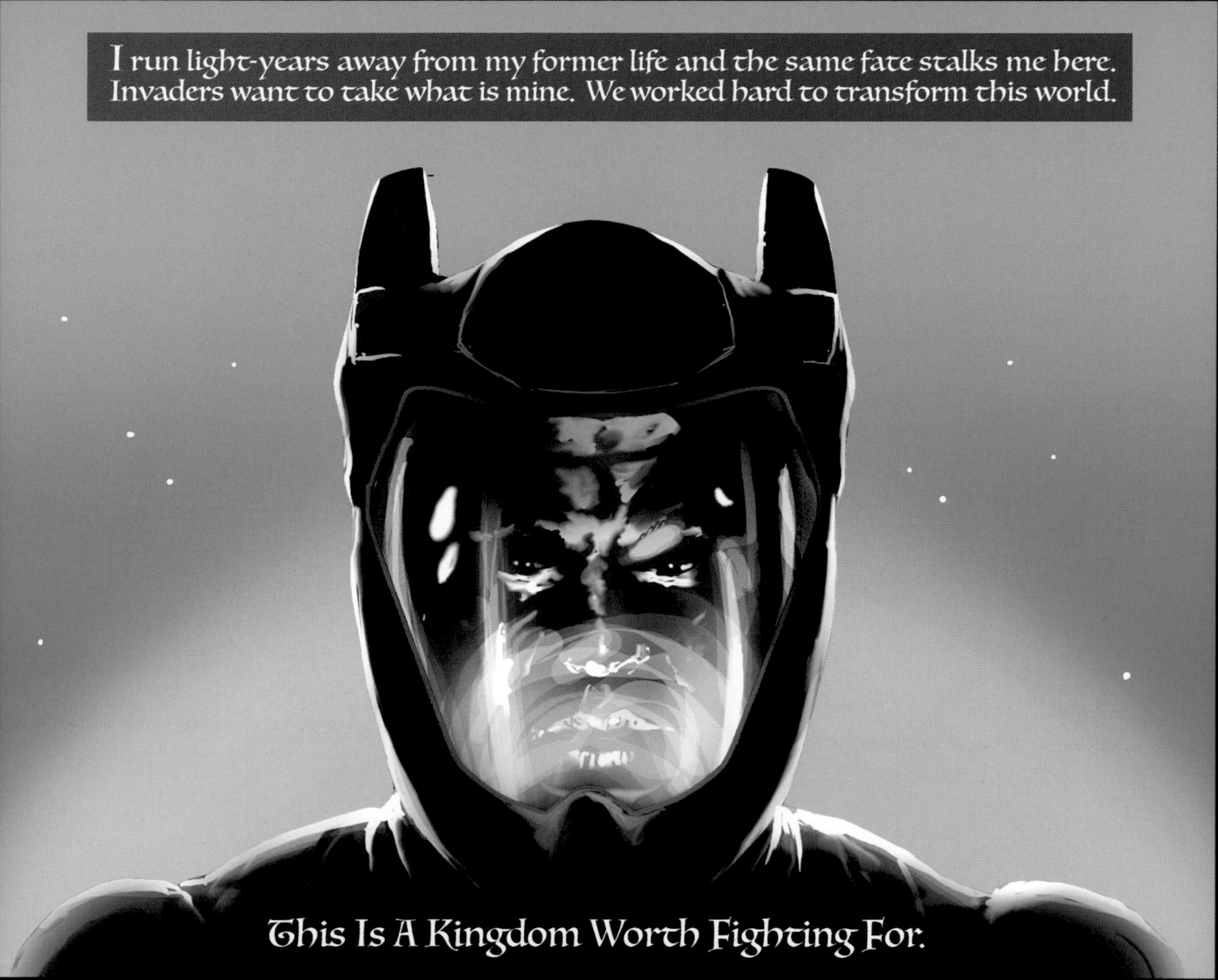
I run light-years away from my former life and the same fate stalks me here. Invaders want to take what is mine. We worked hard to transform this world.
This Is A Kingdom Worth Fighting For.

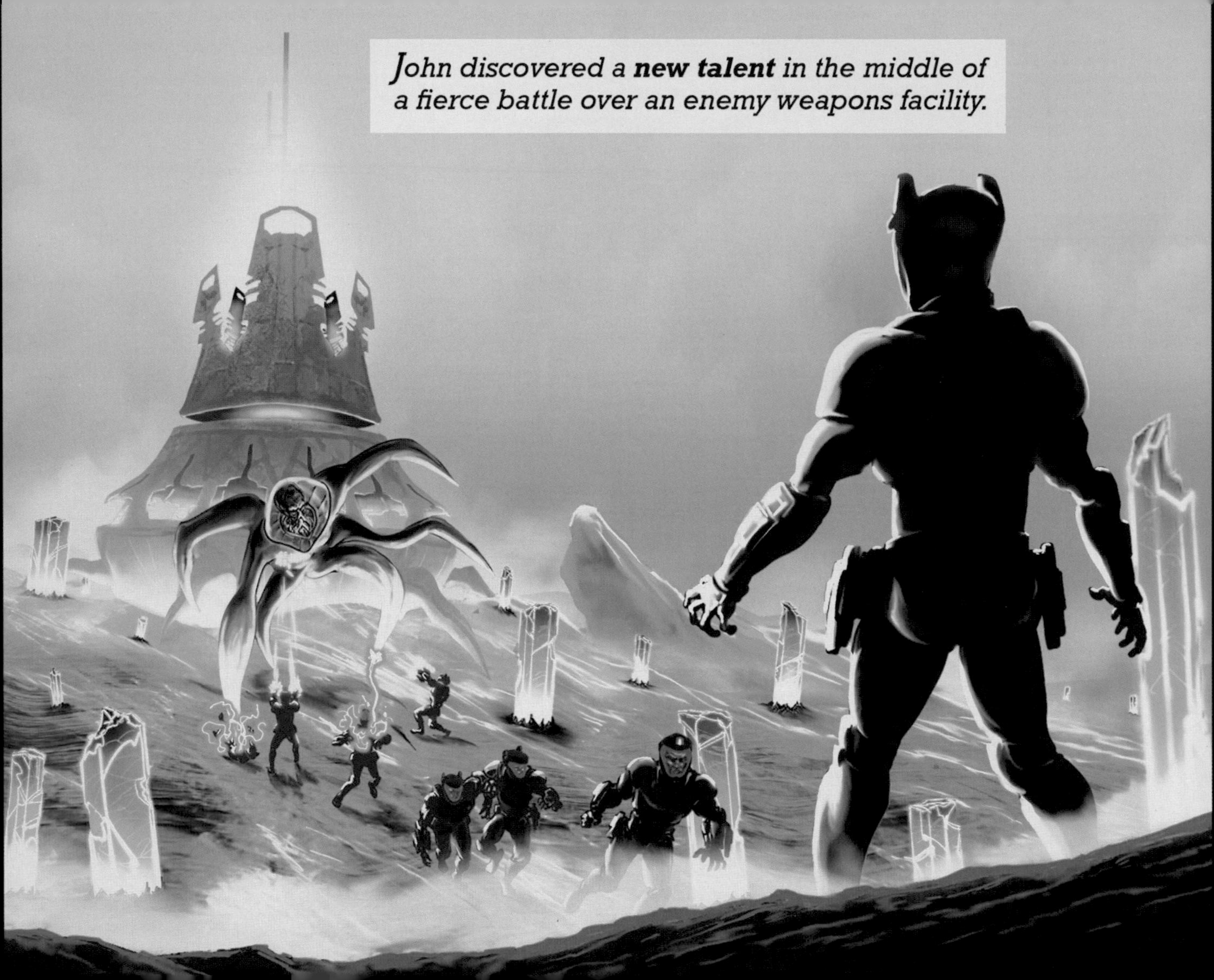
John discovered a **new talent** in the middle of a fierce battle over an enemy weapons facility.

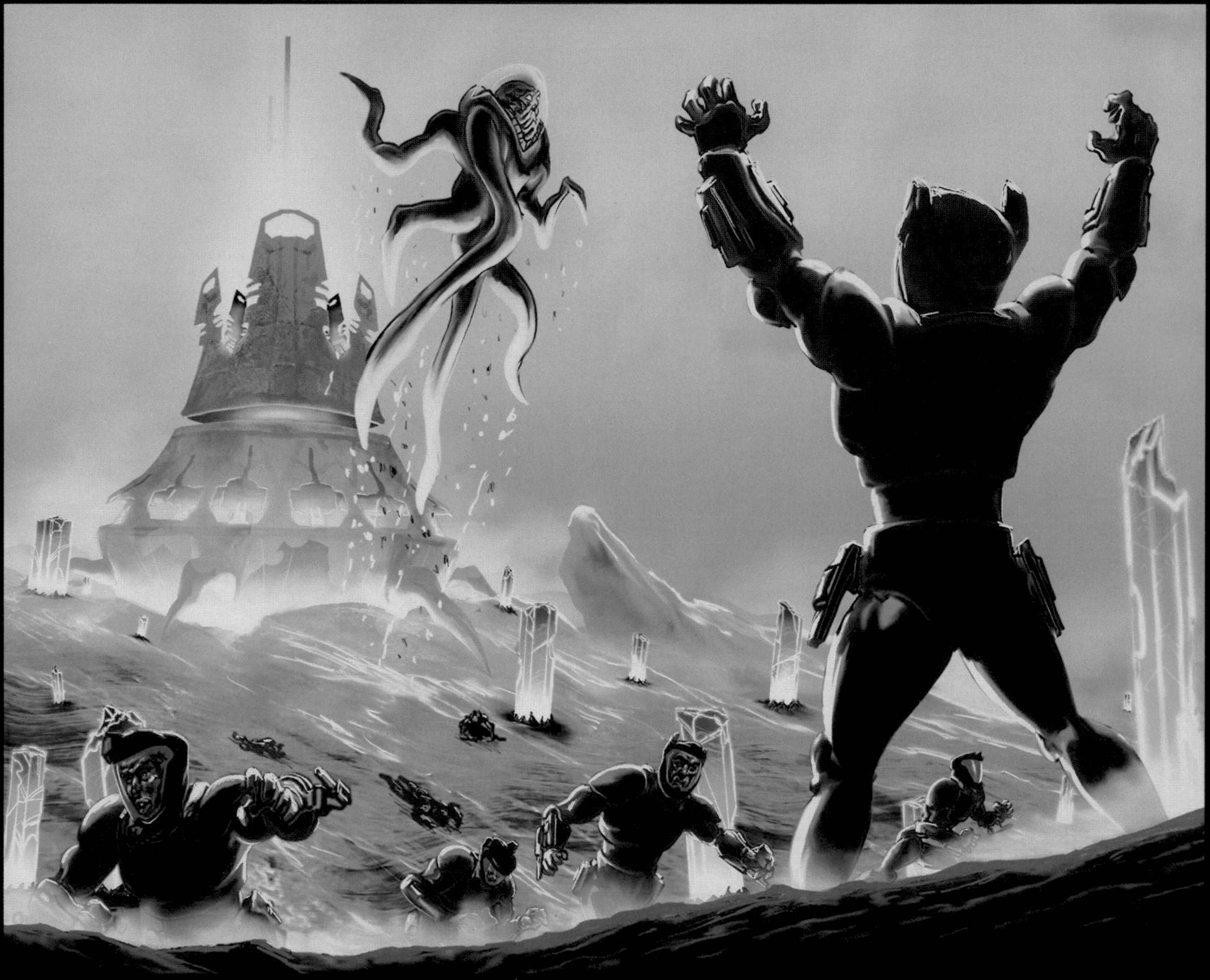

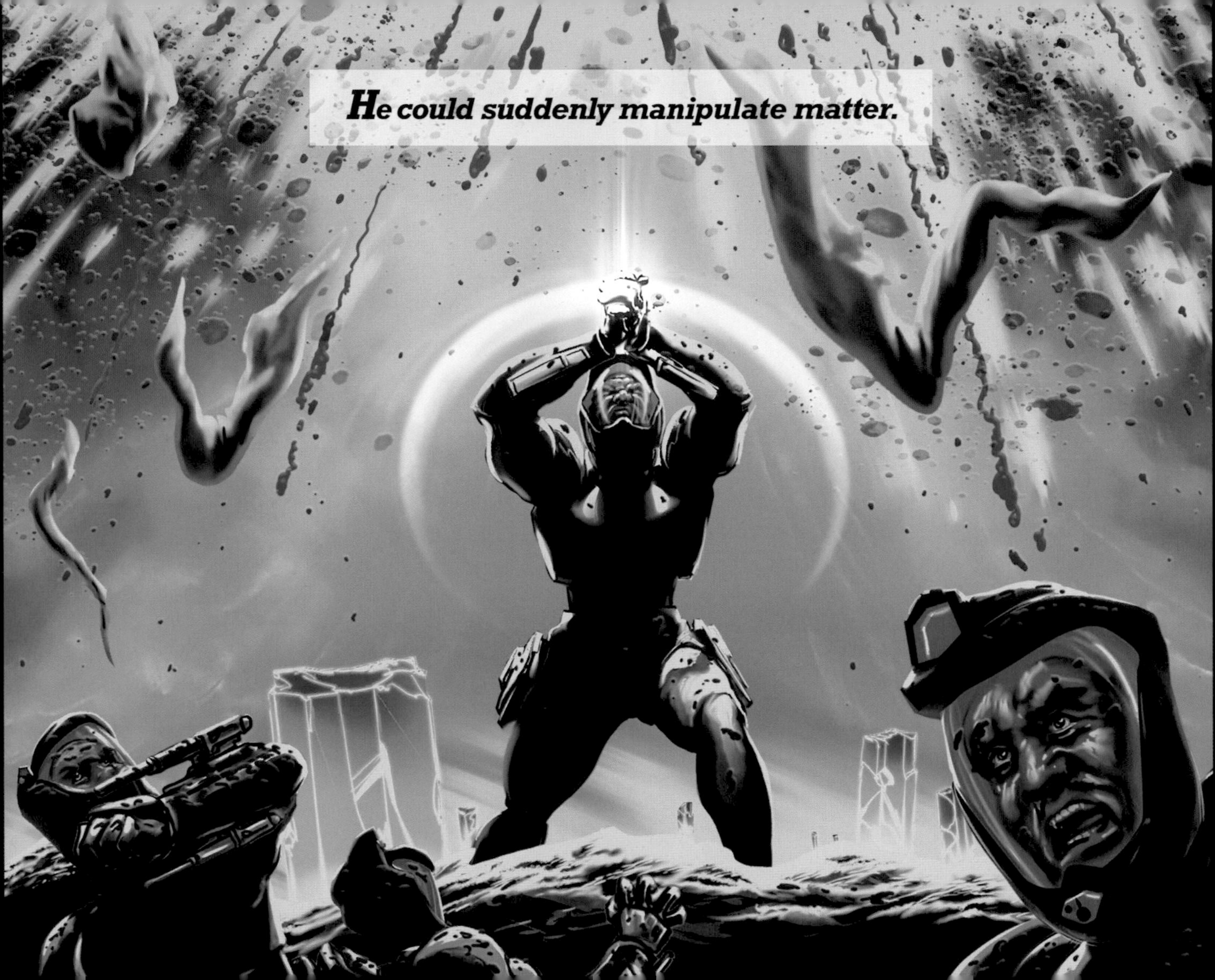
He could suddenly manipulate matter.

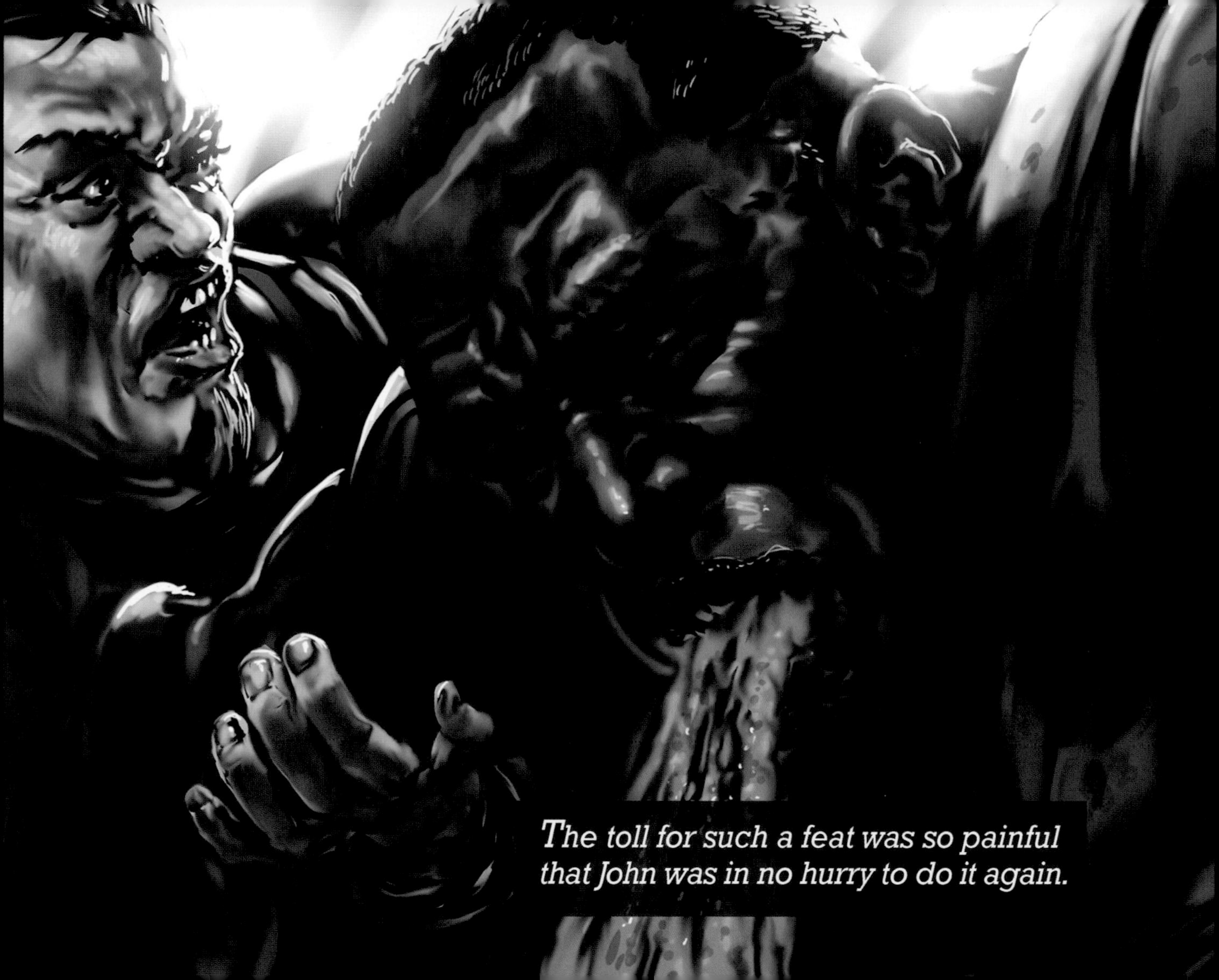
The toll for such a feat was so painful that John was in no hurry to do it again.

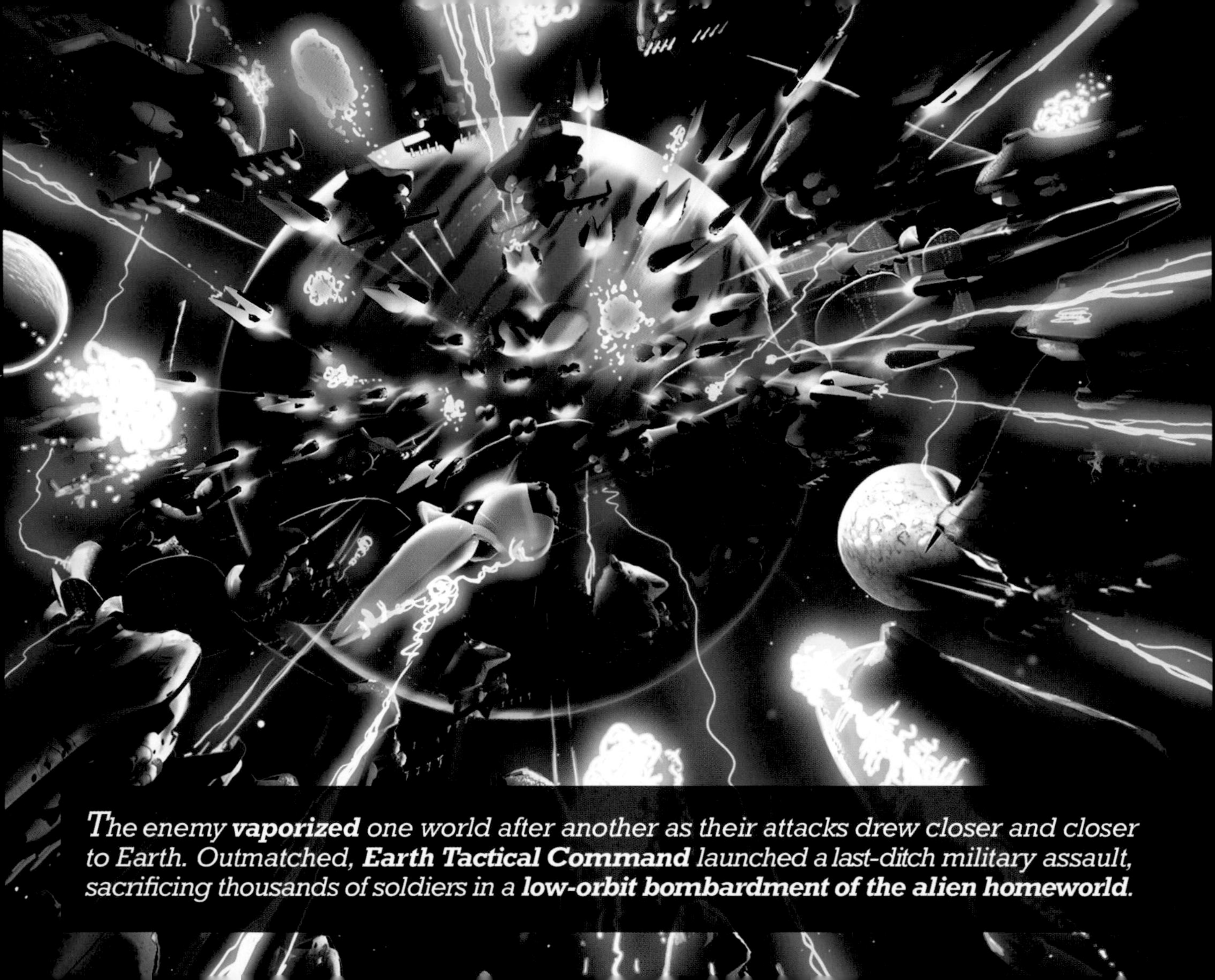

The enemy ***vaporized*** *one world after another as their attacks drew closer and closer to Earth. Outmatched,* ***Earth Tactical Command*** *launched a last-ditch military assault, sacrificing thousands of soldiers in a* ***low-orbit bombardment of the alien homeworld****.*

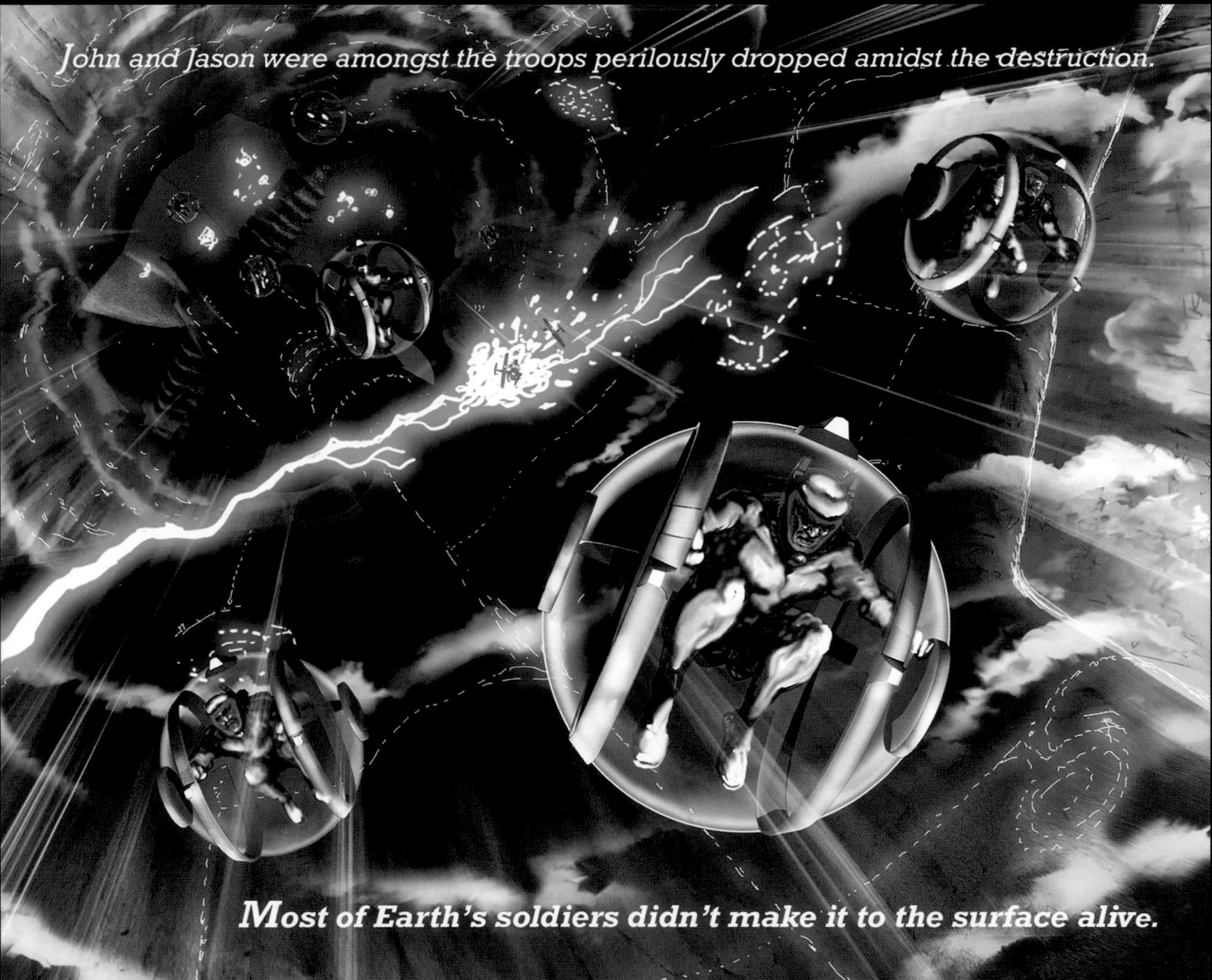
John and Jason were amongst the troops perilously dropped amidst the destruction.
Most of Earth's soldiers didn't make it to the surface alive.

It never occurred to Earth's military intelligence that the enemy's ***most destructive firepower*** *emanated from the* ***molten core*** *of their homeworld.*

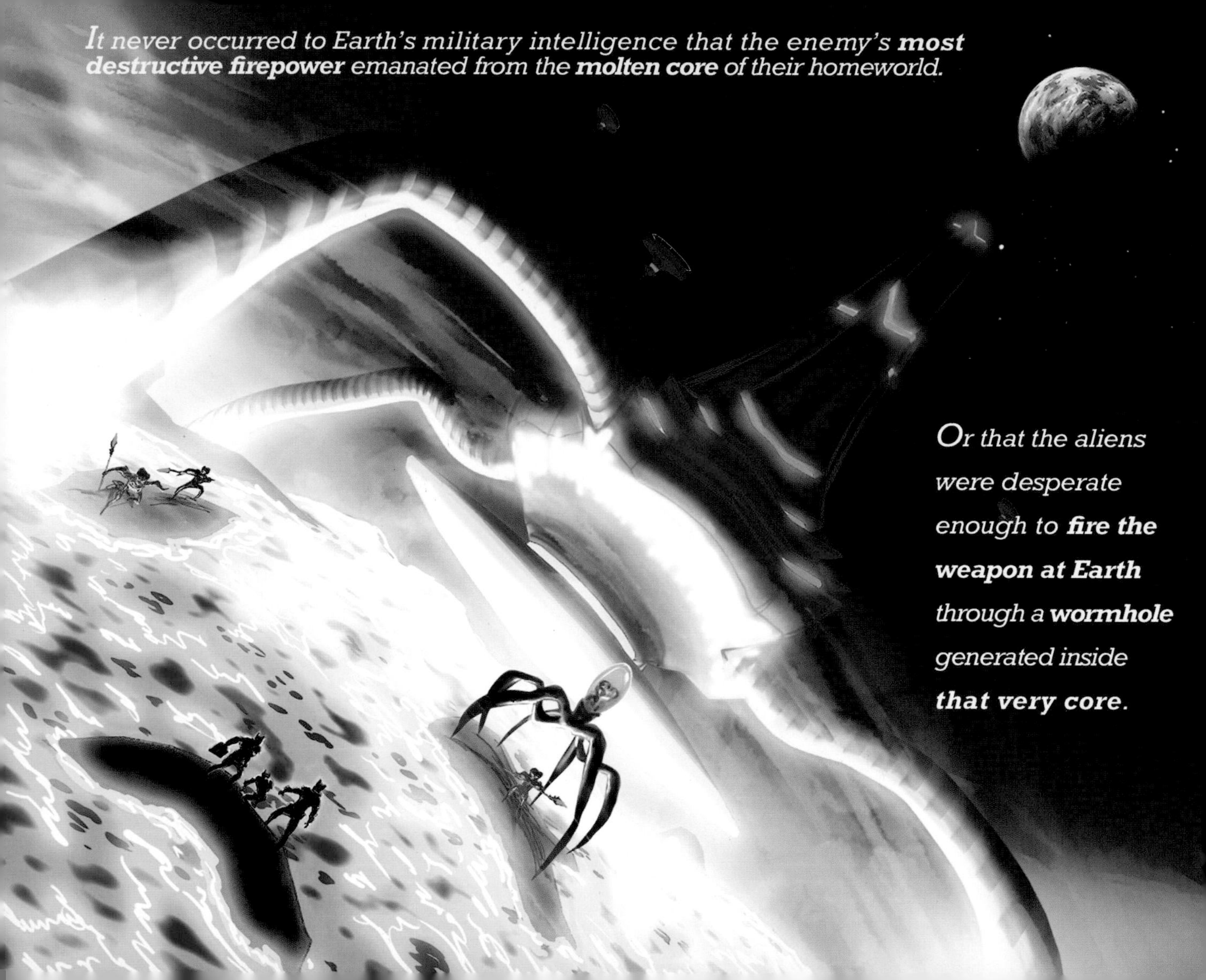

Or that the aliens were desperate enough to ***fire the weapon at Earth*** *through a* ***wormhole*** *generated inside* ***that very core.***

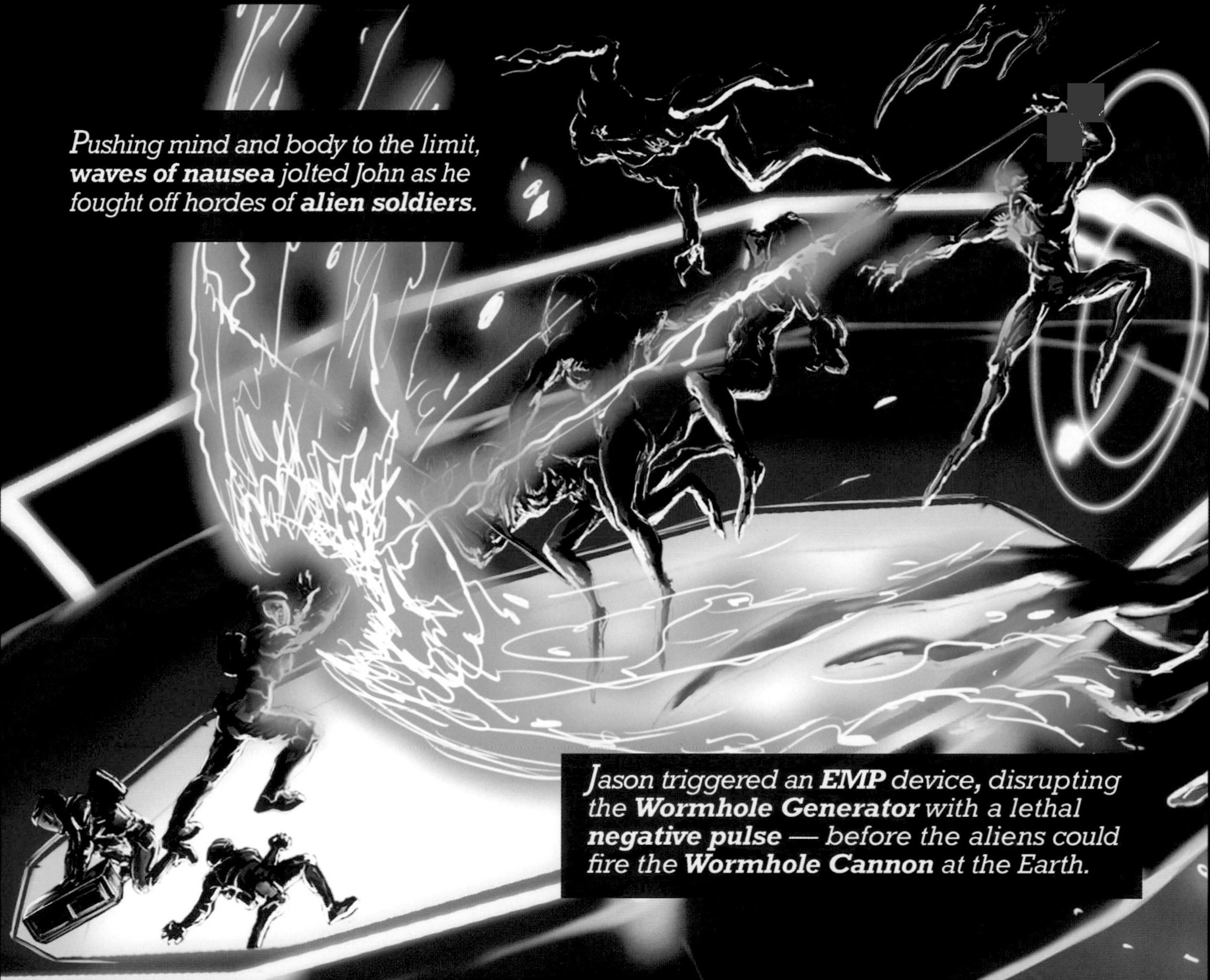
Pushing mind and body to the limit, waves of nausea jolted John as he fought off hordes of alien soldiers.
Jason triggered an EMP device, disrupting the Wormhole Generator with a lethal negative pulse — before the aliens could fire the Wormhole Cannon at the Earth.

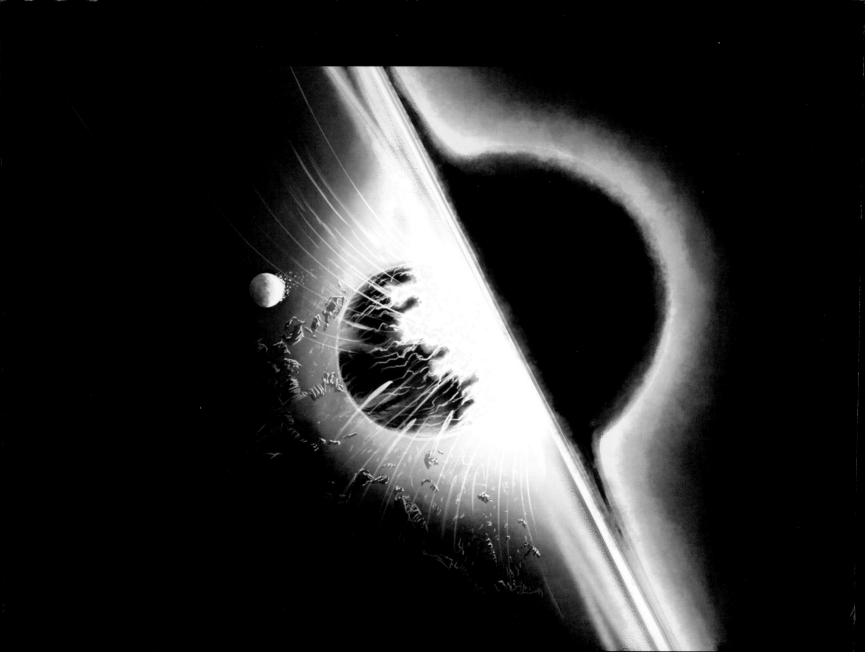

The artificial black hole **collapsed**, taking most of the **alien homeworld** with it.

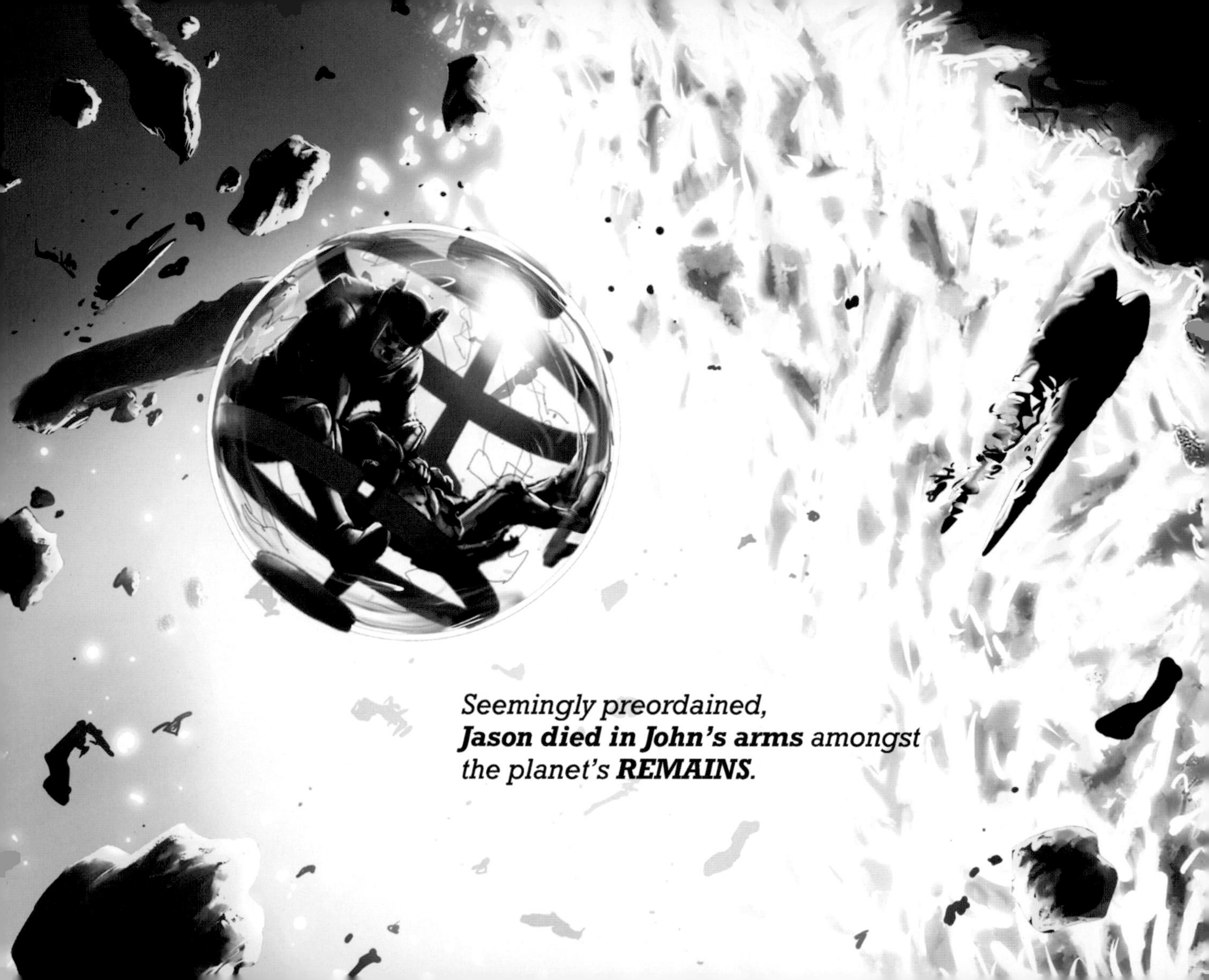
Seemingly preordained,
Jason died in John's arms amongst
the planet's **REMAINS.**

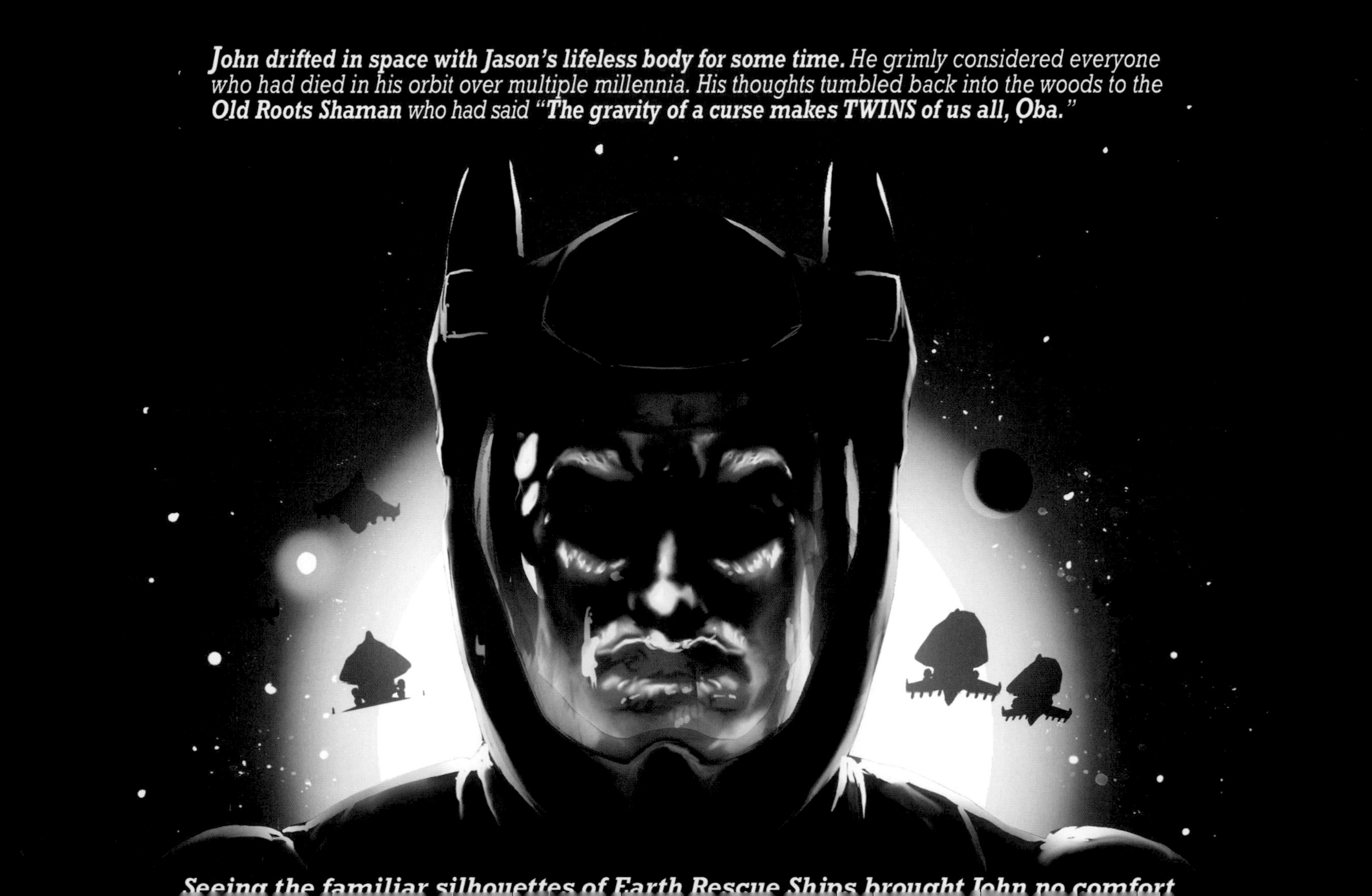
John drifted in space with Jason's lifeless body for some time. *He grimly considered everyone who had died in his orbit over multiple millennia. His thoughts tumbled back into the woods to the* **Old Roots Shaman** *who had said "***The gravity of a curse makes TWINS of us all, Ọba.***"*
Seeing the familiar silhouettes of Earth Rescue Ships brought John no comfort

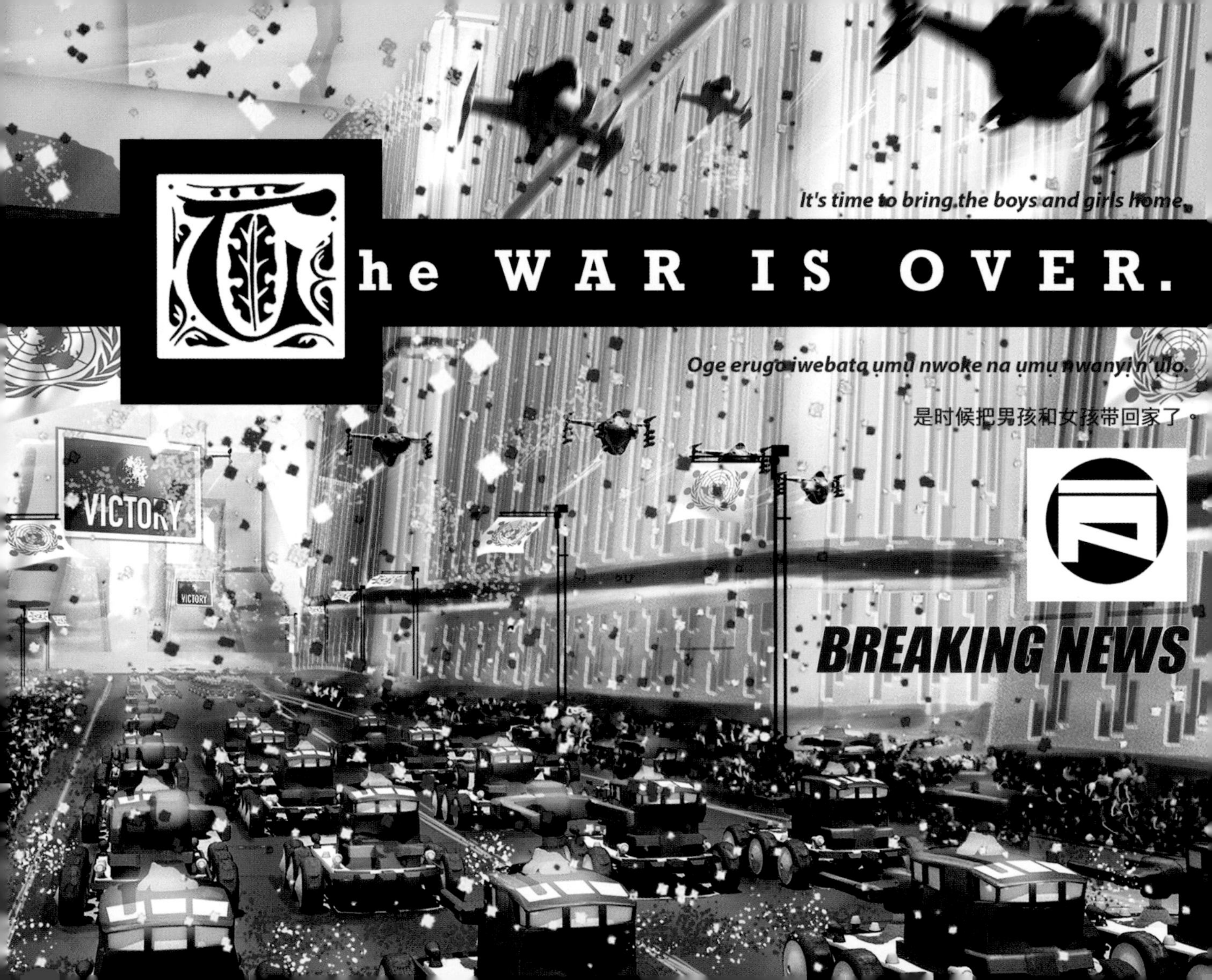
It's time to bring the boys and girls home.
The WAR IS OVER.
Oge erugo iwebata ụmụ nwoke na ụmụ nwanyị n'ulo.
是时候把男孩和女孩带回家了。
VICTORY
VICTORY
BREAKING NEWS

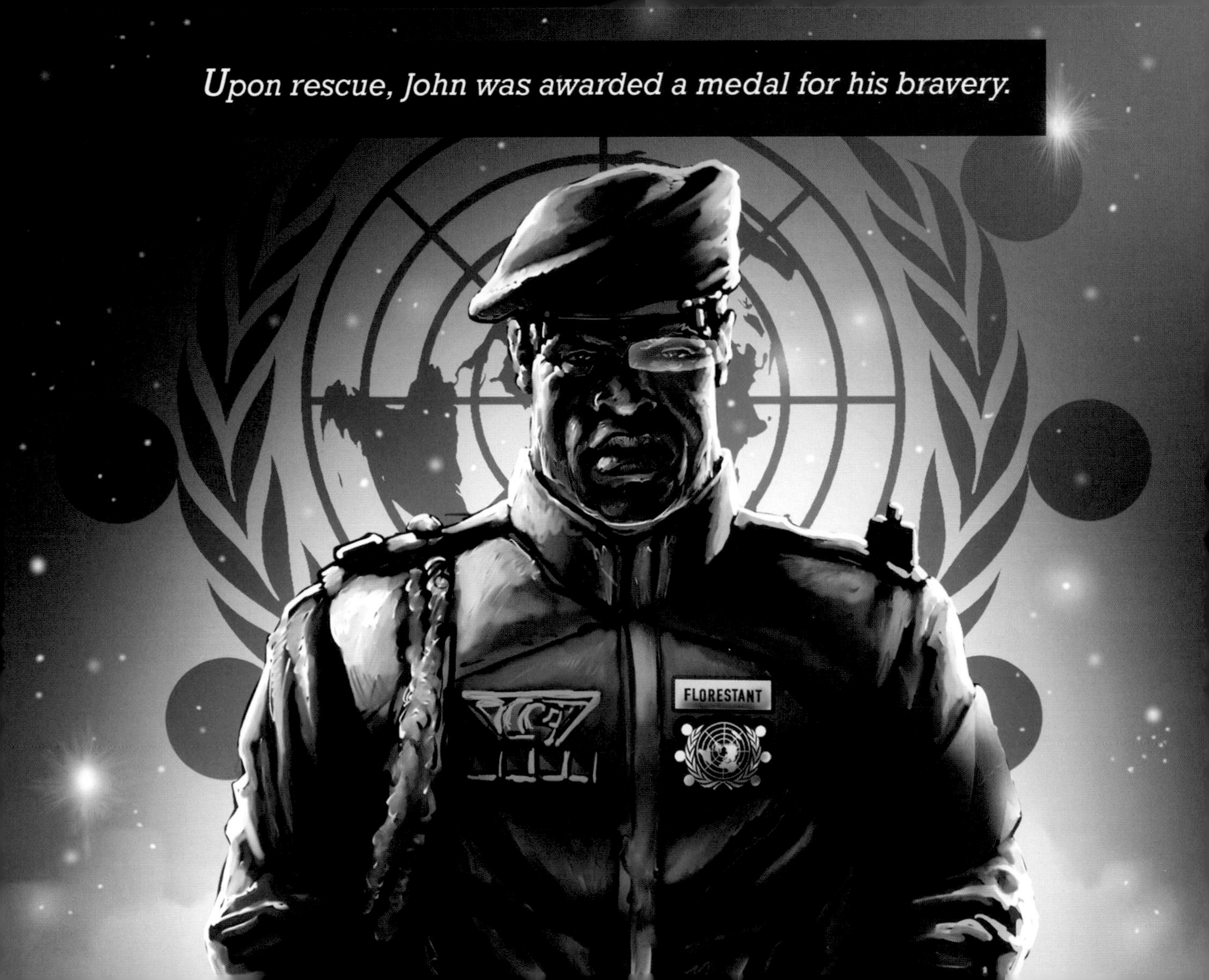
Upon rescue, John was awarded a medal for his bravery.
FLORESTANT

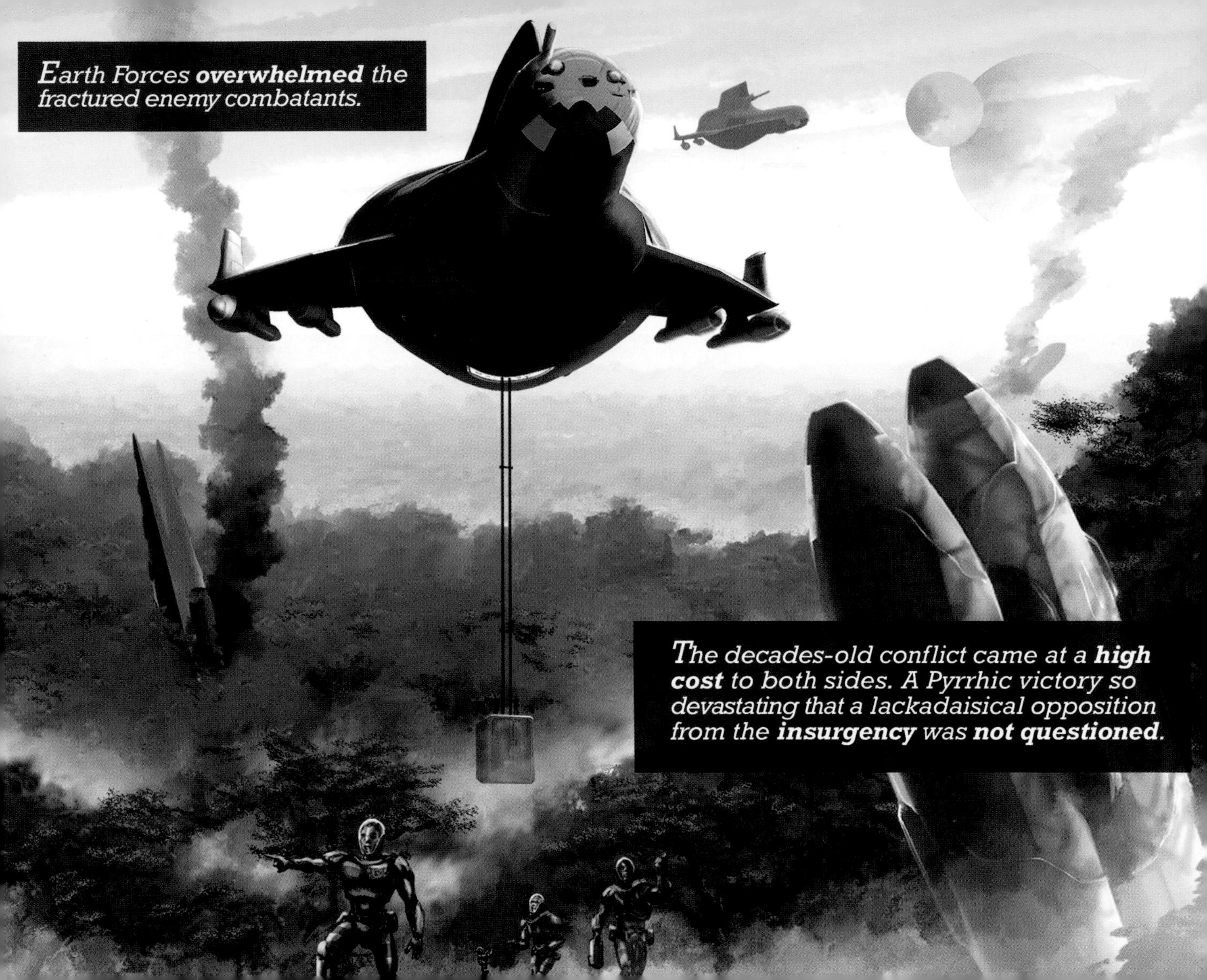
Earth Forces **overwhelmed** the fractured enemy combatants.
The decades-old conflict came at a **high cost** to both sides. A Pyrrhic victory so devastating that a lackadaisical opposition from the **insurgency** was **not questioned**.

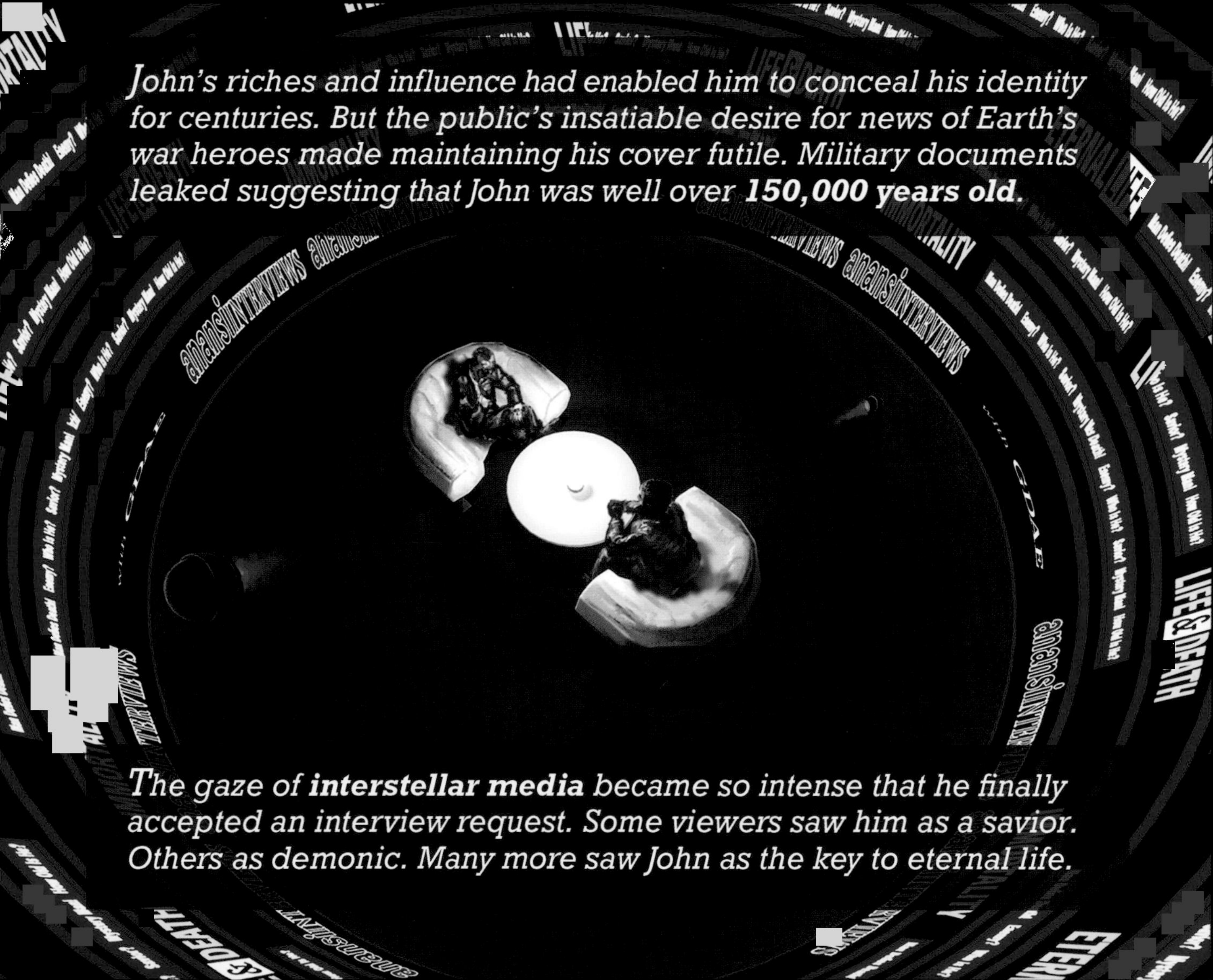
John's riches and influence had enabled him to conceal his identity for centuries. But the public's insatiable desire for news of Earth's war heroes made maintaining his cover futile. Military documents leaked suggesting that John was well over **150,000 years old**.
The gaze of **interstellar media** became so intense that he finally accepted an interview request. Some viewers saw him as a savior. Others as demonic. Many more saw John as the key to eternal life.

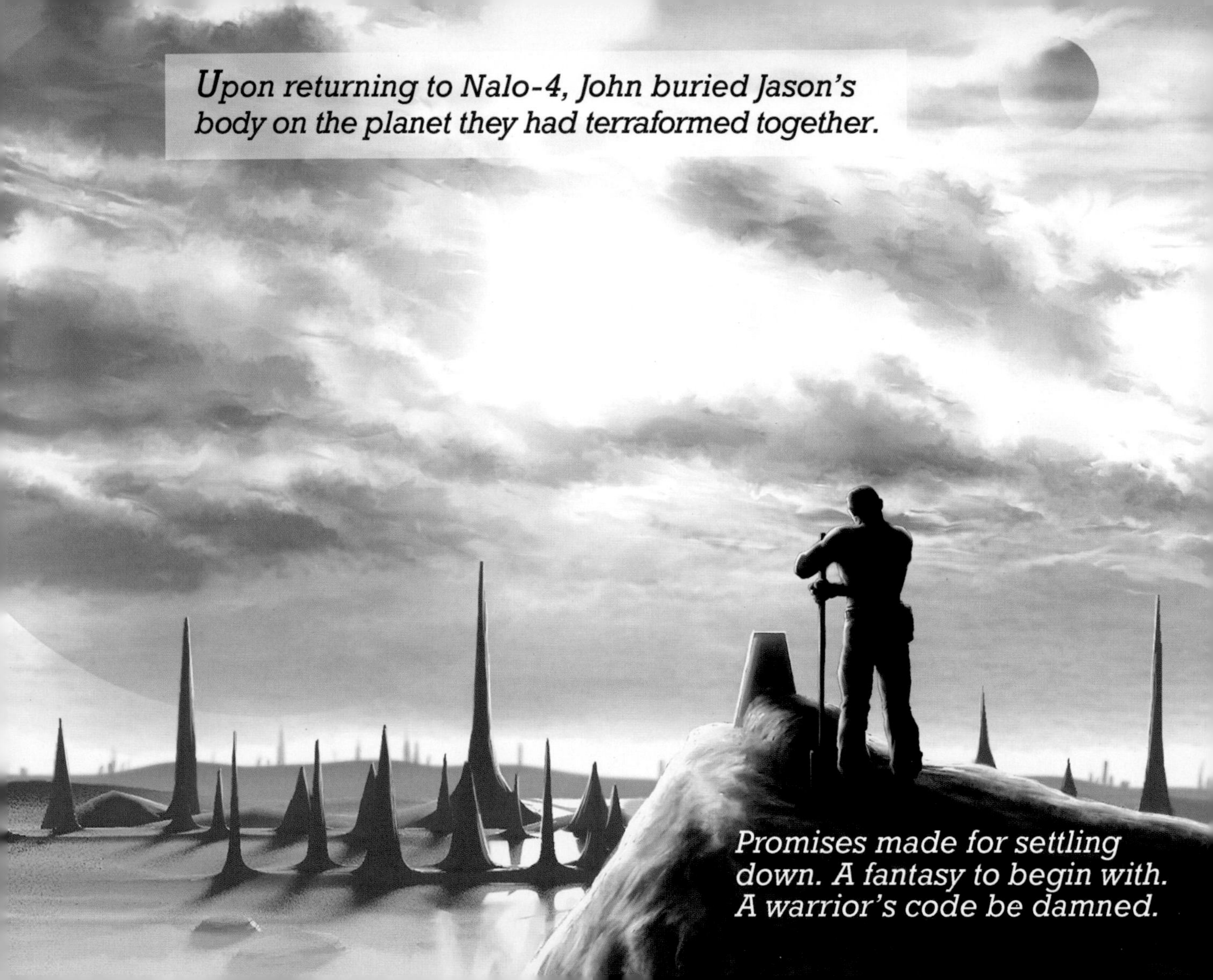
Upon returning to Nalo-4, John buried Jason's body on the planet they had terraformed together.
Promises made for settling down. A fantasy to begin with. A warrior's code be damned.

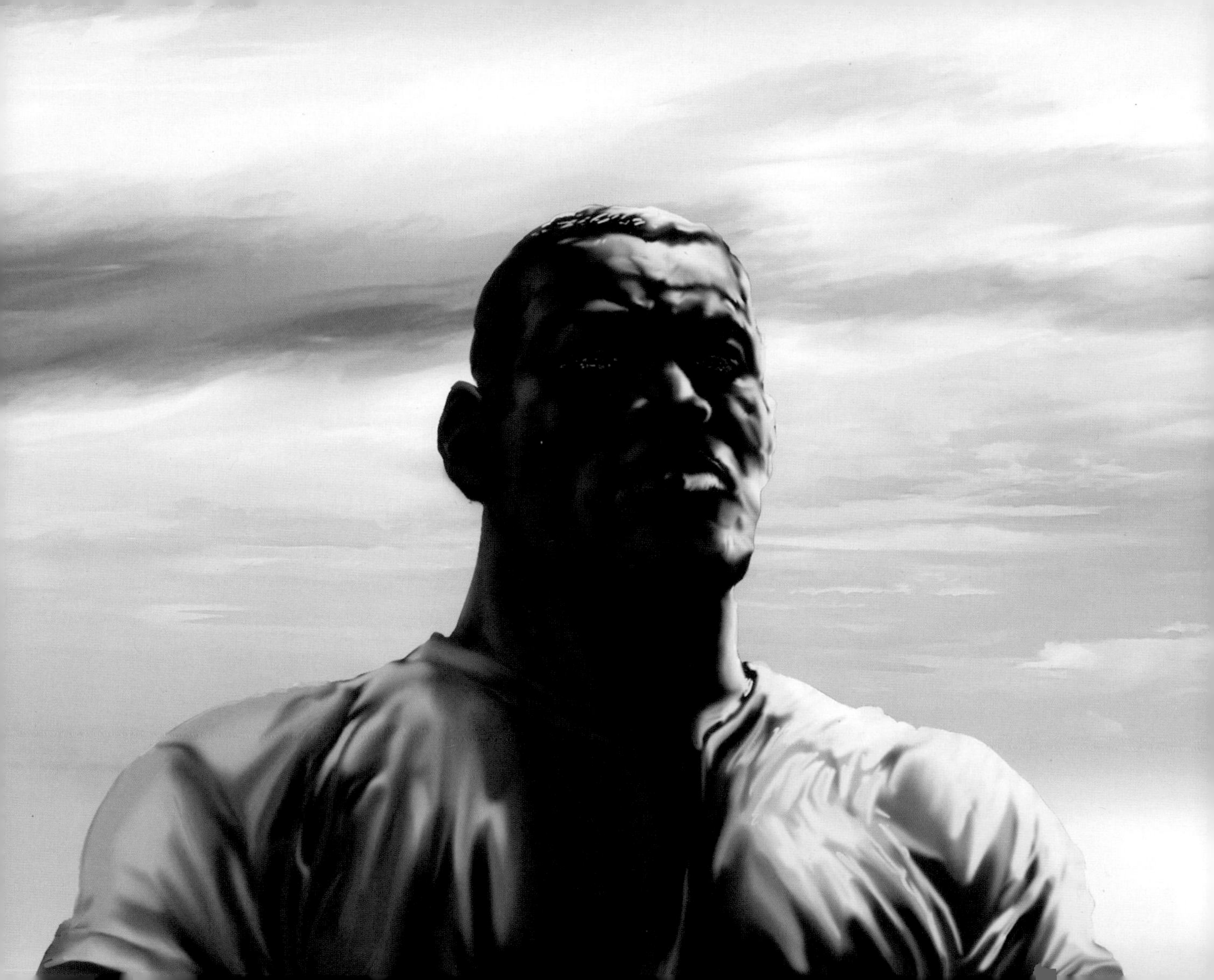

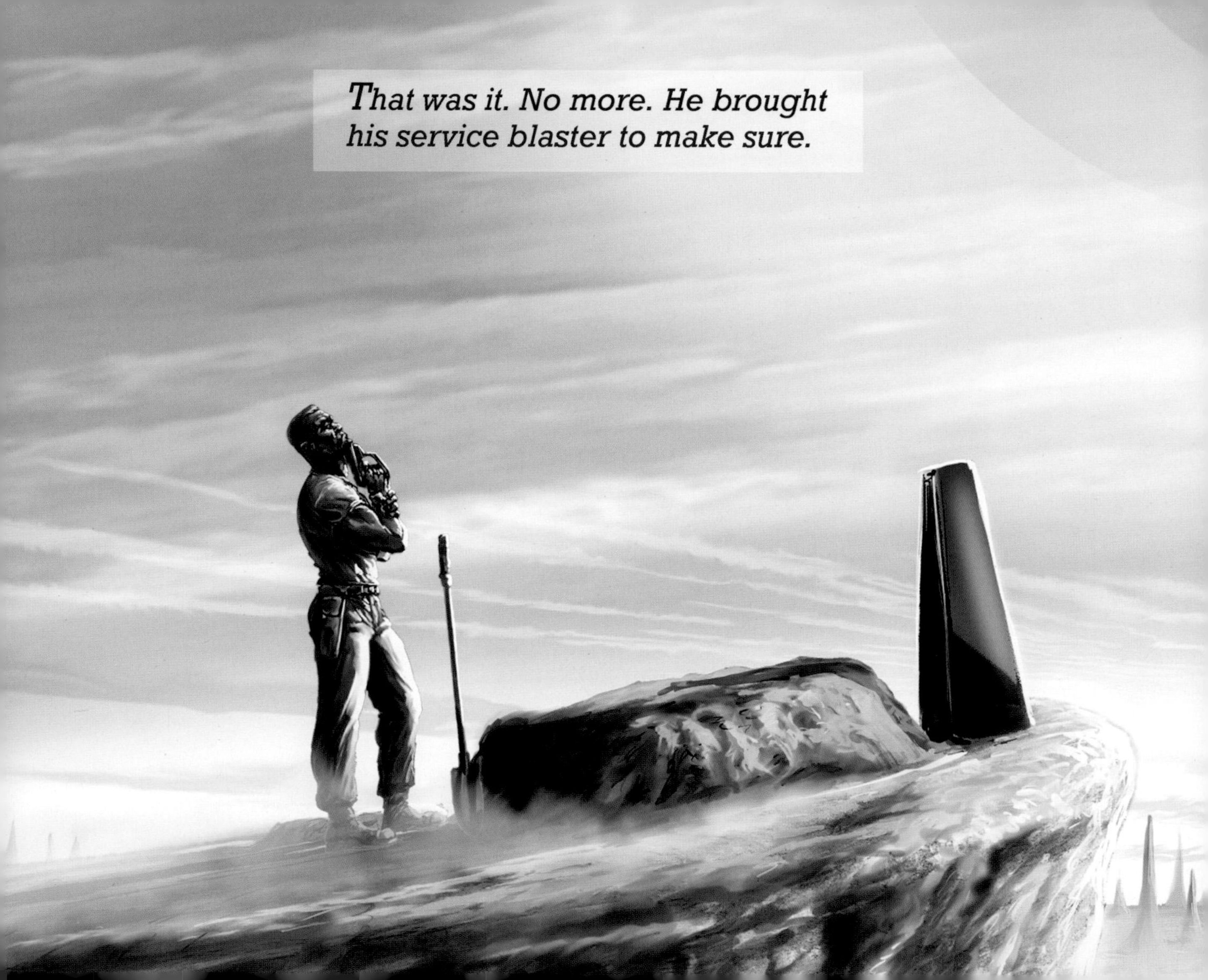
That was it. No more. He brought his service blaster to make sure.

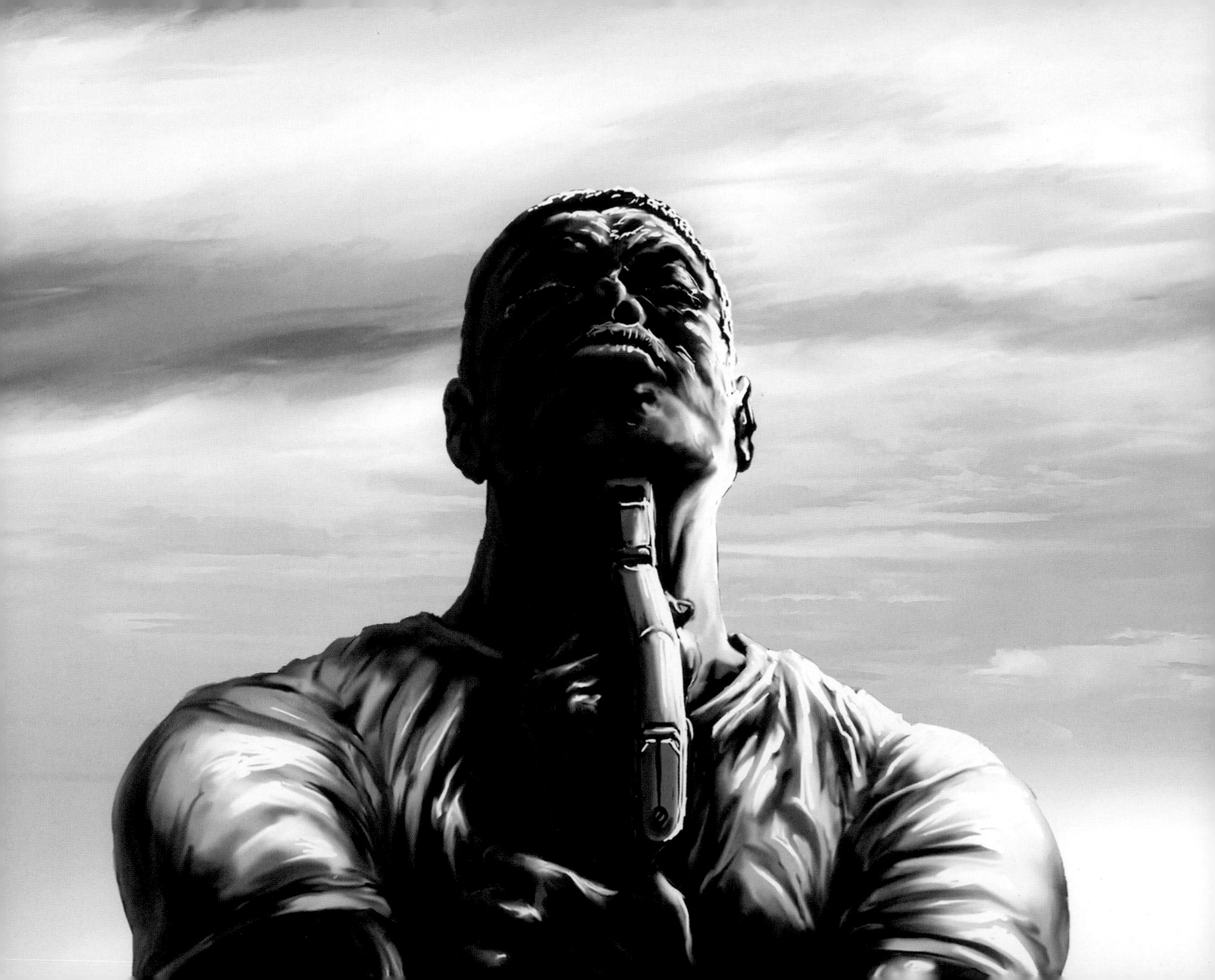

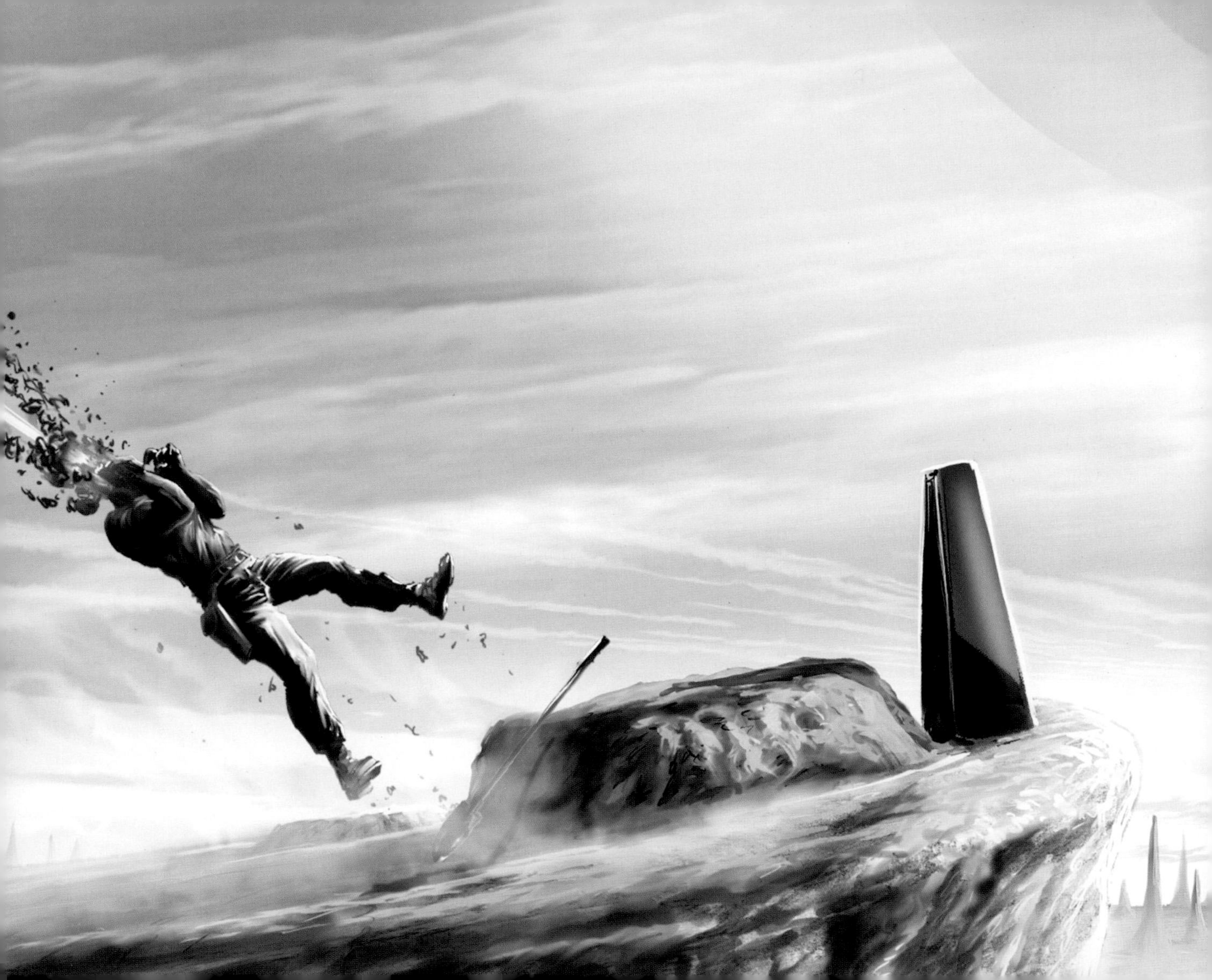

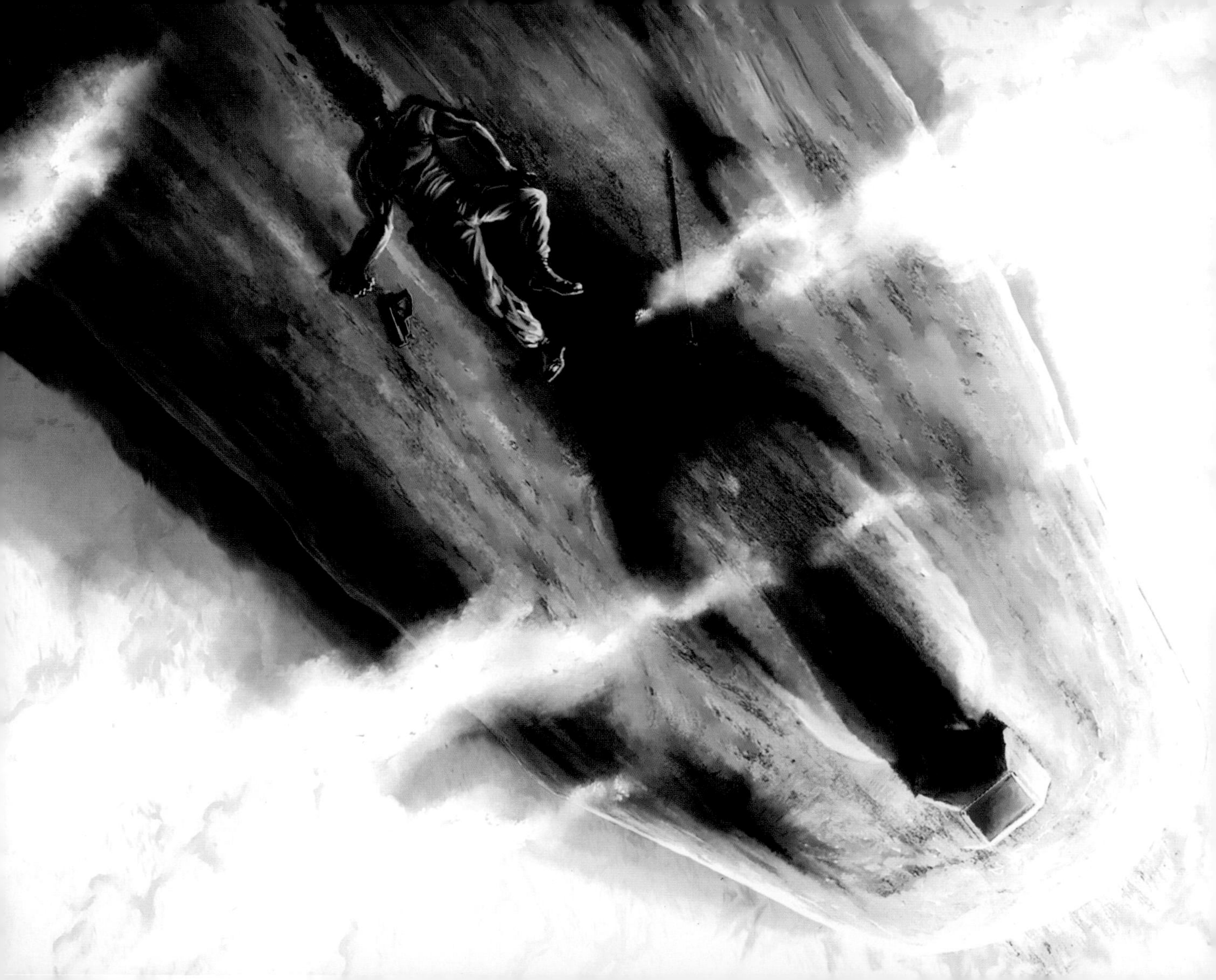

Earth had **pounded** the enemy into submission. Mankind promptly returned to **peacetime interests**. Historians began writing the glorious narrative of the decades-long war...**with humans as righteous victors and the aliens as cowardly failures**.

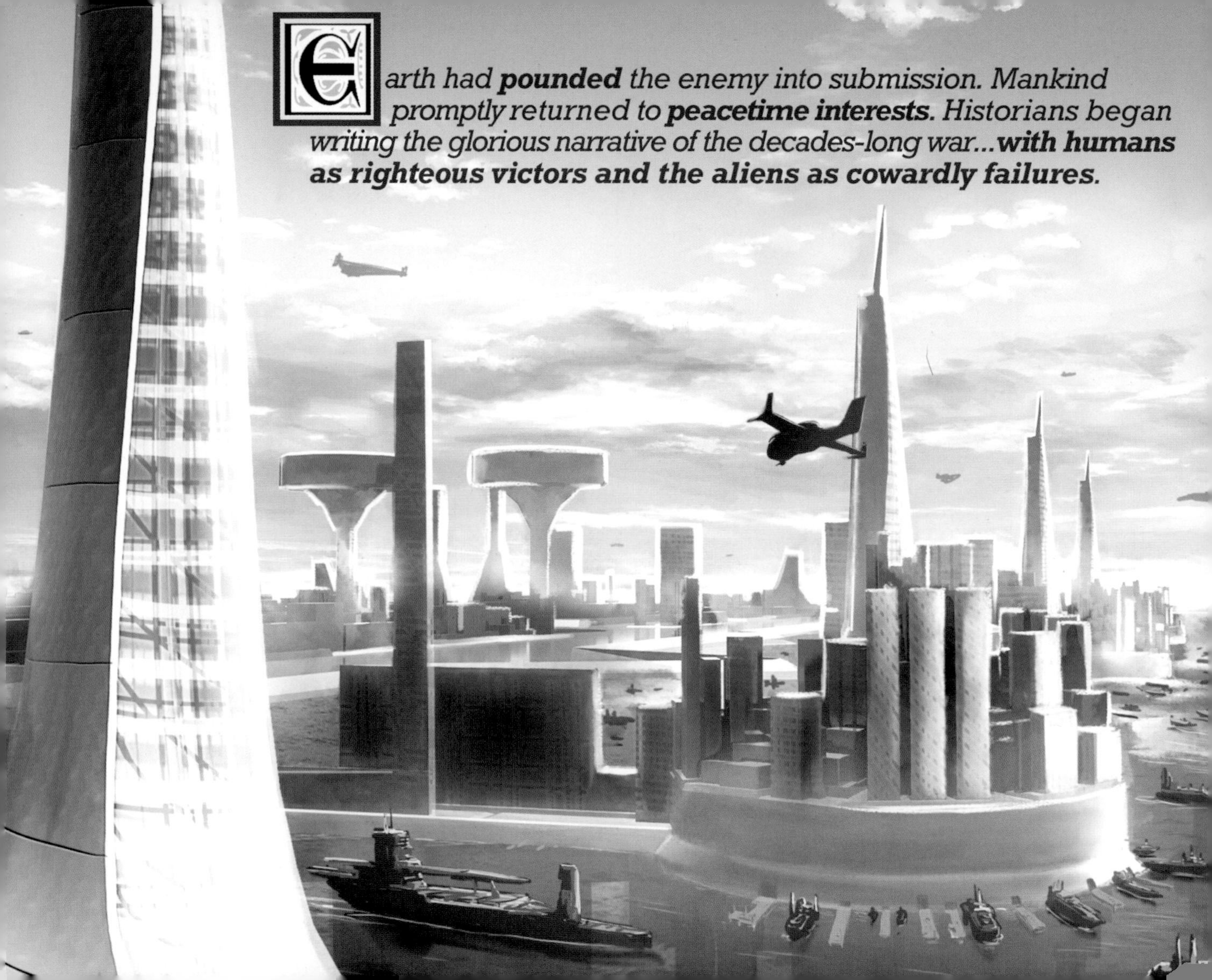

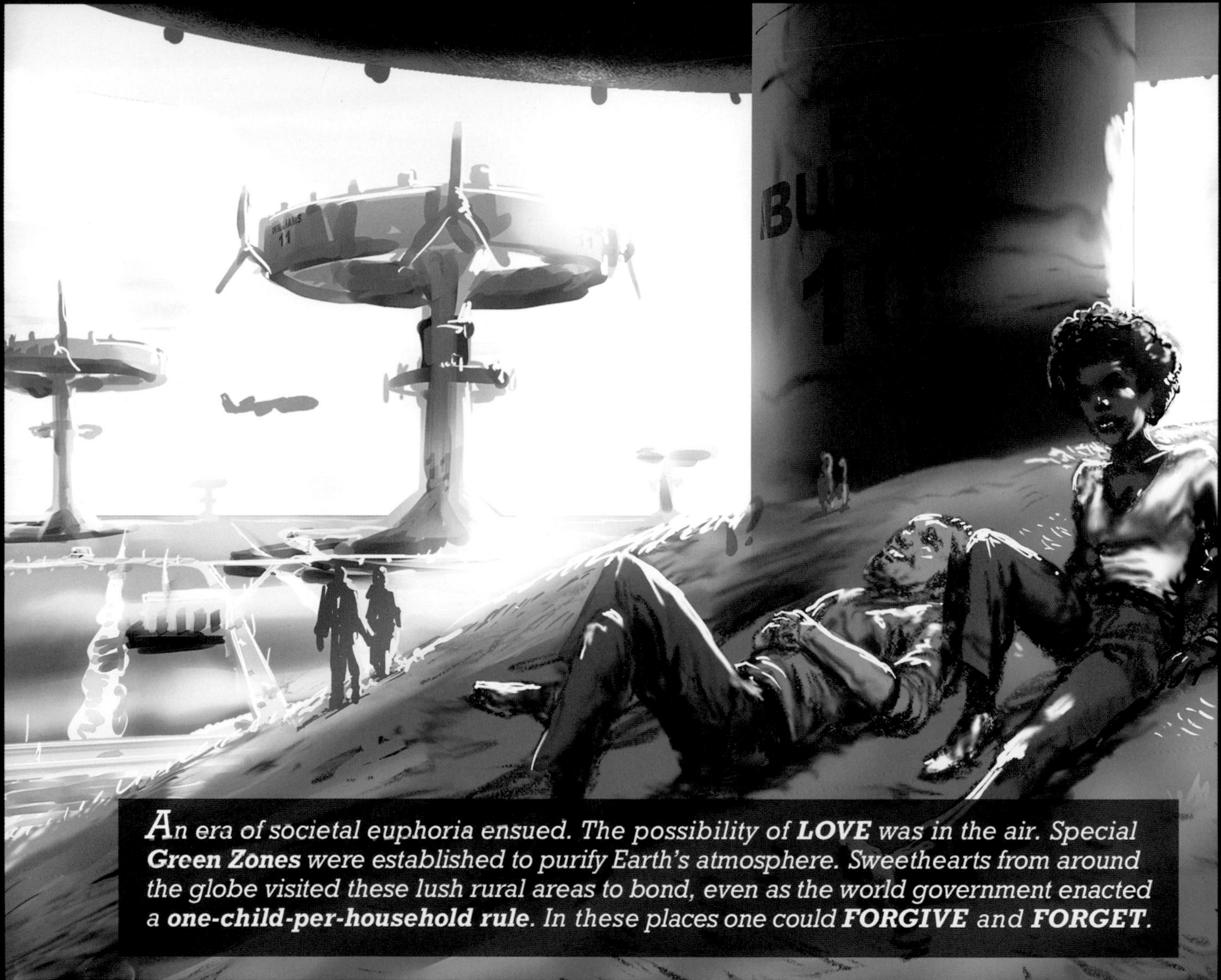
An era of societal euphoria ensued. The possibility of **LOVE** was in the air. Special **Green Zones** were established to purify Earth's atmosphere. Sweethearts from around the globe visited these lush rural areas to bond, even as the world government enacted a **one-child-per-household rule**. In these places one could **FORGIVE** and **FORGET**.

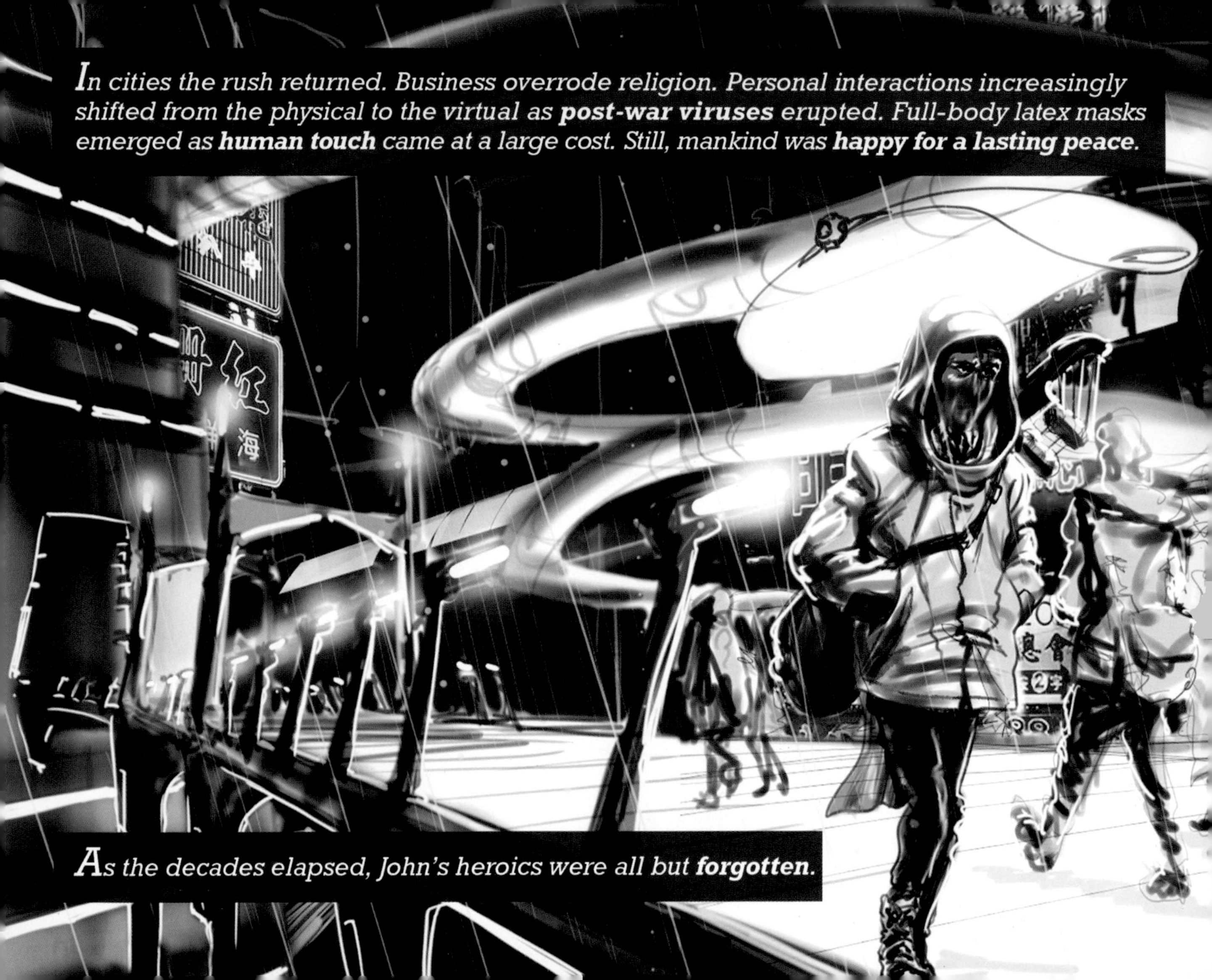
In cities the rush returned. Business overrode religion. Personal interactions increasingly shifted from the physical to the virtual as **post-war viruses** erupted. Full-body latex masks emerged as **human touch** came at a large cost. Still, mankind was **happy for a lasting peace**.
As the decades elapsed, John's heroics were all but **forgotten**.

Augmented reality had become reality to the populace. *The onslaught of addictive content —* ***geo-cosmo politics, cyborg sports, virtual housewives, mutant porn, home break-ins, surgery game shows,*** **The Simpsons*,*** ***etc.*** *— brought families and communities together in a perpetual digital stupor.*

Complacent and lulled to sleep.

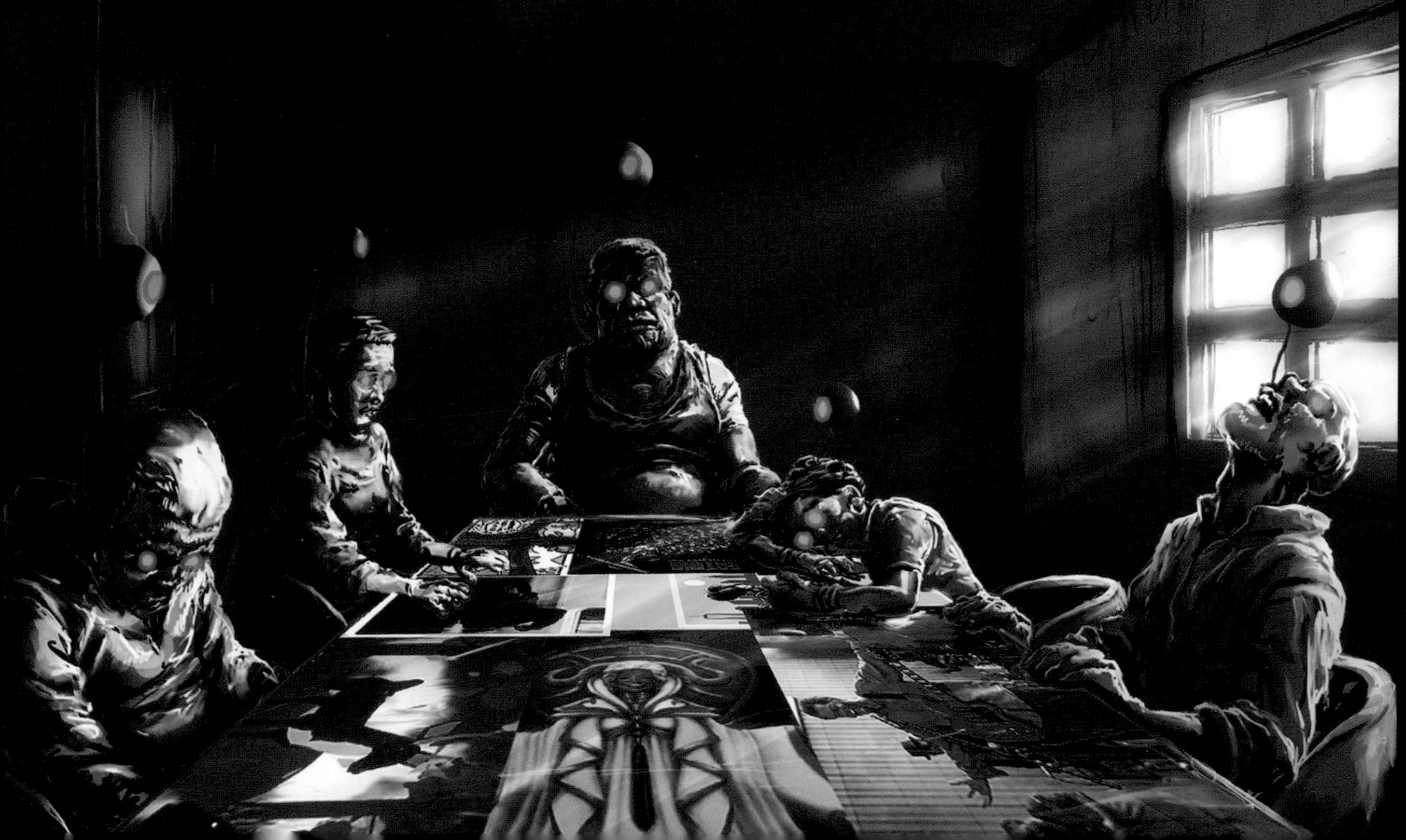

A mortal sleep.

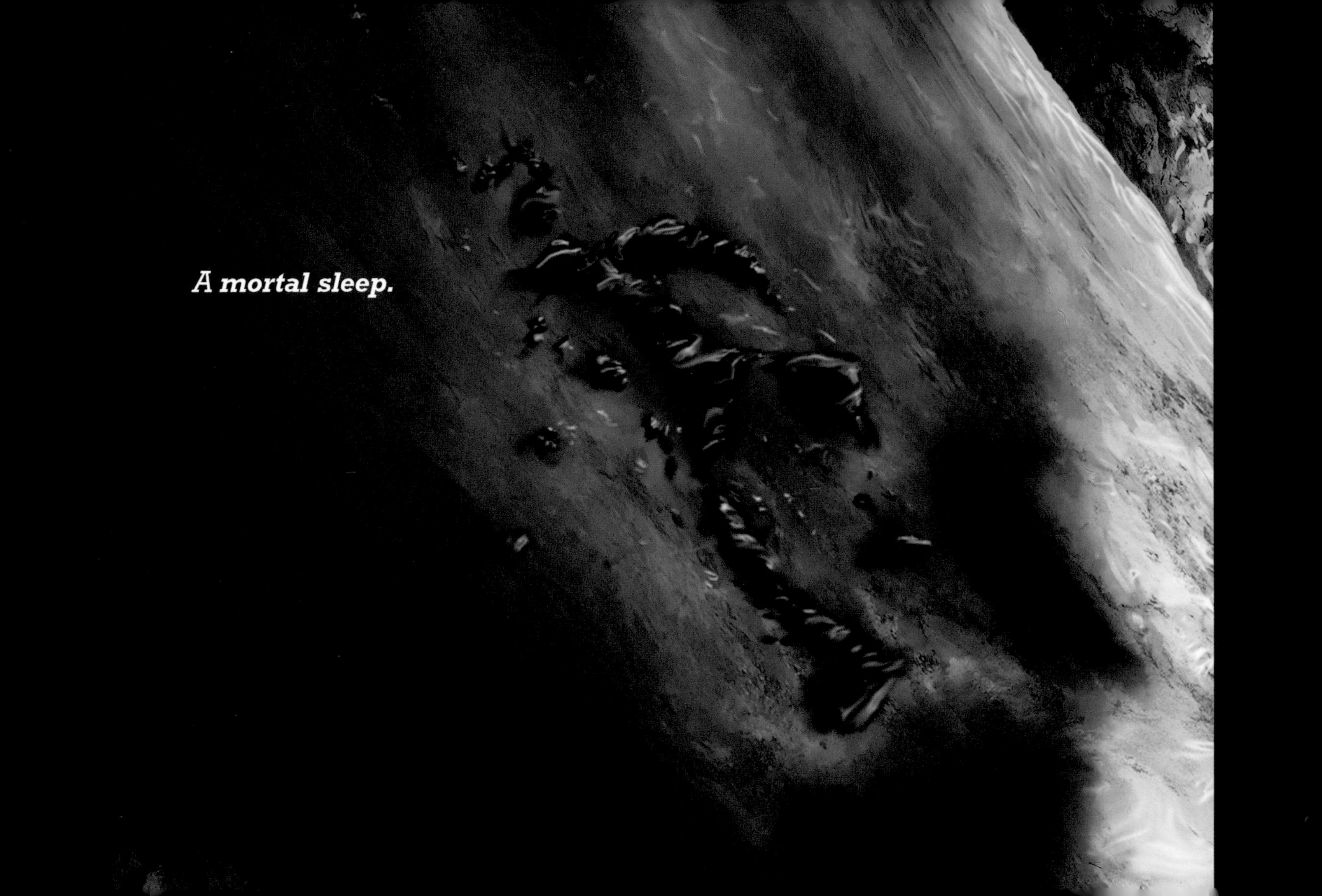

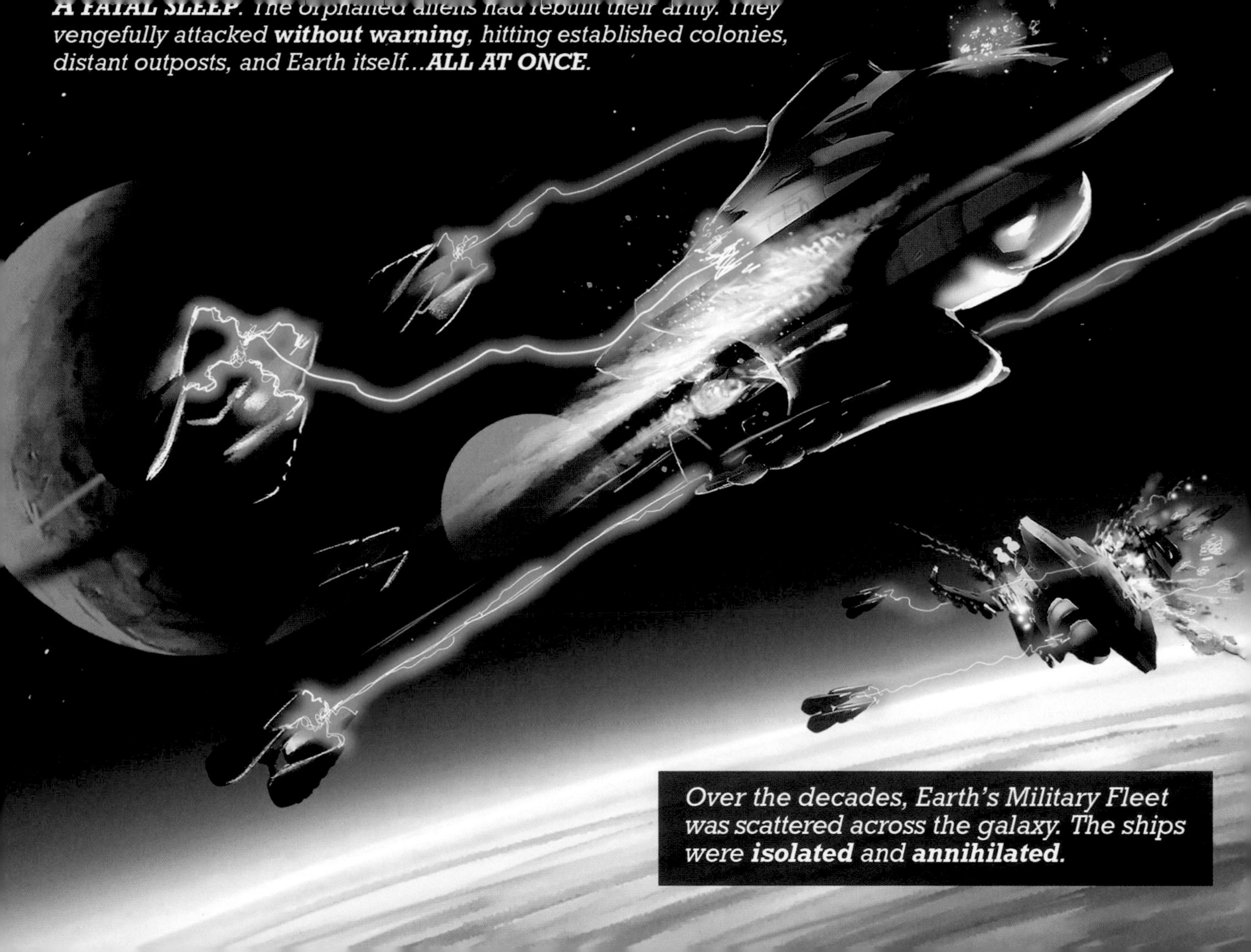
A FATAL SLEEP. The orphaned aliens had rebuilt their army. They vengefully attacked without warning, hitting established colonies, distant outposts, and Earth itself...ALL AT ONCE.
Over the decades, Earth's Military Fleet was scattered across the galaxy. The ships were isolated and annihilated.

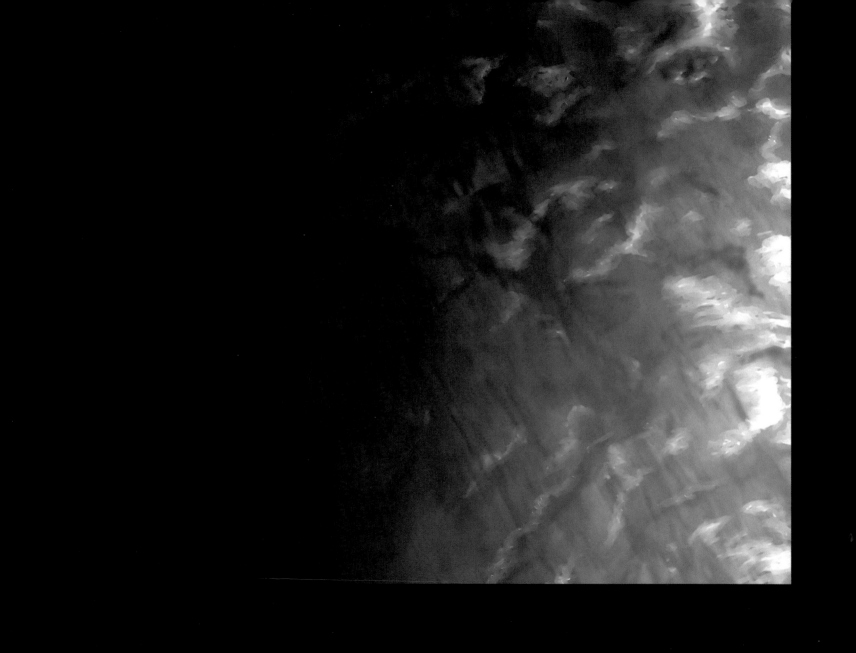

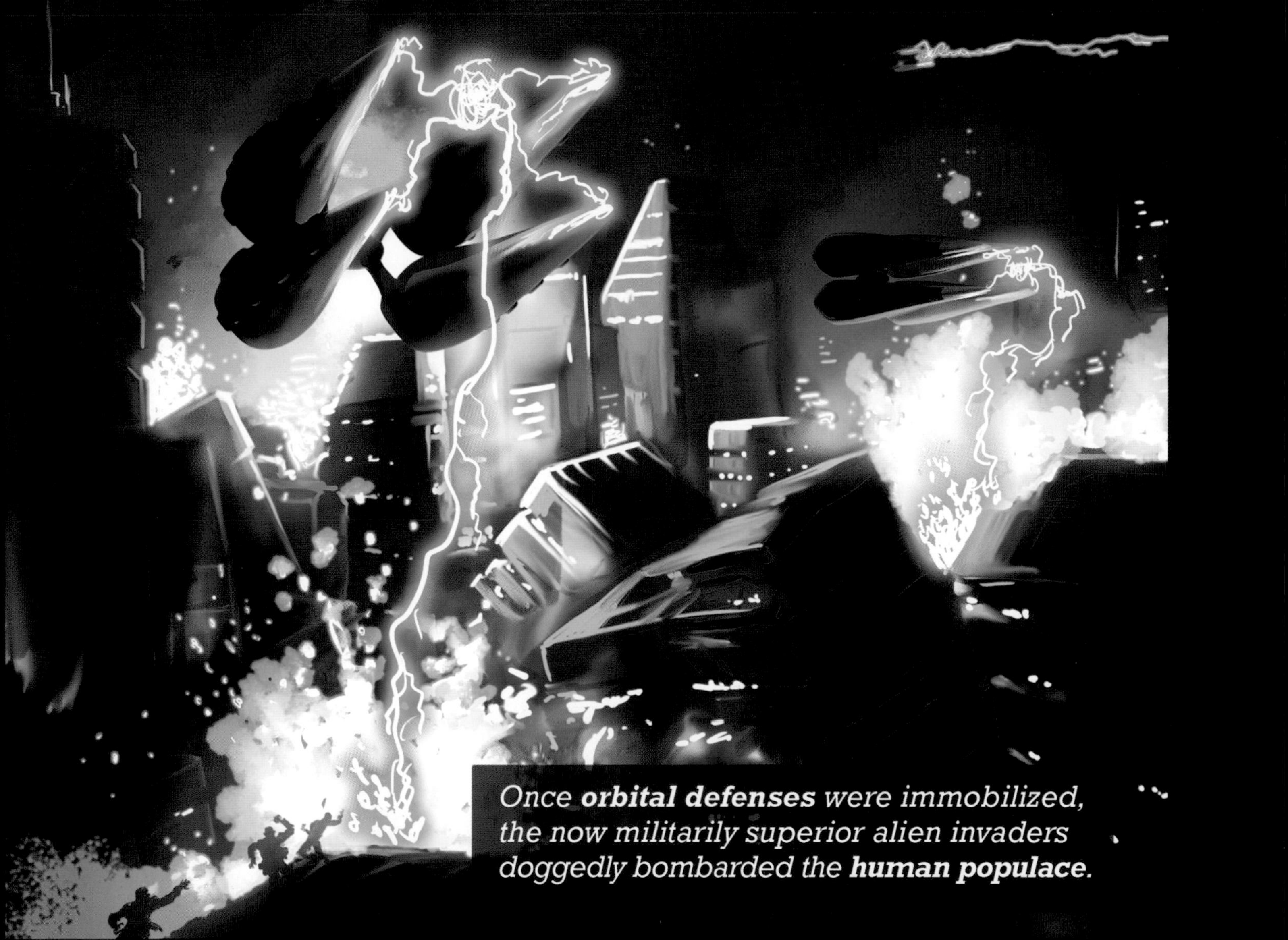
Once **orbital defenses** were immobilized,
the now militarily superior alien invaders
doggedly bombarded the **human populace**.

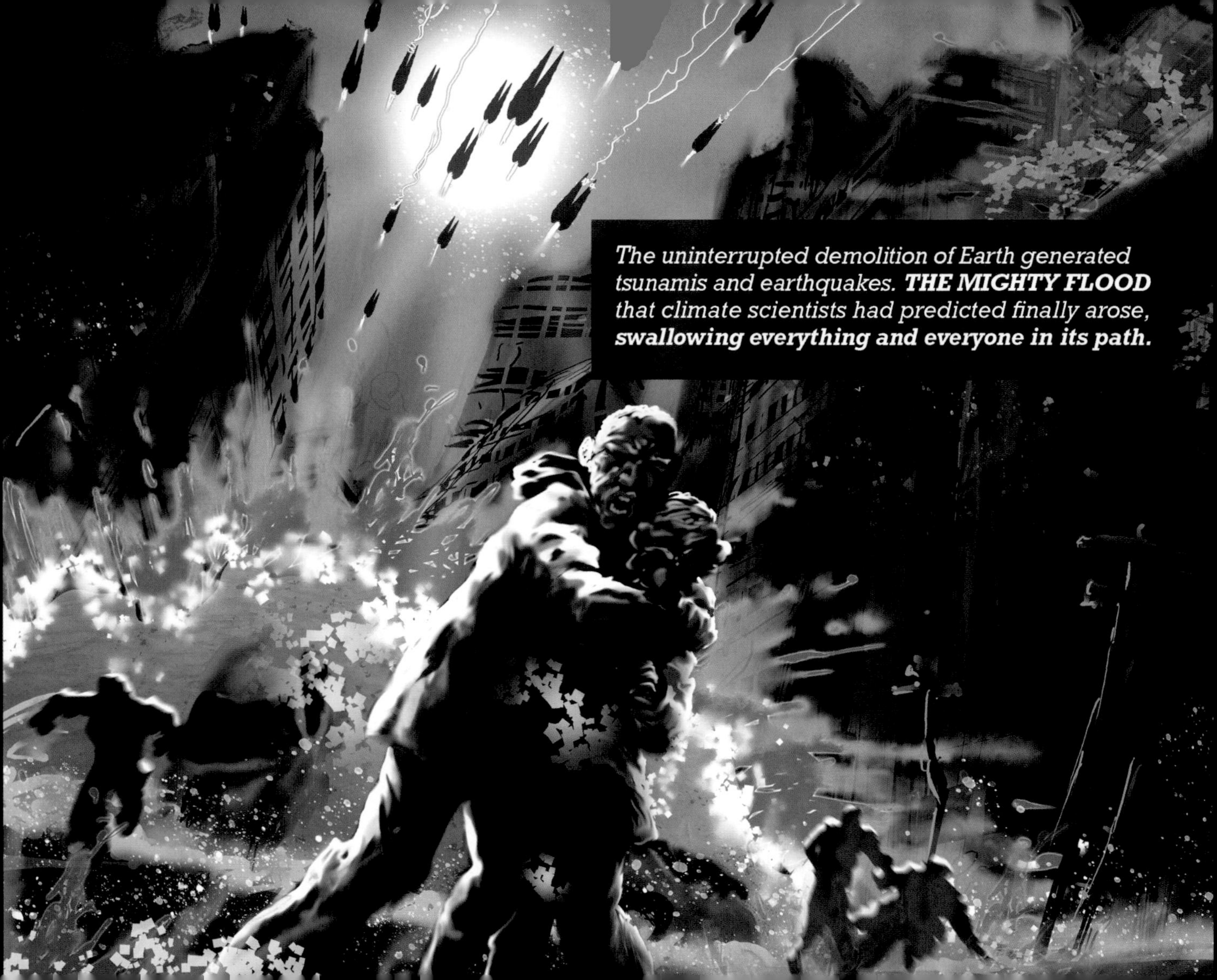
The uninterrupted demolition of Earth generated tsunamis and earthquakes. **THE MIGHTY FLOOD** that climate scientists had predicted finally arose, **swallowing everything and everyone in its path.**

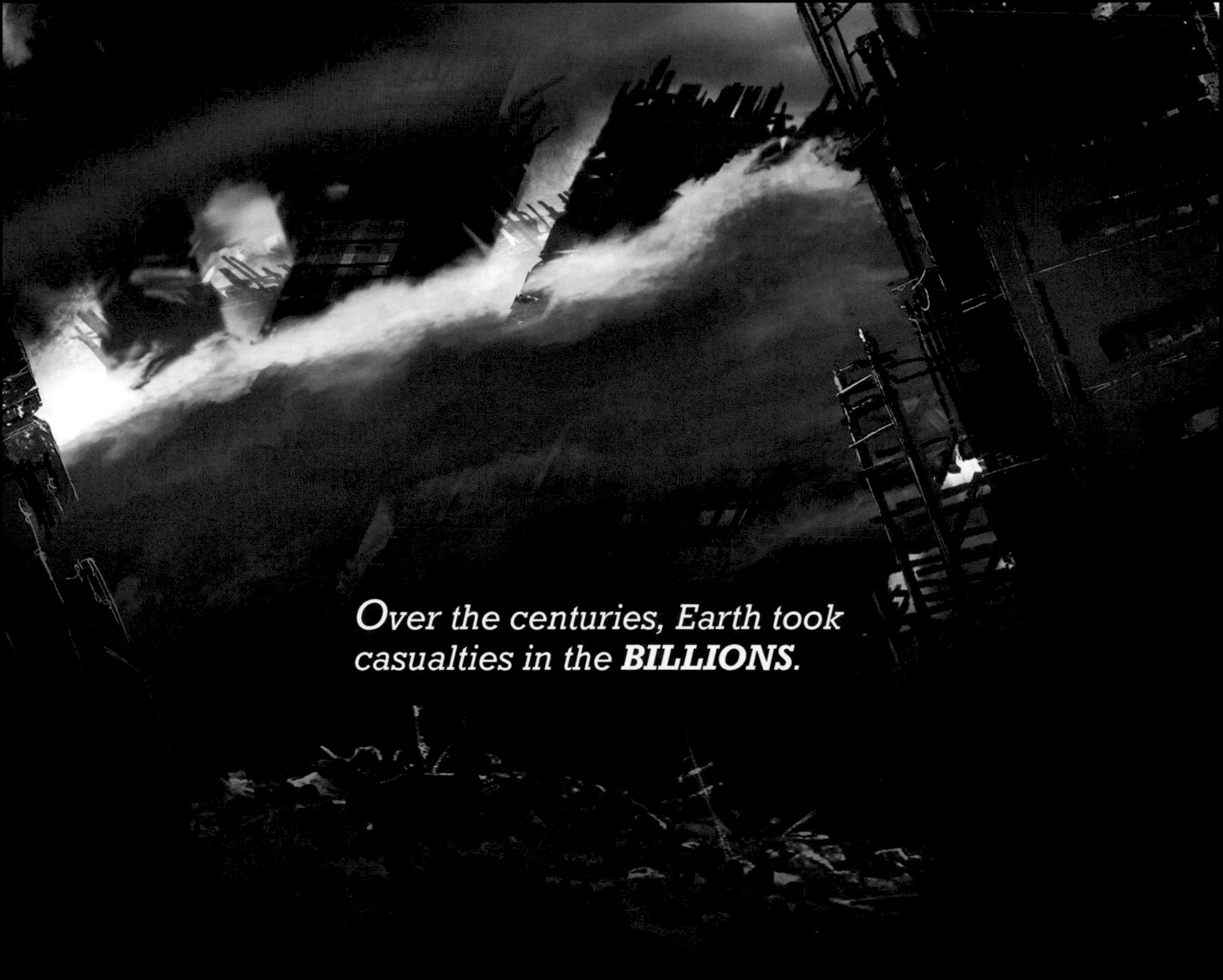
Over the centuries, Earth took casualties in the BILLIONS.

Ọba!

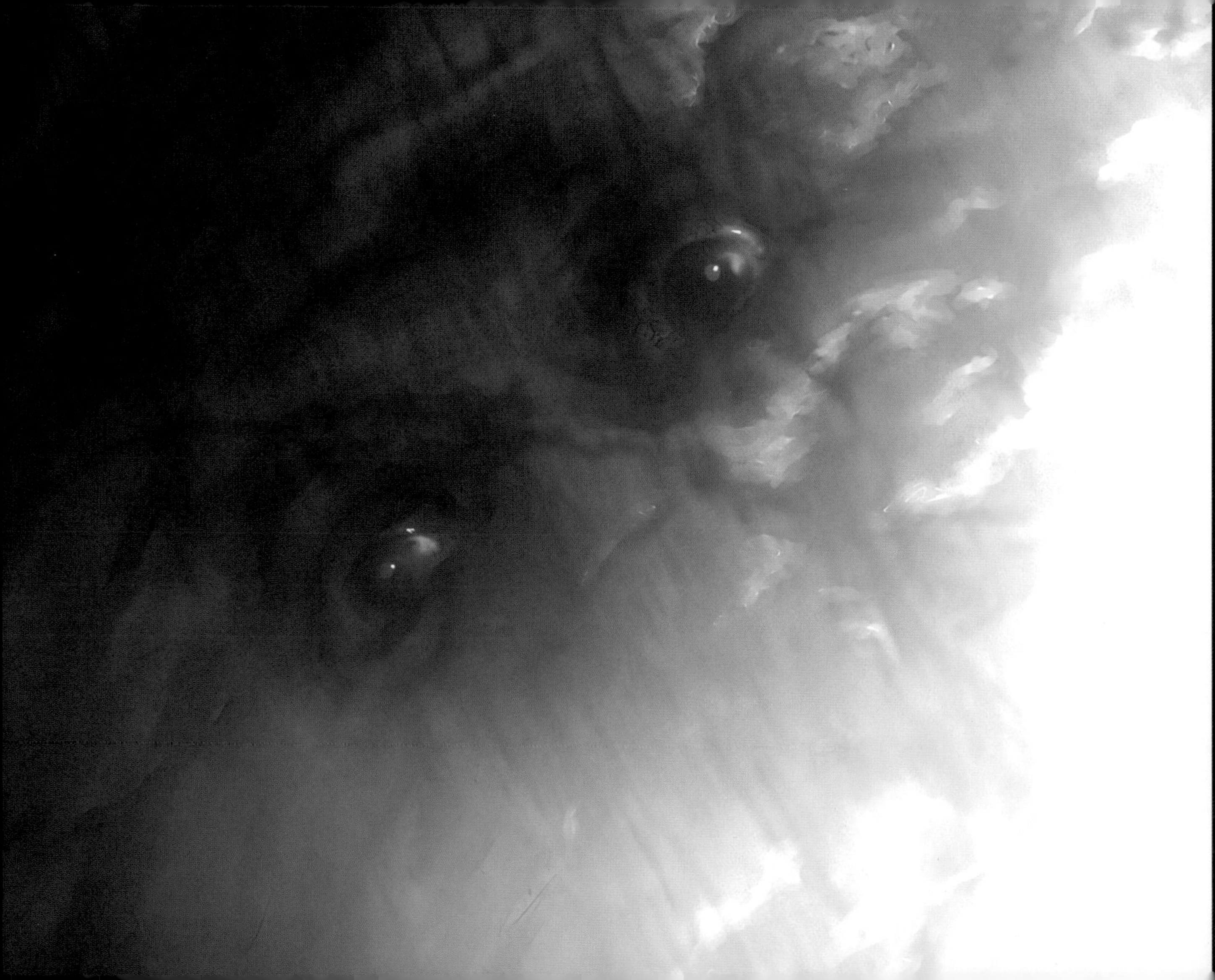

A Thousand years had passed. The Sun and its sibling stars emitted life and light giving radiation well into the universe's middle age. All forms of gravity and nuclear fire had enabled it to fulfill its biological imperative.

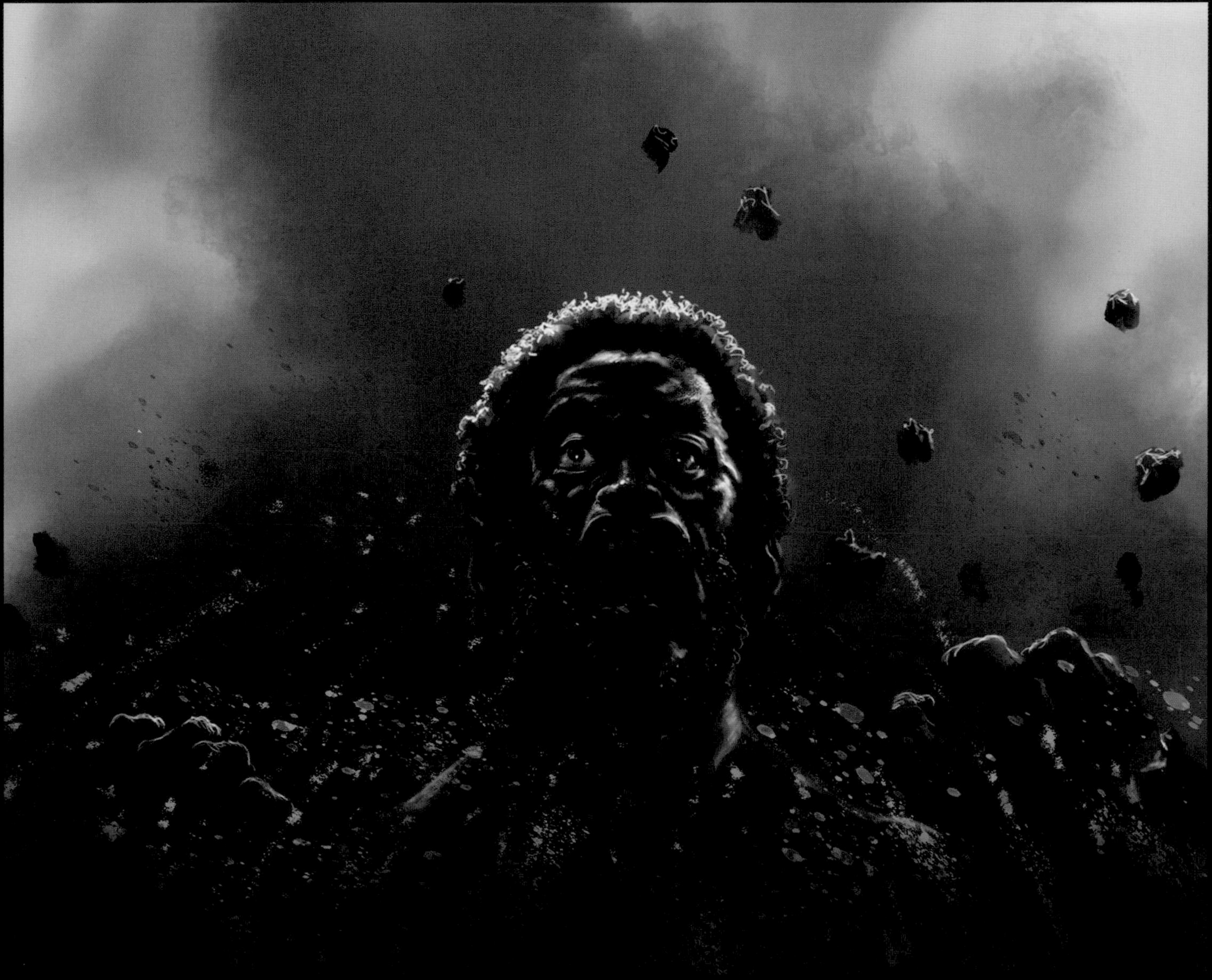

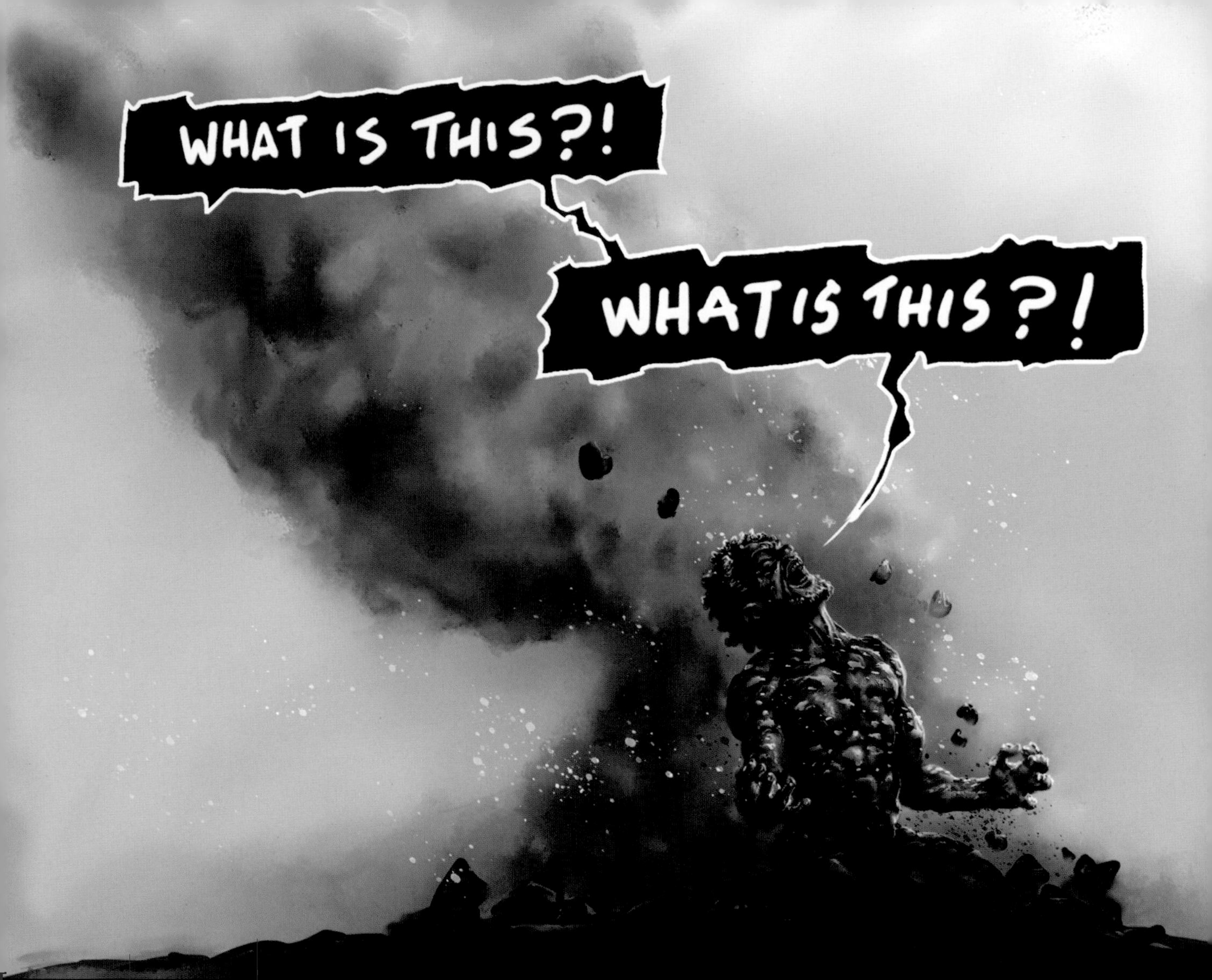
WHAT IS THIS?!
WHAT IS THIS?!

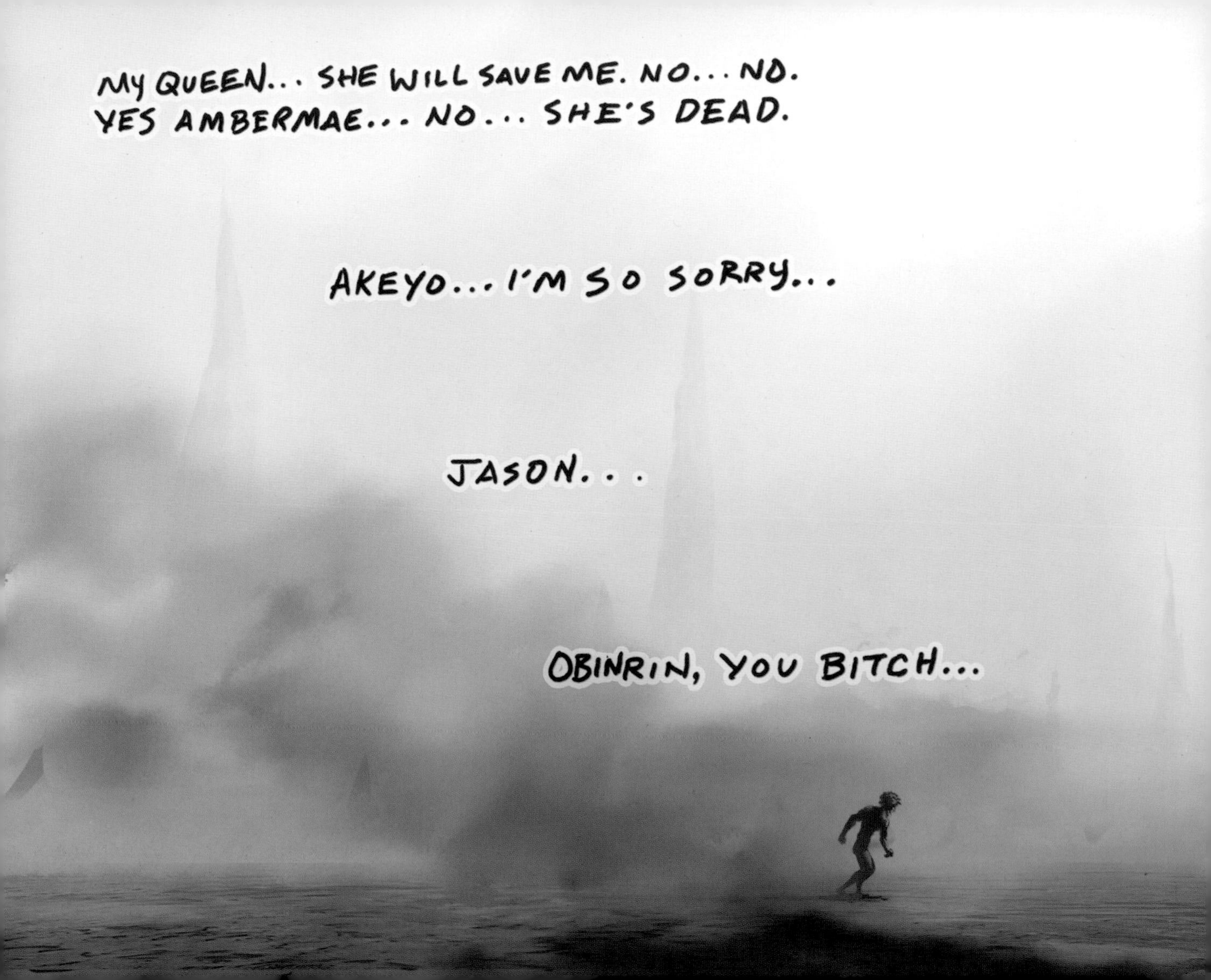
MY QUEEN... SHE WILL SAVE ME. NO... NO.
YES AMBERMAE... NO... SHE'S DEAD.
AKEYO... I'M SO SORRY...
JASON...
OBINRIN, YOU BITCH...

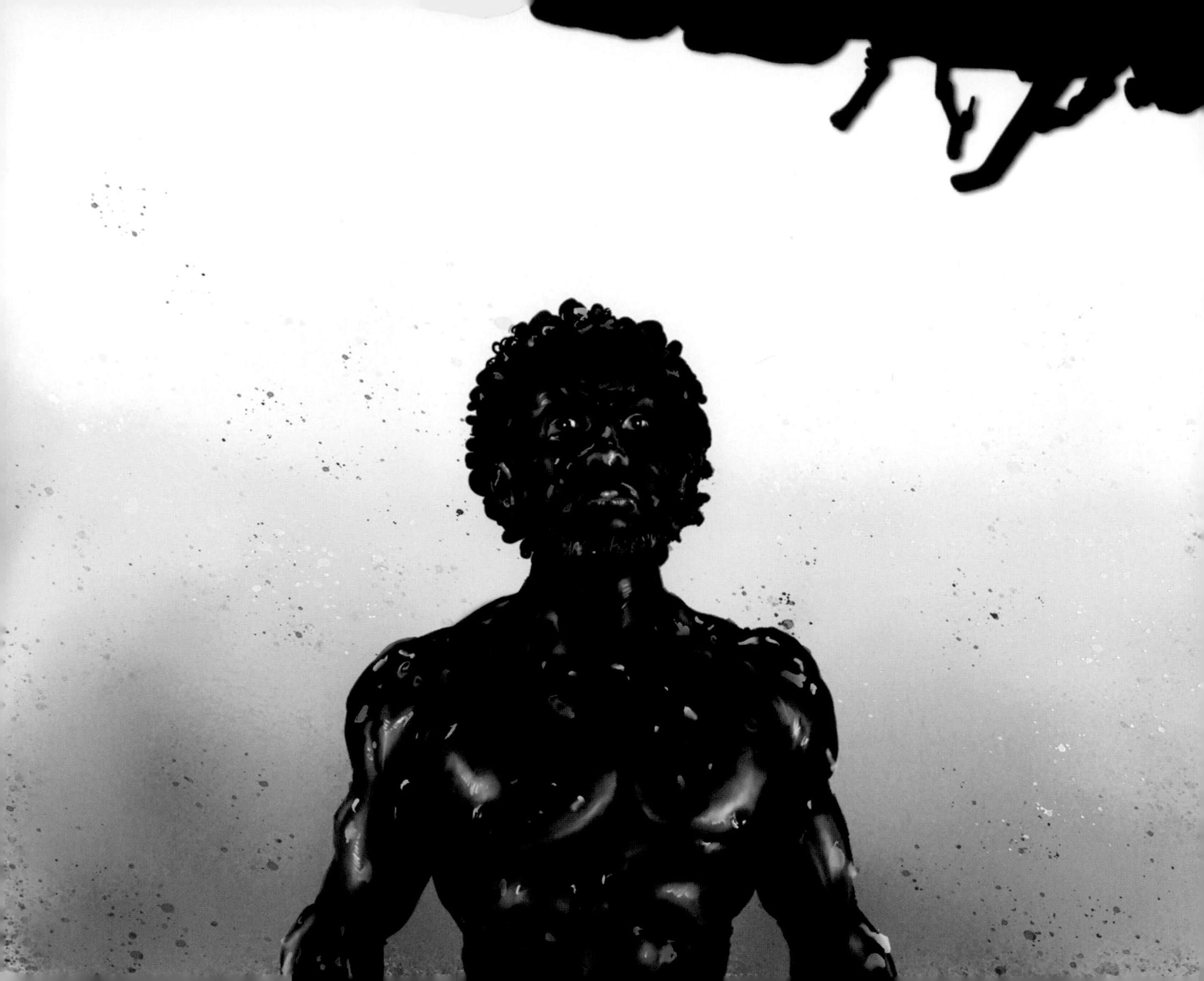

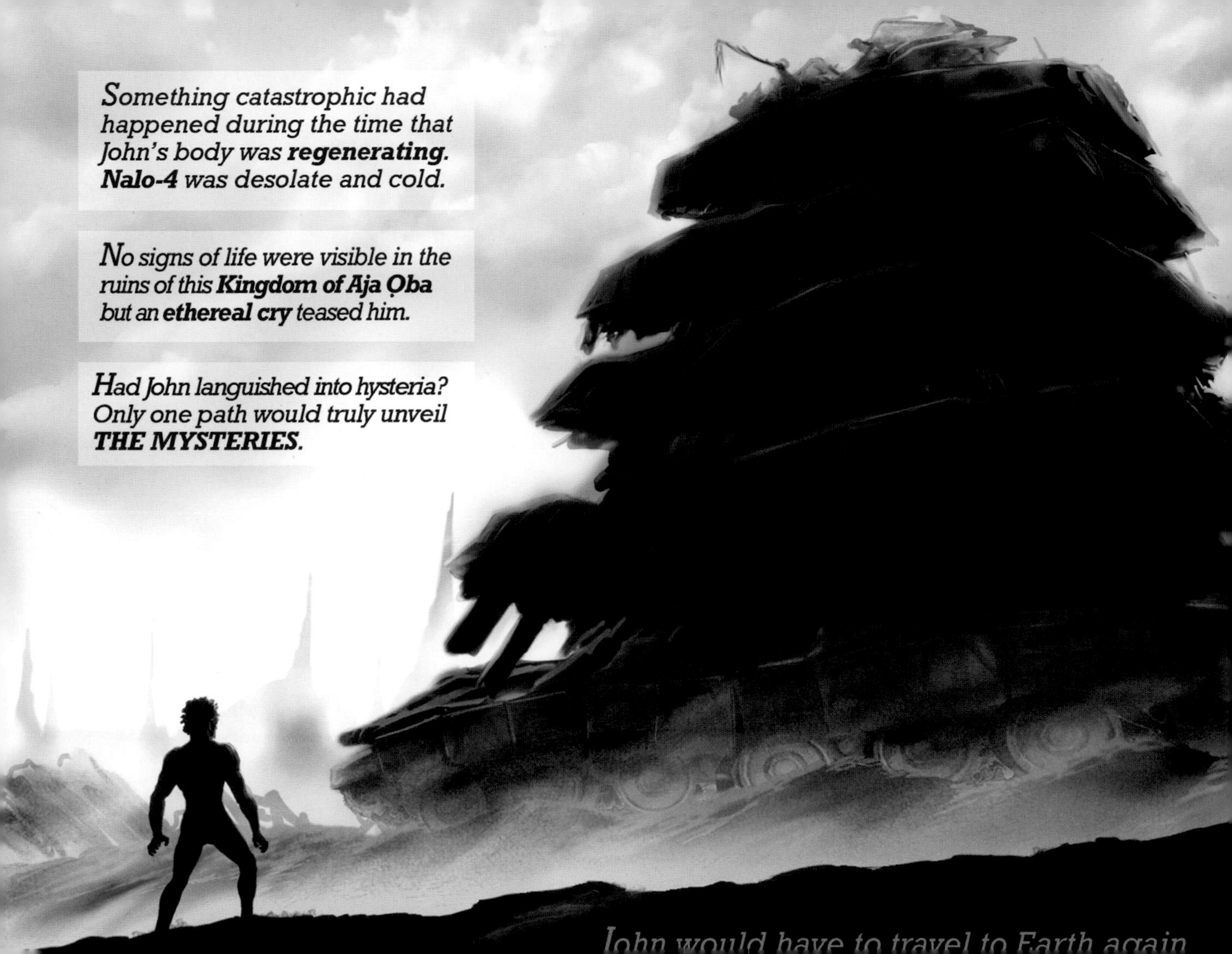
Something catastrophic had happened during the time that John's body was **regenerating**. **Nalo-4** was desolate and cold.
No signs of life were visible in the ruins of this **Kingdom of Aja Ọba** but an **ethereal cry** teased him.
Had John languished into hysteria? Only one path would truly unveil **THE MYSTERIES**.
John would have to travel to Earth again

After

some

modifications,

John was

able to revive

a

***Derelict Ship*.**

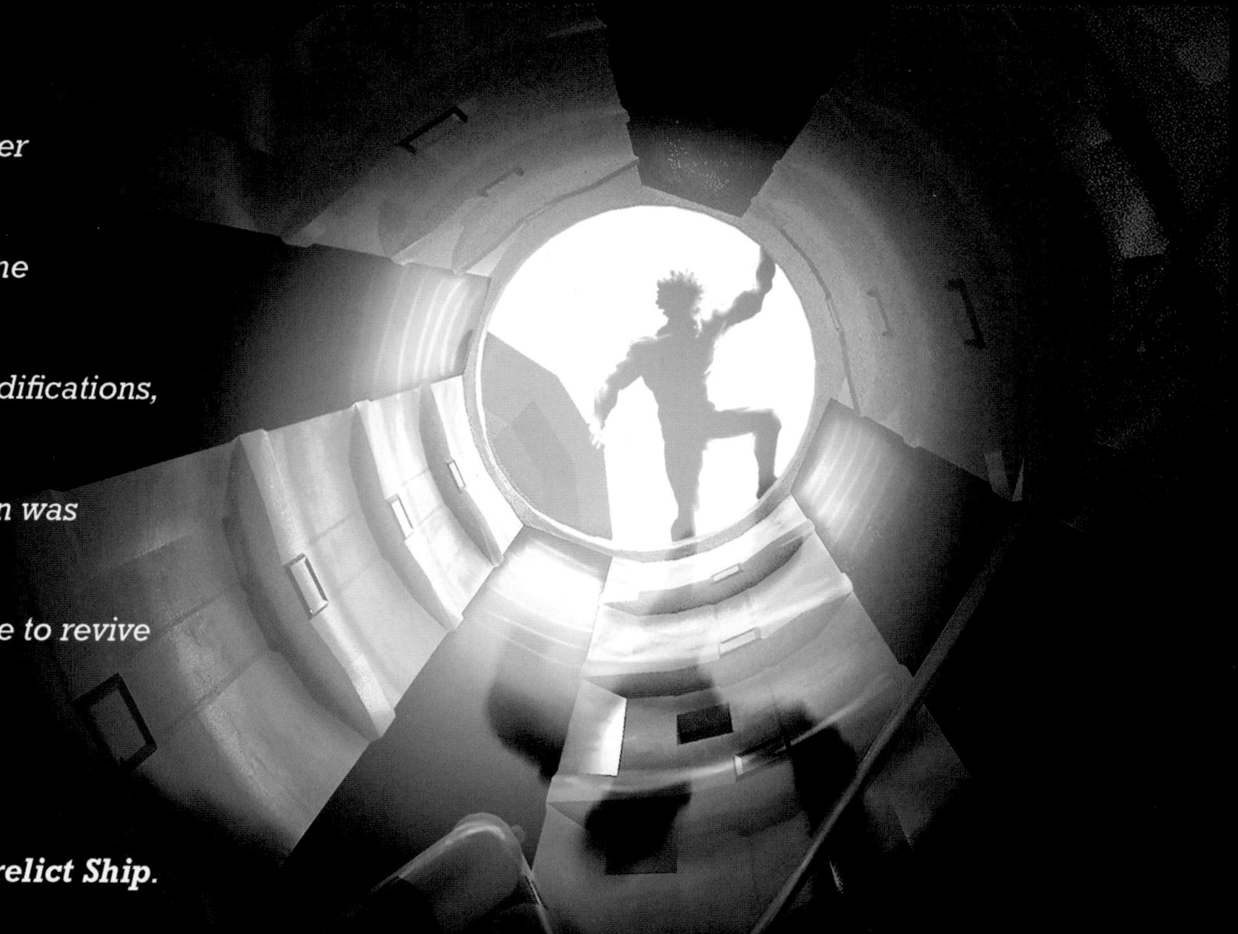

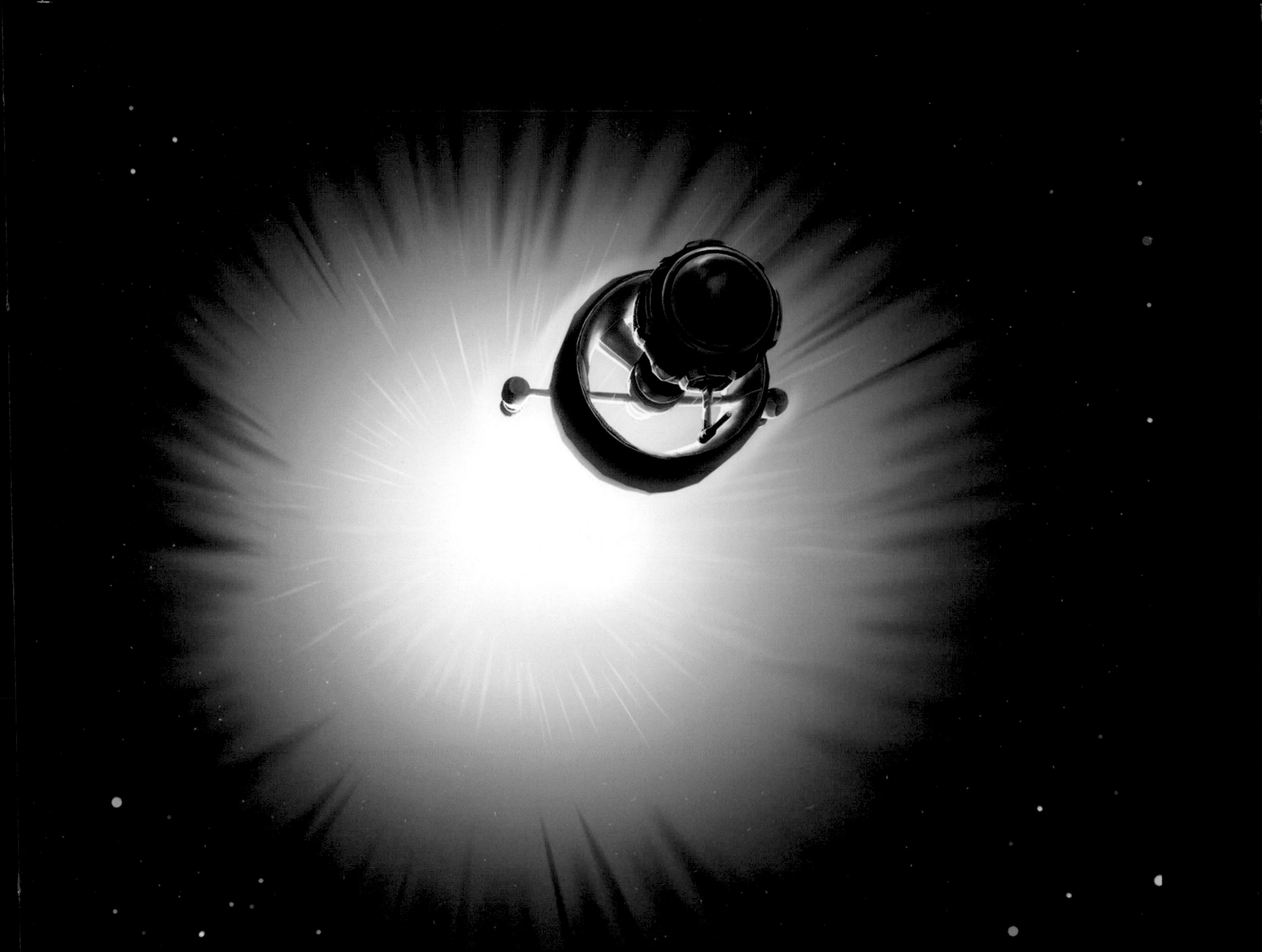

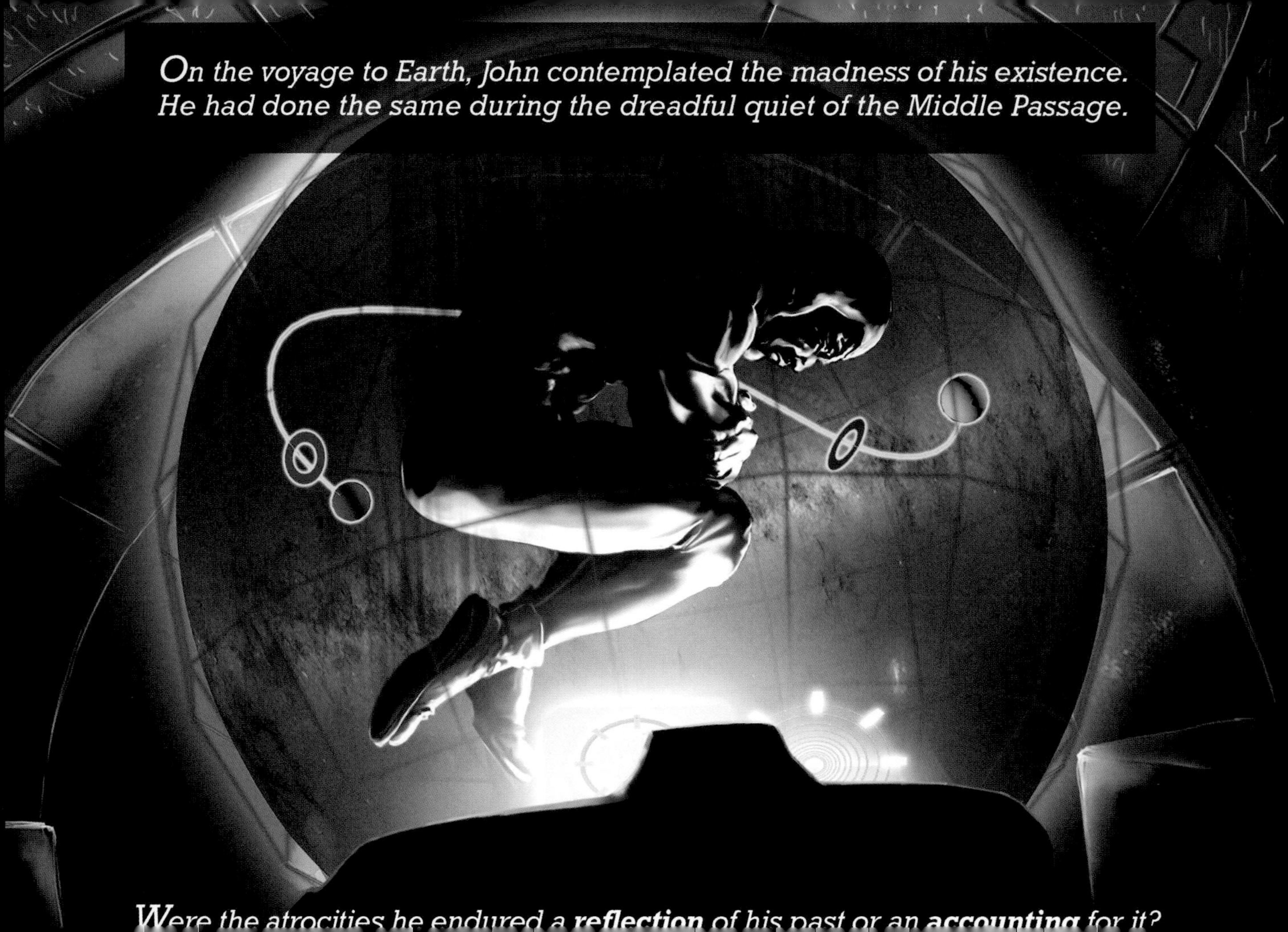
On the voyage to Earth, John contemplated the madness of his existence.
He had done the same during the dreadful quiet of the Middle Passage.
Were the atrocities he endured a **reflection** of his past or an **accounting** for it?

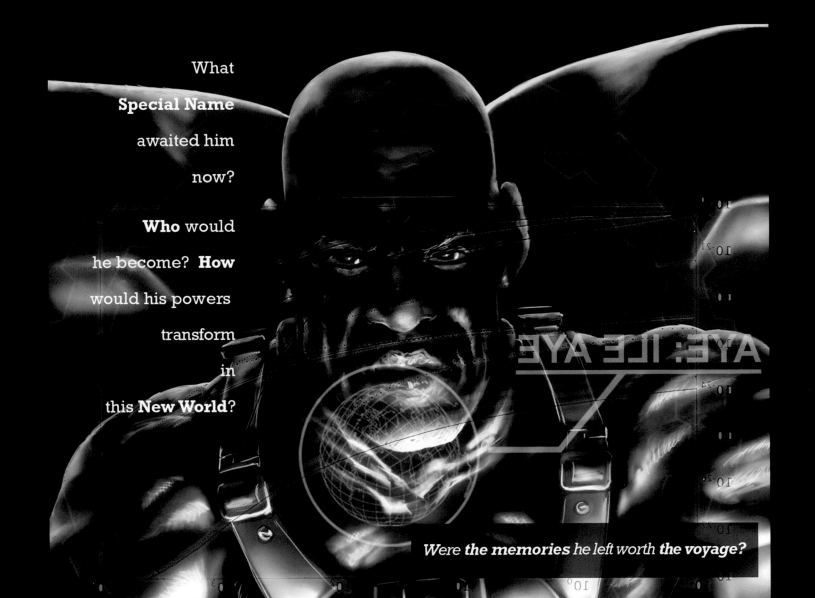

What **Special Name** awaited him now?

Who would he become? **How** would his powers transform in this **New World**?

*Were **the memories** he left worth **the voyage**?*

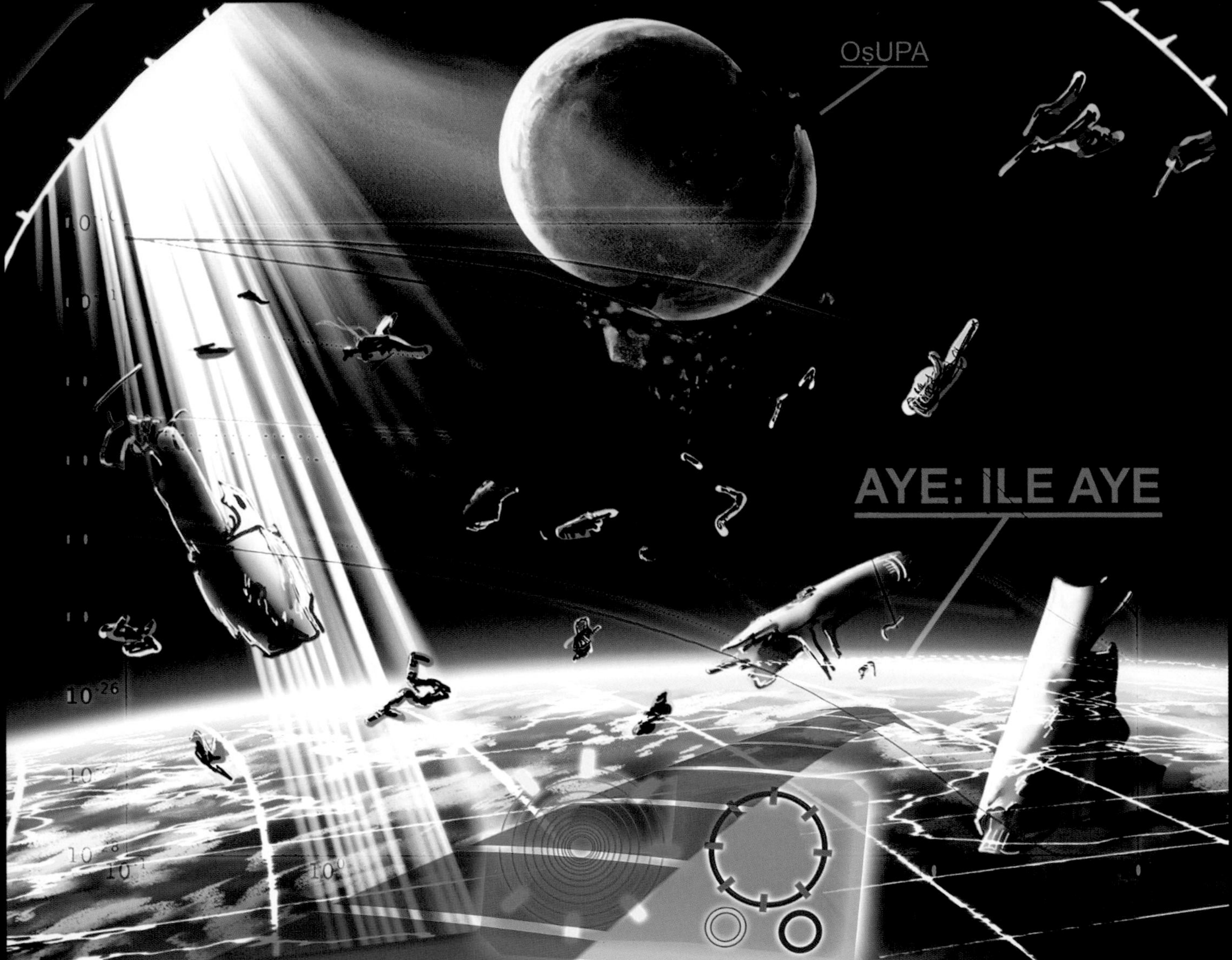

OṣUPA
AYE: ILE AYE

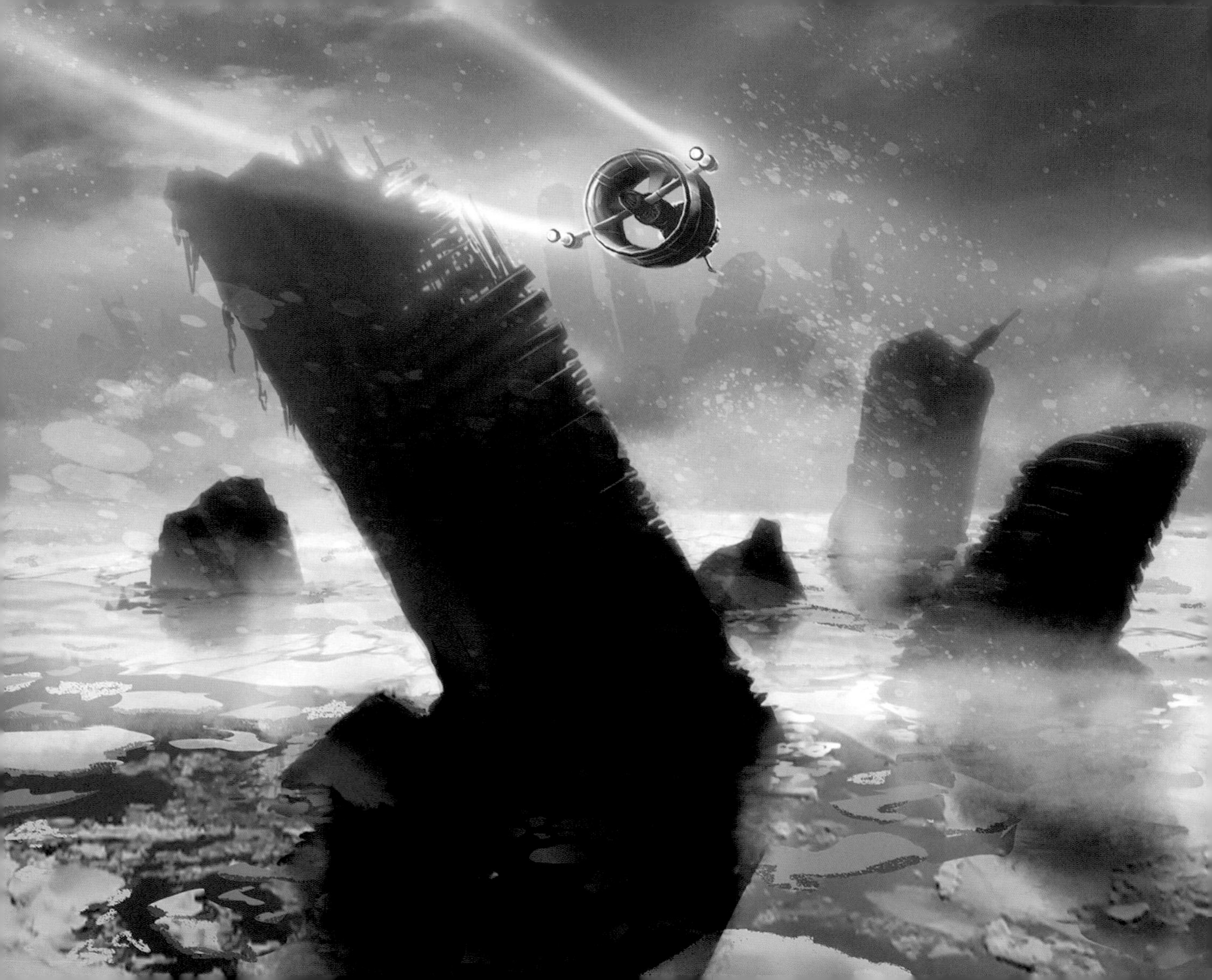

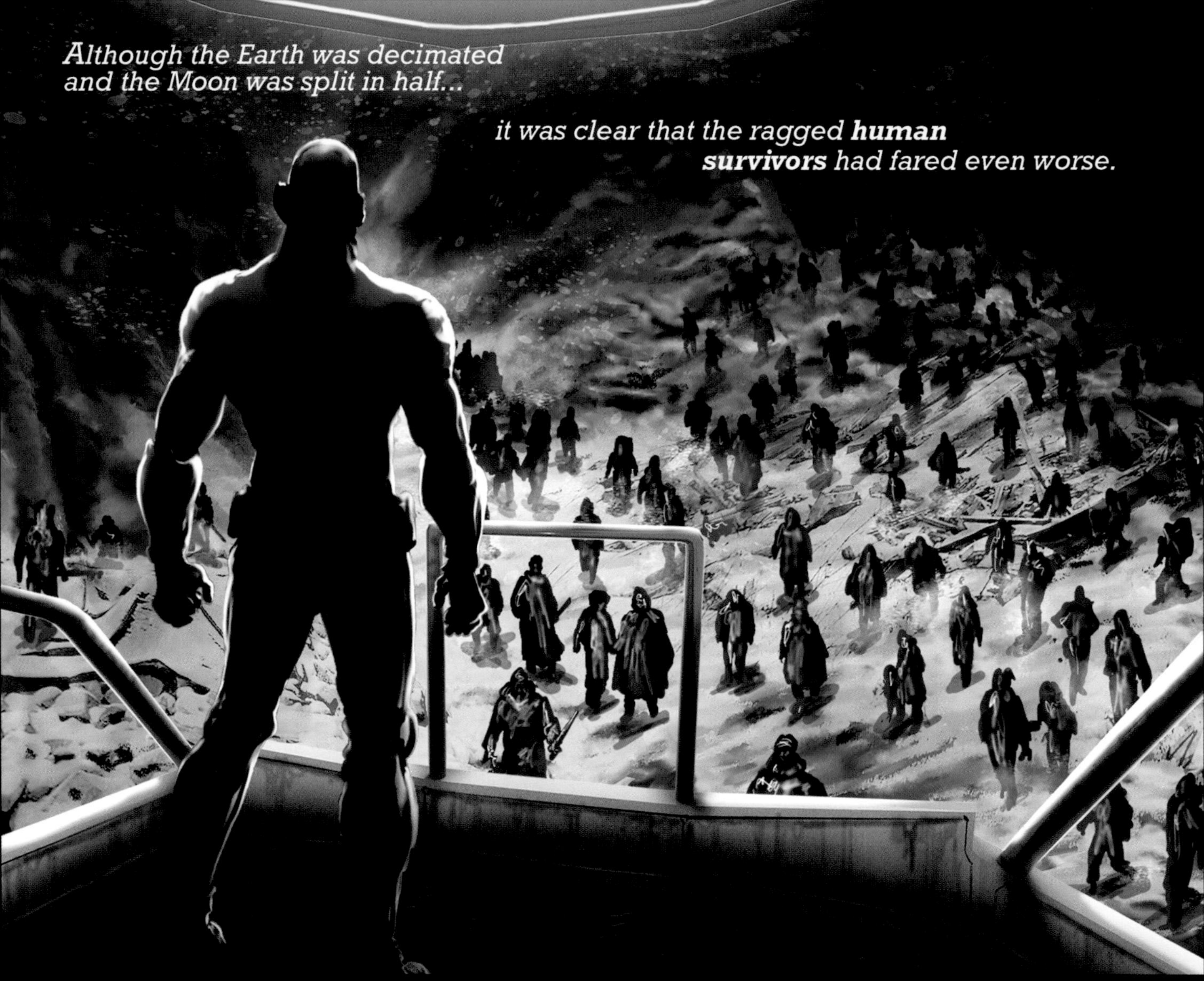
Although the Earth was decimated and the Moon was split in half...
it was clear that the ragged **human survivors** had fared even worse.

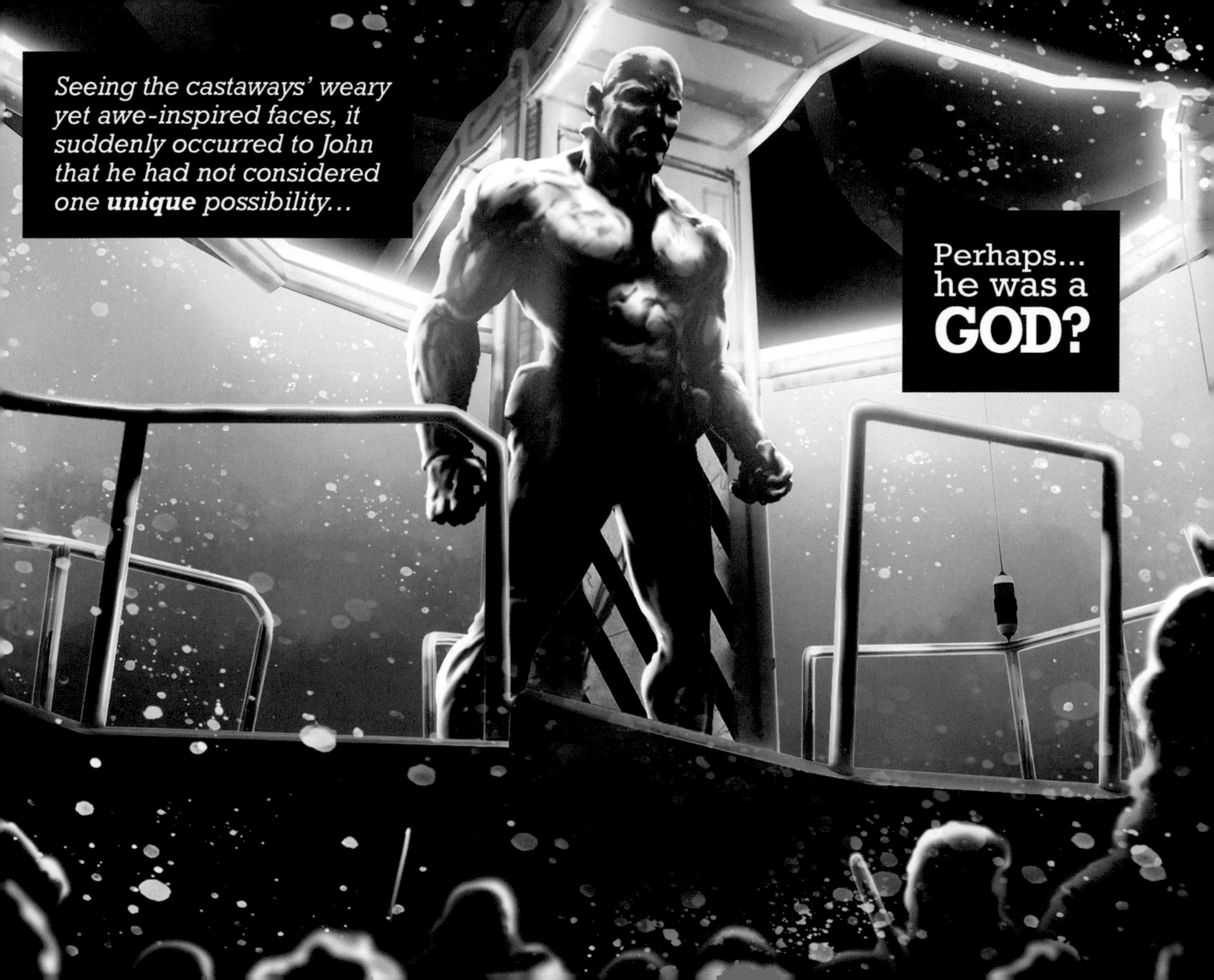

Seeing the castaways' weary yet awe-inspired faces, it suddenly occurred to John that he had not considered one **unique** possibility...
Perhaps... he was a **GOD?**

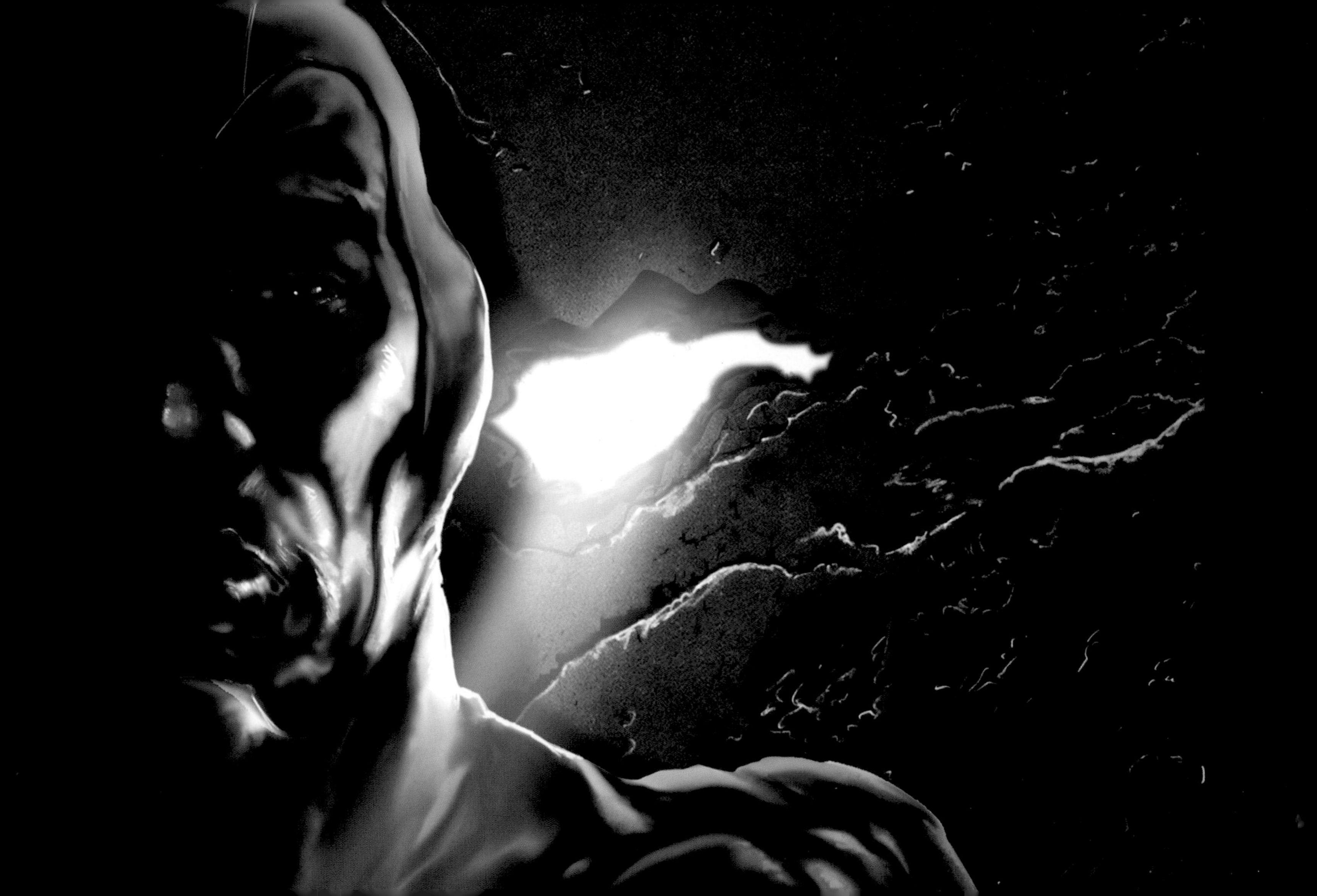

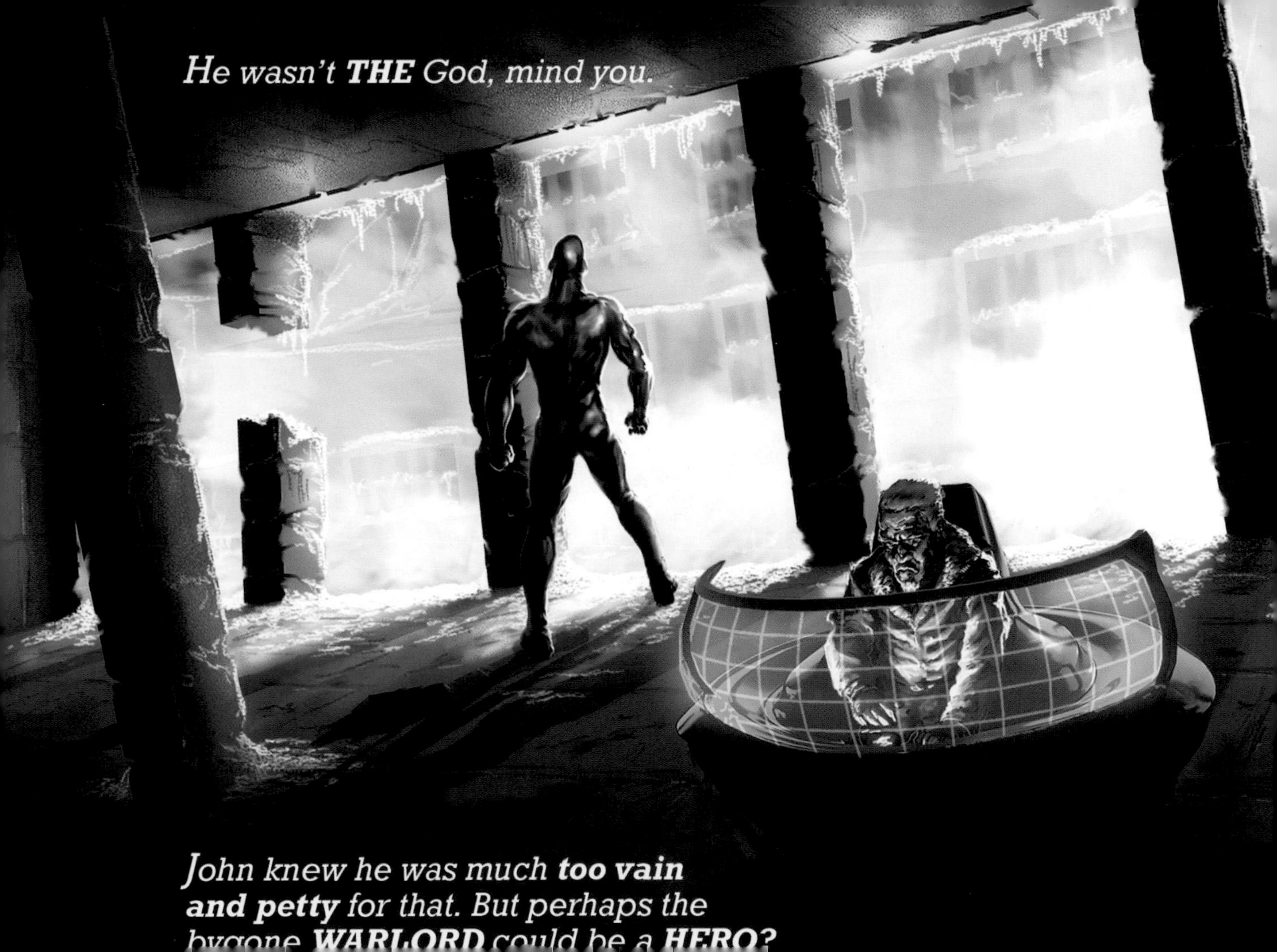
He wasn't ***THE*** *God, mind you.*
John knew he was much ***too vain and petty*** *for that. But perhaps the bygone* ***WARLORD*** *could be a* ***HERO?***

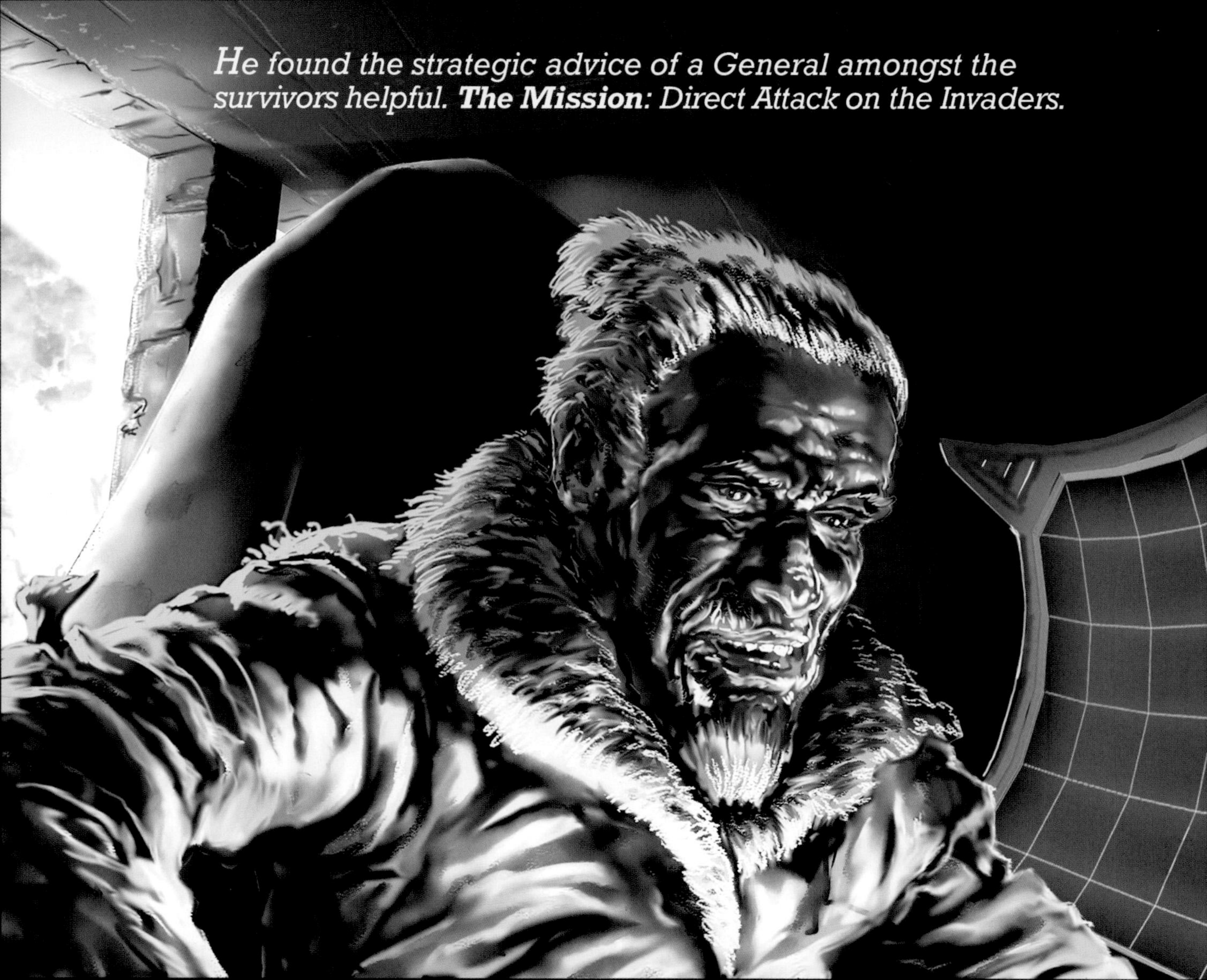
He found the strategic advice of a General amongst the survivors helpful. The Mission: Direct Attack on the Invaders.

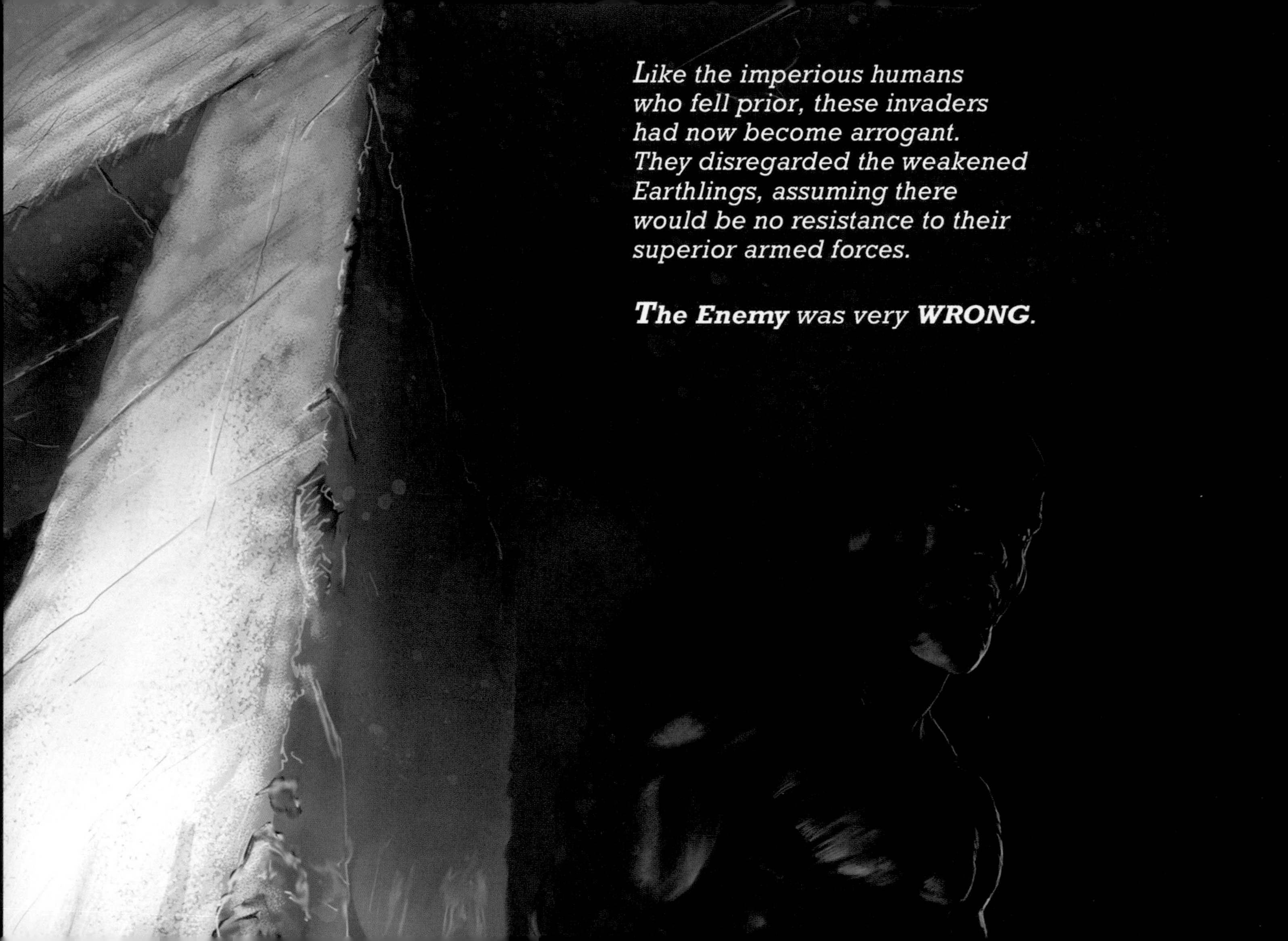
Like the imperious humans who fell prior, these invaders had now become arrogant. They disregarded the weakened Earthlings, assuming there would be no resistance to their superior armed forces.
The Enemy was very **WRONG**.

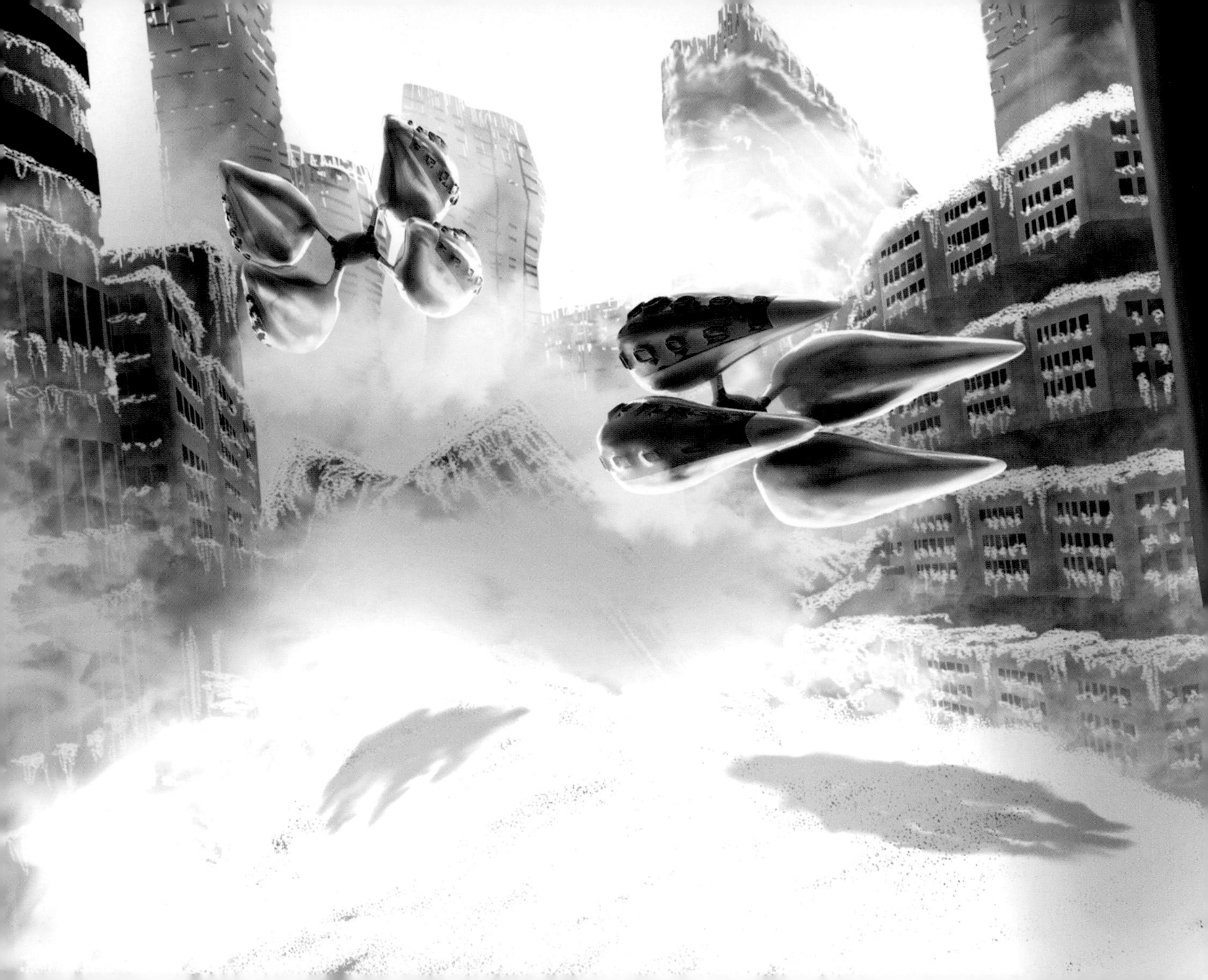

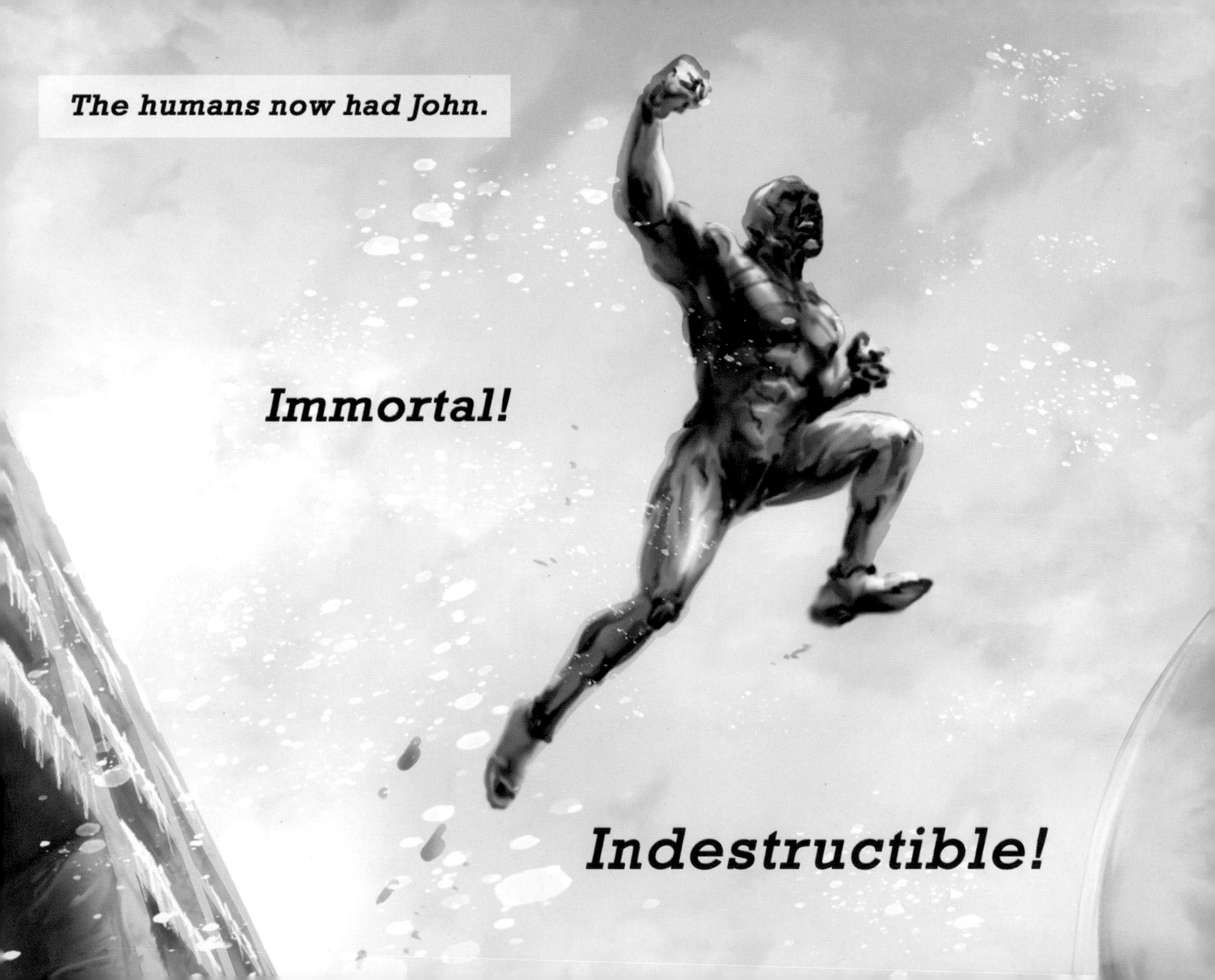
The humans now had John.
Immortal!
Indestructible!

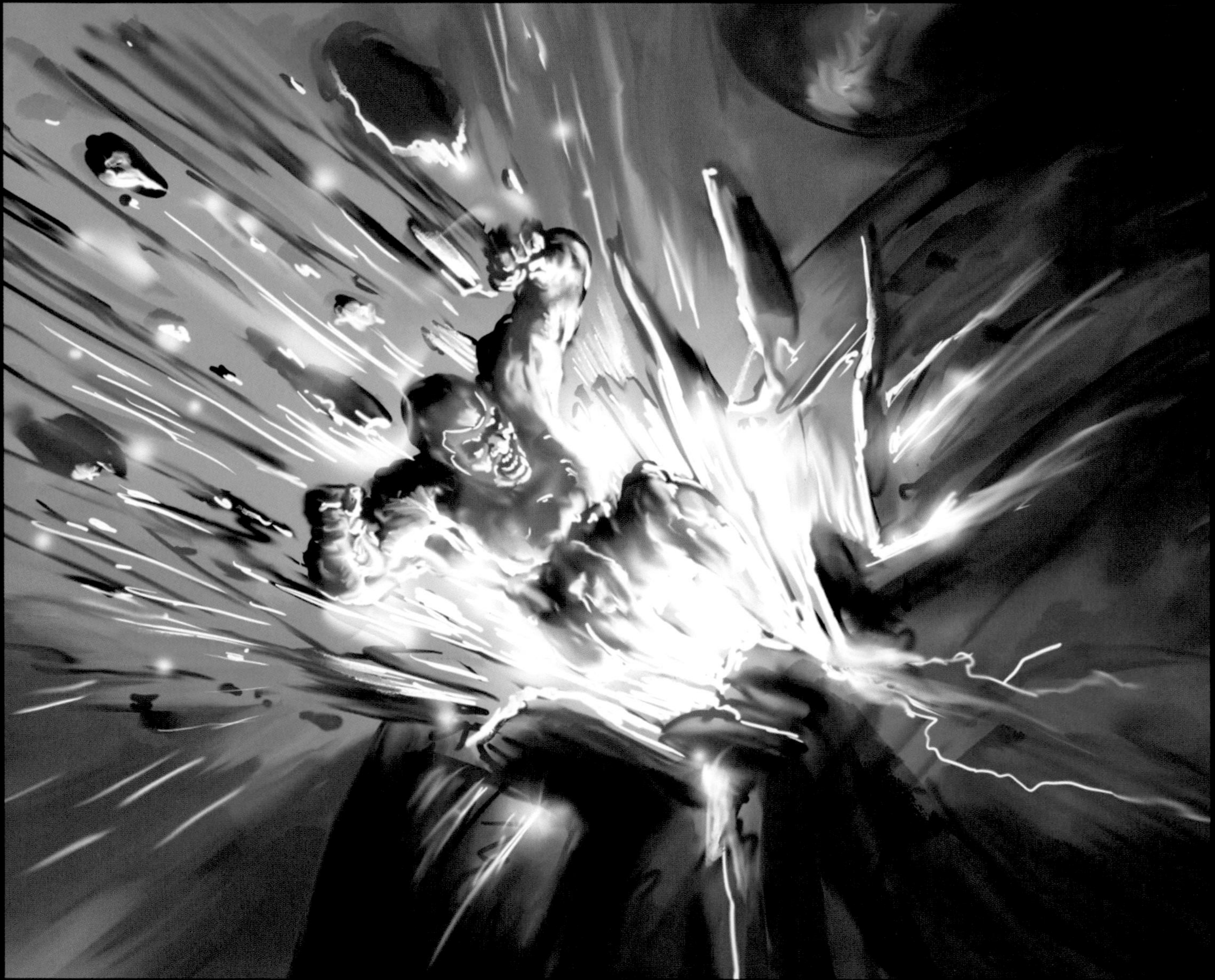

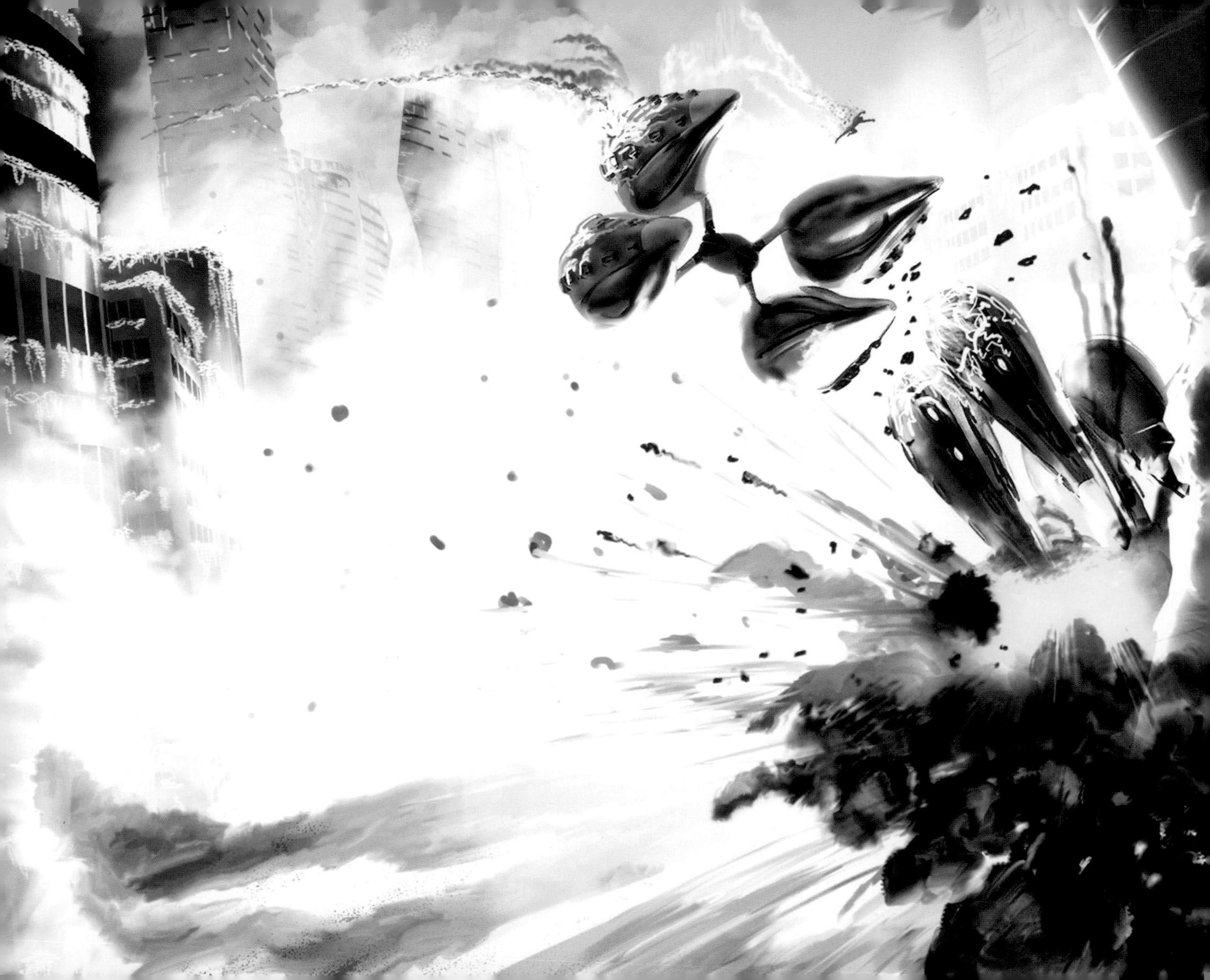

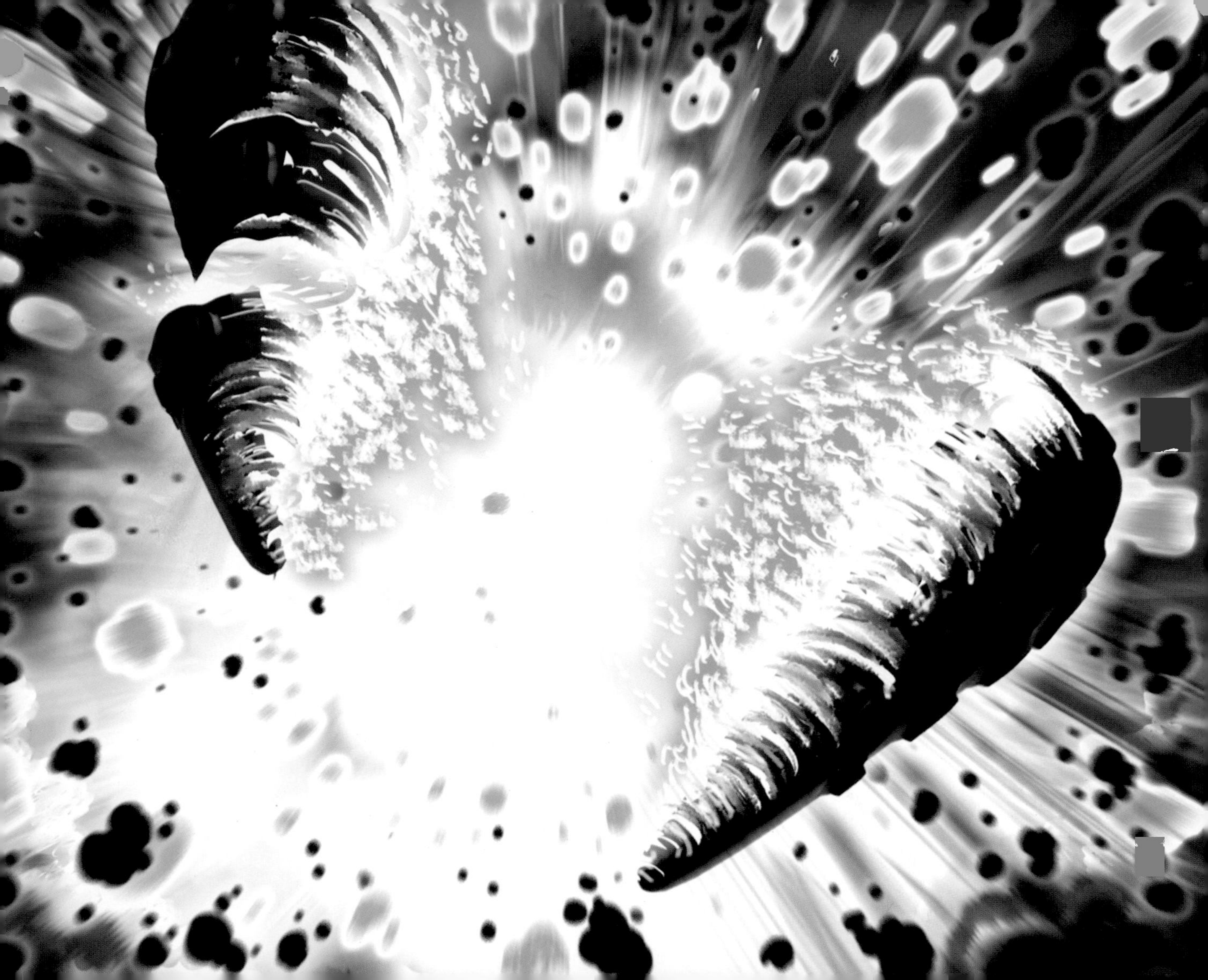

*With each fiery explosion, the Earthlings cried out as they were laid low by the **loss of their savior**…*

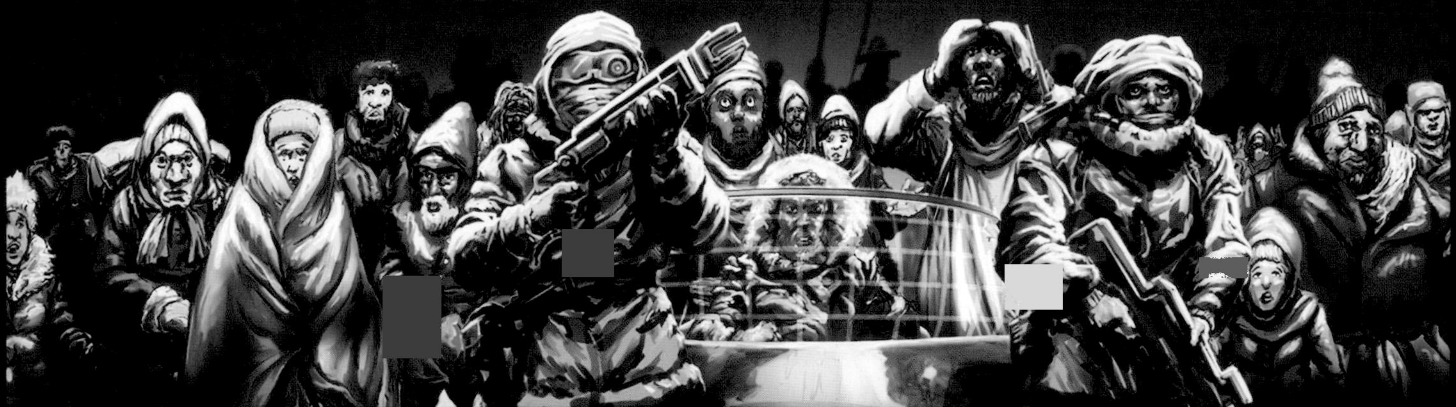

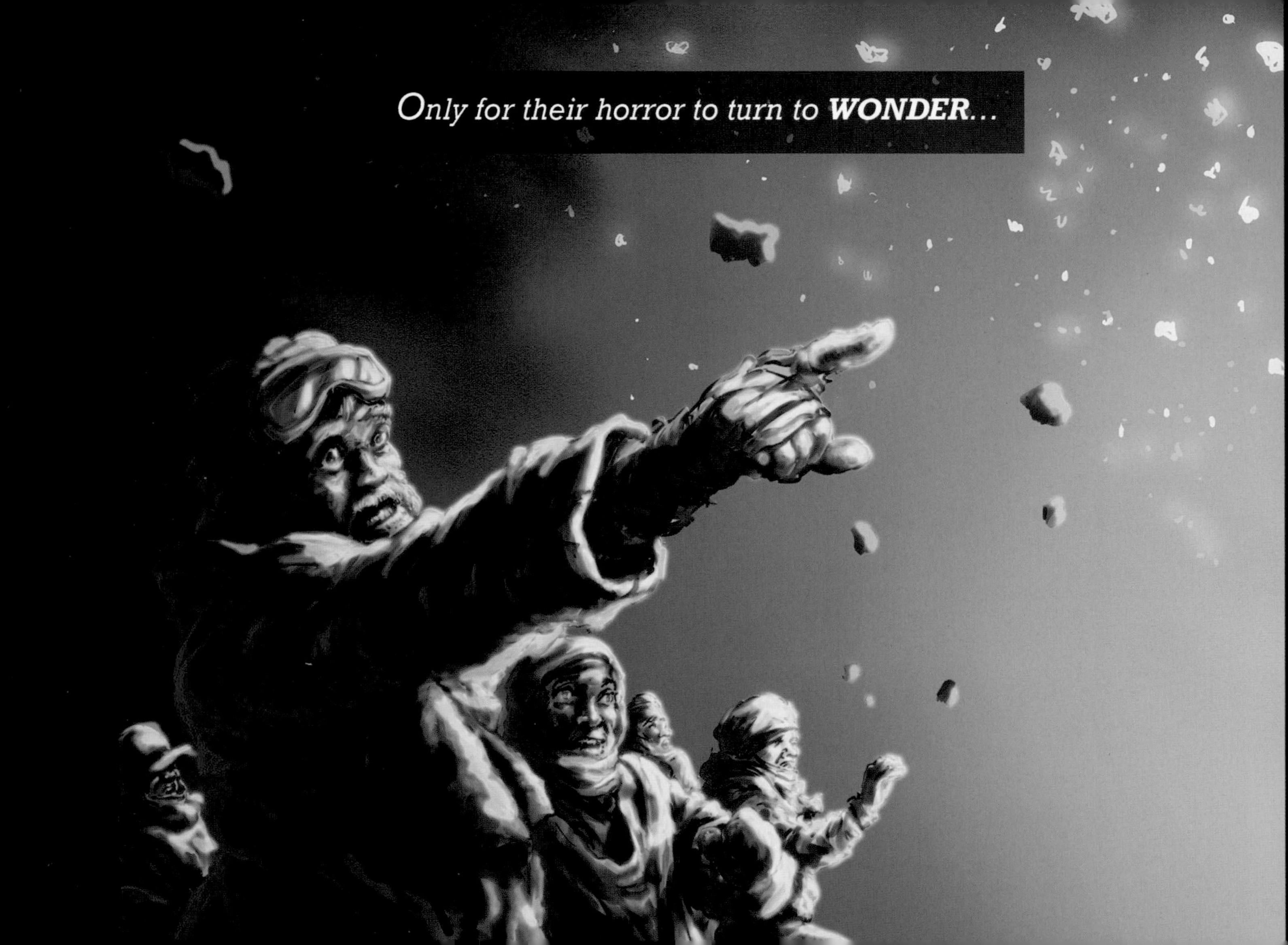
Only for their horror to turn to ***WONDER****...*

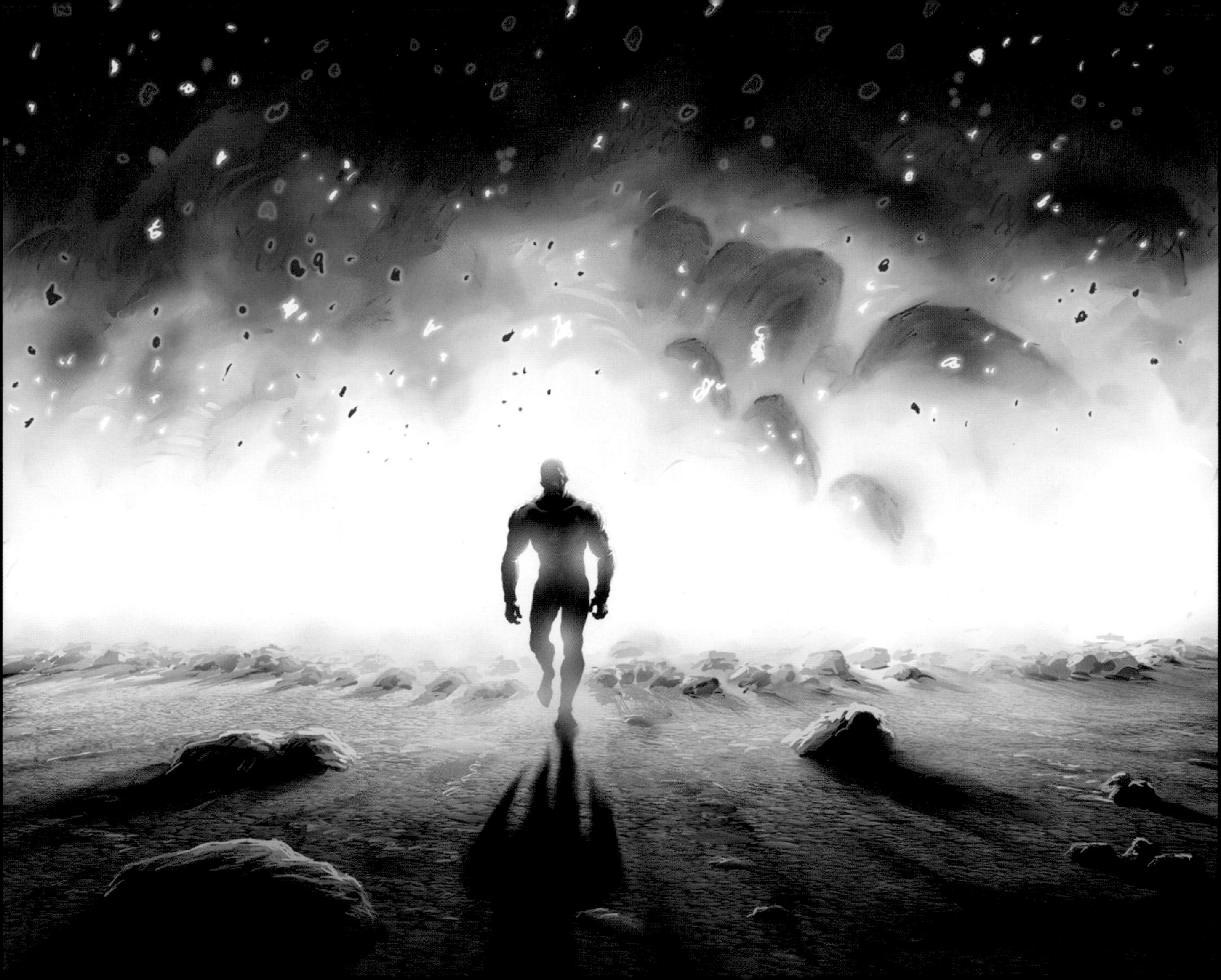

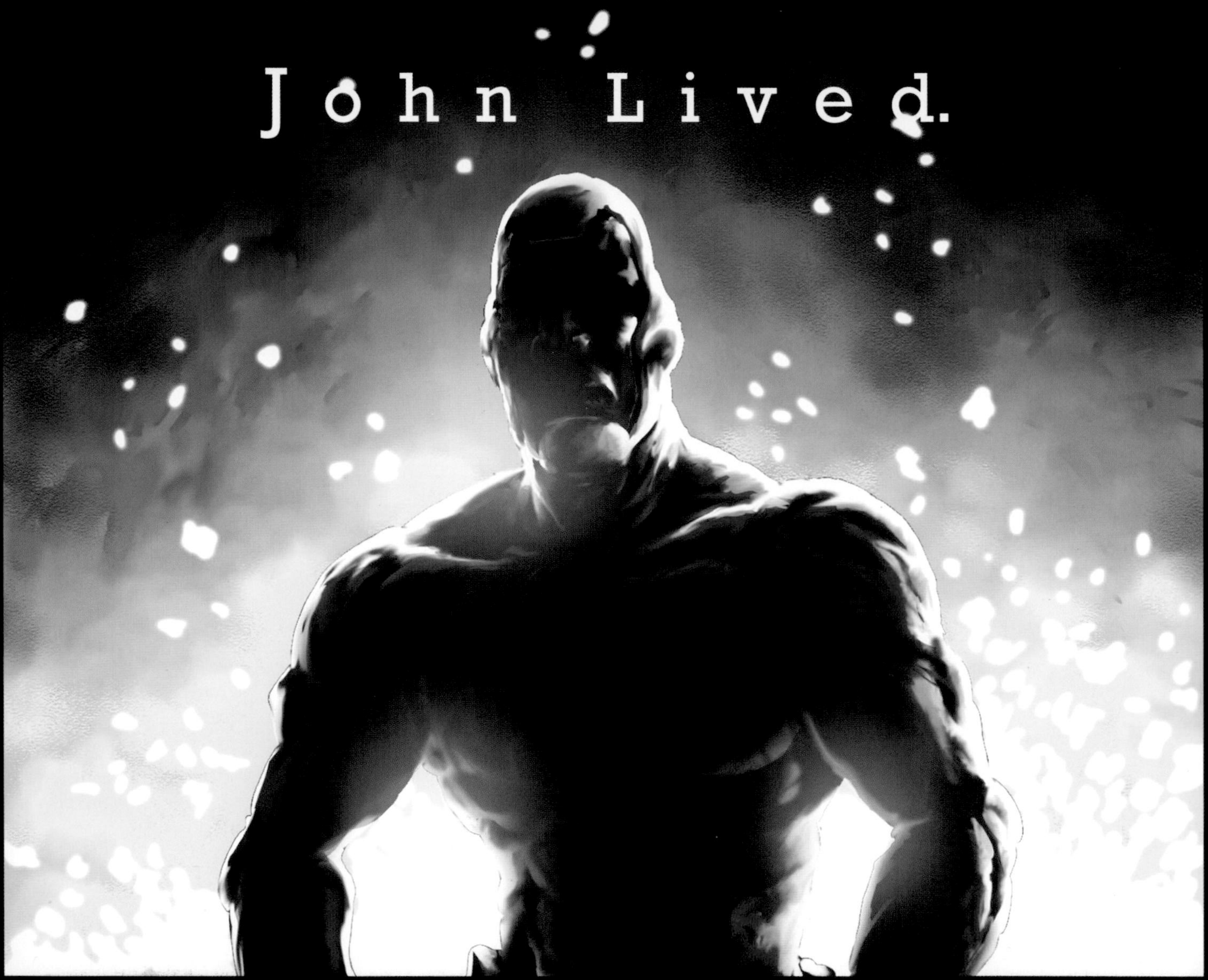
John Lived.

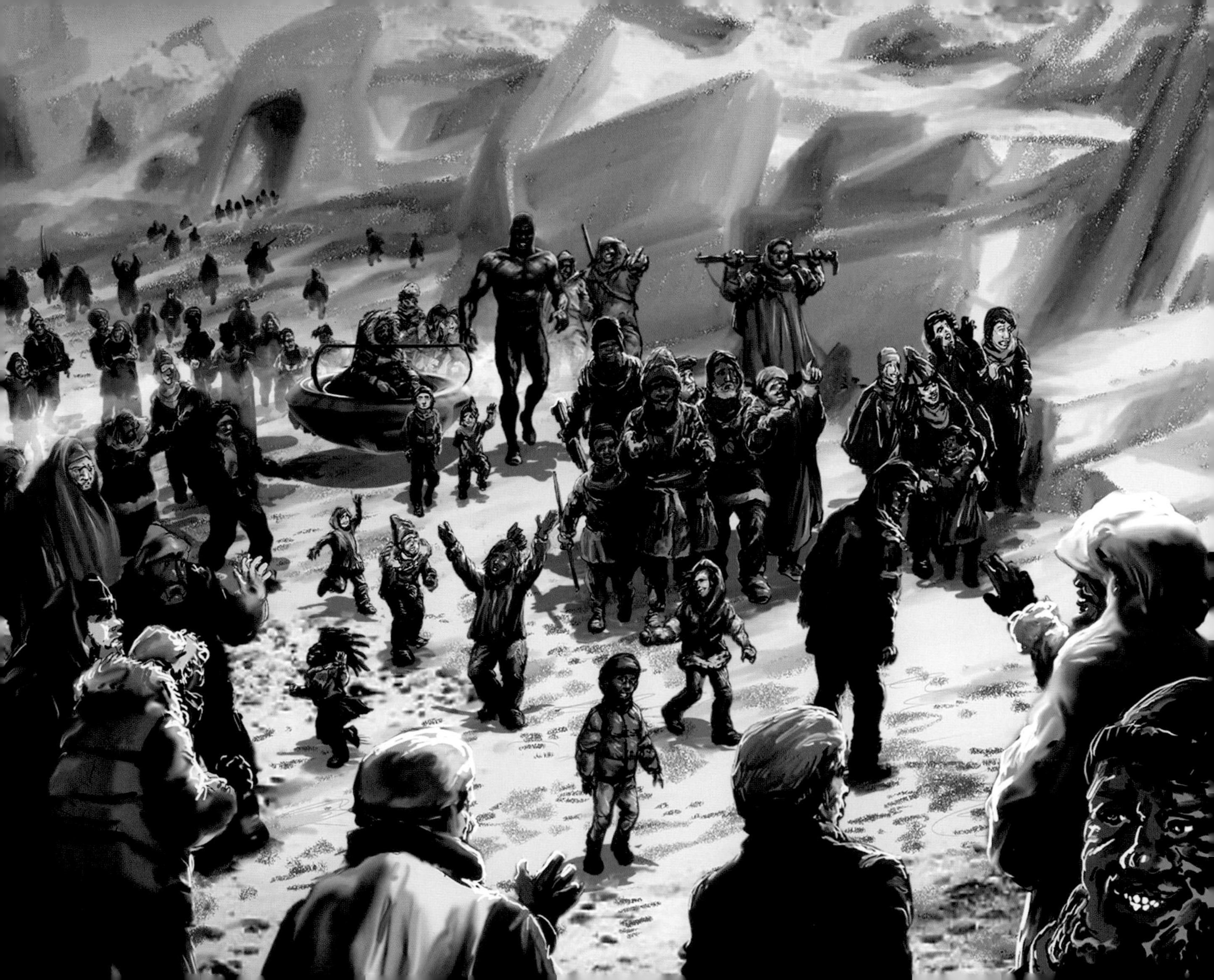

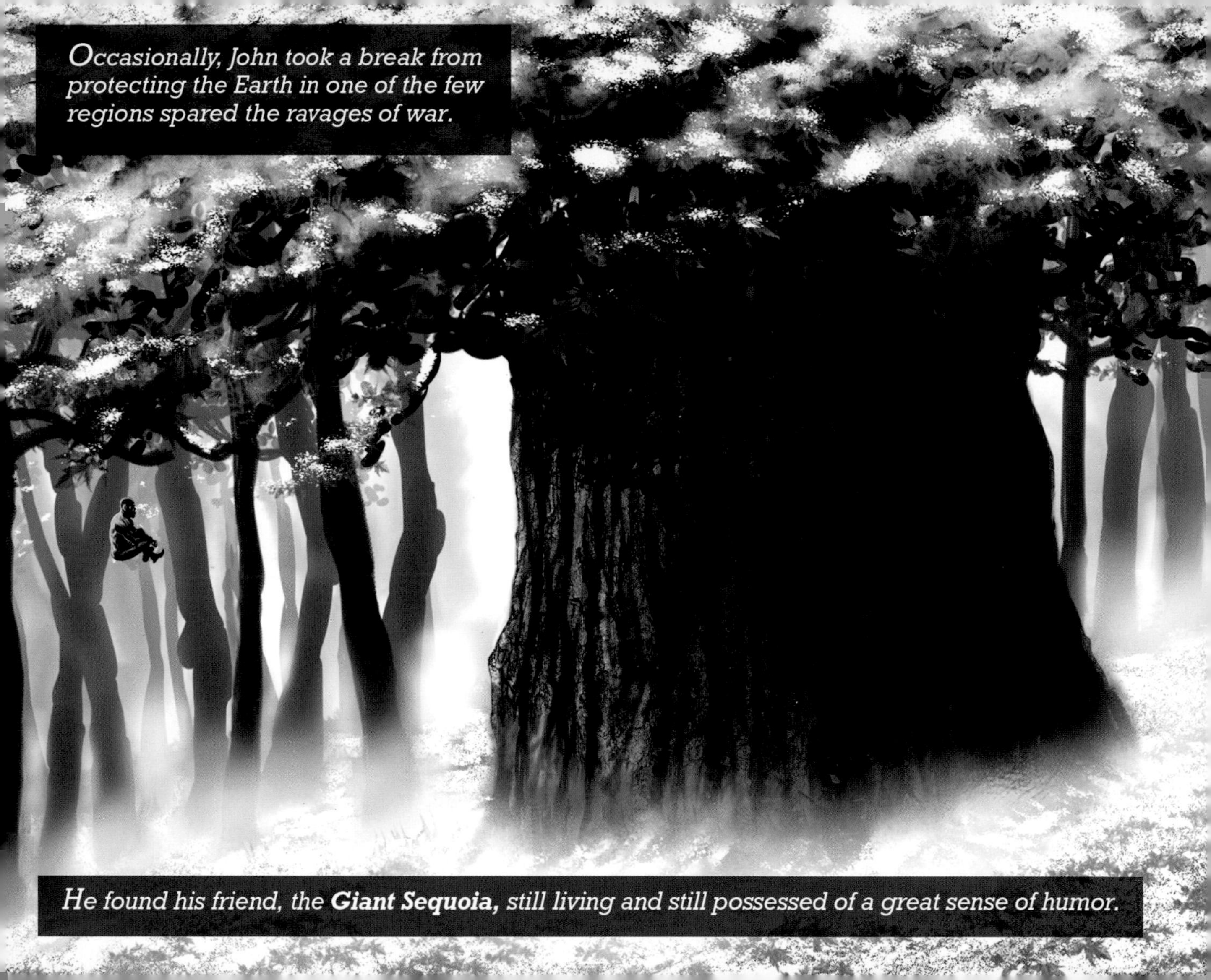
Occasionally, John took a break from protecting the Earth in one of the few regions spared the ravages of war.
He found his friend, the **Giant Sequoia,** still living and still possessed of a great sense of humor.

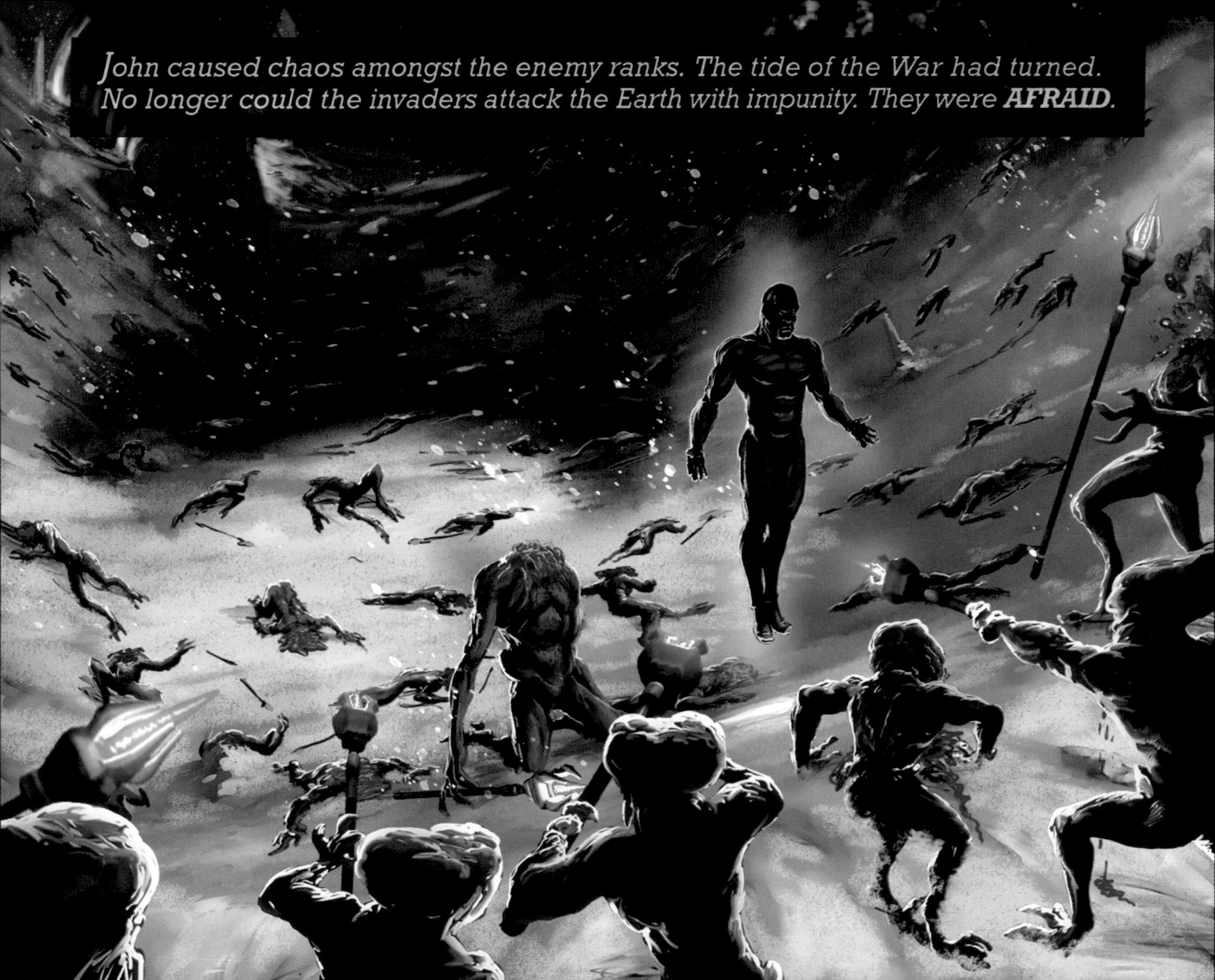
John caused chaos amongst the enemy ranks. The tide of the War had turned. No longer could the invaders attack the Earth with impunity. They were **AFRAID**.

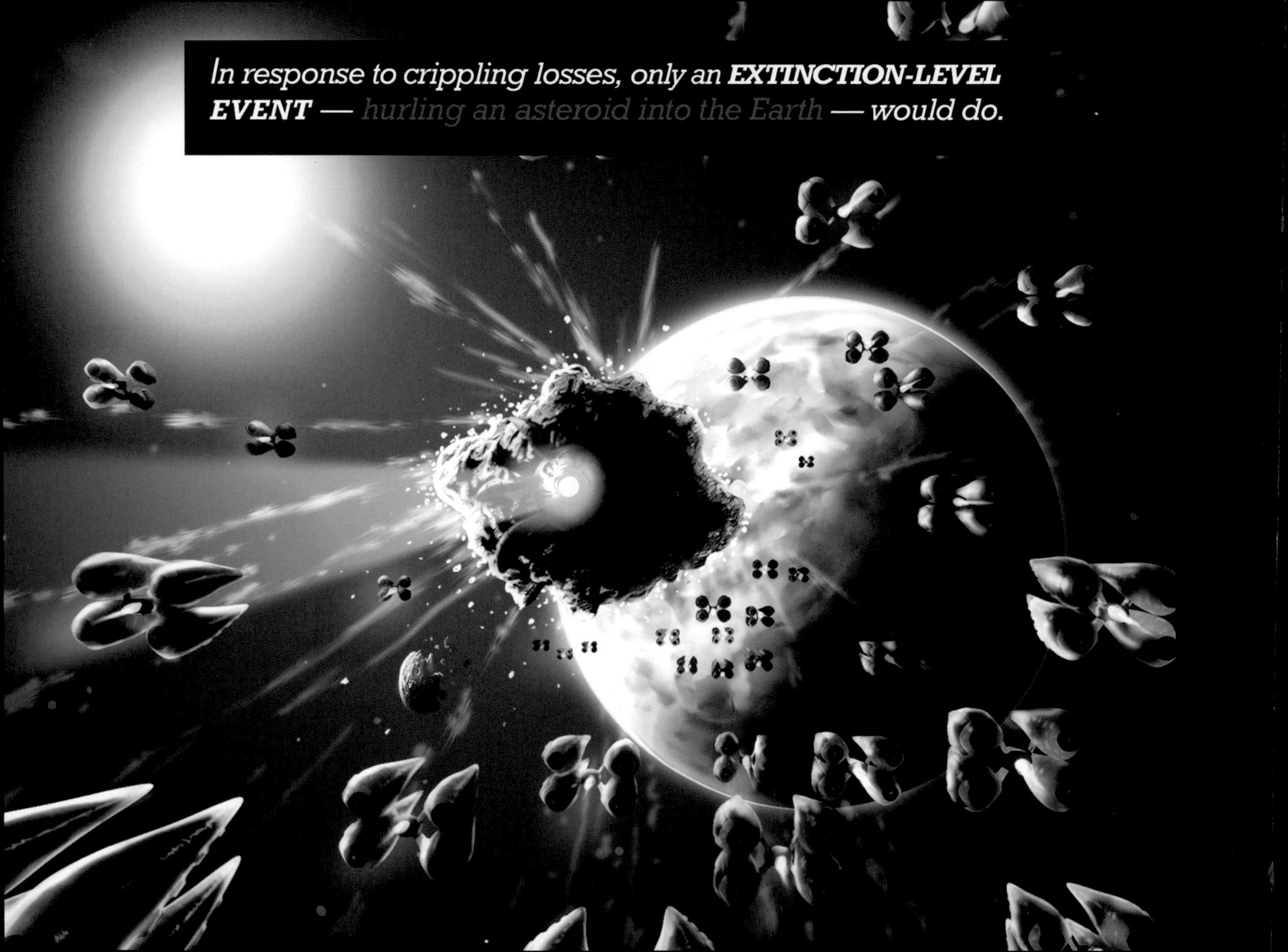

In response to crippling losses, only an ***EXTINCTION-LEVEL EVENT*** *— hurling an asteroid into the Earth — would do.*

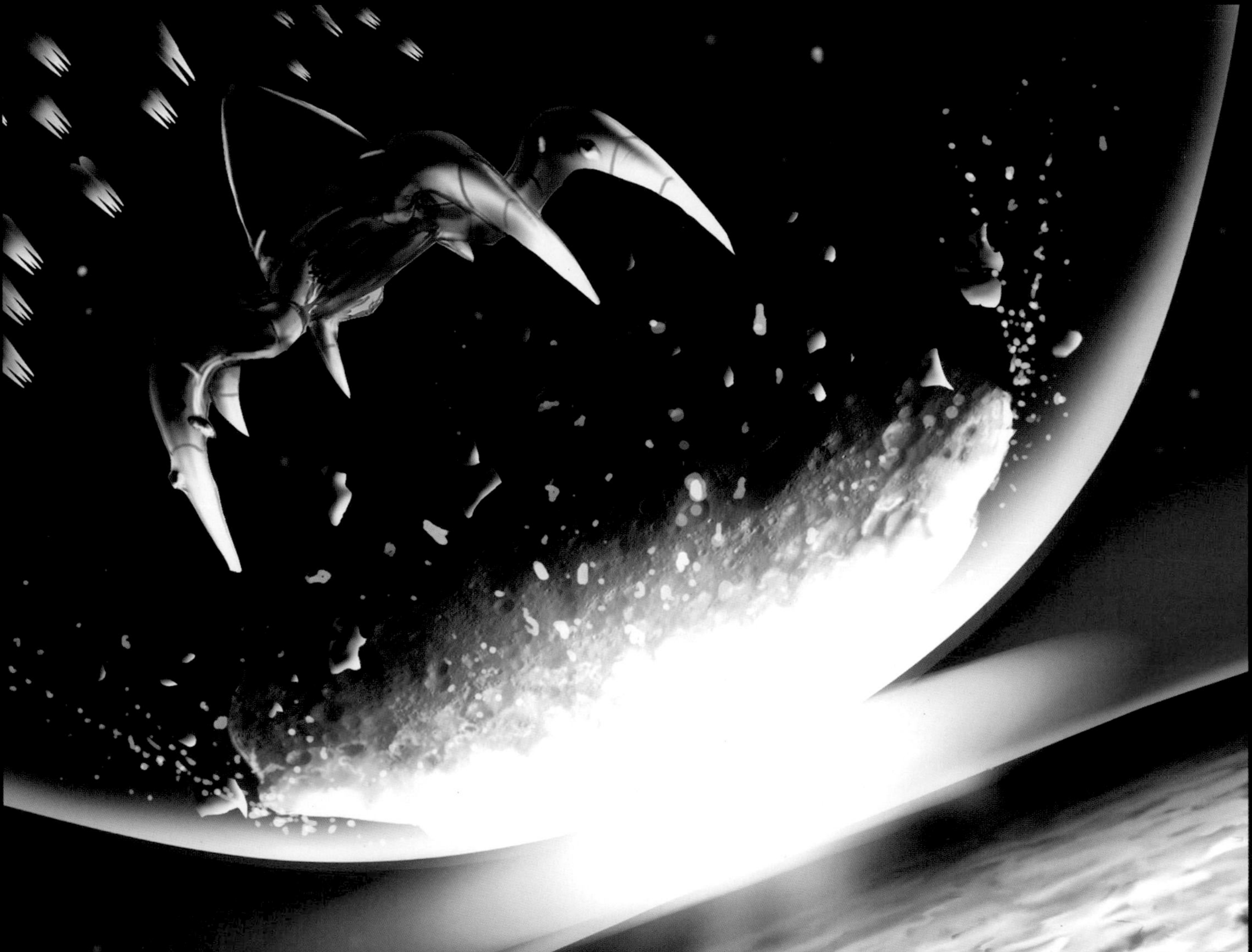

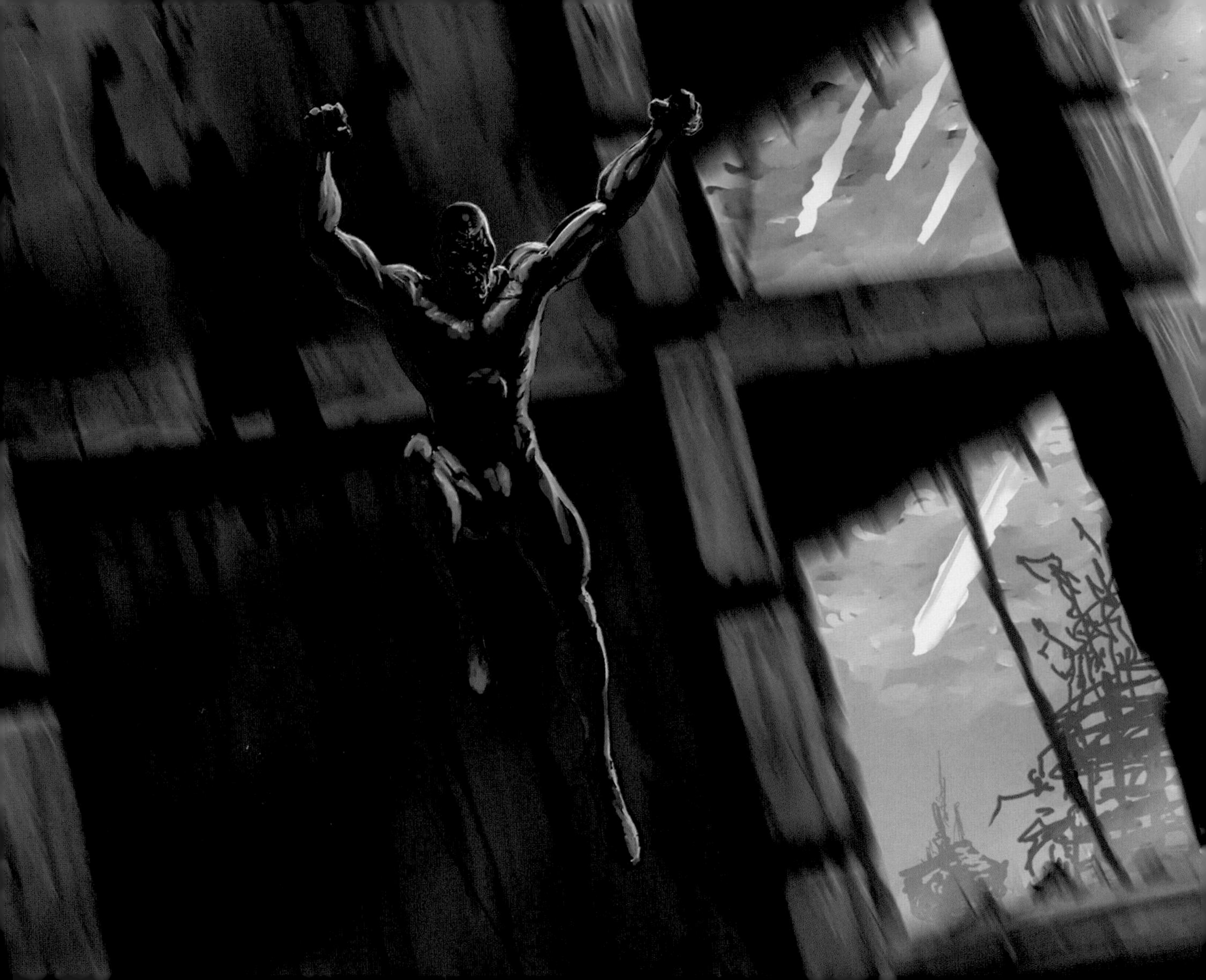

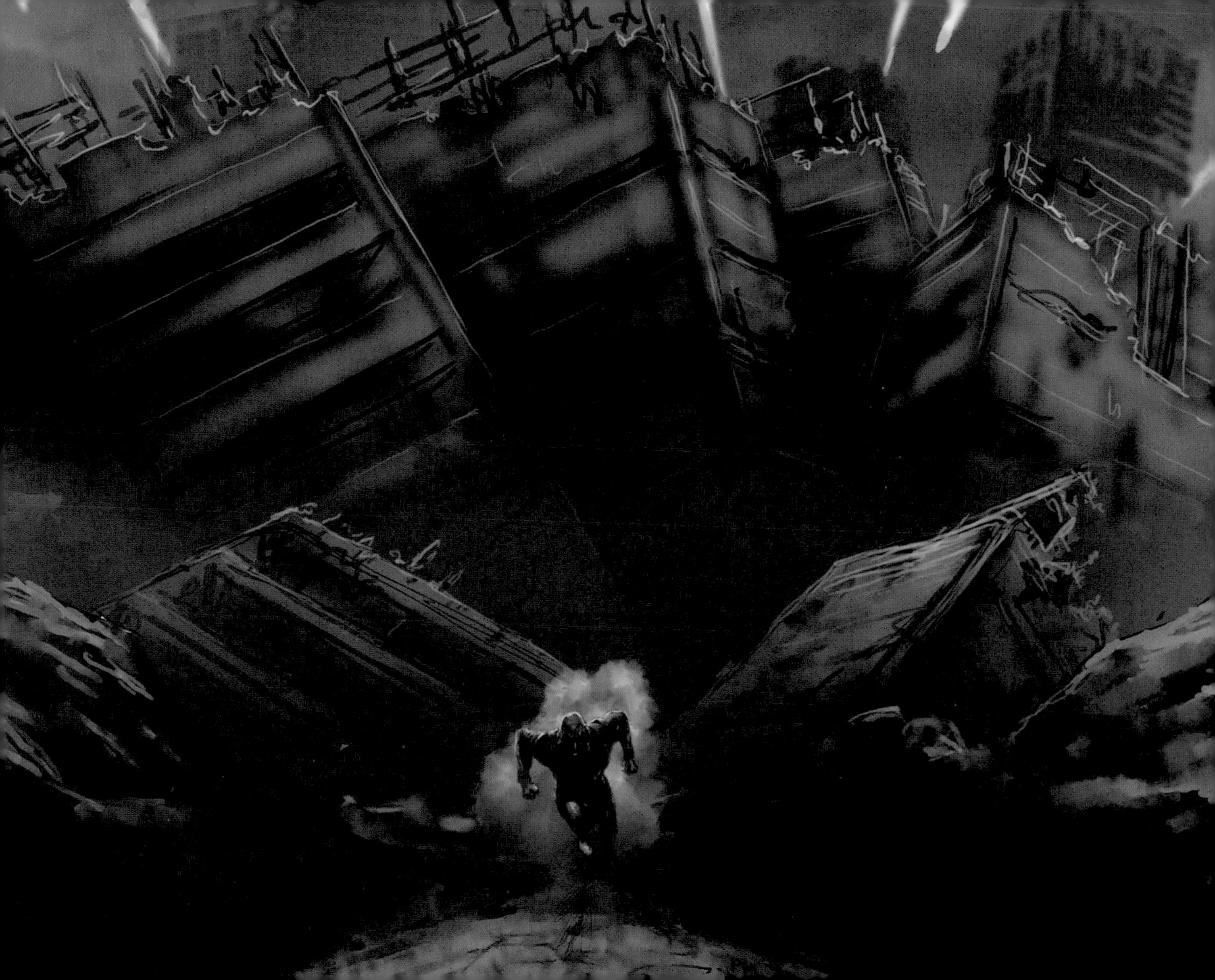

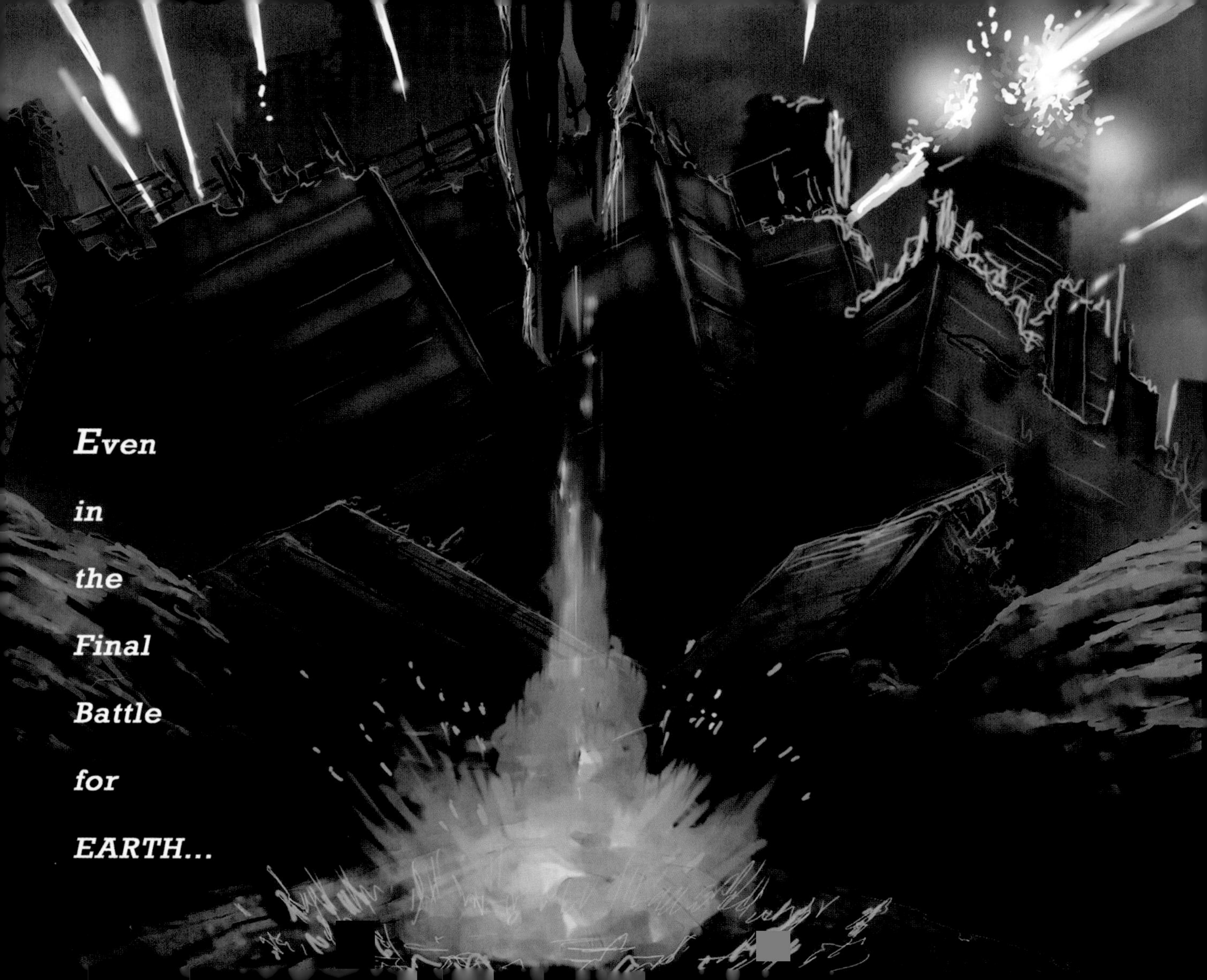
Even
in
the
Final
Battle
for
EARTH...

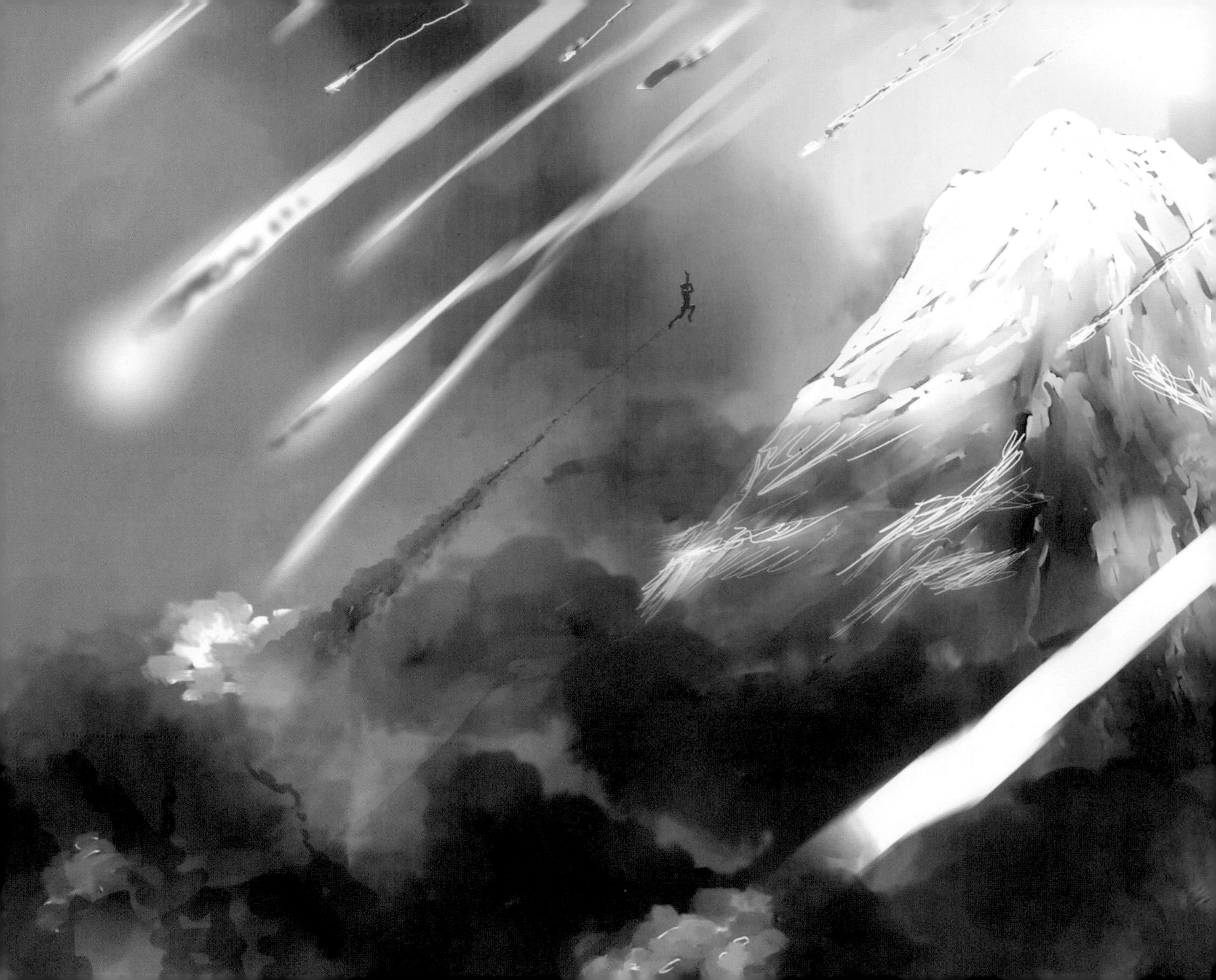

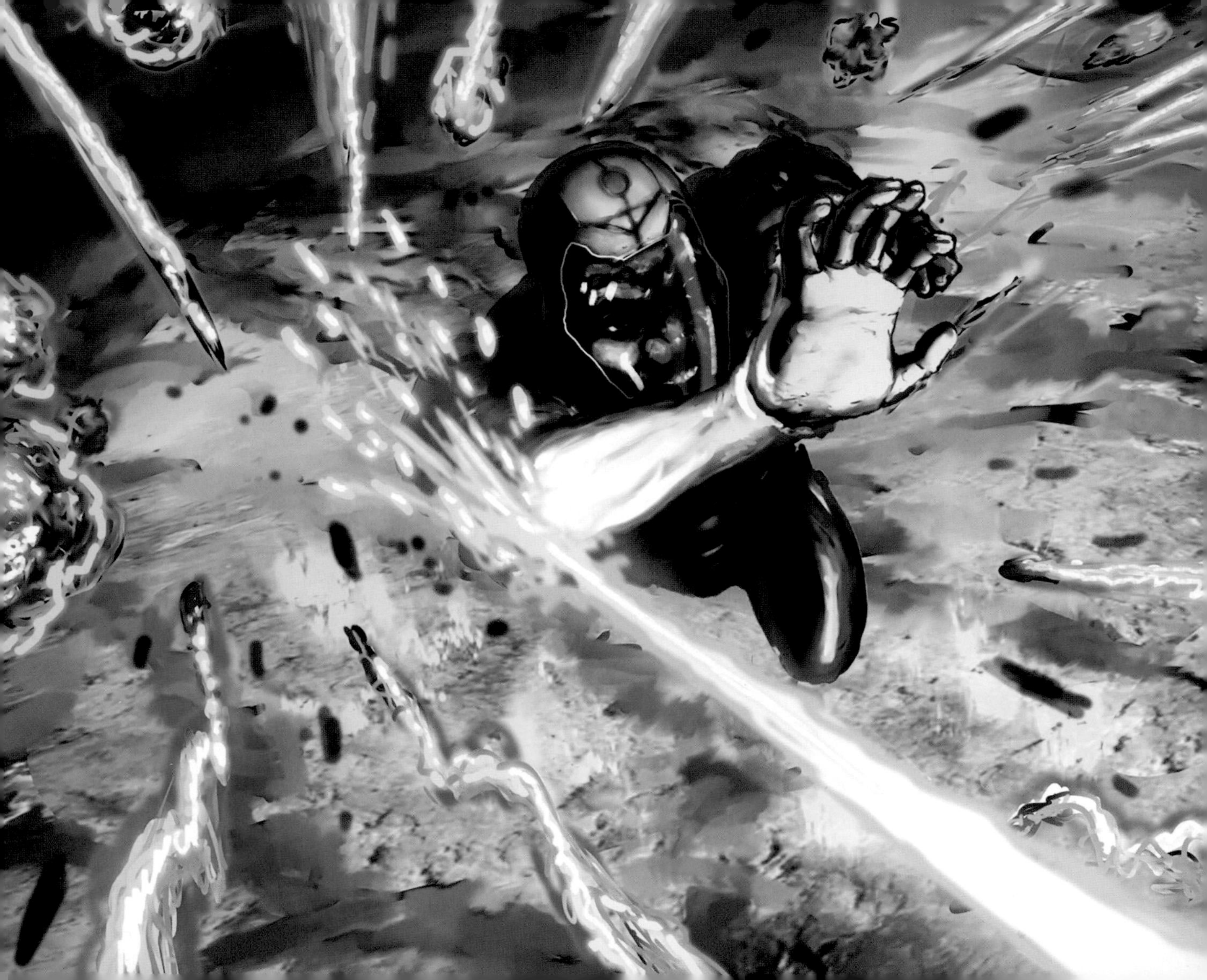

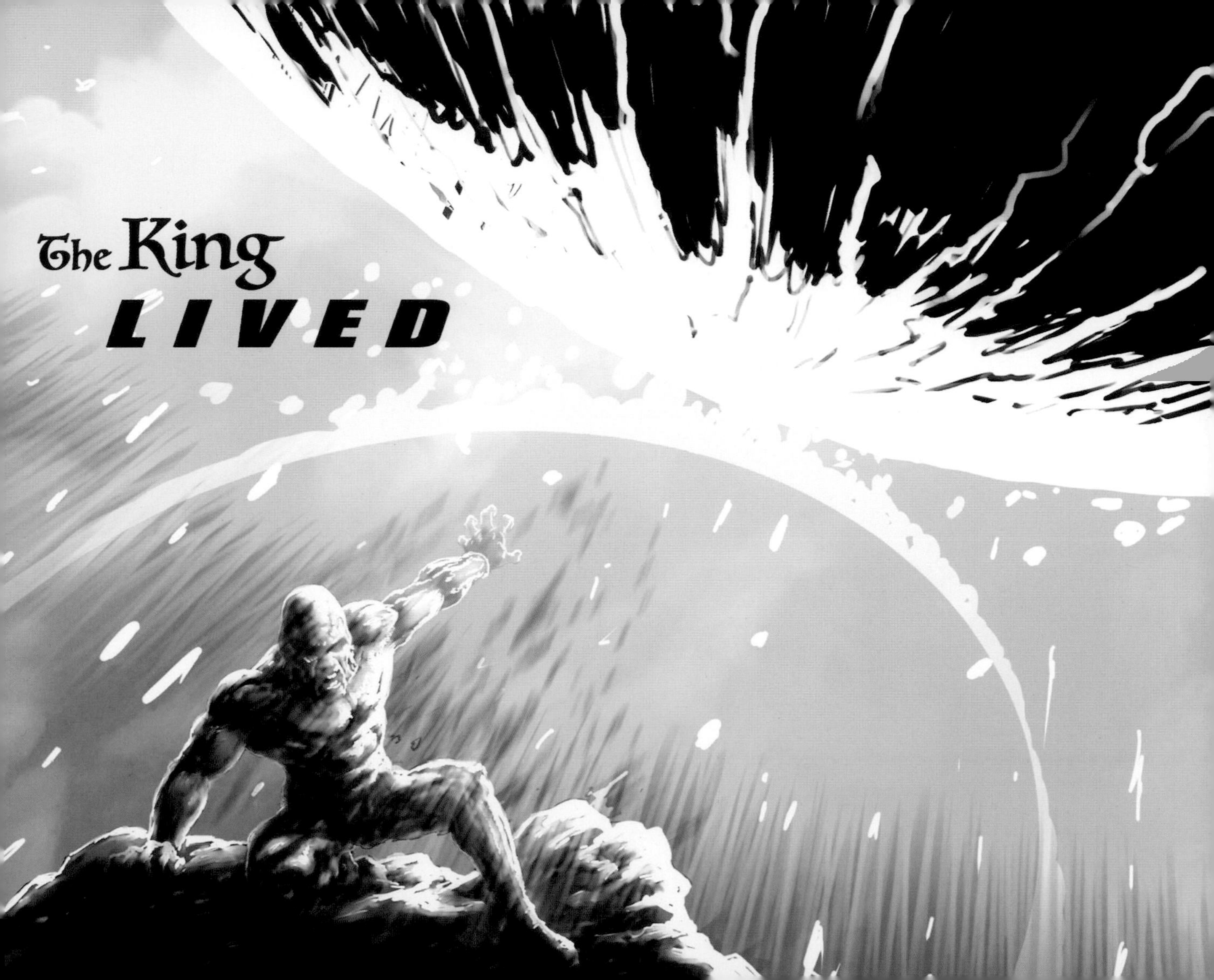
The King
LIVED

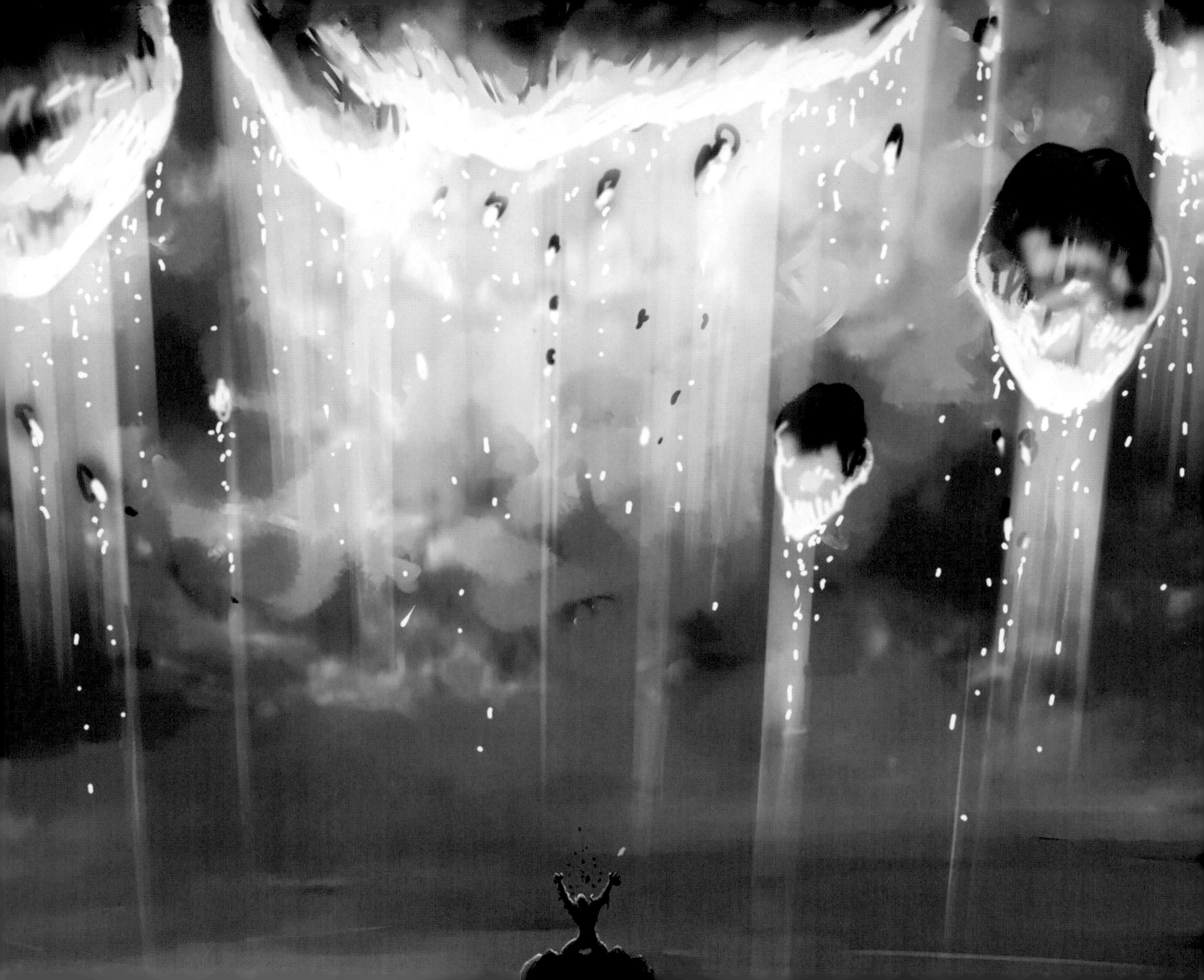

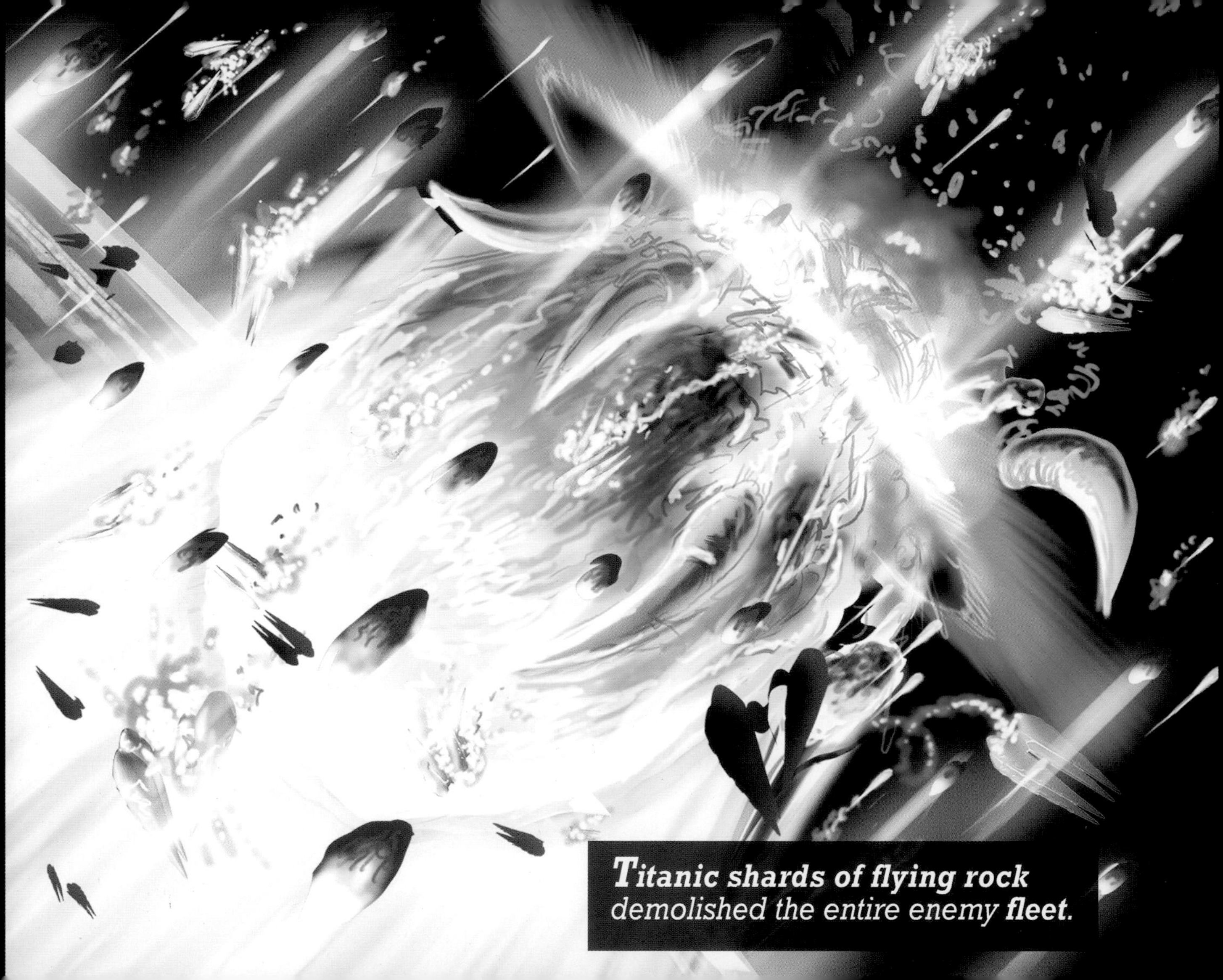

***T**itanic shards of flying rock*
demolished the entire enemy ***fleet****.*

***In the end** John only needed **his** thoughts to **END THE WAR**.*

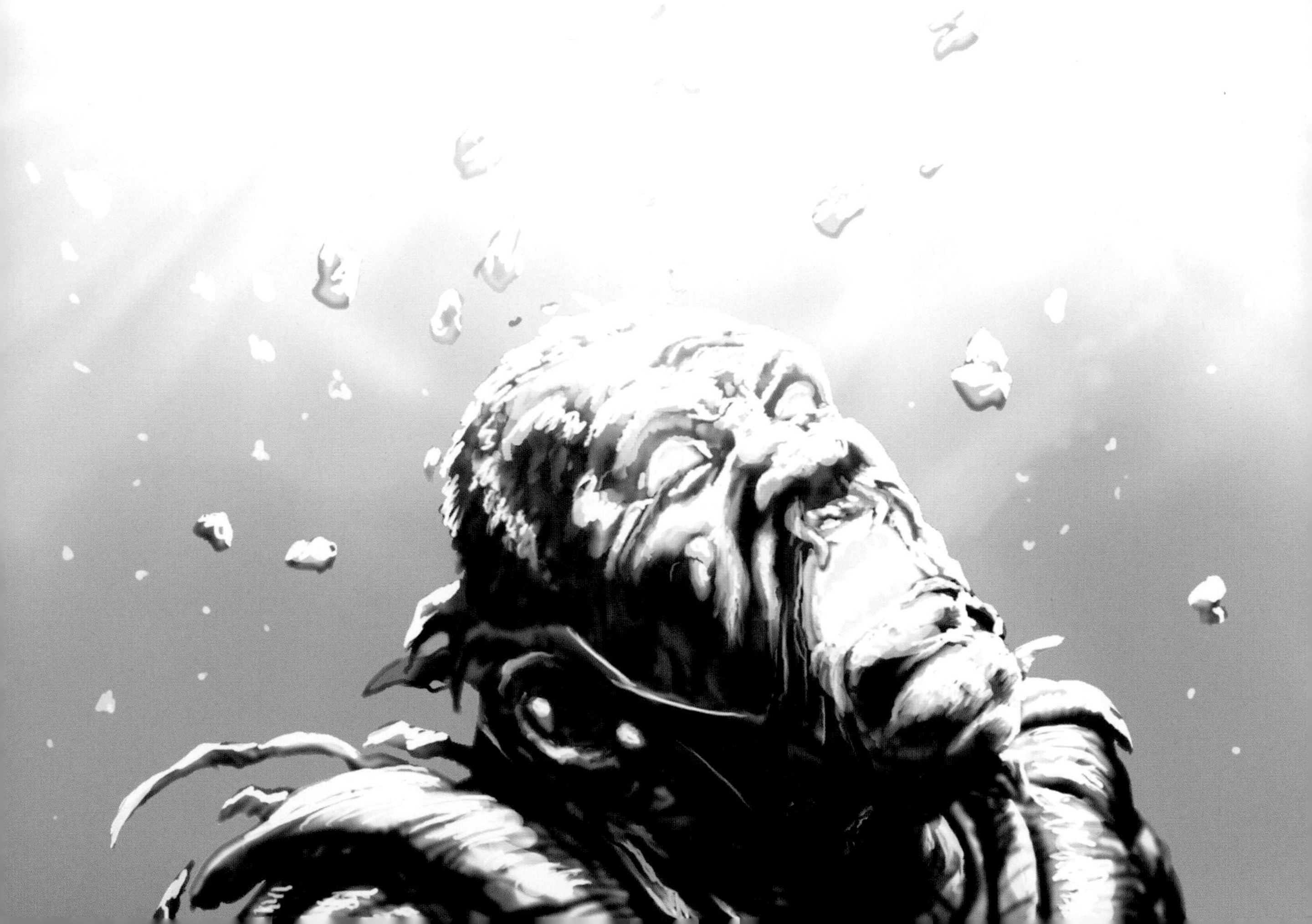

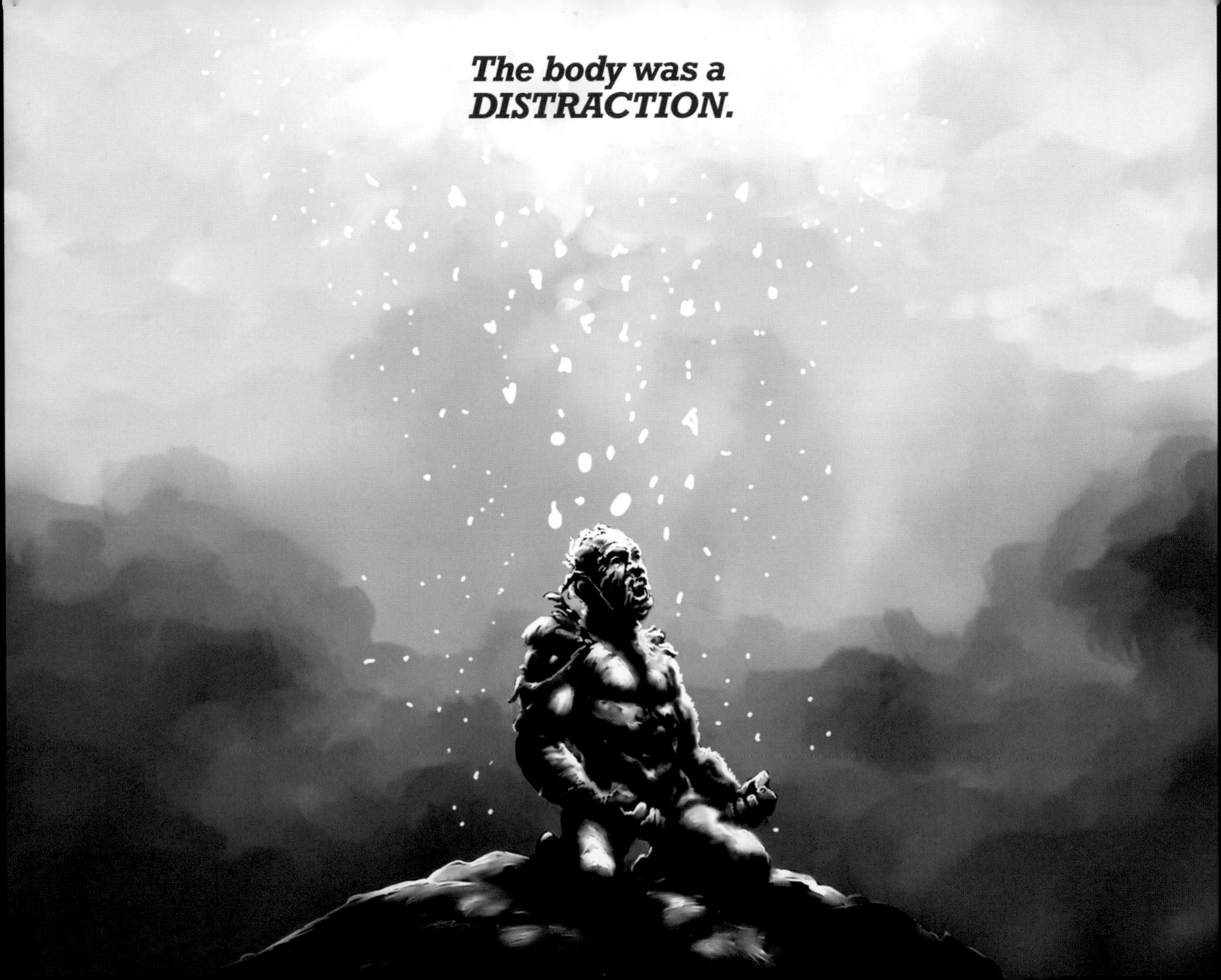
The body was a
DISTRACTION.

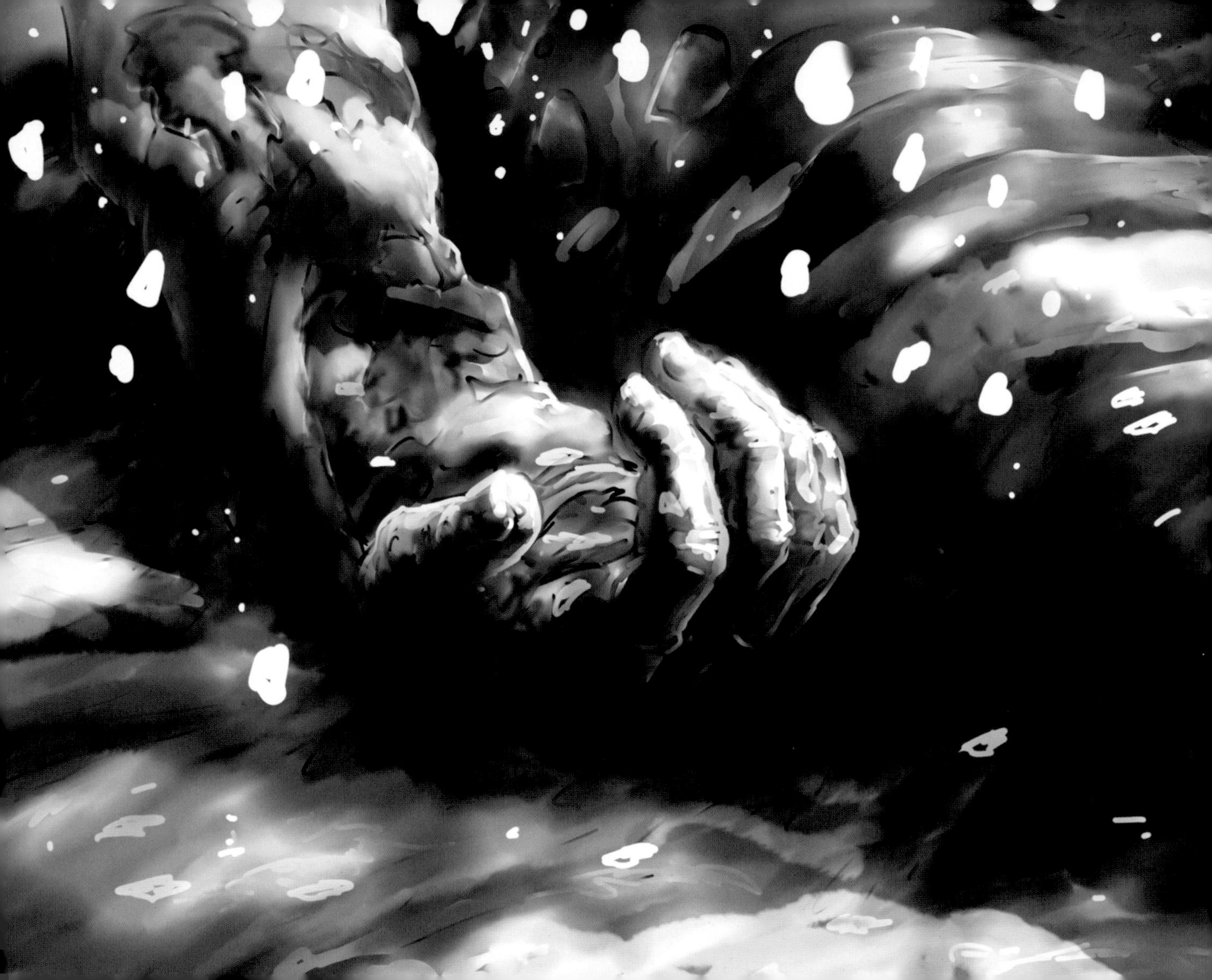

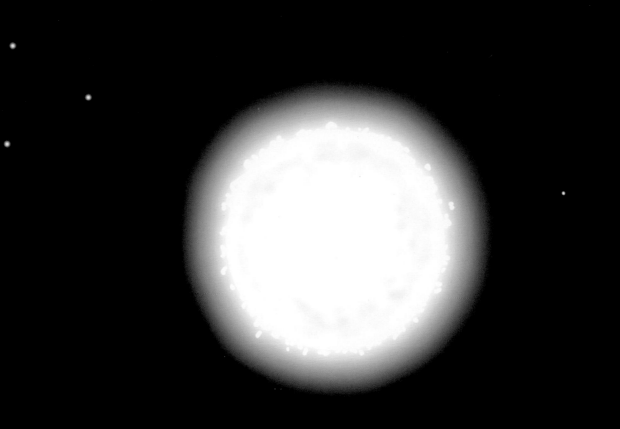

Multiple millennia passed. The Sun and its sibling stars began one by one to spark away into the far beyond. By this time, there were far many older stars than young.

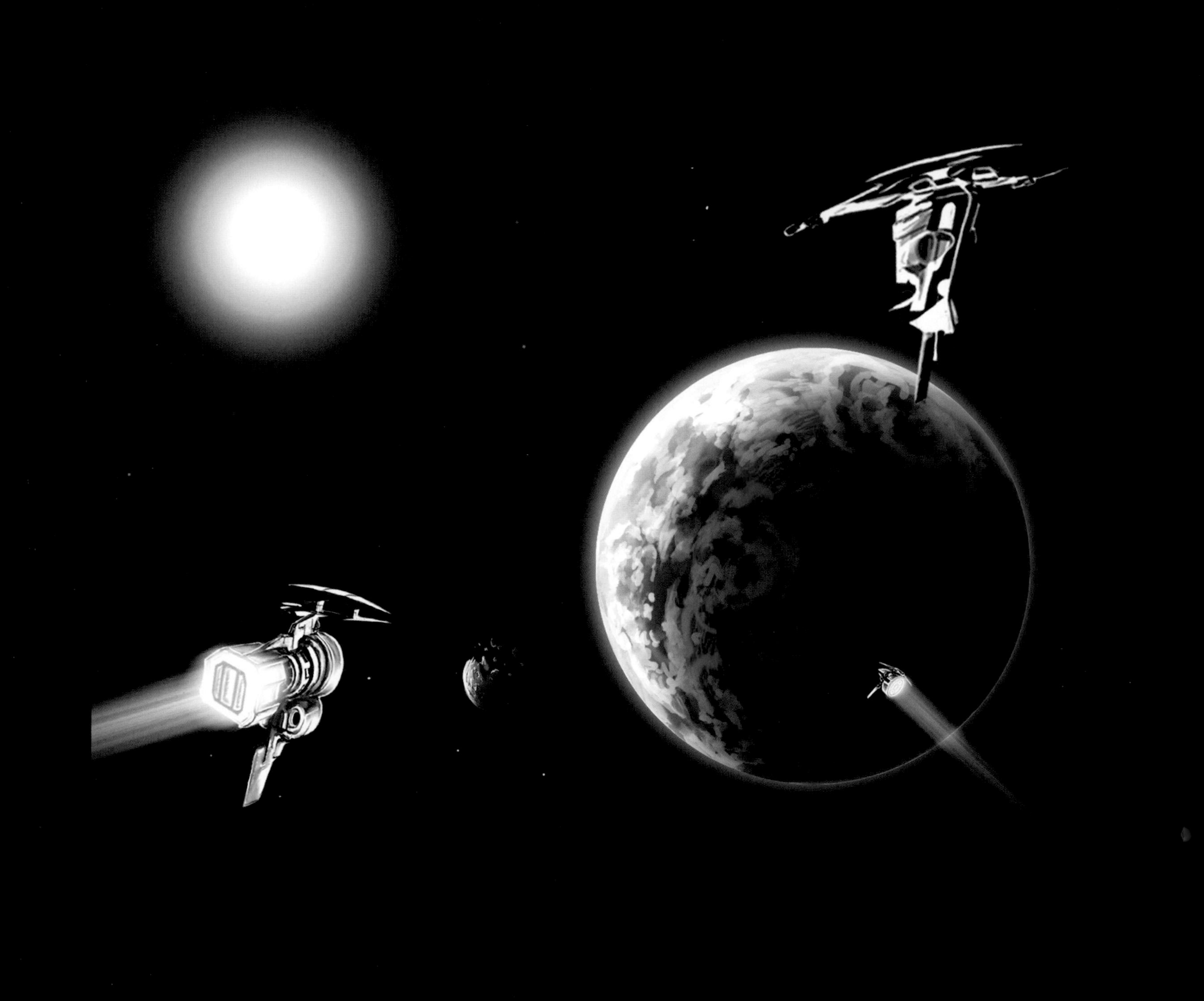

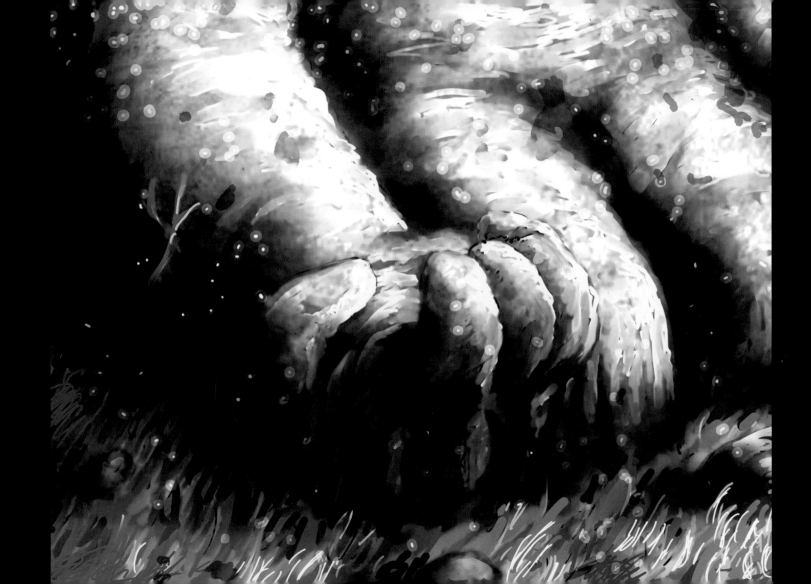

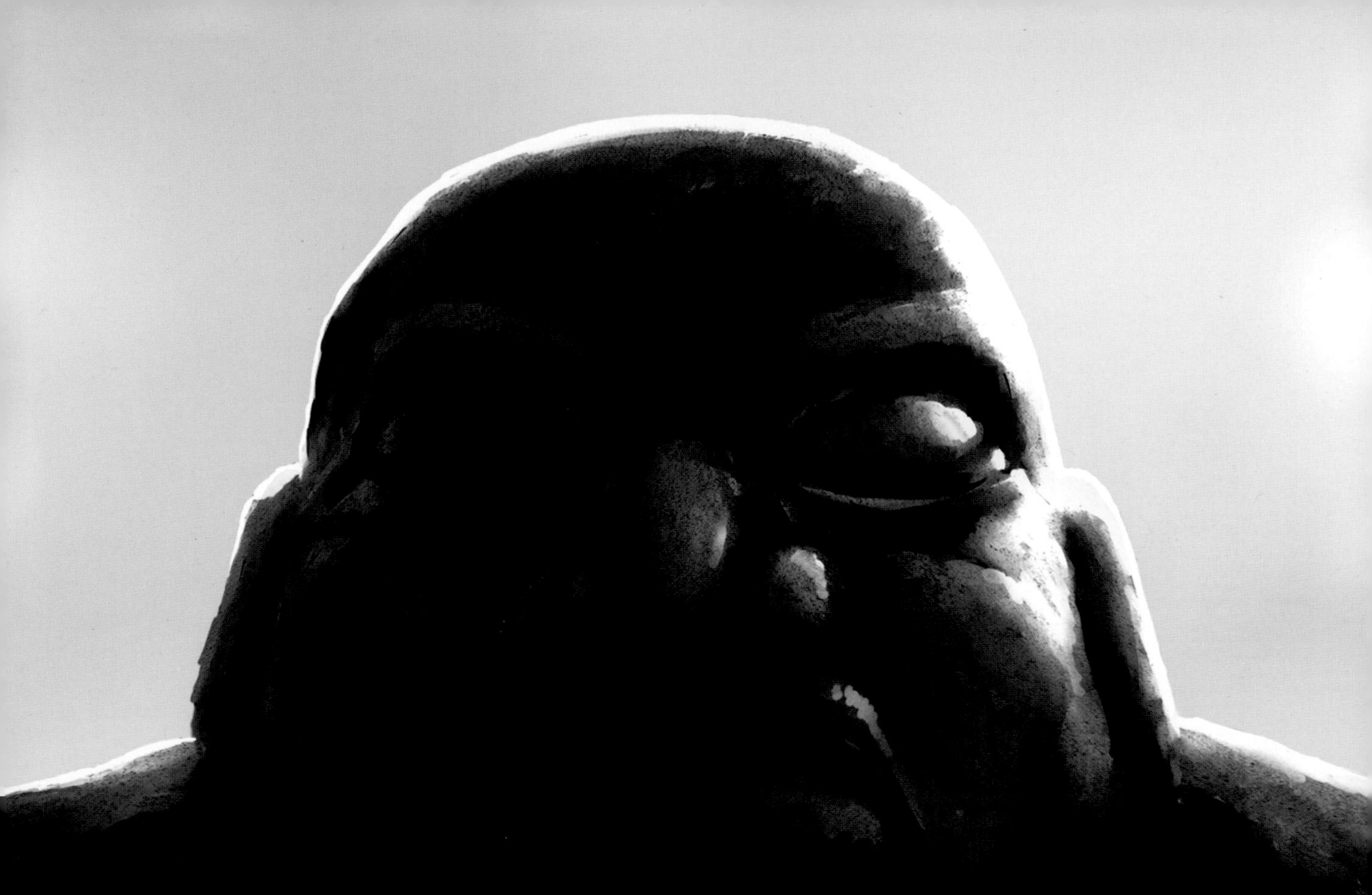

*Nature **reclaimed** John's body into the Earth. Soil, plant life, and detritus encased his still-living form into that of a **solid mountainous statue***

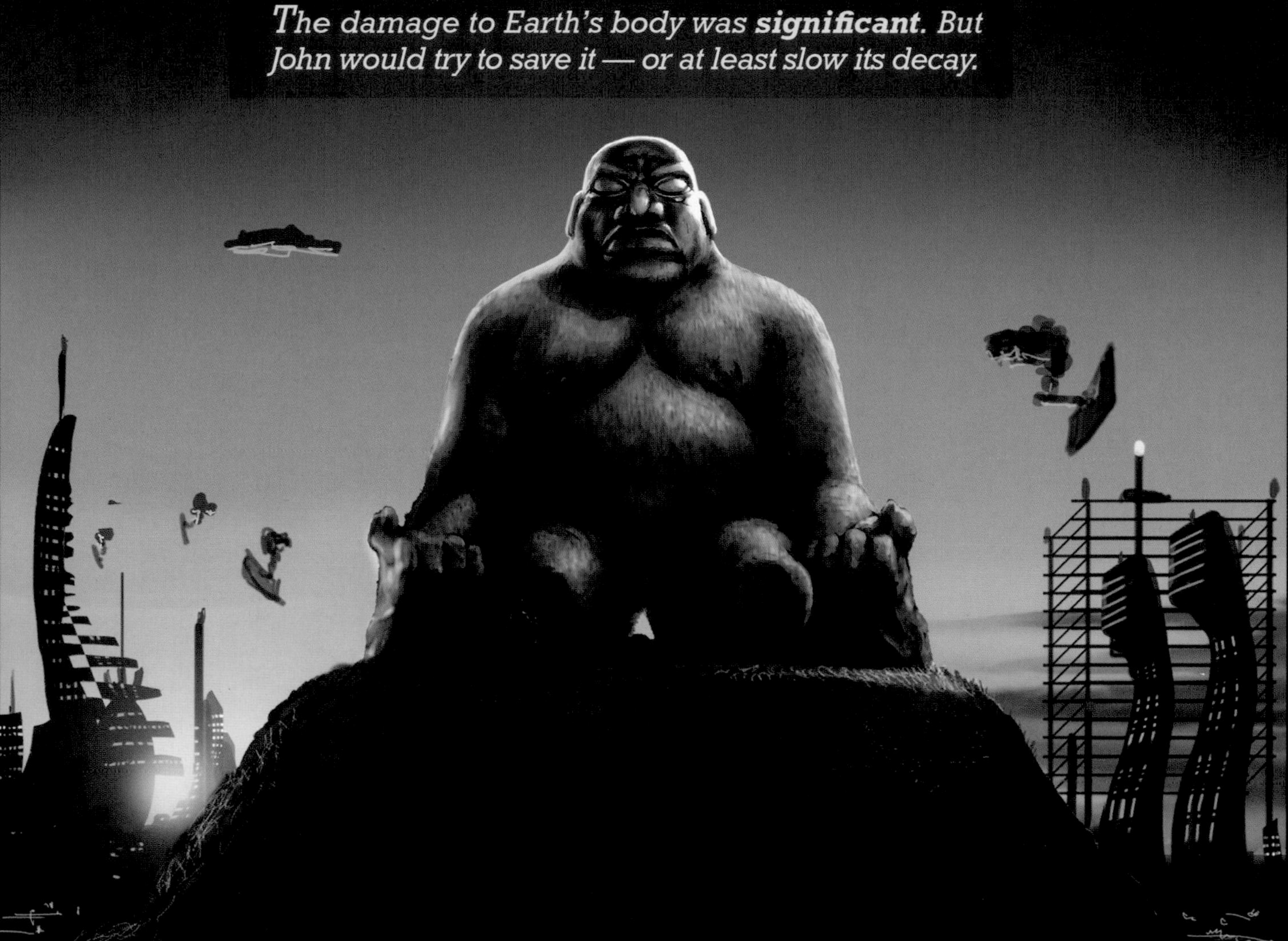
The damage to Earth's body was ***significant****. But John would try to save it — or at least slow its decay.*

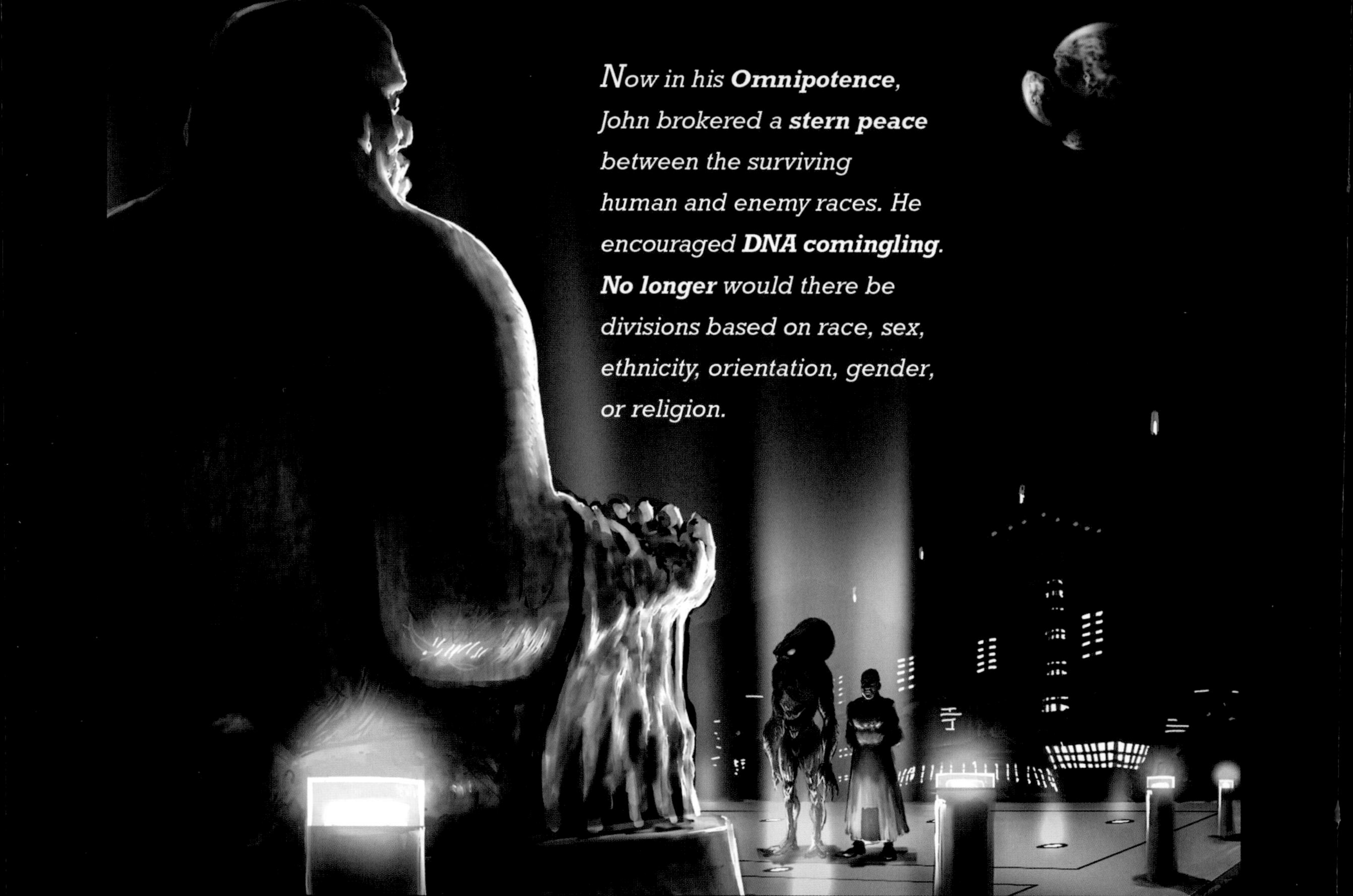

Now in his ***Omnipotence****,*
John brokered a ***stern peace***
between the surviving
human and enemy races. He
encouraged ***DNA comingling****.*
No longer *would there be*
divisions based on race, sex,
ethnicity, orientation, gender,
or religion.

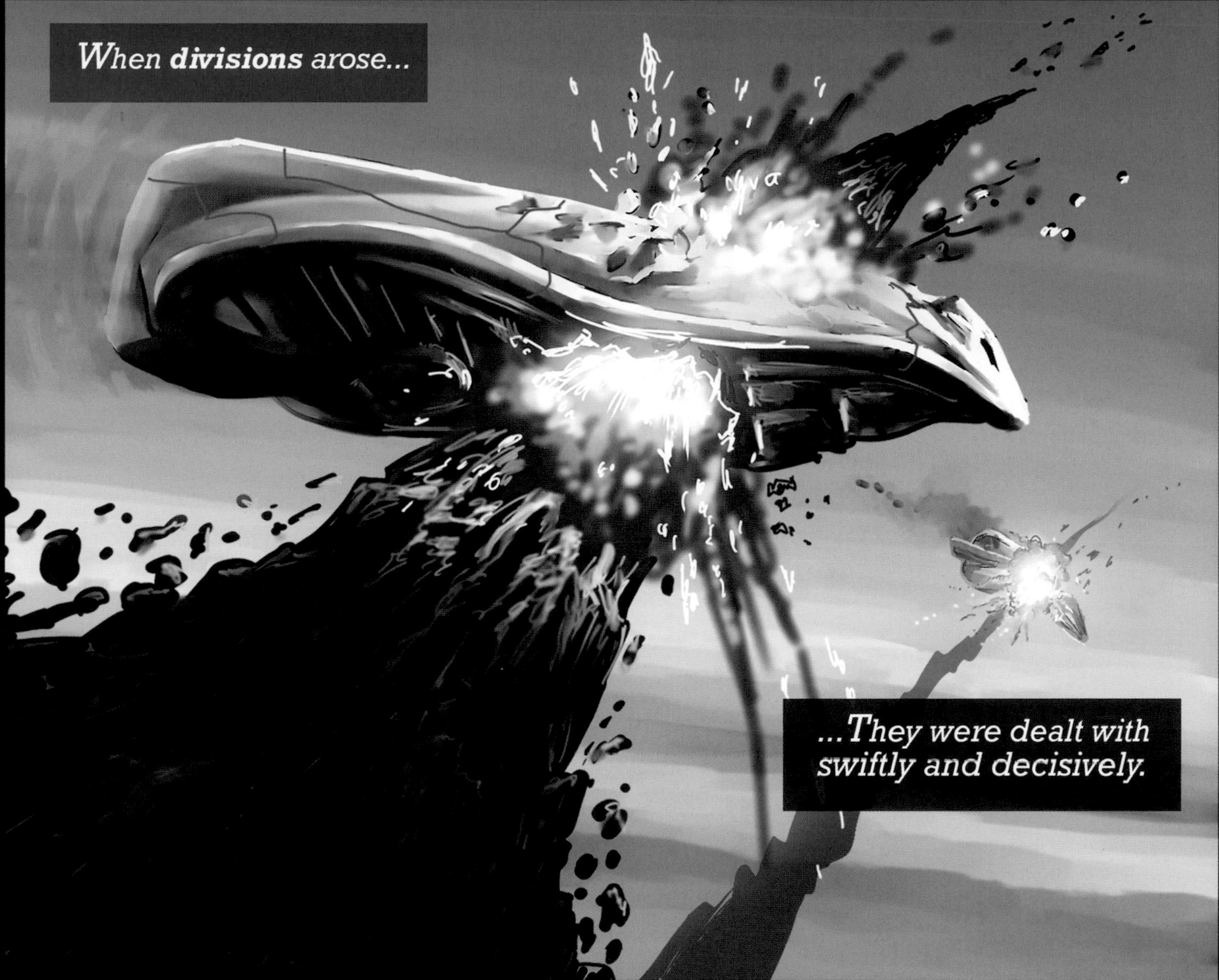
When **divisions** arose...
...They were dealt with swiftly and decisively.

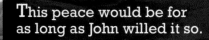

This peace would be for as long as John willed it so.

THIS MEANT FOREVER.

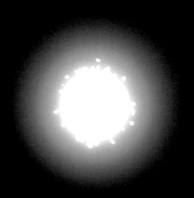

Two Million years had passed. The Sun and its few remaining siblings still played. But not with the energy of their earlier years.

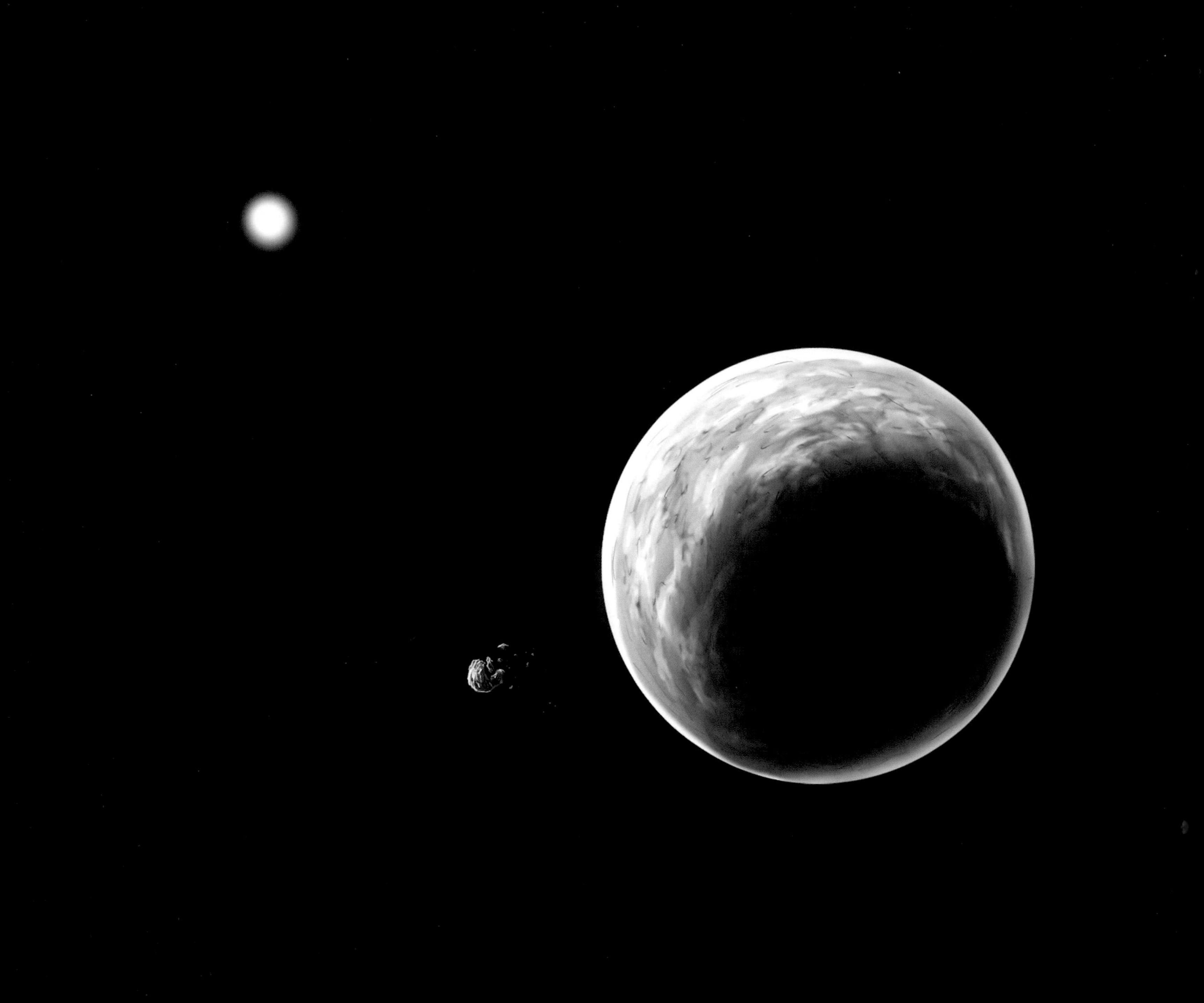

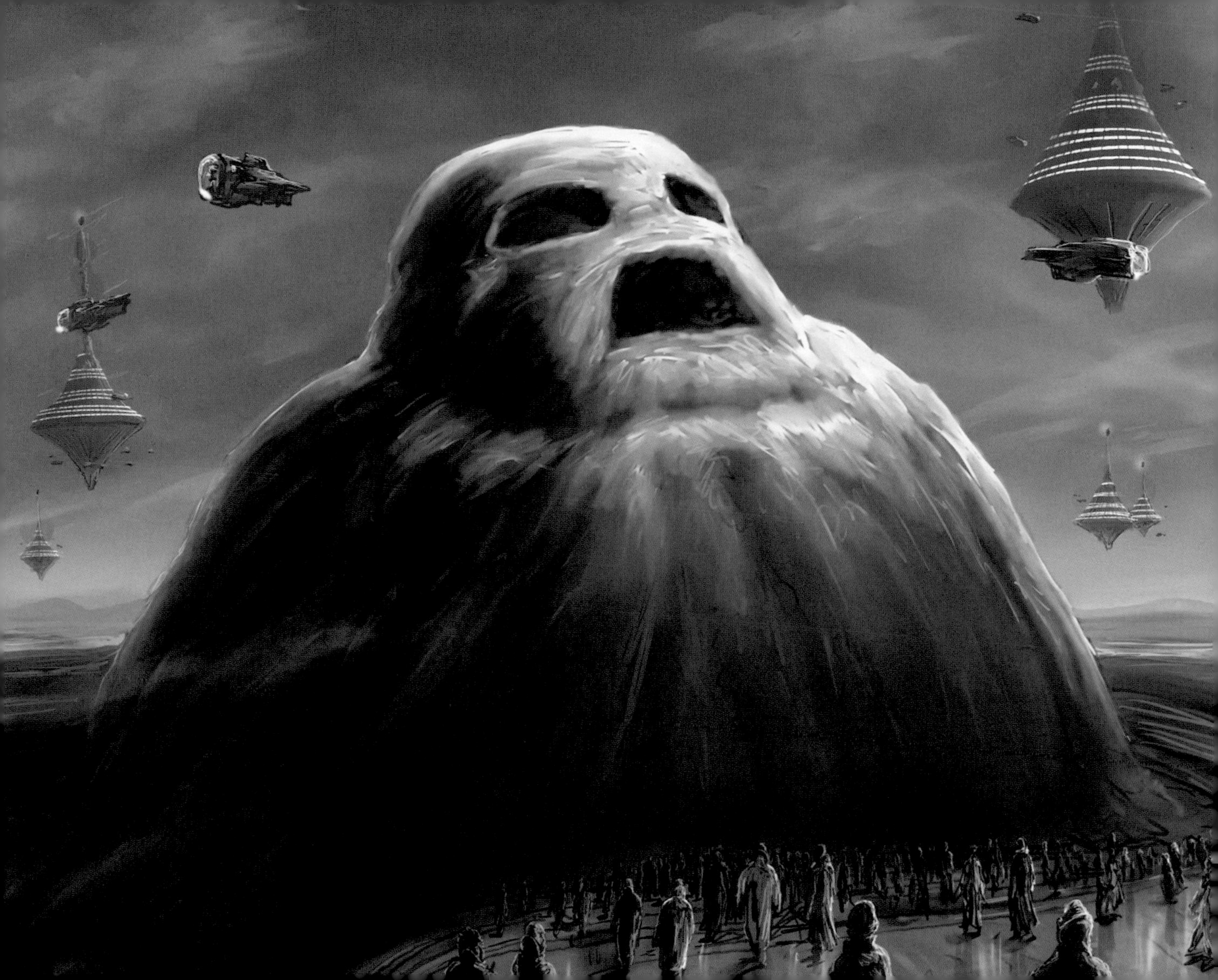

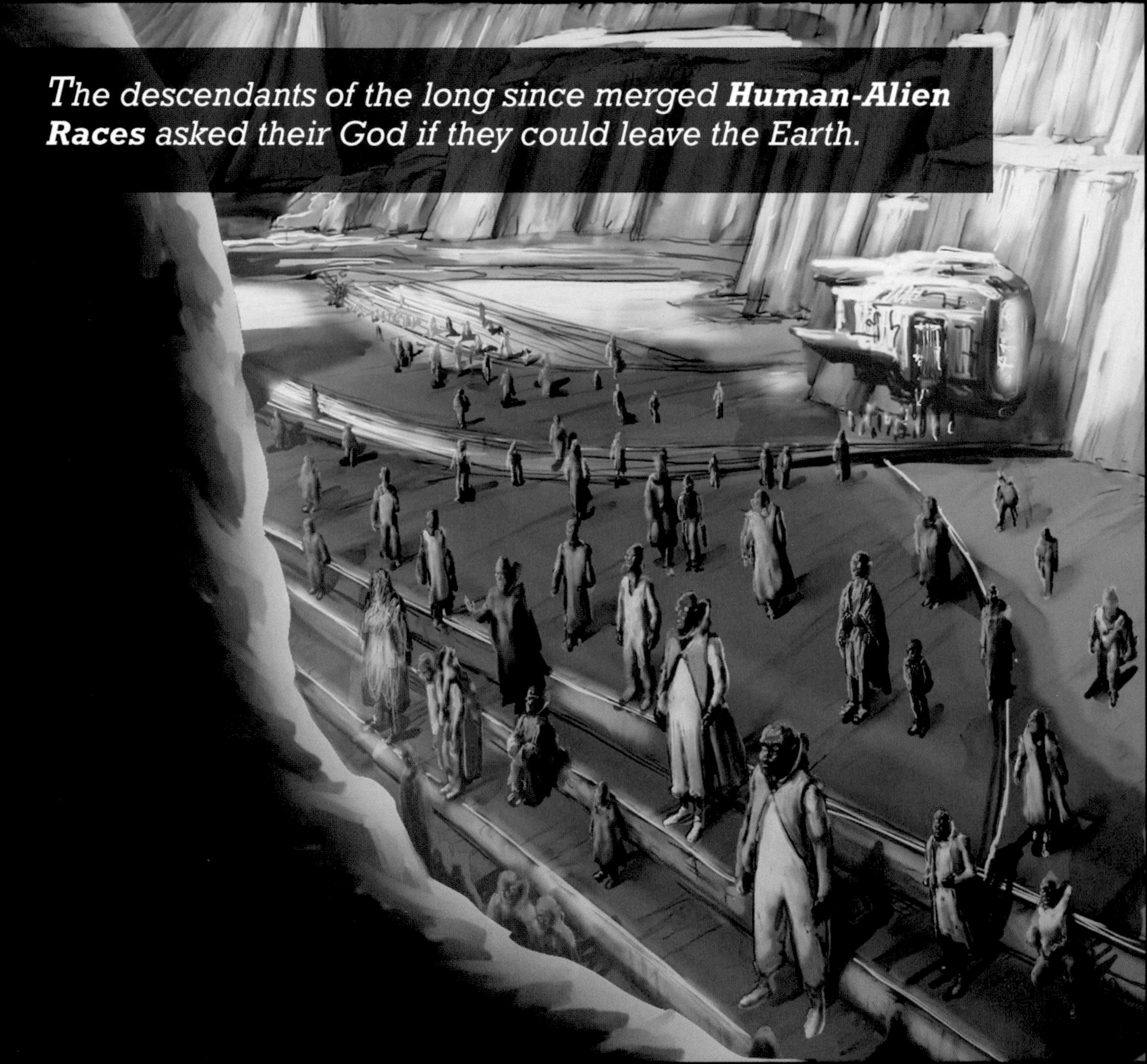
*The descendants of the long since merged **Human-Alien Races** asked their God if they could leave the Earth.*

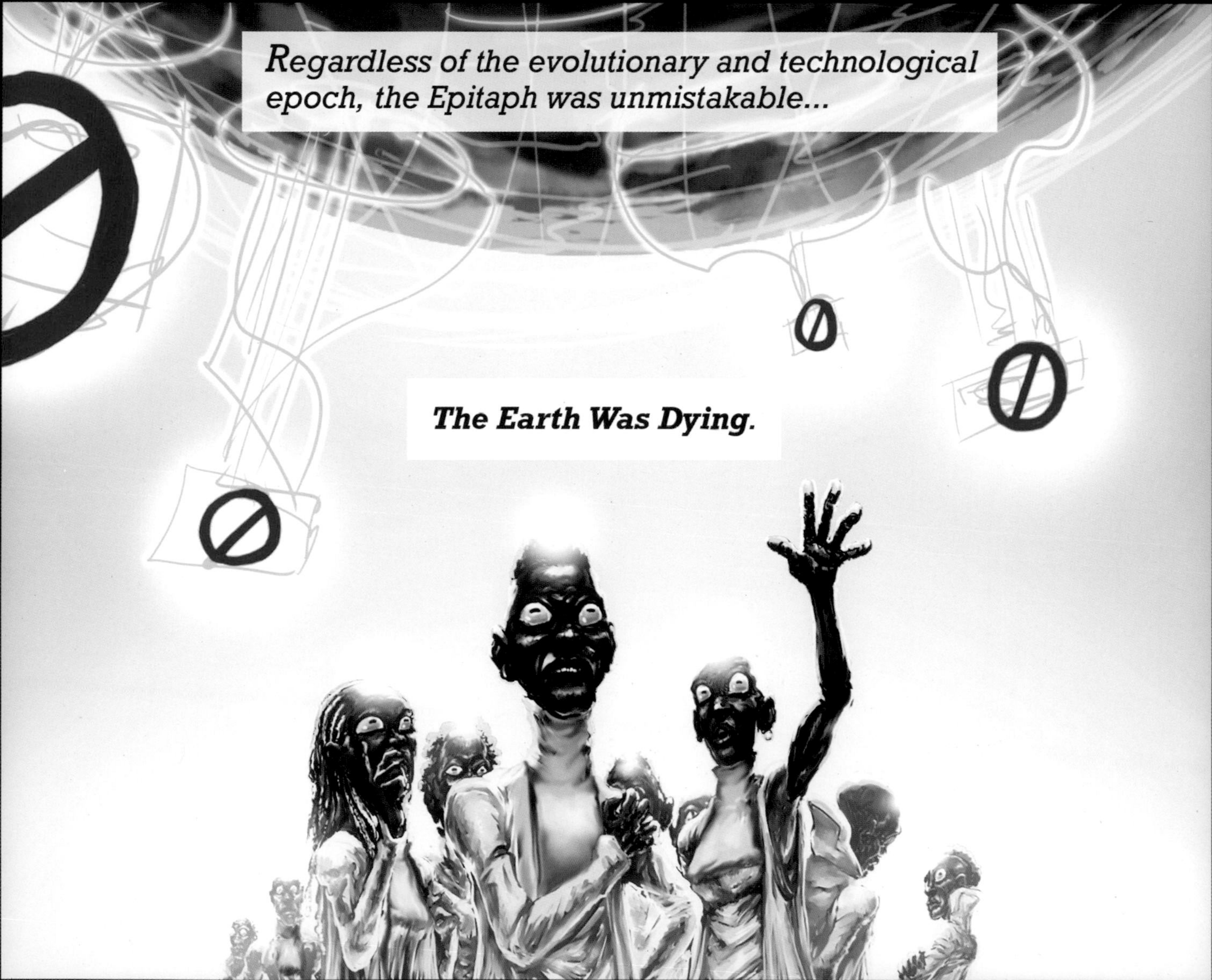
Regardless of the evolutionary and technological epoch, the Epitaph was unmistakable...
The Earth Was Dying.

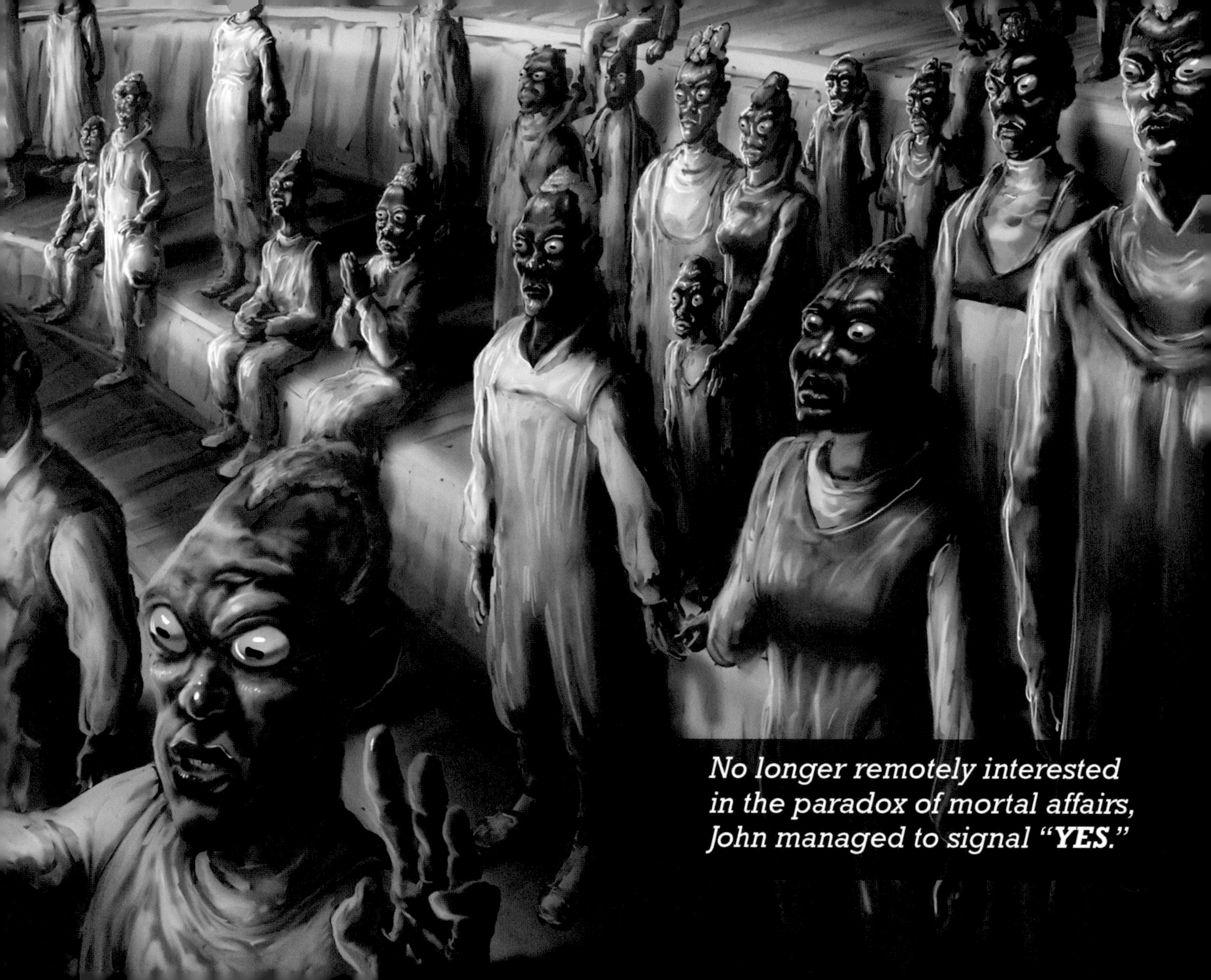
*No longer remotely interested in the paradox of mortal affairs, John managed to signal "**YES.**"*

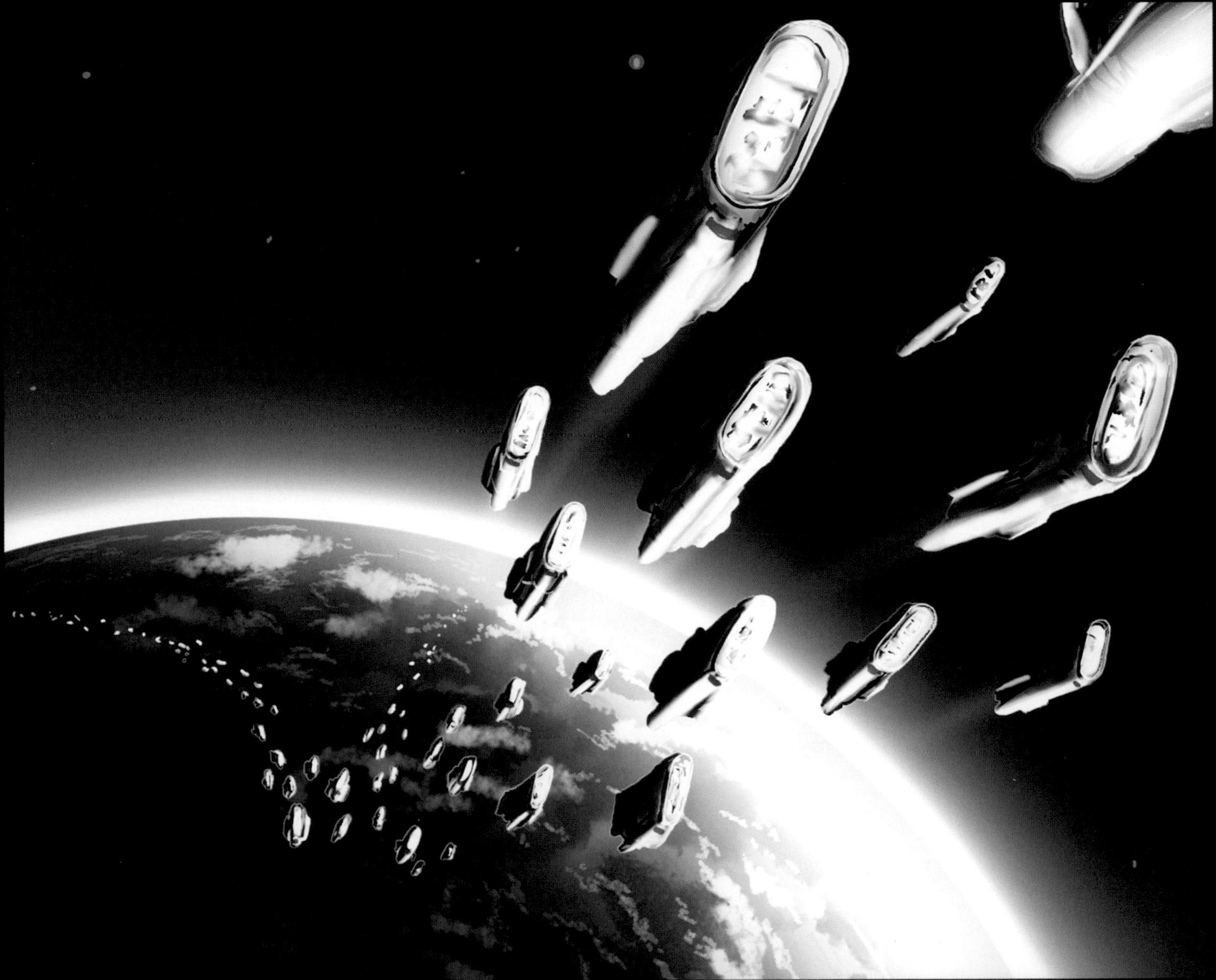

All that was left of life on Earth were ***simple one-celled beings.***

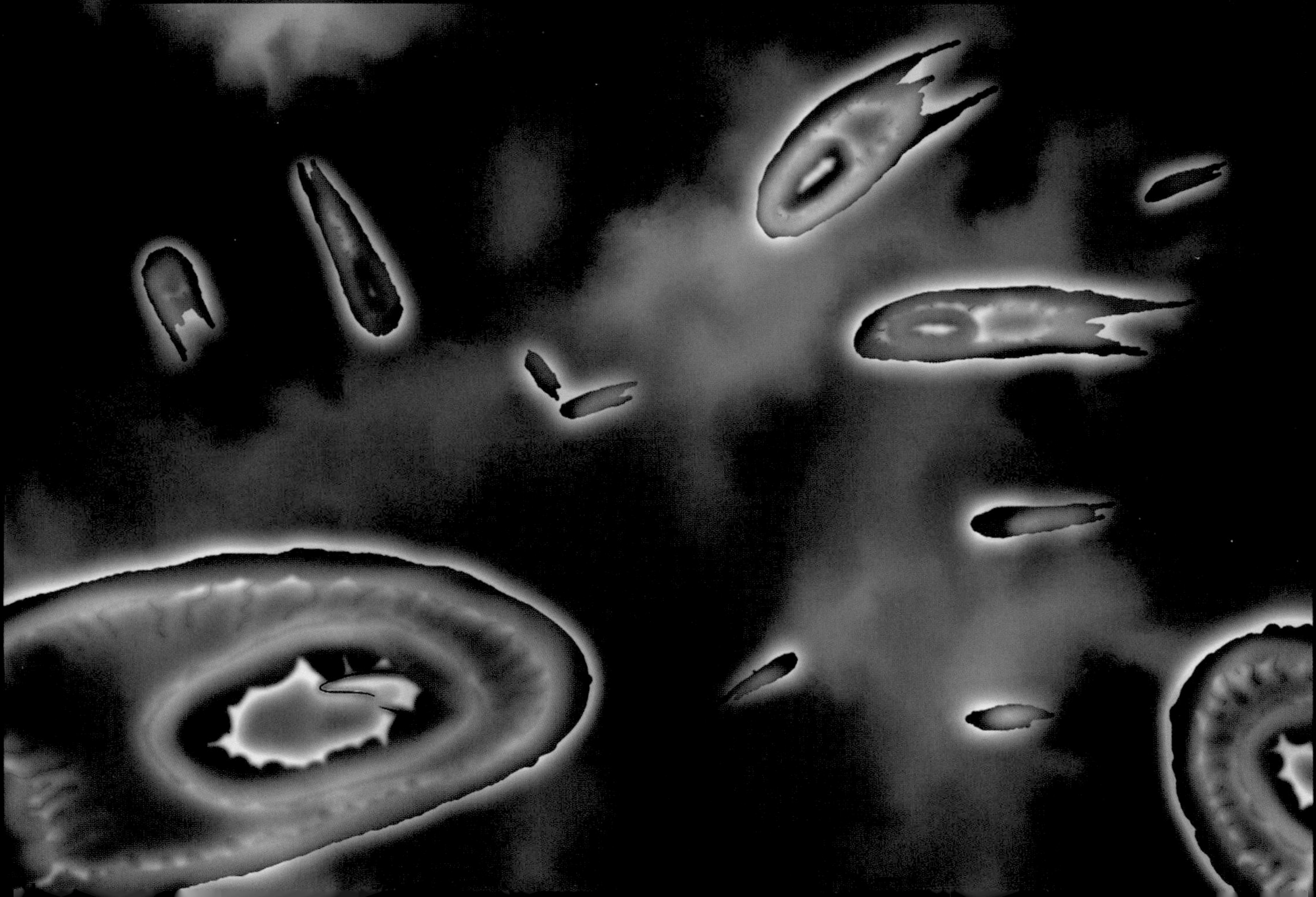

The nutritionless Earth sealed their

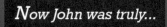

Now John was truly...

Totally...

ALONE.

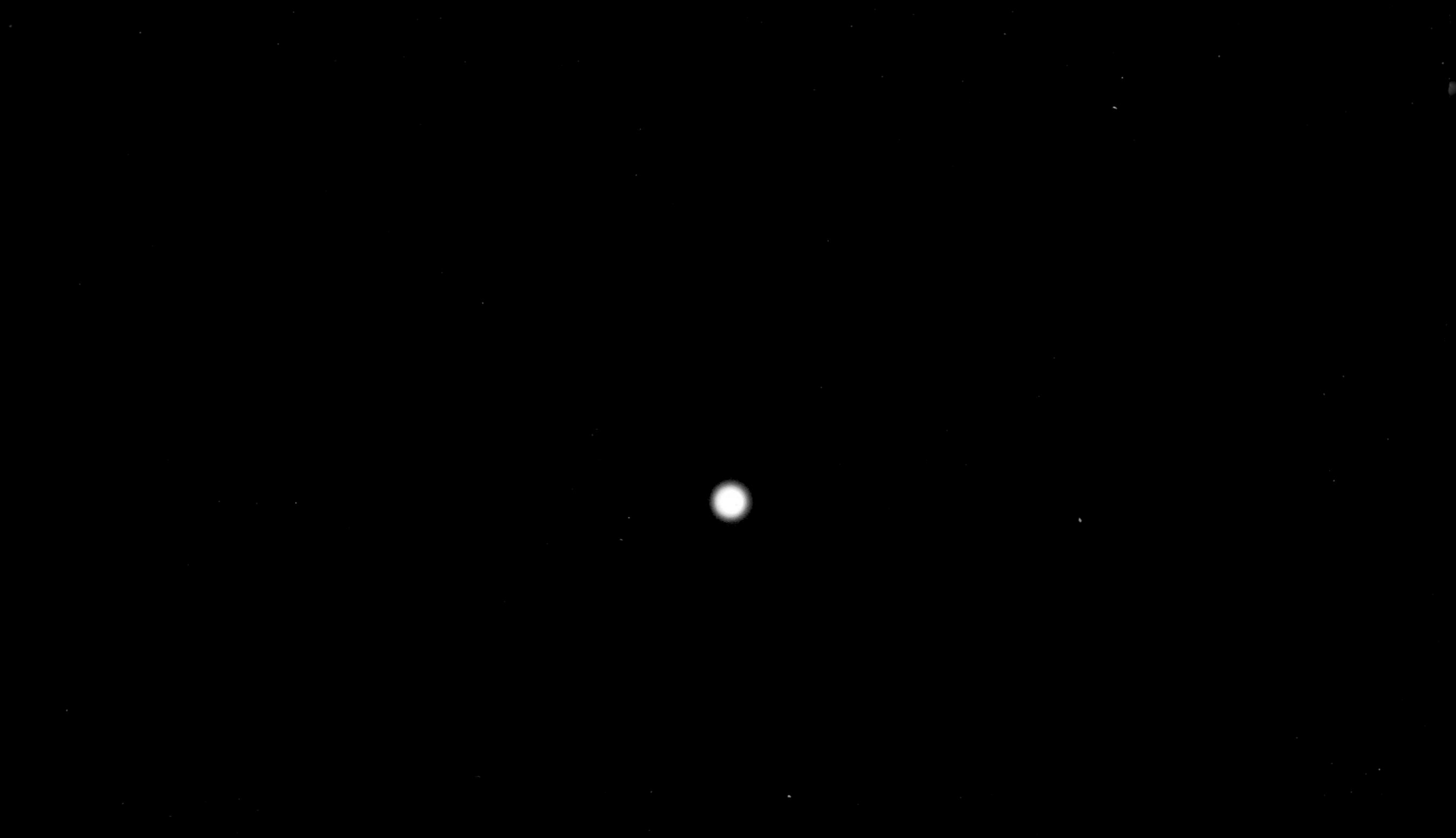

*One Billion years had passed. The Sun was now alone,
and its light had dwindled quite dim and cold.*

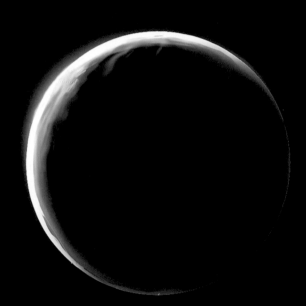

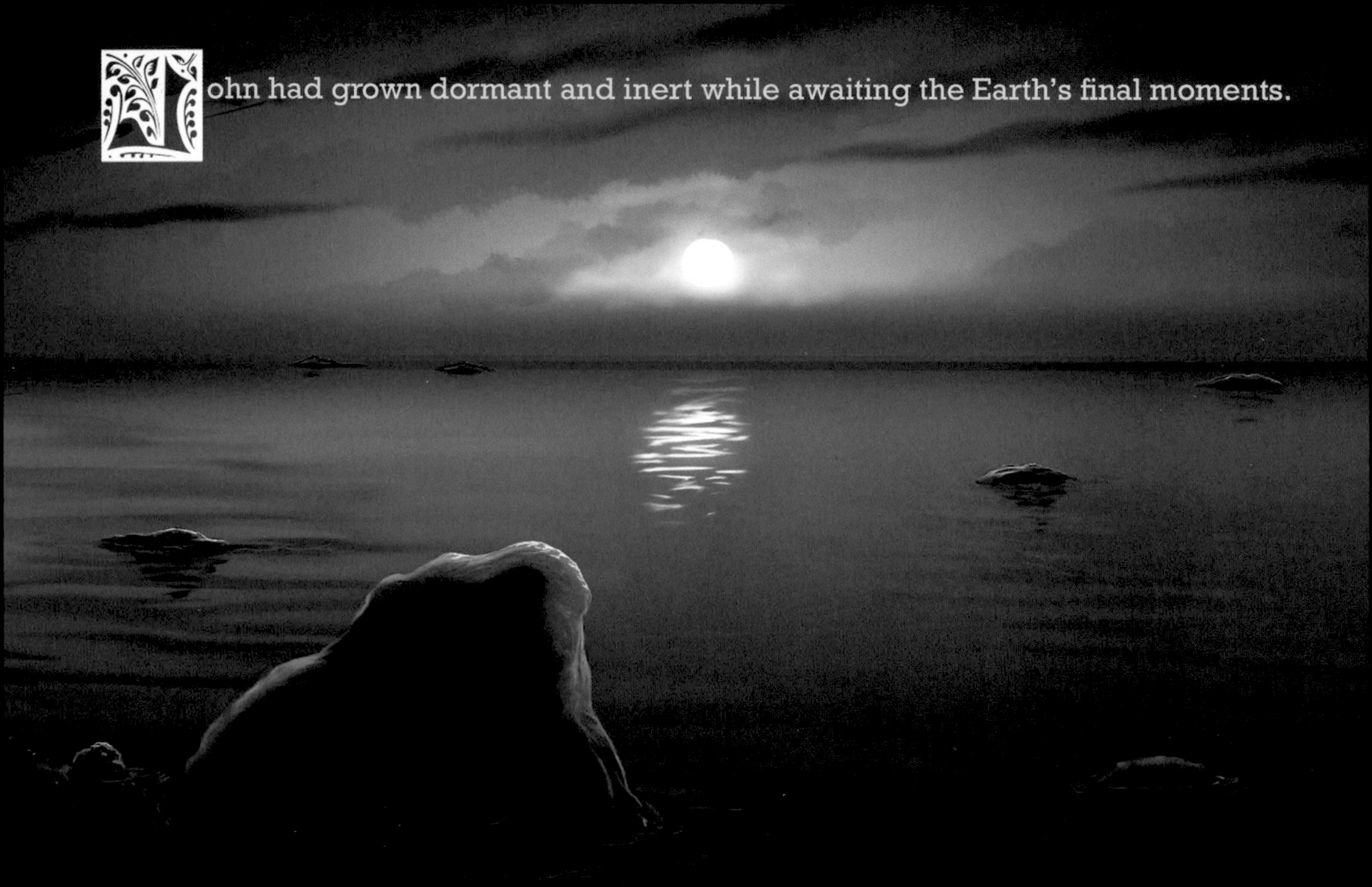
John had grown dormant and inert while awaiting the Earth's final moments.

Out
of the darkness
came an apparition.

Obinrin Aje.

John expected he had heard her...out there...over the eons.

Had **she**
finally come to gloat?

He

had been **patient**.

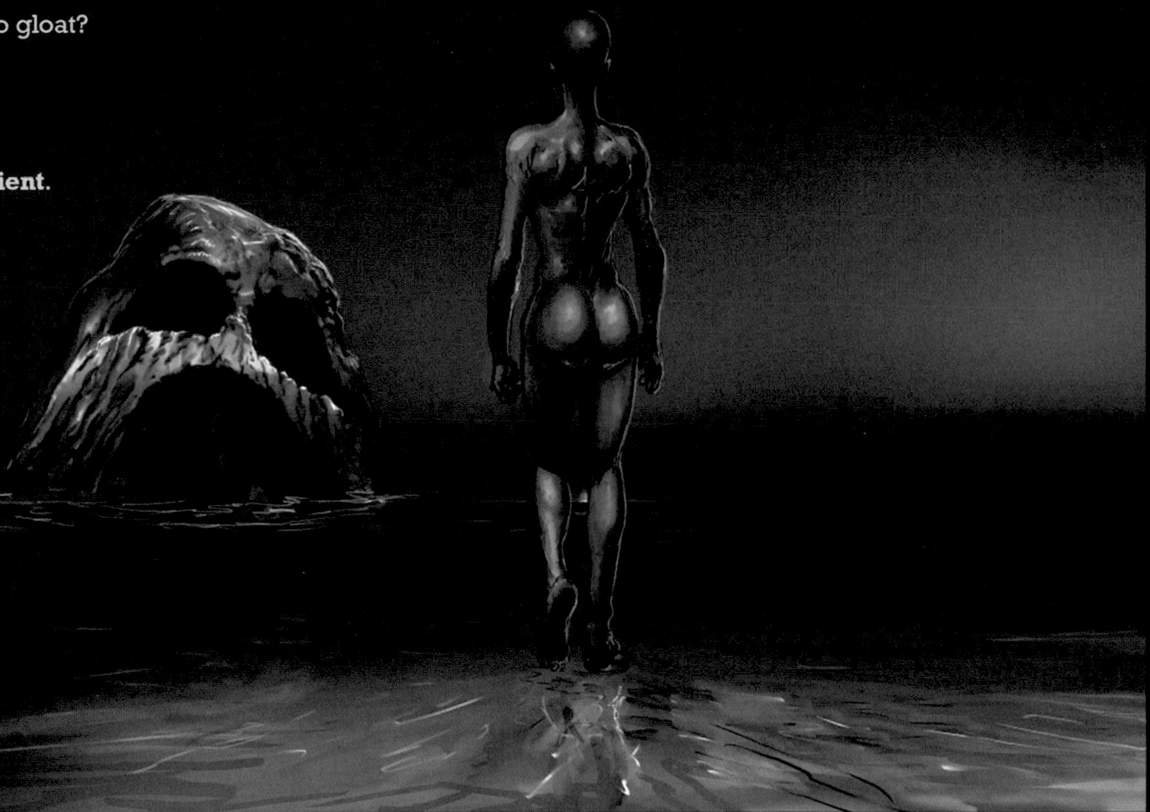

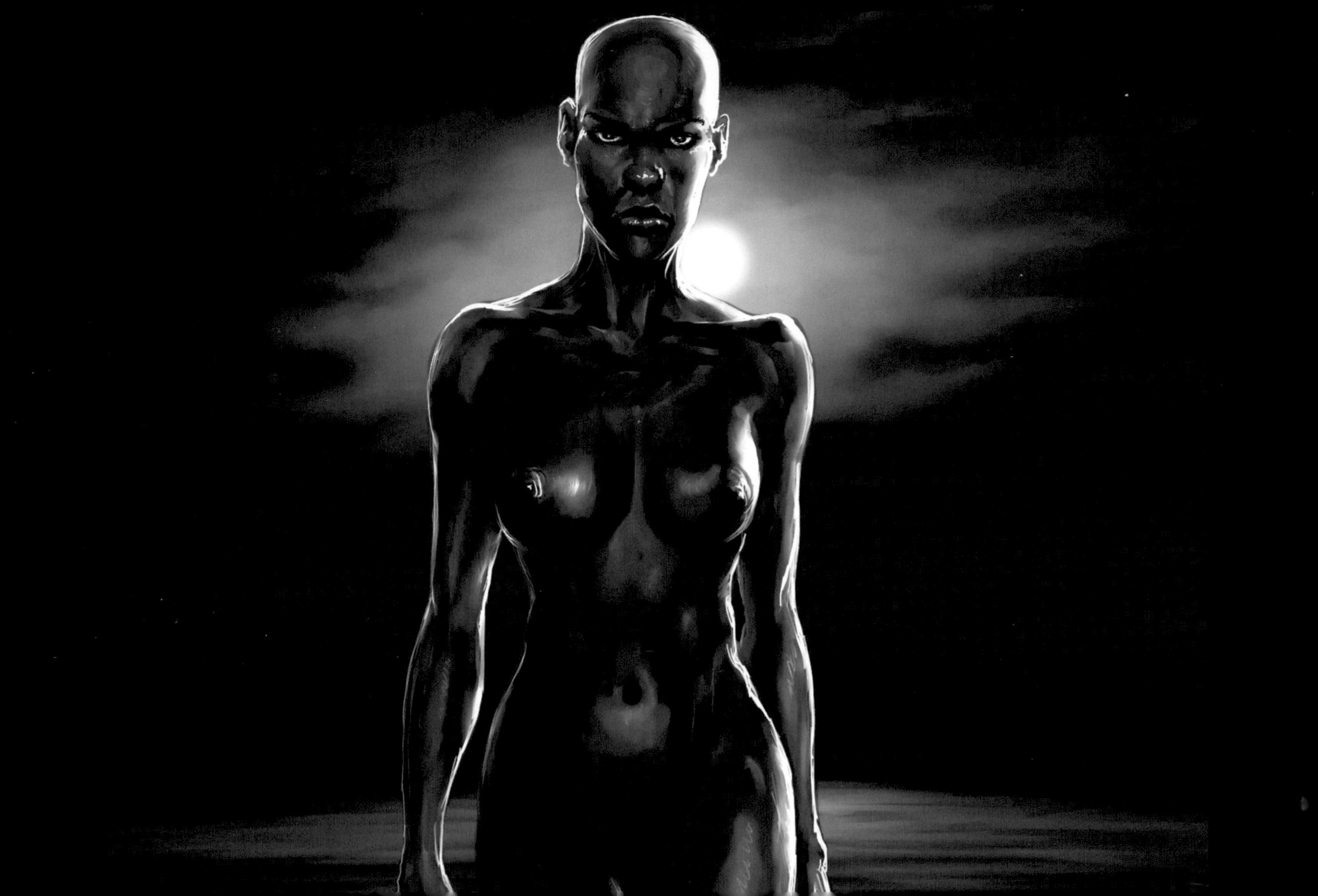

I MUST ASK FORGIVENESS FOR MY HORRENDOUS ACTIONS IN THE PAST.
WE WERE YOUNG THEN.

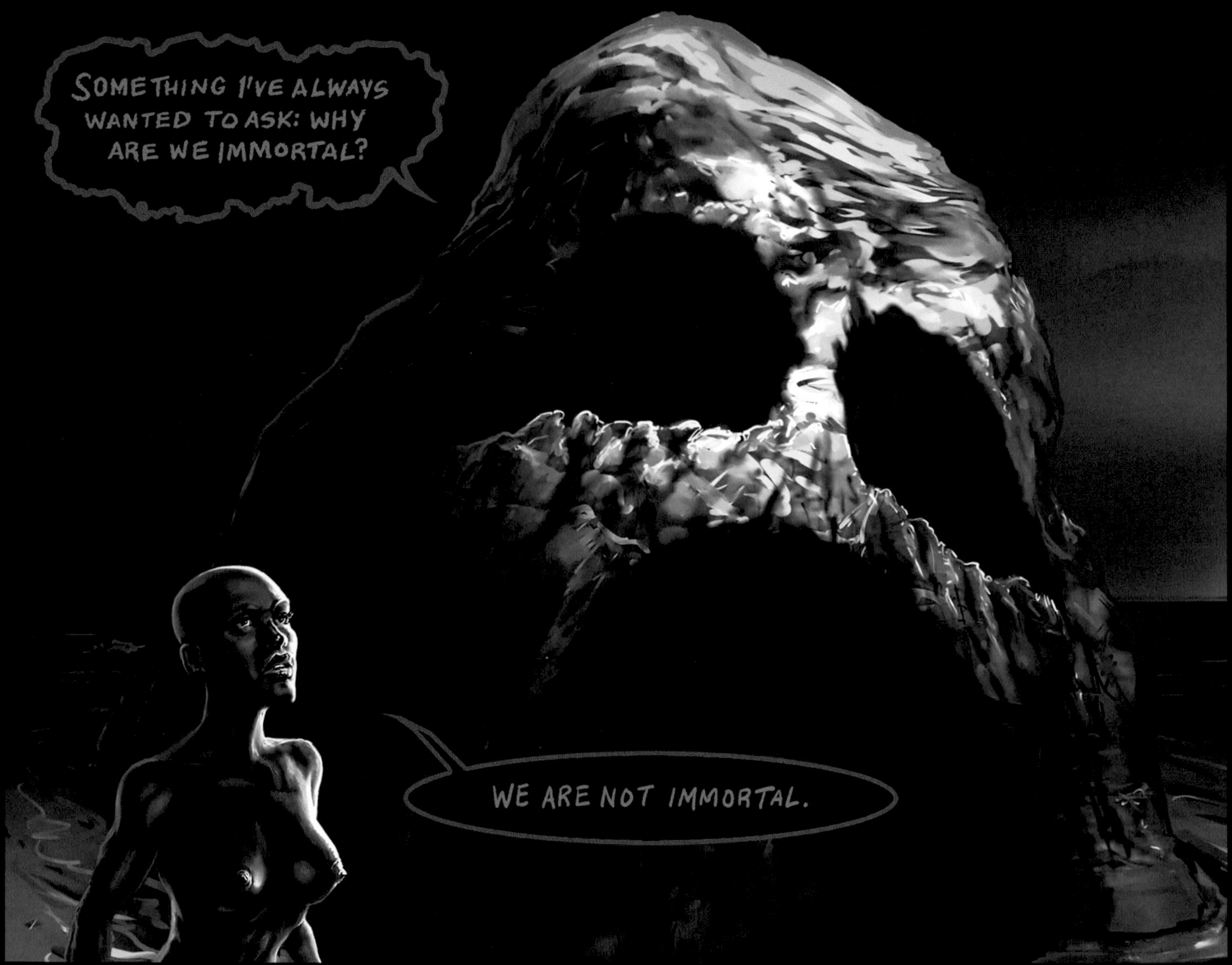
SOMETHING I'VE ALWAYS WANTED TO ASK: WHY ARE WE IMMORTAL?
WE ARE NOT IMMORTAL.

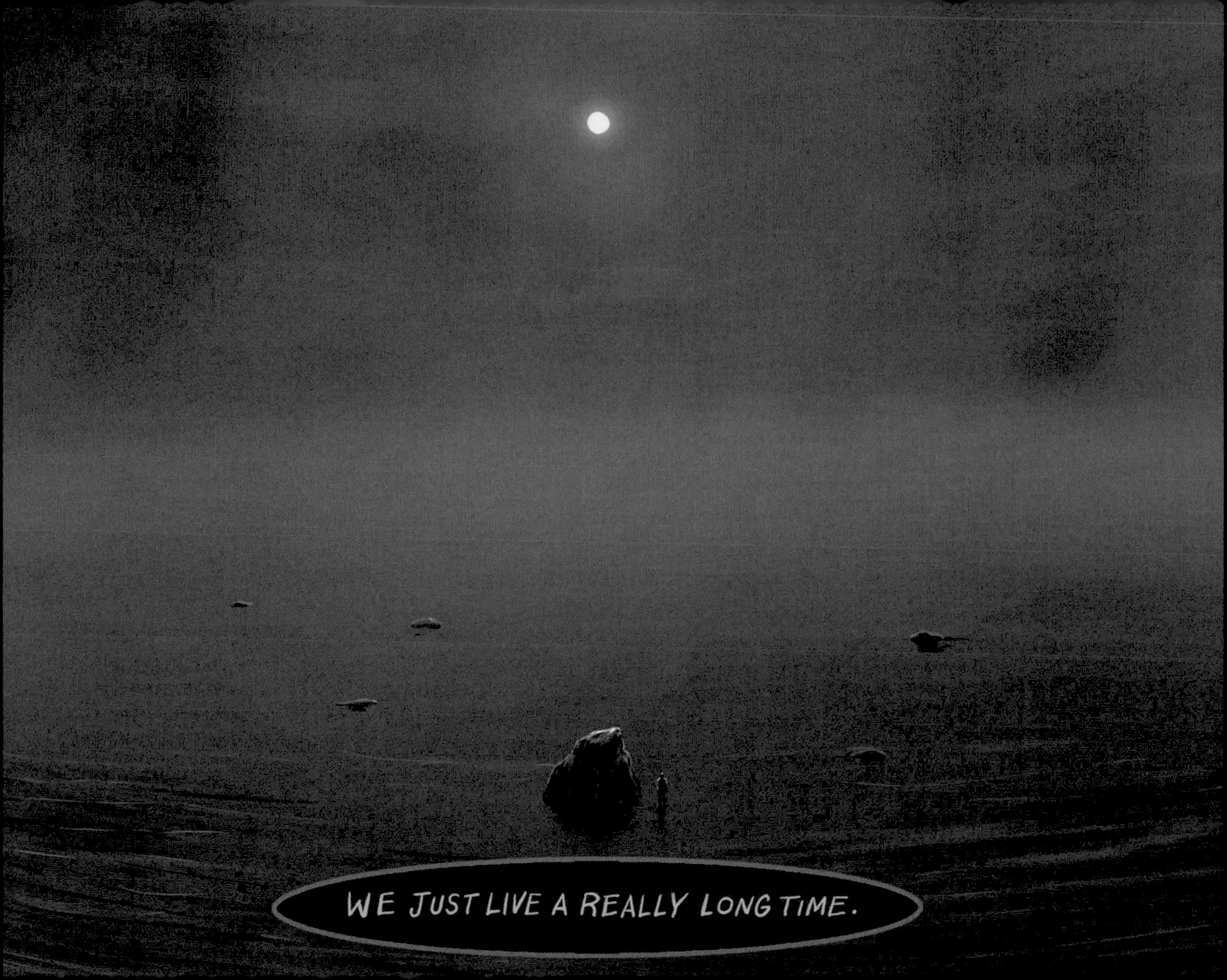
WE JUST LIVE A REALLY LONG TIME.

It had been a long life.

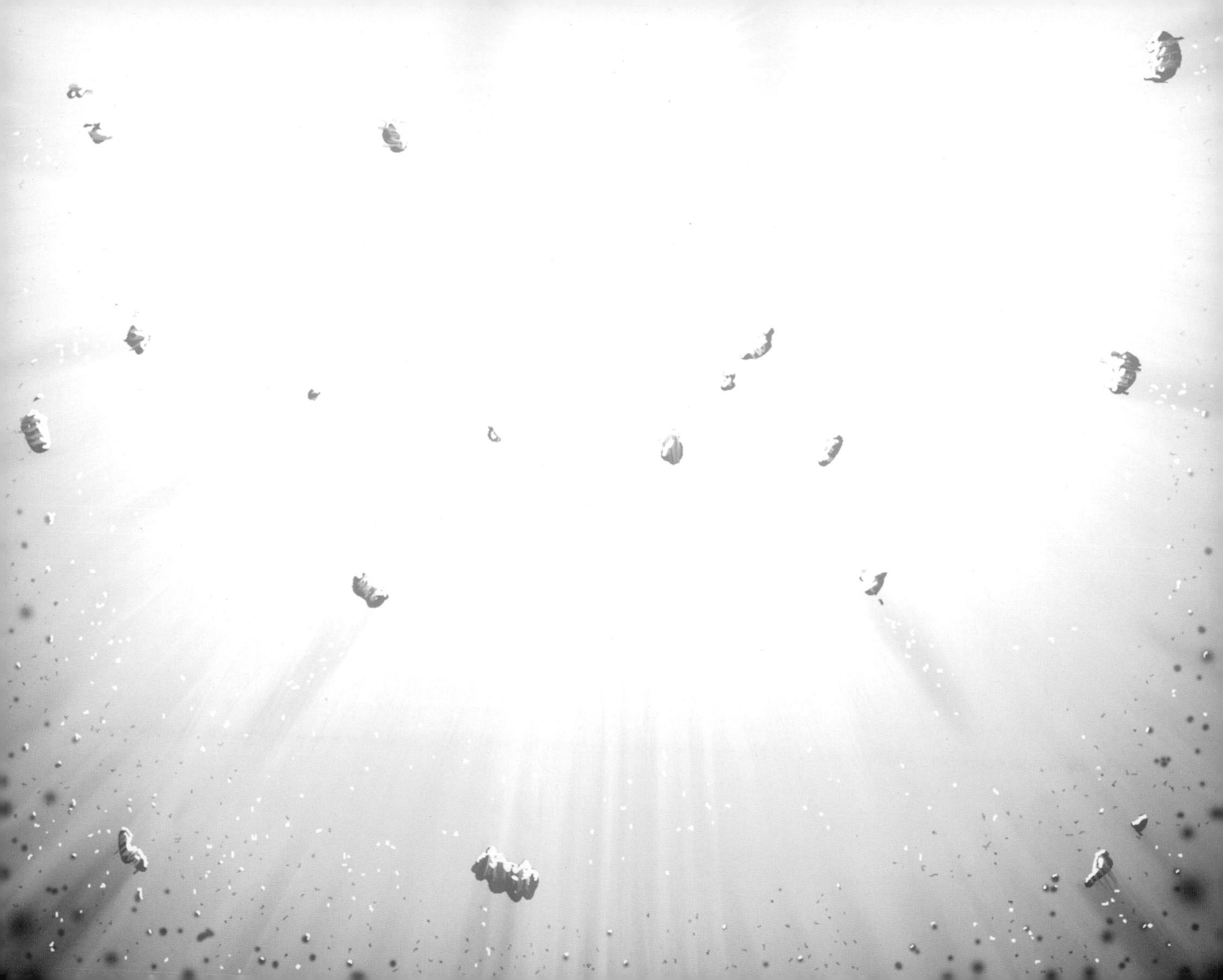

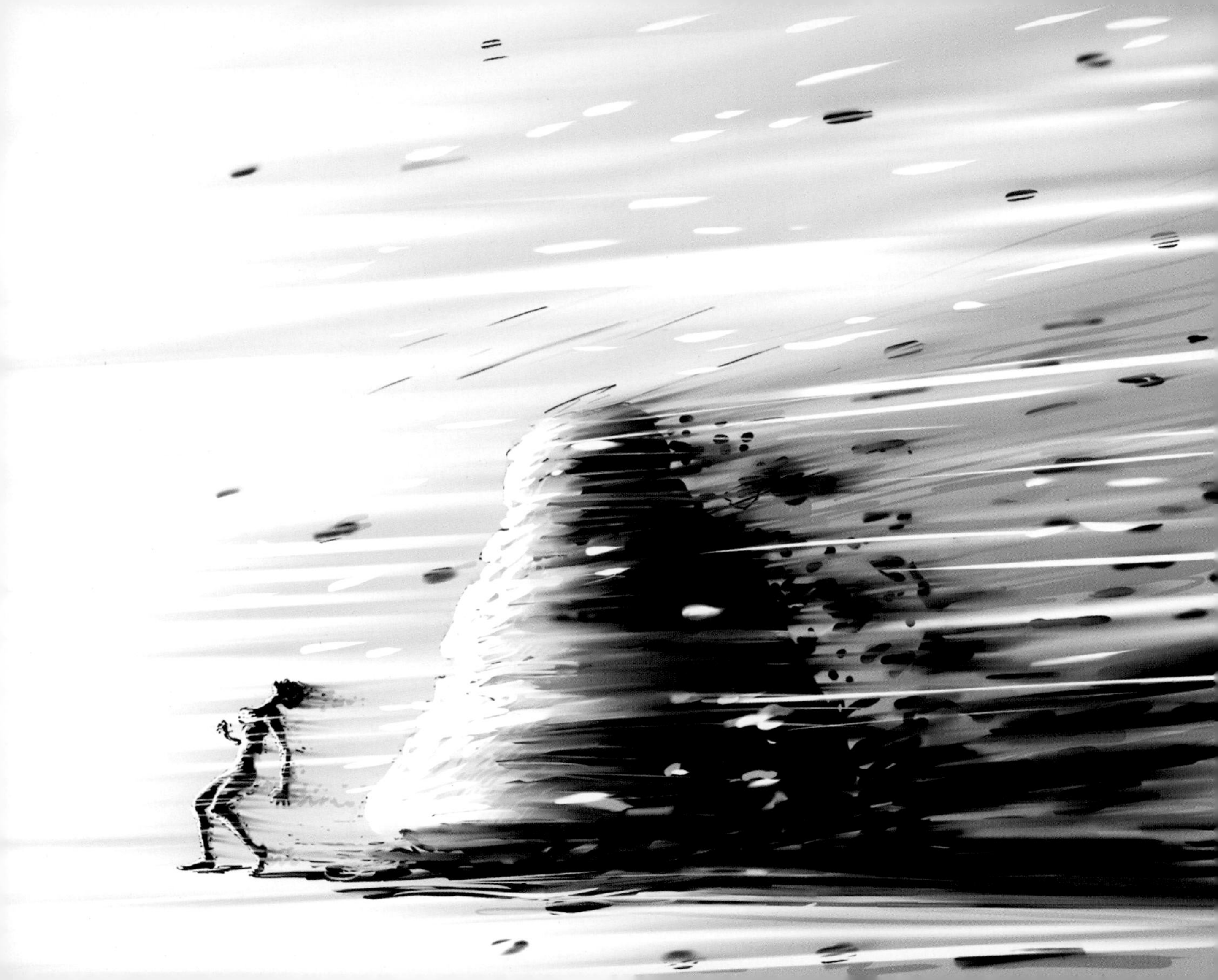

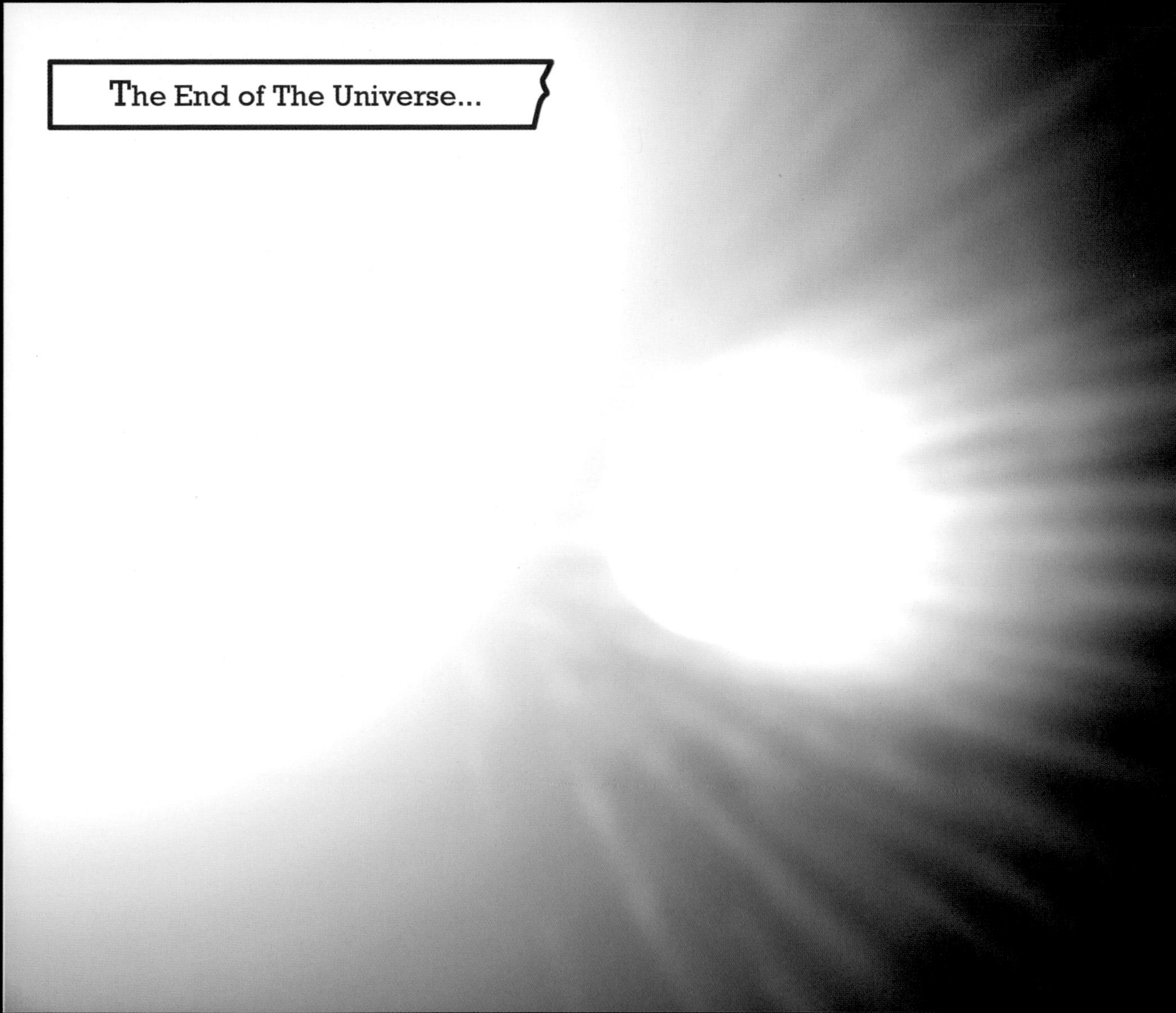
The End of The Universe...

Came and Went.

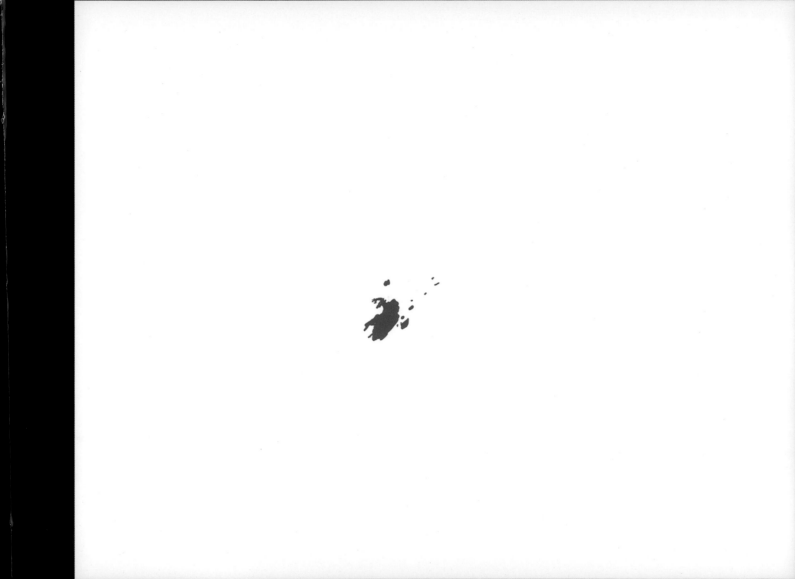

But the King did NOT die.

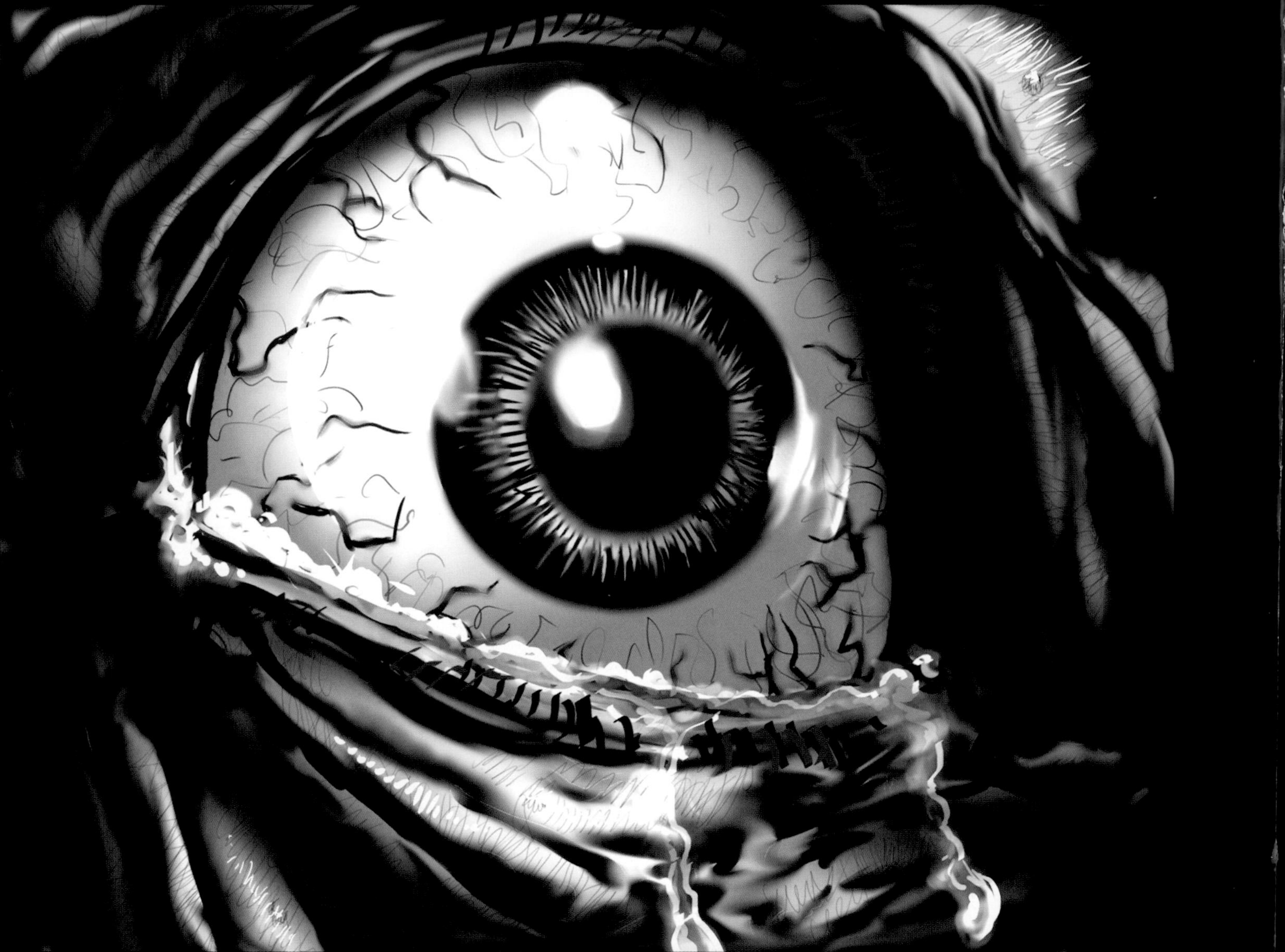

the end

∎ afterword

There's really too much to say, but I'll start here.

If my youngest sibling is anything like me, and Tim most certainly is, he was born in a daemon's headlock. By which I mean, he was born in the grip of fundamentally metaphysical forces. Forces that have shaped the terms of both how he sees and responds to the world, artistically and otherwise. And these terms, this **Black Being**, are the inescapable event horizon for anyone forged by the Mississippi Delta. Any significant difference between how he, **being a Twin**, and I, and our brothers (four Black boys, no girls), experienced growing up in the late sixties, early seventies **Mississippi Delta**, probably comes down to that reality, **his being a Twin**.

Like me, Tim grew up primarily in Clarksdale, oft claimed to be the capital of the Delta, **birthplace of the Blues** (which, laughably, "blues" being synonymous with "depression," multiple Delta towns lay competing claims to). For us, this question of origins (as is always the case with the **narratives of metahumans**) can only be fully understood in light of the fact that we actually grew up in two very different worlds.

The four of us were all born in Tupelo, Mississippi (as was our mother, and, yes, Elvis Presley). But from '67, when we relocated to Clarksdale, this movement, back and forth between the two cities, profoundly shaped us. Tupelo was the model **post-integrated** Southern city, relatively progressive, while Clarksdale was decidedly, being for all intents and purposes **segregated, not**. So our movement, typically weekly, between the two social contexts was as much traveling back and forth in time as it was traveling to and fro through space. **And this travel, leaving us alienated in both contexts, made us** aliens.

Our father remarked much later that if he'd had any daughters, he'd have evacuated Mississippi twenty years earlier. It was, as Dad put it, an environment saturated with, among other forms of violence, "sexual depravity." As it was, we all, including Tim, spent our formative years in this "**Armaghetto**."

I've often joked that if ever I write a memoir, it'll be titled **Dark and Lovely**. Our upbringing, as I experienced it, was a cross between **the Brady Bunch** and **The Color Purple**. A steady diet of 4th World Gods, Soul/Rock music, horror films, hog guts, Encyclopedia Britannica, alternative comics (European and underground), bell bottoms, and high waters (in combination with the Mississippi Delta) made for a strange brew. And in the early seventies, we were **that** family.

Experience, though, is slippery. Which of these things are true, which are just imagined? My brother, Boston, has pointed out that the account of my epochal encounter with Kubrick's **2001: A Space Odyssey** (see my essay, "My Black Death") was accurate save for my complete erasure of him from the actual occurrence. Who figured? Perhaps, on some fundamental level, the true and the imagined are more alike than not.

Hence, **our epic summer '72 trip across America**. Nearly three months on the road. I was eleven, which would have made Tim and his twin, Jim, five. I remember a lot of things, from unprecedented access to episodes of **Speed Racer** and **Thunderbirds** to my brother almost drowning in the Pacific. But a couple of related events stand out: eyeing the only copy I'd ever seen of the mythic (for us, given the vagaries of comic book distribution at the time) **second issue of Jack Kirby's Forever People**—after midnight, in the lobby of some fleabag hotel in Iowa City we were checking into. We'd driven there, against Dad's wishes (Mom may have insisted), to wait out a

deluge of biblical proportions. Under any other circumstance, it would have been impossible to deter me from drawing a beeline directly to the rare comic. But only a few hours earlier, in one of the most traumatic episodes of my then young life, we were parked on the side of the road while our dad, searching the trunk of our '71 Cadillac Eldorado for a flashlight, flew into a rage (in his defense, he was getting drenched in the downpour): "These damn comic books are everywhere." At which point he proceeded to fling our carefully preserved comics onto the side of the muddy road. As is often the case with any truly traumatic experience, I have no memory beyond the four of us, in our tiny green space capsule waiting out the torrent, all crying profusely at the loss of our treasure.

The fantastical, in all its permutations, despite the inevitable normalization that occurs from growing up in any place, is the only way to truly describe what Mississippi (and the Delta in particular) was like. It's a **haunted region**, one in which some of the more horrific incidents of the 20th century (the murder of Emmett Till and the murders of Chaney, Goodman, and Schwerner) transpired. This violence was real and had a half-life that permeated the environment. **We grew up in this fallout,** or at least in its aftermath. All of which went down in a period ten years prior to and within a hundred-mile radius of us moving to the Delta. So while, paradoxically, the Mississippi Delta is, as I've mentioned a thousand times in talks, ground zero in terms of Black American musical culture, which means it was ground zero in terms of American musical culture, which, in the 20th century, means it was ground zero in terms of American culture, period (and consequently, the dominant cultural form

of the 20th century, as asserted by David Hickey). It is also the Black Jurassic Park and the penultimate state of abjection. Hence, Black folks en masse got the hell out as soon as they could.

But what of those who stayed behind, beyond the point at which whatever imagined gifts (like the Incredible Hulk, X-Men, or Godzilla) resulted from proximity to this Black Chernobyl?

For us, a drive to escape this defined our early lives. And often I've wondered if the life I've lived was anything more than a Sixth Sense–like daydream. One from which, inevitably, I'll awaken to discover myself still living in Clarksdale. This drive, this longing for a larger world, for space (the final frontier), found voice for us in comics, science fiction, and horror films. All of which resonated with **Black Being**, when understood as a being in a constant state of emergency, a constant state of emergence, of coming into, by day and by night.

My brothers and I were weird. **Black unicorns, mythical Black nerds, mutants,** unaware at the time that a herd, a horde, a swarm of our kind existed just over the horizon. **And comics**—Kirby, Heavy Metal, Ron Cobb, Star Wars, Corben, Trashman, and Alien—shaped us.

Tim was and is our Kwisatz Haderach, or maybe our Gully Foyle, the emergent one. And he/we, like all Black folks (at the end of the day) are survivors. Which, prior to having read INFINITUM, I'd imagined it must be about—**survival**. Now, having read it many, many times, I wonder.

Arthur Jafa, 2020

acknowledgments ∎

To KJ and Rowena Fielder, thank you for being great parents and allowing me to be an artist. Jim, my partner/clone in crime since before birth, "Here All Is Forgiven." To Boston, for being my guide, motivator, and, when necessary, enforcer. To Art, for the tongue-lashing forty years ago. To my daughter, Johnnie, Dad loves you no matter how annoying you may find me . . . it's my job. To my numerous nieces, nephews, cousins, and extended family. And to my wife, the magnificent beauty and artistic genius, Melanie Maria Goodreaux-Fielder. Love in Vermont calls us as always.

Tremendous appreciation and respect for longtime running dude, Marc E. Florestant, and Beijing buddy, David Littlefield. Love to my New Orleans and Vermont families. Thanks for the prayers and food supply, Monica and Ms. Carmelite. Special nod to the amazing Floyd Hughes, Jeff Smith, and Alison Bechdel for advice along the way. Thanks to my Brothers in Afrofuturism, Junot Díaz, Professor John Jennings, Professor Stacey Robinson, Mark Dery, and Professor Reynaldo Anderson. And Sisters in Afrofuturism, Professor Kinitra Brooks, Deidre Holman, Professor Toniesha L. Taylor, Ytasha Womack, and Sheree Renée Thomas. Comic colleagues Greg Anderson Elysée, Jason Reeves, Jerry Craft, and Alex Simmons. God-siblings Dorothea Smartt, Kadija Sesay, and Isis Barra-Costa. Many thanks to Julie Anderson and Blossom Blair. Special nod to Dawoud Bey: yes, man, you were right.

To Amistad/HarperCollins Publishers editorial director Tracy Sherrod, thank you for choosing INFINITUM. And finally, a salute to the GREAT Calvin Reid.